Marriages of
WILKES COUNTY, NORTH CAROLINA

1778-1868

STATE of NORTH-CAROLINA.

KNOW all men by these presents, That we *William Adams and John Hall Jun.* are held firmly bound unto *Abner Nash Esq.* governor and commander in chief of the said state, in the just and full sum of *five hundred pounds* current money of the state aforesaid, to be paid to *the said Abner Nash* his successors and assigns: To which payment well and truly to be made and done, we bind ourselves, our and each of us, our heirs, executors and administrators, jointly and severally, firmly by these presents. Sealed with our seal and dated this *Sixteenth* day of *April* Anno Dom. 178*1*.

THE condition of the above obligation is such, That whereas the above bound *William Adams* hath made application for a licence for a marriage to be had and solemnized between *the said William Adams & Omea Hall* of the county of *Wilkes* Now in case it shall not appear hereafter that there is any lawful cause to obstruct the said marriage, then this obligation to be void; otherwise to remain in full force and virtue.

Sealed and delivered in the Presence of } *G Wheatey*

William his ✕ mark Adams

John Hall

A marriage bond dated April 16, 1781. *See p. 3.*

Marriages of
WILKES COUNTY, NORTH CAROLINA

1778-1868

Compiled by
BRENT H. HOLCOMB

Indexed by
Deborah G. Sherr & Richard W. Lewis

CLEARFIELD

Reprinted for
Clearfield Company, Inc. by
Genealogical Publishing Co., Inc.
Baltimore, Maryland
1993, 1998

Copyright © 1983
Genealogical Publishing Co., Inc.
Baltimore, Maryland
All Rights Reserved
Library of Congress Catalogue Card Number 82-83913
International Standard Book Number 0-8063-1008-1
Made in the United States of America

INTRODUCTION

THIS VOLUME contains abstracts of all marriage bonds extant for Wilkes County, North Carolina (formed in 1777 from Surry County). The abstracts were made from a microfilm copy of the bonds and are listed here in alphabetical order by groom, with brides and bondsmen indexed. All original bonds are in the North Carolina Archives in Raleigh.

Marriage bonds are the only public records of marriage prior to 1851. The marriage bond law was enacted in 1741 and remained in force until 1868. In 1851 the clerk of the county court was required to keep a register of marriages performed by license (issued with the bond). The bonds alone are not proof that a marriage took place, only that a marriage was intended. Marriages could also be performed after publication of banns, and therefore no bond, license, or other public record of the marriage was kept. Occasionally, only a license is extant. In this case, no bondsman is shown. For some reason unknown to the compiler, a number of returns in the 1840s are found with the bond. These returns sometimes give the exact date of the marriage but almost always give the name of the person who performed the marriage. This practice was a bit unusual; fortunately, it provides proof that the marriage did take place.

BRENT H. HOLCOMB, C.A.L.S.
Columbia, South Carolina

WILKES COUNTY MARRIAGES, 1778-1868

Abesher, Isaac & Merinda Eskew, 19 Jan 1866.

Abshear, Ezekiel & Jinny Brown, 1 Nov 1824; Robin Hall, bm.

Abshear, Ezekiel & Elisabeth Brown, 29 July 1833; Goin Abshear, bm.

Abshear, Jacob & Sally Hall, 9 April 1831; Walter Brown, bm.

Absher--see also Apshar

Absher, Alfred B. & Elizabeth Whitly, 15 Sept 1846; Ezekiel Abshear, bm.

Absher, Alfred J. & Martha Johnson, 22 Feb 1847; James Gwyn Jr., bm.

Absher, John L. & Amelia Shomall, 1 Feb 1842; John Hall, bm.

Absher, William & Jain Hains, 14 Jan 1821; Alexr Brown, bm; Marry Marting, wit.

Abshier, Going & Sarry Wheatly, 23 Jan 1818; John Absher, bm.

Abshier, John & Mary Vannoy, 16 Nov 1836; Ezekiel Absher, bm.

Abshir, Wm & Polly Jinnings, 20 Oct 1850; R. R. Hall, bm; Wm. E. Reynolds, wit; m Feb 1851.

Abshire, Abram & Nancy Walker, 31 Jan 1852; Joseph H. Adams, bm; m 5 Feb 1852 by L. Sebastian, J. P.

Abshire, Adam & Letty J. Brown, 23 July 1851; Abram Absher, bm; m 30 July 1851 by L. Sebastian, J. P.

Abshire, Benjamin F. & Nancy Brown, 8 Jan 1862; J. F. Owens, bm; m 19 Jan 1862 by P. R. McGrady, J. P.

Abshire, Going & Jane Abshir, 3 May 1862; John Holbrook, bm; consent from John Abshier, father of Jene.

Abshire, Walter & Nancy Brown, 7 July 1821; William Abshir, bm.

Abshire, William & Betsy Abshire, 10 Feb 1820; Owen Hall, bm.

Adams, Allen & Judy Adams, 17 Feb 1836; Reuben Hays Jr., bm.

Adams, Benjamin & Alesebeth Campel, 21 Feb 1809; Abner Candill, bm.

Adams, Byard & Mary Morris, 13 April 1849; James Morris, bm.

WILKES COUNTY MARRIAGES, 1778-1868

Adams, Calvin & Polly Jones, 4 Dec 1839; William Sebastian, bm.

Adams, Chapman & Dolly Higgins, 26 Dec 1812; A. Robinett, bm.

Adams, Charles & Elizabeth Hopper, 7 Sept 1779; James Sheffield, bm.

Adams, Charles & Elizabeth Wilds, 8 Dec 1835; Abraham Buttery, bm.

Adams, Charles & Rachel Johnson, 19 Sept 1857; m 19 Sept 1857 by Eli Grimes, L. D. of M. C. S.

Adams, Charles, son of Wily Adams & Marthy Hall daughter of Larken Hall, 23 March 1868; m 25 March 1868 by A. B. Dancey, J. P.

Adams, Ellison & Vicey Richardson, 1 Dec 1834; Moses Adams, bm.

Adams, Franklin M. & Nancy E. Tinsley, 10 Jan 1867; W. M. Rhodes, bm; m 10 Jan 1867 by Henry Jinnings, J. P.

Adams, G. W. & Martha Wilcoxson, 30 Aug 1863; Harrison Adams, bm; m 30 Aug 1863 by A. B. Dancey, J. P.

Adams, G. W. & Sarah C. Adams, m 16 July 1868 by William Hall, C. C.

Adams, Gibson & Suanna(?) Hampton, 17 Aug 1815; Isaiah Hampton, bm.

Adams, Harper & Martha Gentle, 29 March 1861; Harvey Smithy, bm; m 31 March 1861 by Wm. H. Hubbard, J. P.

Adams, Harrison & Susan Adams, 15 Dec 1853; m 15 Dec 1853 by Tobias Long.

Adams, Henry & Nancy Meirs, 12 Aug 1841; Wm. M. Deason, bm.

Adams, Henry & Nancy C. Brown, 18 Dec 1866; M. N. Dancy, bm; m 19 Dec 1866 by P. R. McGrady, J. P.

Adams, Henry & Nancy Wyatt, 13 Nov 1835; George Wyatt, bm.

Adams, Isaac & Susanna Walser, 30 July 1813; Eli Pettey, bm.

Adams, Isaac & Sintha Roberds, 18 Oct 1817; John Roberds, bm.

Adams, Jackson & Sarah Burchett, 25 Dec 1860; m 25 Dec 1860 by A. B. Dancey, J. P.

Adams, James F. & Prudence E. Woodruff, 9 Oct 1851; James Mastin, bm; m by S. D. Swaim.

Adams, Jesse & Nancy Lovelace, 21 Oct 1795; Robert Foster, bm.

Adams, Jesse & Peggy Byrd, 10 March 1807; Jno Adams, bm.

Adams, Jesse & Lucy Tandley, 22 Sept 1834; Garland Lane, bm.

Adams, Jesse P. & Jincey Sparkes, 29 Oct 1846; Reuben Sparkes, bm.

WILKES COUNTY MARRIAGES, 1778-1868

Adams, John & Roda Johnson, 22 Sept 1806; Reubin Kilbey, bm.

Adams, John & Aby Adams, 25 Jan 1813; Henry Adams, bm.

Adams, John & Polly Adams, 13 Nov 1838; Reubin Hayes Jr., bm.

Adams, John & Emiline Nance, 29 April 1850; Andrew Porter, bm.

Adams, John H. & Elizabeth McDaniel, 14 Oct 1835; Thos. McDaniel, bm.

Adams, John M. & Matilda Richeson, 2 Nov 1841; Stephen Caudell, bm.

Adams, Joseph & Catharine McGrady, 23 March 1854; no bm; m 30 March 1854 by L. Sebastian, J. P.

Adams, King David & Louiza Y. Burehot, 14 April 1866; Wm. Herrald, bm; m 15 April 1866 by A. B. Dancey, J. P.

Adams, King M. & Rachal Handy, 25 Aug 1841; Wm. Adams, bm.

Adams, Moses & Salley Hawkins, 19 Sept 1826; Daniel Call, bm.

Adams, Nipper & Sarah Ryon, 6 Dec 1779; William Adams Snr, bm.

Adams, Sollomon & Francis Church, 8 Sept 1841; Welborn Adams, bm.

Adams, Spencer & Tasy Johnson, 11 March 1818; Abner Caudill, bm.

Adams, Spenser & Elizabeth Smith, 25 Sept 1799; James F. Fletcher, bm.

Adams, Spenser & Pegga Adams, 29 July 1813; Wm. Williams, bm.

Adams, Thomas & Eunice Johnson, 16 May 1829; George Sheppard, bm.

Adams, Wellborn & Susanah Church, 25 Aug 1837; James Wellborn, bm.

Adams, Wiley & Rosanah Huffman, 22 March 1836; Andrew Cox, bm.

Adams, William & Omea Hall, 16 April 1781; John Hall, bm; G. Wheatley, wit.

Adams, William & ____, 27 Oct 1807; John Hickerson, bm.

Adams, William F. & Elizabeth Walker, 10 March 1835; Wm. Walker, bm.

Adams, William M. & Permelia Brook, 29 May 1852; Mathew Brooks, bm; m by M. H. Wheatley, J. P.

Adams, William Vicry & Charity Jinnings, 28 Dec 1854; John D. Jinnings, bm; Siler Brewer, wit.

Adams, William W. & Leanah Brown, 26 Dec 1851; Calvin Adams, bm; m 17 Dec 1852 by J. E. Reynolds, J. P.

Addams, James & Mary Gunter, 8 Aug 1816; Joshua Morgan, bm.

WILKES COUNTY MARRIAGES, 1778-1868

Adie, Andrew C. & Catherine D. Morgan, 2 Nov 1814; A. Nesbitt, bm.

Adinger, Frederic & Elizabeth McCray, 10 March 1820; Christopher McCray, bm.

Adkerson, Calvin & Delphia Smith, 22 March 1832; W. C. Emmit, bm.

Adkins, Alfred & Marthy Oliver, 12 March 1860; m 13 March 1860 by Wm. H. Hubbard, J. P.

Adkins, D. P. & Emily Pryer, 2 March 1862; Wm. A. Lipford, bm; m 10 March 1862 by J. H. Brown.

Adkins, John & Mary Boman, 13 May 1856; Alferd Adkins, bm; m 13 May 1856 by A. M. Foster, J. P.

Adkins, Lewis & Sarah Lipps, 10 March 1849; Wm. Dyer, bm.

Aesque, Pinckney & M. E. Spicer, m 23 April 1865 by Eli Grimes, L. D. M. E. C. S.

Aeyrs, James & Marey Sanders, m 28 June 1853 by E. B. Philips, J. P.

Aldridge, Isham & Diannah Parker, __ Dec 1792; Isaac Walker, bm.

Aldridge, Prince William & Maryann Coons, 18 Feb 1793; Isaac Walker, bm.

Alexander, Colby & Susannah Gambill, 14 Nov 1825; Spencer Adams, bm.

Alexander, Colby & Susannah Gambril, 7 Jan 1826; Spencer Adams, bm.

Alexander, J. H. & Catherine C. Porter, m 14 Nov 1854 by S. C. Williams, J. P.

Alexander, J. T. & Catherine Thompson, m 10 June 1867 by W. Joines, J. P.

Alexander, James & Catharine Overstreet, 12 Sept 1780; Wm. Overstreet, bm; Benjamin Yeargain, wit.

Alexander, Jesse & Fanny Woolfolk, 27 April 1814; Reuben Aprks, bm.

Alexander, Jesse & Elisabeth Billings, 19 June 1828; William Alexander, bm.

Alexander, John & Ann Simpson, 11 March 1779; Benja. Cleveland, bm.

Alexander, Linsey & Mary Alexander, 24 Oct 1815; Solomon Alexander, bm.

Alexander, Nelson & Jane E. Brewer, 21 Feb 1851, m by Eli Grimes, L. D. of M. E. Church South.

Alexander, Randolph & Sary Allexander, 7 July 1819; W. Shackelford, bm.

WILKES COUNTY MARRIAGES, 1778-1868

Alexander, William & Sary Dimmet, 27 Dec 1855; Isham L. Dickerson, bm; m by John Brewer, Esq.

Alexander, William F. & Elizabeth Demmett, 6 Jan 1853; J. H. Alexander, bm; m 6 Jan 1853 by Wm. F. Adams, minister of the Gosspel of the Baptist Denomination.

Alexander, Willis & Sukey Holebrooks, 1 May 1789; Ralph Holbrook, bm.

Alford, Joseph & Elizabeth Darnell, 28 Aug 1804; James Darnall, bm.

Alford, William & Betsy Cannon, 30 April 1804; James Shephard, bm.

Alison, Wm & Charity Elmore, 22 Nov 1793; Geo. Hulme, bm.

Allen, Gideon & Sarah Milliner, 1 Feb 1799; Simeon Perkins, bm.

Allen, John & Eliza Coffey, 1 Sept 1818; Jesse Compton, bm.

Allen, Joseph & Elisabeth Parkes, 3 Feb 1801; Uriah Parkes, bm.

Allen, Joseph & Peggy Parks, 22 Aug 1807; Reuben Parks Junr, bm.

Allen, Richard Junr. & Margaret A. Hampton, 11 Aug 1818; J. Allen, bm.

Allen, Thos & Milley Loven, 1 Oct 1796; Jesse Stamper, bm.

Allen, Wm. & Fanny Cheek, (no date, during admn. of Gov. Nathaniel Alexander); Samuel Cheek, bm.

Allen, Wm. & Martha Renols, 20 June 1783; George Cook, bm.

Allison, Benjamin & Caty Bradly, 2 Jan 1804; James Bradly, bm.

Allexander, Solomon & Salley Caogile, 30 March 1816; Linza Allexander, bm.

Allexander, William & Sary Sparks, 18 March 1820; James Johnson, bm.

Allin, Darlin & Susanna Wallice, 1 April 1809; William Keeton(?), bm.

Alison, David & Patsy McGee, ____ 180_; Bluiforrt McGee, bm; Betsy Lenoir, wit.

Allison, Henery & Susanna Ayleson, 19 April 1781; Benjamin Elledge, bm.

Allison, James & Mary Calton, 29 March 1817; Orrel Livingston, bm.

Allison, Samuel & Polly Brooksher, 10 May 1806; James Ellison, bm.

Allison, Thomas & Casandrew Bird, 17 Aug 1779; Benjamin Bird, bm.

WILKES COUNTY MARRIAGES, 1778-1868

Allowey, John & Elizabeth Waters, 19 Aug 1803; Michael Israel, bm.

Allred, Albertt & Sallie Gordon, m 16 Jan 1853 by David G. Bodenhamer.

Alvey, Elisha & Lucy Brown, 18 April 1808; James Denny, bm.

Alvey, Enoch & Patsy Denney, 25 Oct 1825; Enoch Sale, bm.

Anderson, Albert & Mary Ann Anderson, 24 Feb 1867; Nathaniel Baily, bm.

Anderson, Ausborn (Osborn) & Matilda Johnson, 24 Feb 1851; David Johnston, bm.

Anderson, Cornelius & Alla M. Queen, 4 Aug 1840; James Queen, bm.

Anderson, Eales & Biddy Tedder, 6 Feb 1851; Eanes Anderson, bm; H. O. Waugh, wit.

Anderson, Enos & Nancy Stanley, 11 Oct 1813; A. Nisbett, bm.

Anderson, Enos & Sarah Moore, 17 Feb 1847; James Moore, bm.

Anderson, Enzor & Polly Penix, 27 March 1851; Henry Windle, bm.

Anderson, Evan & Rebecah Smithy, 22 Dec 1823; Wm. Smithy, bm.

Anderson, George & Nancey C. Ferguson, 21 Sept 1865; Alex Bailey, bm; m 22 Sept 1865 by A. B. Dancey, J. P.

Anderson, Jesse & Anny Moore, 18 Jan 1853; Enzor Anderson, bm; m 22 Jan 1853 by W. W. Wright, J. P.

Anderson, Jesse & Sarah Coumbs, 1 Jan 1822; Samuel Anderson, bm.

Anderson, John & Sary Ellis, 11 Oct 1815; Benjamin Ellis, bm.

Anderson, John & Ibby Harris, 26 April 1834; William Anderson, bm.

Anderson, John Alfred & Mary Evans, 24 Dec 1866; T. J. Vannoy, bm.

Anderson, John T. & Sarah C. Hutson, 1 Dec 1863; Henry W. Lane, bm; m 1 Dec 1863 by A. A. Whittentough.

Anderson, Martin & Delita Nance, 24 Dec 1856; Wesley Anderson, bm.

Anderson, Nelson & Amy Matthis, 21 March 1825; Reuben Standley, bm.

Anderson, R., son of Robert & Keziah Anderson, & Levina Johnson, daughter of Noel & Sethe Johnson, 20 Oct 1868; m 22 Oct 1868 at Noel Johnstons, by Oliver Hendren, J. P.

Anderson, Osborn & Matilda Johnson, 24 Feb 1851; m 28 Feb 1851 by Wm. Goforth, minister.

Anderson, Rhesha & Elizabeth Duke, 25 Jan 1822; William P. Johnson, bm.

WILKES COUNTY MARRIAGES, 1778-1868

Anderson, Richd & Clarinda Swinney, ___ 1849(?); Wm. Brown, bm.

Anderson, Richmond & Milley Duncan, 13 May 1841; Chapman Duncan, bm.

Anderson, Robinett & Rebecca Curry, 26 March 1828; Robert Moore, bm.

Anderson, Samuel & Elizabeth Smitsney, 22 May 1819; Jesse Smitsney, bm.

Anderson, Wesly & Dicey Combs, 29 Jan 1833; Robinett Anderson, bm.

Anderson, William & Polly Harris, 28 Dec 1852; John Joines, bm; m 28 Dec 1852 by Thos. S. Wellborn, J. P.

Anderson, William C. & Emily Smithey, 23 Feb 1854; m 28 Feb 1854 by L. J. Bicknell, J. P.

Anderson, William H. & Eada Dula, m 5 Nov 1865 by J. H. Brown.

Andrew, James & Sary Gregory, 23 Dec 1814; Joseph Ray, bm.

Andrew, Robart & Lusey Harvin, 2 Dec 1800; Richard Parker, bm.

Andrews, George & Sarah A. Livingston, 16 Sept 1855; Thomas Andrews, bm; m 16 Sept 1855 by Pickens Carlton, J. P.

Angelly, John & Sary Gray, 21 Jan 1819; Briant Marymen, bm.

Apshar, Jacob & Ann Bradley, 18 Sept 1779; Laurance Bradley, bm.

Armstrong, James C. & Mary Johnson, 10 Aug 1850; John Brown, bm.

Armstrong, J. C. & Mary McBride, 4 April 1863; John Holleman, bm; m 5 March 1863 by S. D. Swaim, Minister of the Gospel in the Baptist denomination.

Armstrong, Thomas & Nansey McBride, 3 April 1866; J. C. Armstrong, bm.

Arnold, S. S. & Susa Sails, 17 Oct 1846; William F. Parker, bm.

Arowood, Jesse & Elizabeth Yeats, 1 Sept 1812; John Yeats, bm.

Arrington, Jno & Mary Stevingson, 27 Dec 1783; Wm Allen, bm.

Asbury, James T. & Sarah A. Allen, 8 July 1846; L. B. Carmichael, bm.

Ashley, John & Marcy Alford, 8 March 1799; Thomas Allin, bm; Richd Allen, wit.

Ashley, Joseph & Hannah Parr, 23 Oct 1804; Abner Parr, bm.

Ashley, Burgess & Susana Wilborn, 9 May 1844; John Welborn, bm.

Ashley, Thomas M. & Caroline Owen, 5 July 1865; m by William Church, J. P.

Ater, James & Bethany Hall, 24 Oct 1854; G. W. Triplett, bm; m 24 Oct 1854 by Thomas Land, J. P.

WILKES COUNTY MARRIAGES, 1778-1868

Atkins, Jonathan G. of Graycon Co., Va. & Cinderella Bryan, 23 April 1843; Robert B. Bryan, bm.

Atkerson, William C. & Mary Shores, 17 Jan 1832; David Rousseau, bm.

Ausbon, Jonathan & Sarah Benge, 11 Sept 1825; Benj. H. Martin, bm.

Austen, Nathan & Marcy Barnes, 11 Sept 1834; Wm Pool, bm.

Austin, William & Sally Dimmit, 3 Nov 1832; Thos Holcomb, bm.

Ayers, Robert & Mary Eve, 26 Jan 1787; James Fletcher, bm.

Ayres, James & Milley Laws, 24 March 1831; Moses Ayres, bm.

Ayres, William & Betsey Hubbard, 27 July 1831; James Mitchell, bm.

Badger, Joshua & Sabrough Gibson, 9 June 1779; Stephen Harris, John Alexander, bm.

Badger, William & Sarah Profitt, 9 Nov 1804; Robert McHay, bm.

Bagbey, Elisha & Rebecah Sale, 9 April 1824; Wm. Gilliam, bm.

Bagby, Edmund & Anne Martin, 7 Oct 1808; Richd Cunningham, bm.

Bagwell, Hiram & Vancey Rash, 12 Dec 1854; Mancy Rash, bm.; m 13 Dec 1852 by Wm. Goforth, minister.

Bailey, Anselm & Elizabeth Bradley, 11 April 1789; James Demoss, bm.

Bailey, Benjamin & Anna Pearce, 13 May 1803; John Walker, bm.

Bailey, Robert P. & Famett Jones, 26 July 1833; Thos R. Tate, bm.

Baird, Joseph & Hannah Lay, 27 Nov 1794; William Dula, bm.

Baker, George & Susanna Morris, 29 Aug 1778; John Baker, Henry Morris, bm.

Baker, Gosten & Elizabeth Meadows, 10 April 1827; John Baker, bm.

Baker, Howell S. & Sarah E. Gilreath, 3 Sept 1861; m 5 Sept 1861 by Eld. Wm. J. Chaffe(?).

Baker, Isaac & Martha Medows, 5 April 1831; Enoch Baker, bm.

Baker, John & ___, 10 Sept 1779; George Morris, Charles Rowland, bm; Spruce Macay, wit.

Baker, John W. & Kizzah Ceareley, 3 April 1830; Clement Cearcley, bm.

Baker, Martin & ___ Vannoy, 1 Aug ___; Nathanael Vannoy, bm.

Balden, John & Pheby Tompkins, 20 Nov 1791; William Tompkins, bm.

WILKES COUNTY MARRIAGES, 1778-1868

Baldwin, John K. & Polly Pourter, 5 March 1829; Benj. Sabastian, bm.

Baldwin, John K. & Sary Warren, 18 Feb 1854; m by John Brewer Esqr.

Baldwin, Joseph & Sally McQuary, 12 Dec 1810; John McQuary, bm.

Ball, George J. & Rachel L. Phrophet, 30 Nov 1866; T. D. Hall, bm.

Ball, Biram & Elizabeth Rash, 18 Jan 1825; Levi Ball, bm.

Ball, Javan & Elizabeth Vicar, 4 Aug 1815; Jno Smoot, bm.

Ball, Javan & Fatana Nance, 22 Jan 1862; Alexander Moore, bm; m 23 Jan 1862 by Wm. Tedder, Baptist minister.

Ball, J. C. & Cenia Marlen, 14 Dec 1865; Wilborn J. Ball, bm; m 15 Dec 1865 by H. Hayes, J. P.

Ball, Joel & Elizabeth Jarvis, 17 Feb 1820; John Ball, bm.

Bawl (Ball), John & Balinona Davis, 19 Nov 1859; Archabel Speakes, bm.

Ball, John & Mary Moore, 8 Jan 1868; m 12 Jan 1868 by Wm. J. Chafe, Baptist minister.

Ball, John B. & Elizabeth Keys, 5 Nov 1854; J. J. L. Church, bm.

Ball, Johnson & Nancy Brown, 3 June 1834; Hamson Miller, bm.

Ball, Levi & Alce Jarvis, 29 Aug 1817; Imlah Ball, bm.

Ball, Nelson & Edney Jerden, 17 Oct 1827; Wm. S. Spencer, bm; Nathl Gordon, wit.

Ball, Sampson & Rosanna Norman, 21 Oct 1811; Asa Rash, bm.

Ball, Silas & Jincey Browder, 29 Aug 1828; Thos Rutherford, bm.

Ball, Wesley & Amy Standly, 6 Feb 1836; Miles Nance, bm.

Ballard, John M. & Elizabeth Sale, 8 March 1864; Milton J. Walker, bm; Eli Grimes, wit.

Ballow, Uriah, son of N. B. & Elisabeth Ballow, & Mary Jane Witherspoon, daughter of William P. & Nancy Witherspoon, 9 April 1868; m by Joel H. Brown, 28 April 1868.

Baltrip, Gabriel & ___, 25 April 1833; Lewis Underwood, bm; F. W. Cass, wit.

Baly, Alexander & Susanah Jones, 7 Dec 1854; John Hall, bm; Silas Brewer, wit.

Bange, Thomas & Patsey Brown, 15 Dec 1867; John Martin, bm.

Bankis, John & Delila Greenstreet, 1 Nov 1808; John Chambers, bm.

Banker, Henry & Cathrine Pruet, 16 Sept 1807; William Laws, bm.

WILKES COUNTY MARRIAGES, 1778-1868

Banks, Johnson & Mary Adams, 23 Feb 1814; Henry Banks, bm.

Banks, Saml & Rebecah Yates, 1 Feb 1814; Henry Banks, bm.

Banks, Westley & Jane Adams, 7 Feb 1797; John Banks, bm.

Barber, Mathew L., son of James & Rilla Barber, & Mary Williams, daughter of Judah Williams, colored, 28 Sept 1867; m 28 Sept 1867 by R. W. Barber.

Barber, R. W. & Mary S. Peden, 22 June 1853; m 23 June 1853 by John H. Parker, minister of the Protestant Episcopal Church.

Barker, John N. & Elizabeth M. Whittington, 19 Nov 1860; m 20 Nov 1860 by Wm. H. Hubbard, J. P.

Barker, Lewis & Elizabeth Childers, 29 Dec 1817; Hezekih Saberstin, bm.

Barker, Lewis & Charety Lawes, 2 Feb 1853.

Barker, Marida & Maryann Suttle, 24 Dec 1855; James P. Cockerham, bm; m 25 Dec 1855 by J. M. Gomhill(?), J. P.

Barker, Meradeth & Sarah Cockerham, 19 Oct 1851; John Durham, bm; m 19 Oct 1851 by Wm. F. Adams, Baptist minister.

Barker, Nathl. & Milley Cockerham, 14 Nov 1829; John Durham, bm.

Barker, Solomon & Mary Wilson, ___ 1820; William Barker, bm.

Barker, William & Elizabeth Wheatly, 20 Nov 1816; John Sabastin, bm.

Barker, William & M. C. Davis, 19 June 1850; James Wellborn, bm.

Barlow, Braxton & Charlotte Catton, 21 Jan 1834; Livingston Catton, bm.

Barlow, Eliphelet & Nancy Bradley, 11 Feb 1823; Thomas Stone, bm.

Barlow, H. H. & Amanda Ferguson, 25 Oct 1861; m by J. H. Brown.

Barlow, Henry & Patsey Dula, 14 Jan 1832; Eliphalet Barlow, bm.

Barlow, Henry & Matilday Kilbey, 22 March 1832; W. M. Forester, bm.

Barlow, J. C. & Susanna Pennel, 9 Dec 1858; m by E. B. Philips, J. P.

Barlow, John & Elizabeth Merrit, 20 April 1803; Thomas Isbell, bm.

Barlow, John & Susannah Rauswell, 19 March 1808; Morton Jones, bm.

Barlow, John & Nancy N. Nulby, 20 Oct 1842; Reubin W. Kilby, bm.

WILKES COUNTY MARRIAGES, 1778-1868

Barlow, Joseph & Louisa Laxton, 24 April 1828; Lewis Laxton, bm.

Barlow, Larkin & Edy Knight, 22 Aug 1840; Newman J. Holder, bm.

Barlow, Thomas & Susannah Isbell, 28 Jan 1794; Ambrose Parks, bm.

Barlow, Thomas & Sarrah Kilby, 20 Feb 1822; Thornton Kilby, bm; consent from Humphrey Kilby, guardian for Sarah.

Barlow, Thomas L. & Elizabeth A. Ferguson, 14 Dec 1859; Henry H. Barlow, bm; m 23 Dec 1859 by E. B. Philips, J. P.

Barlow, William & Jane Burch, 22 Dec 1818; George Ferguson, bm.

Barnes, Archibald & Lucinda Mallby, 20 April 1840; John Watts, bm.

Barnes, E. F. & A. E. Fletcher, 13 April 1866; Peter Q. Barker, bm; m 15 April 1866 by James Kerby, minister.

Barnes, George & Mary Parkes, 28 Sept 1819; Wm Watts, bm.

Barnes, George & Salley Mitchell, 3 April 1824; John Barnes, bm.

Barnes, Isaac & Elizabeth Barnes, 23 July 1827; George W. Jones, bm.

Barnes, Jesse & Anna Marley, 13 Dec 1806; John Marley (Marlow), bm.

Barnes, John & Polly Swim, 25 May 1811; Peter Barnes, bm.

Barnes, John & Cynthia Mackconer Parkes, 21 May 1821; Solomon Barnes, bm; Mary Martin, wit.

Barnes, John & Nancy Mitchel, 4 April 1823; George Mitchel, bm.

Barnes, John & Nelley Lanes, 1 Oct 1857; m 1 Oct 1857 by Charles Carlton, J. P.

Barnes, Joshua & Sary Murphrey, 28 May 1819; Thos Barnes, bm.

Barnes, Peter & Martha Swaim, 6 Feb 1806; Michael Swaim, bm.

Barnes, Peter & Mary Bryant, 14 April 1817; John ___, bm.

Barnes, Solomon & Elizabeth Phillips, 21 Sept 1813; Peter Barnes, bm.

Barnes, Solomon & Mary A. Ferguson, m 31 Oct 1867 by Smith Ferguson.

Barnes, Thos & Ann Murpha, 7 March 1813; Archable Murphe, bm.

Barnet, James & Mary Baker, 3 Nov 1779; Pritchet Alexander, bm.

Barnett, Hamilton & Mary Ann West, 1 Aug 1866; J. W. West, bm; m 8 Aug 1866 by J. W. Church.

Barnett, James & Nancy Holder, 4 Oct 1823; John Dula, bm.

Barnett, James & Margaret Call, 6 Nov 1855.

WILKES COUNTY MARRIAGES, 1778-1868

Barnett, James Jur. & Martha Williams, 28 Dec 1852.

Barnett, John & Tempy Dostridg, 10 Oct 1818; Isaac Paxsley, bm.

Barnett, Mark & Nesa Beach, 28 Nov 1840; Bennet Dula, bm.

Barnett, Robert E. & Emaline Tuder, 25 Dec 1854; m 25 Dec 1854 by J. D. Hubbard, J. P. (return has Emaline Tedder).

Barnett, Randolph S. & Eliza Ann Chapel, 2 Oct 1860.

Barns, Brinsly & Sarah Barns, 2 Feb 1796; George Brown, bm.

Barns, John & Nancy Brown, ___ 1800; John Brown, bm; consent dated 9 Jan 1800 from George Brown, father of Nancy and John Brown.

Barns, Thomas & Polley Stinson, 27 March 1831; Isaiah Lowe, bm.

Barton, Benjamin & Lucy Wilburn, 10 March 1779; Wm. Wilburn, Isaac Welburn, bm.

Bass, William & Eliza Sulivan, 17 Sept 1856; Chapman Duncan, bm.

Bates, John & Sarah Hawkins, 21 April 1801; James Tugman, bm.

Baty, Moses & Martha McCoy, 23 Feb 1853; John Robertson, bm; m 24 Feb 1853 by W. W. Wright, J. P.

Bauguss, Osburn & Fanny Roberts, 13 Oct 1843; David K. Bauguss, bm.

Baugess, Rheuben & Eveline Richardson, 9 April 1862; John Hall, bm.

Baugess, William & Sary Waddle, 19 Feb 1819; C___ Waddle, bm.

Baugess, Emanuel & Amelia Sparks, 26 Sept 1817; Joseph Speer, bm.

Baugess, Vinson & Nancy Creed, 10 Jan 1843; Henry Creed, bm.

Bauges, John & Nancy Caudle, 2 Nov 1821; Jesse Caudle, bm.

Baugus, Reubin & Francis Gambell, 27 Jan 1834; William C. Slone, bm.

Baugus, Solomon & Nancy Adams, 5 Dec 1855.

Baugus, Vinson & Suana Hanks, 7 Jan 1817; James Hanks, bm.

Bauguss, Richard & Lidia Waddell, 26 Oct 1831; Mason Johnson, bm.

Bauguss, Richard & Elisabeth Lacky, 29 March 1835; Nelson Hagins, bm.

Bauguss, Saml J. & Leafy Yeates, 15 Nov 1840; Jno. E. Mastin, bm.

Bawl, Eliga & Lewenday Redding, 12 Dec 1844; James Gregory, bm.

Beach, Oliver C. & Selah Forgason, 9 Jan 1833; Mariman Walker, bm.

WILKES COUNTY MARRIAGES, 1778-1868

Beach, William & Elsy Kurby, 27 Dec 1831; Owen Mereman, bm.

Beams, James & Nancey Lay, 3 Sept 1793; Jesse Lay, bm.

Beasley, Edmund & Nancey Moore, 26 Sept 1787; Joseph Forguson, bm.

Beaty, John W. & Cathrine Wagoner, 4 Oct 1841; Wm. L. Cooper, bm.

Bebber, Elisha & Serah H. Fletcher, 6 Sept 1858; m 14 Sept 1858 by Wm. H. Hubbard, J. P.

Bebber, John G. & Irenah Jines, 3 Jan 1855; m 3 Jan 1855 by E. B. Philips, J. P.

Beck, Joel L. & Mary E. Foster, 1 Sept 1841; Elisha B. Phillips, bm.

Beck, Wm. D. & Rebecka Brown, 10 Dec 1816; Wm. Dotson Senr., bm.

Becknall, Benj. & Rebecca Lewis, 10 Sept 1813; J. Waugh, bm.

Becknel, Pleasant & Mary Campble, 27 Feb 1821; Reuben Standley, bm.

Becknall, Meriday & Rebeccah Hanley, 18 Dec 1823; Wm. Nance, bm.

Becknall, Merril & Sarah Lewis, 11 Aug 1829; Reuben Standley, bm.

Becknell, A. A. & Amanda A. Kemp, 10 May 1864; R. M. Smith, bm; m 30 Jan 1865 by Rev. R. W. Wooton.

Becknol, Benja. E. & Sarah Hardin, 14 Jan 1853; m 18 Jan 1853 by R. W. Wooton, J. P.

Becknell, Lewis & Jane Felts, 12 July 1819; Henry Cook, bm.

Beeman, Charles & Mathey Currey, 28 April 1800; John Currey, bm.

Bell, Archabald & Mary Bustle, 4 Dec 1851; Ausborn Anderson, bm.

Bell, George & Polley Runt, 23 Sept 1783; Jacob Stanley, bm.

Bell, Ivin & Fanney Johnson, 5 March 1839; John Curry Jr., bm.

Bell, Manuel & Nina Pruitt, 2 Oct 1851; James Parker, bm; m 3 Oct 1851 by Wm Goforth, minister.

Bell, Reason & Mary Smitsney, 5 Nov 1816; David Bell, bm.

Bellee, Tho. & Sarah Eve, 16 Sept 1788; Robert Ayers, bm; Russel Jones, William Jacks, Thos Land, wit.

Bell, Thomas S. & Malinday Anderson, 23 Feb 1854; m 28 Feb 1854 by L. J. Bicknell, J. P.

Bell, William & Aladelpha Speaks, 1 Feb 1816; Joseph James, bm.

13

WILKES COUNTY MARRIAGES, 1778-1868

Bell, Zadock & Elizabeth Becknall, 6 Feb 1827; Wm Bell, bm.

Bemon, George C. & ___, 25 March 1867; Thomas C. Minter, bm.

Benge, James C., son of Willis and Sarah Benge, and Rebecca C. Younce, daughter of Wm H. Parsons and Sinthy Parsons, 7 Sept 1867; m 8 Sept 1867 by J. W. Church, J. P. at W. W. Whites.

Benge, James & Elizabeth Fedor, 17 ___ 1820; Jeremiah Gibson, bm.

Bently, Henry & Sarah Stevens, 10 March 1865; Daniel Bently, bm; m 12 March 1865 by J. W. Church.

Bentley, James & Elizabeth Laws, 25 Feb 1806; William Laws, bm.

Bentley, John & Polley Laws, 31 Jan 182_; James Laws, bm.

Bentley, John & Nersisey Payn, 6 March 1856; m 6 March 1856 by A. Gilreath, minister.

Bentley, Martain & Nancy Feeland, 27 March 1834; Robert Sloan, bm.

Bentley, Thomas & Hannah Bentley, 12 May 1824; Squire Bentley, bm.

Benton, Abram & Susannah Caul, 8 Nov 1808; Joseph Ray, bm.

Benton, Warren & Frances Mathes, 3 Jan 1817; William McDaniel, bm.

Berry, Franklin & Jenny Curtis, 18 May 1805; David Humphry, bm.

Berry, Jesse & Merey Colvard, (no date, during admn. of Gov. Wm. R. Davie); Wm Colvard, bm.

Beshears, John, son of Aaron & Aley Beshears, and Selenia V. Church, daughter of William and Sally Church, 24 Oct 1867; m 27 Oct 1867 by J. W. Church, J. P.

Bever, Isaac & Ann Bryant, 21 July 1820; John Person, bm.

Bevoly, John & Milley Suttle, 1 Dec 1779; Benja. Cleveland, bm.

Becknell, Jordon & Mary Harriett Byers; J. W. Clendennin, bm; 5 Oct 1866.

Bicknell, Larkin J. & Marinda Hammons, 29 Dec 1834; J. J. Bryan, bm.

Billings, Elijah & Elisabeth Fuget, 27 March 1827; John Fugit, bm.

Billings, Daniel & Nancy Baugess, 26 Dec 1865; John Bauges, bm; m 31 Dec 1865 by R. Sparks, Ll. d.

Billings, Elisha & Nancy Hawkins, 4 Nov 1831; William Wiles, bm.

Billings, Elisha & ___, 9 Nov 1837; Thomas Wiles, bm.

Billing, Hiram & Rosannah Minton, 20 March 1828; John Church Jr., bm.

WILKES COUNTY MARRIAGES, 1778-1868

Billings, Aderson & Susan Holebrook, 12 March 1854; m by
Eli Grimes, L. D. of M. E. C. S.

Billings, Hiram & Sally Kilbey, 24 March 1864; Daniel Jinings,
bm.

Billings, James H. & Arrena R. Sparks, 5 Aug 1860; m 6 Aug
1860 by John Gentry.

Billings, Jasper, son of Thomas & Nancy Billings, and Dicey
Davis, daughter of John and Bethania Davis, 19 Oct 1867;
m 20 Oct 1867 by Daniel Welborn, Baptist minister.

Billings, Jessa & Emely E. Buttery, 17 Dec 1851; m 17 Dec 1851
by Eli Grimes, L. D. of M. E. Church S.

Billings, Jesse & Lucinda Riley, 28 Dec 1822; Claborn Wadel,
bm.

Billings, Jesse & Candis Blackburn, 12 April 1843; John
Bauguss, bm.

Billings, John & Pheba Combs, 15 Jan 1841; Jery Alexander, bm.

Billings, John & Susan Bauguss, 20 Feb 1847; John Baugess, bm.

Billings, Joseph, son of Hiram Billings, & Sarah Jane Wilcoxson,
daughter of William C. Wilcoxson, m 1 March 1868 by Wm. A.
M___ J. P., at the house of Wm. A. M___.

Billings, Thos. & Franky Combs, 4 Aug 1835; Jery Alexander, bm.

Billings, Thos & Nancy Wiles, 28 Sept 1845; Thomas Wiles, bm.

Billings, Thomas & Frances Bowers, 16 Sept 1864; Adam Grimes,
bm; m 26 Sept 1864 by Eli Grimes, L. D. of M. E. C. S.

Billings, Thomas & Sary Elles, 28 Jan 1867; James Walker, bm.

Billings, Wilborn & Catharine Holbrooks, 6 June 1858;
A. Waddel, bm; m by P. Grimes.

Billings, Wellborn & Sally M. Higgins, 25 Dec 1852; Reuben R.
Hall, bm; m 25 Dec 1852 by L. Sebastian, J. P.

Billings, William & Winney Allexander, 10 April 1816; Linsy
Allexander, bm.

Billings, Wm. & Salley Childers, 8 April 1831; William W.
Couthern, bm.

Bingham, Benjamin & Nancy Prophit, 19 March 1818; John Prophit,
bm.

Bingham, D.A. & Hulda Handy, 2 Dec 1865; N. P. Canter, bm.

Bingham, Joseph T. & Minerva Adaline Linear(?), 23 Nov. 1846;
Saml Stelman, bm.

Bingham, R. S. & Elisabeth Parker, 26 Oct 1861; J. W. Kilbey,
bm; m 26 Oct 1861 by A. A. Whittenton, J. P.

Bingham, Wm. & Frances Case, 19 Feb 1818; Joseph Howard, bm.

WILKES COUNTY MARRIAGES, 1778-1868

Birchitt, Isom & Mary J. Edwards, 26 Nov 185; Maraday Thorton, bm.

Bird, Thomas & Elizabeth Heatley, 6 Jan 1784; Thomas Allison, bm.

Bird, William & Elizabeth Gregory, 27 Oct 1858; Wm. Iscore, bm; m 28 Oct 1858 by John Brown, J. P.

Bishop, Abraham & Phebe Jones, 3 Nov 1795; William Laws, bm.

Bishop, Abraham & Nancey Phillips, 1 Feb 1834; Larkin Bishop, bm.

Bishop, Alfred & Nancey Holt, 25 Aug 1855; N. A. Foster, bm.

Bishop, Calvin & Carline Church, 2 Sept 1841; Larkin Bishop, bm; m by Saml Walsh, J. P.

Bishop, George W. & Christenas Hicks, 13 Sept 1862; John J. Foster, bm; m 21 Sept 1862 by J. F. Tugman, J. P.

Bishop, Hiram & Mary Watson, 30 March 1835; David Watson, bm.

Bishop, Jesse & Nancy Crain, 21 Dec 1840; John Dockry, bm.

Bishop, John & Elizabeth Smith, 16 June 1827; John Watson, bm.

Bishop, John R. & Eliza Ann Minton, 24 Feb 1853.

Bishop, Larkin & Sarah Mitchell, 7 Feb 1833; Elihue Watson, bm.

Bishop, Lindsey, son of Abraham & Nancy Bishop, & Margret E. Hix, daughter of Charles & Charlotte Hix, m 18 July 1867 by J. W. Church, J. P.

Bishop, Roger & Jane Adams, 10 April 1801; John Banks, bm.

Bishop, Saml & Nelly Adams, 7 Oct 1799; William Adams, bm.

Bishop, Samuel & Huldah Summerlin, 26 Oct 1842; Wesly Hamby, bm; m Oct 1842 by Saml Walsh, J. P.

Blackbern, Spencer & Viry Wiles, 10 Feb 1853; m by John Brewer, J. P.

Blackborn, Miles & Martha Harras, 2 Jan 1866; L. H. Carter, bm; m 4 Jan 1866 by John K. Rose, Bapt. minister.

Blackburn, Andrew J. & Frances Farchilds, 9 Dec 1842; Enoch Holman, bm.

Blackburn, C. F., son of W. B. Blackburn and Sarah Crouse, & Katherine Blackburn, daughter of Henry and Mahaley Crouse, 29 Nov 1867; m 2 Dec 1867 by John Gentry, J. P.

Blackburn, Eli & Polley Caudell, 7 Dec 1827; Thomas Caudell, bm.

Blackburn, Francis E. & Nancy E. Spence, 22 Dec 1859; Wm. Johnson, bm; m 22 Dec 1859 by Wm. H. Pardue.

Blackburn, James W. & Dianna Waddill, 20 April 1861; m 24 April 1861 by Jno M. Brown.

WILKES COUNTY MARRIAGES, 1778-1868

Blackburn, John & Winney Rivett, 17 Oct 1818; Joel Sparks, bm.

Blackburn, John & Milly Dyer, 23 Dec 1832; John Mitchell, bm.

Blackburn, John & Charlotte Hendricks, 2 July 1844; Joel Sparks, bm.

Blackburn, John N. & Delthe Goforth, 5 April 1862; Wm. A. Keller, bm; m 26 March 1862 by Rev. J. McNeill.

Blackburn, Lambeth & Nancy Hanks, 29 Nov 1822; Vincen Baugus, bm.

Blackburn, Moses E. & Abigail Spicer, 5 Dec 1855; Samuel Hanks, bm; Ansel Parks, wit; m 6 Dec 1855 by Ansel Parks.

Blackburn, Perry A., son of Wm. B. & Sarah Blackburn, & Mary Thomas, daughter of Henry & Susan Thomas, m 23 Aug 1867, by J. P. Parks, J. P.

Blackburn, William C. & Susanah Brewer, 23 May 1863; Jesse Blackburn, bm.

Blackburn, William & Catherine Hanks, 13 Aug 1819; Vinson Baugus, bm; W. W. Martin, wit.

Blackburn, Wm. & Sarah McNiel, 23 Oct 1841; James McNeil, bm; m 24 Oct 1841 by Wm. Church.

Blackburn, William Burton & Sarah McCan, 4 April 1846; James Durham, bm.

Blackburn, Wm. J. & Nancy E. Hembee, 29 Dec 1864; J. D. Walker, bm; m 29 Dec 1864 by Eli Grimes, L. D. of M. E. C. S.

Blackburn, Wm. J. & Margaret Cordill, 4 Nov 1857; L. M. Blackburn, bm; m 12 Nov 1857 by R. C. Sparks.

Blackburn, John & Polly Holbrook, 14 Nov 1861; J. F. Walker, bm; m 16 Nov 1861 by Wm. Hall, minister.

Blake, Hugh & Nancy Wellborn, 17 Aug 1799; G. Jones, bm; Edd. Jones, wit.

Blankinship, E. A. & Mary A. Church, 21 Jan 1854; John Adkins, bm; m 21 Jan 1854 by A. M. Foster, J. P.

Blakingship, John T. & Fanny L. Walsh, 25 Dec 1865; m 31 Dec 1865 by J. W. Church.

Blaylock, John & A. H. Ginning, 9 March 1866.

Blevens, William & Roady Prewit, 4 Feb 1816; Jeremiah Caudell, bm.

Blevins, Elisha & Nancy Adams, 1 m Jan 1854 by S. J. Gambill Esqr.

Blevins, John & Nancy Pruet, 7 Jan 1824; Wm. Blevins, bm.

Blevins, John & Susanah Hays, 25 Oct 1849; Ezekael Hawkins, bm.

WILKES COUNTY MARRIAGES, 1778-1868

Boarin, William & Mary Johnson, 9 July 1817; Ambrose Johnson, bm.

Boaz, Edmond T. & Susanah Joyner, 12 Sept 1846; Willis Demmet, bm.

Bolejack, William & Nelley Forrester, 23 Aug 1817; John Forester, bm.

Bowles, Simpson & Elizabeth Brown, 24 Oct 1861; W. M. Forester, bm; m 24 Oct 1861 by J. A. Haynes, J. P.

Boling, Justus & Pattie Baker, 8 Jan 1782; Jesse Ray (Wray), bm.

Boman, Alfred & Elizabeth Boman, 1 Aug 1854; Calvin J. Cowles, bm; m 29 Nov 1854 by A. M. Foster(?).

Boman, James & Elizabeth Webb, 7 Sept 1811; William Hamby, bm; Mary McCord, wit.

Boman, John W. & Jane E. Foster, 18 March 1856; L. C. Ferguson, bm; m 18 March 1856 by A. M. Foster, J. P.

Bomar, Thomas & Elizabeth Spencer, 1 Nov 1847; Wm. D. Allison, bm.

Bond, Jesse & Rebecca Opkins, 19 Dec 1780; Samuel Simpson, bm.

Boothe, James & Polley Mullis, 26 Feb 1820; John Coleman, bm.

Borders, Eli & Sarah Jarman, 21 April 1827; William Moony, bm.

Bottom, Franklin & Sintha Mahathes, 20 Jan 1855; James Myers, bm.

Bouchill, Thomas Slater & Miss C. J. E. Finly, 26 Dec 1826; Th. W. Wilson, bm.

Bouchelle, Augustus W., son of Thomas S. & Clarinda J. E. Bouchelle, & Elizabeth E. Mastin, daughter of William and Rebecca A. Mastin, 22 Dec 1868; m 24 Dec 1868 by R. W. Barber.

Bouchelle, Thos S. & Sarah A. Hackett, 25 Jan 1864; W. W. Vannoy, bm; m 26 Jan 1864 by J. D. Wilson.

Boulam, A. J. & Mary J. Stone, 7 March 1866.

Bowen, Isaac & Mary Roy, 11 May 1785; Thos Ray, bm.

Bowers, Findley & Rebeca Myres, 11 June 1861; m by Alfred Warren, J. P.

Bowers, George & Nancy Bryan, 10 Feb 1825; Benj. J. Parks, bm.

Bowers, George & America C. Rousseau, 7 Nov 1839; B. F. Pettey, bm.

Bowers, Giles & Elizabeth Robinson, 2 Aug 1860; John Duncan, bm; m 26th Aug 1860 by S. J. Ginnings, J. P.

Bowers, Wm & Milley Brotherton, 1 Oct 1833; Wm Redding, bm.

WILKES COUNTY MARRIAGES, 1778-1868

Bowers, William & Mahaley Walker, 17 Dec 1868, m by A. W. Myers.

Bowles, E. & Matilda Perdew, 15 Aug 1866; L. F. Madison, bm.

Bowman, Peter & Elizabeth Wilson, 9 June 1780; William McGill, bm.

Boyd, John & Ann Bone, 16 Nov 1779; James Bones, bm.

Bozwel, William & Elisabeth Winfree, 24 Dec 1816; James Hemby, bm.

Bradbury, John & ___; James Bradbury, bm; (no date).

Bradley, George S. & Sarah E. Howel, 8 March 1842; Jackson W. Bradley, bm.

Bradley, James & Hannah Pogue, 1 May 1806; Joseph Pogue, bm.

Bradley, Levi & Jane Barlow, 29 April 1828; Eli Stone (Story), bm; consent from James and Hannah Bradley, parents of Levi Bradley.

Bradly, Richard & Sally Mooney, 27 Nov 1805; James Walker, bm.

Bradly, George W. & Lucinda Pain, 14 Feb 1834; Anthony Lepford, bm.

Brady, Spencer & Mary Simcock, 4 Oct 1817; Thomas Bryant, bm.

Brandon, Joseph & Susannah Chambers, 28 May 1814; Wm. B. Sharp, bm.

Brandon, Thomas & Cyntha Horn, 17 March 1828; Joseph Horn, bm.

Bratcher, Seth & Anna Low, 10 Dec 1784; Isaac Loe, bm.

Bray, Moses & Lucy Walker, 4 Jan 1822; Mere Walker, bm.

Brewer, Albert P. & Martha L. Porter, 21 June 1838; George Whatley Jr., bm.

Brewer, Charles N. & Sarah Jane Madison, 30 June 1867; m by J. N. Haynes.

Brewer, Eli & Jane Higgins, 30 Oct 1855; John Brewer, bm.

Brewer, Felix & Sarah Wiles, 26 June 1859; m 26 June 1859 by Eli Grimes, L. D. of M. E. C. S.

Brewer, Henry L. & Milly Call, 4 Aug 1846; Josiah Brewer, bm.

Brewer, Joel & Nancy Adams, 27 Dec 1838; Wm. Adams, bm.

Brewer, John D. & Nancy Hutchison, 28 Aug 1856; m 28 Aug 1856 by L. Sebastian, J. P.

Brewer, Siler & Franses A. Johnson, 18 April 1864; Adam Jones, bm; m 20 April 1864 by Jno. M. Brown, J. P.

Brewer, William & Phana Risdin, 19 April 1781; William Cocram, bm.

Briant, John & Sally Kerby, 14 March 1807; John Kerby, bm.

WILKES COUNTY MARRIAGES, 1778-1868

Bridges, Nathaniel & Sarah Fox, 27 Dec 1836; Benjamin Clary, bm.

Brient, R. A. & Catherine Head, 24 Dec 1856; m 25 Dec 1856 by John Brown, Esqr.

Brinegar, Jacob & Tasann Johnson, 9 Feb 1832; John Brown Jr., bm.

Brock, Allen & Nancy Rains, 30 Dec 1837; John E. Mastin, bm.

Brock, Lensey & Tabetha White, 10 March 1828; Lemuel Doss, bm.

Brock, Martin & Agness Gilreath, 6 Oct 1835; James Underwood, bm.

Brock, Rainey W. & Elizabeth Ragsdell, 28 Dec 1848; James J. Ragsdell, bm.

Brogden, William & Salley Perdue, 25 March 1844; Edmond Day, bm.

Brookes, Robert & Amey Pendergrass, 11 April 1860; Roley Pendergrass, bm.

Brookes, Vinson & Edney M. Strane(?), ___ 1840; Manson Wood, bm.

Brooks, Eli A. & Mary Brewer, 4 Nov 1846; Wm. E. Reynolds, bm.

Brooks, James & Nancy Edwards, 17 Oct 1807; William Miller, bm.

Brooks, James & Mary A. Tomlinson, 5 March 1835.

Brooks, John & Francis Benton, 26 Jan 1826; Eli Pettey, bm.

Brooks, Larkin & Mary Brown, 15 Nov 1843; James M. Brown, bm.

Brooks, John N. & Susana Jinnings, 26 Dec 1866; Wm. McGrady, bm; m 27 Dec 1866 by Henry Jinnings, J. P.

Brooks, John S. & Sarah Elledge, 20 Dec 1866; J. P. Pruitt, bm; m 25 Dec 1866 by W. Joines, J. P.

Brooks, Robert & Sarah Royaland, 5 May 1867; m 14 July 1867 by Rev. William J. Combs.

Brooks, Stokes & Clarasey Reynolds, 1 Jan 1822; J. A. Barrit, bm.

Brooks, Zachariah & Sarah Baugus, 7 March 1821; James Byrd, bm.

Brookshire, Elisha & Mary Ann Kirk, 9 Oct 1858; Enoch Brookshire, bm.

Brookshire, James & Elizabeth Tilley, 21 Aug 1827; Benjamin Shearwood, bm.

Brookshire, N. B. & Sarah Miller(?), 5 Aug 1861; John J. Foster, bm.

Brookshire, William & Nancy Triplette, 13 Nov 1817; W. T. Campbell, bm.

WILKES COUNTY MARRIAGES, 1778-1868

Brookshire, Wm & Matilda Kilby, 14 Sept 1858; John Pearson, bm; m 17 Sept 1858 by John Parker, J. P.

Brookshire, William & Matilda Cesell, 7 April 1867; m 7 April 1867 by J. W. Church.

Brookshire, Wilis, son of Joel & Nancy Brookshire, & Sarah Wellborn, daughter of Daniel & Susan Wellborn, m 23 Jan 1868 by Smith Ferguson.

Brothertin, Hugh B. & Alsa Cook, 16 Dec 1843; Alfred Quinn, bm.

Brothertin, James & Elizabeth Wysong, 26 Feb 1839; Isaac Brothertin, bm.

Brotherton, John M. C. & Amelia M. Wright, 4 Oct 1850; James W. Wright, bm.

Brotherton, Levi & Jane Queen, 27 March 1828; Elis Queen, bm.

Browlan, John & Marray Fletcher, 12 Aug 1836; Henry Rash, bm.

Brown, A. H. & Mary Shumate, 31 Oct 1854; m 31 Oct 1854 by L. Sebastian, J. P.

Brown, Aaron & Elender Shomate, 27 Jan 1841; William Sabastion, bm.

Brown, Abraham & Lucy Edwards, 24 Oct 1821; John Brown, bm.

Brown, Abraham & Nancy L. Brown, 30 June 1864; G. H. Brown, bm; m 30 June 1864 by William Hall.

Brown, Alfred & Elizy Kendall, 21 Feb 1848; William S. Ferguson, bm.

Brown, Archer & Nancy Phillips, 4 Nov 1805; John Brown, bm.

Brown, Benjamin & Nancy Tugman, 26 April 1832; Wellborn Garman, bm.

Brown, Benjamin & Susanah Brown, 1 Nov 1861; Wesley Brown, bm.

Brown, Benjamin H. & Sarah Hubbard, 2 Oct 1826; Henry Gilreath, bm.

Brown, Benjamin H. & Nancy Goar, 16 Dec 1843; D. C. Stinson, bm.

Brown, Brison & Sena Ellige, 3 March 1867; m 17 March 1867 by W. Joines, J. P.

Brown, Charles & Mary Denney, 13 Oct 1783; George Denney, bm.

Brown, Daniel & Elizabeth Fitts, 30 Aug 1814; H. Brown, bm.

Brown, Daniel & Dolly McGrady, 18 Jan 1831; John Brown, bm.

Brown, Daniel & Jinsey Clark, 12 Aug 1824; Tillis Bussell, bm.

Brown, Daniel W. & Lidia Harris, 1 Nov 1848; Tinley Laws or Louther, bm.

Brown, David & Margartt Montgomery, 3 June 1832; Hiram Bushup, bm.

WILKES COUNTY MARRIAGES, 1778-1868

Brown, David & Susanah Hamby, 1 Nov 1842; Charles Hix, bm.

Brown, Edwin & Cyntha McEwen, 29 Sept 1811; John Grier, bm.

Brown, Eli & Betsy Brookshire, 13 Jan 1807; Francis Brown, James Brown, bm.

Brown, Elisha & Elisabeth Redding, 20 Oct 1813; Wm. Redding, bm.

Brown, Ely & Elizabeth Meadows, 13 April 1846; John Brown, bm.

Brown, Ezekael & Susanah Brown, 23 Jan 1849; Zachariah Roberts, bm.

Brown, Ezekiel & Sta(?) Stamper, 16 April 1844; George Wyatt, bm.

Brown, Francis & Nelley Foster, 2 Feb 1808; Joshua Johnson, bm.

Brown, Francis & Mary Mitchel, 17 Nov 1815; John Elledge, bm.

Brown, George & Sally Roberts, 26 April 1806; Joshua Smith, bm.

Brown, George & Nelly Kerley, 11 Oct 1821; Daniel Harrison, bm.

Brown, George & Delphia A. Hampton, 17 Feb 1833; J. J. Bryan, bm.

Brown, George H., son of Wm. H. & Julia Brown, & Olivia A. Smith, daughter of Samp P. Smith Sr. & Amelia M. Smith, 12 Nov 1867; m 12 Nov 1867 by R. Hale(?), Baptist minister.

Brown, George Hamilton & Matilda Blevins, 31 Dec 1859; m 1 Jan 1860 by H. Hutchison, J. P.

Brown, George W. & Vira Marlow, 19 Sept 1848; Elijah Hendrix(?), bm.

Brown, George W. & Amelia Lane, 21 Jan 1851; Jn. W. Pearson, bm.

Brown, H. A., son of Hamilton & Sarahan Brown, & A. S. Guyn, daughter of James and Maryan Guyn, 29 April 1868; m by R. W. Barber, minister Ep. Ch.

Brown, Hamilton & Sarah H. Gorden, 6 Oct 1830; Hugh Brown, bm.

Brown, Henry & Amandy M. Tedder, 9 March 1862; George Roberts, bm.

Brown, Henry J. & Marey Gilliam, 16 March 1849; Elsey A. B. Messick, bm.

Brown, Hugh & Mira E. Gordon, 5 Sept 1827; Thos P. Gwyn, bm.

Brown, Isaac & Famy Eller, 3 Sept 1851; m 6 Sept 1851 by Wm. Church.

Brown, Isaac & Jemima Phillips, 3 Aug 1857; John W. Whittington, bm; m 5 Aug 1857 by Wm. H. Phillips.

WILKES COUNTY MARRIAGES, 1778-1868

Brown, Isaac J. & Martha Ballows, 24 Sept 1862; Wm. Perdue, bm; m 24 Sept 1862 by Isaac N. Haynes, J. P.

Brown, Isaiah M. & Jane H. Woodruff, 30 Dec 1864; Wm. M. Caudill, bm; m 15 Jan 1865 by Rev. R. Sparks, D. D.

Brown, J. A. & Elizabeth McNil, 19 Oct 1858; Elijah Dyer, bm; m 19 Oct 1858 by A. M. Foster, J. P.

Brown, Jackson J. & Sary Wilcockson, 25 Dec 1858; Victory Wiatt, bm; m 26 Dec 1858 by Wm. Hall, M. G.

Brown, Jackson & Martha Gorden, 26 Sept 1866; Wm. M. Forester, bm.

Brown, James L. & Carolina Mahaffey, 18 June 1862; W. Mahaffey, bm; m 19 June 1862 by J. N. Haynes, J. P.

Brown, James & Nancy Brookshair, 30 Sept 1801; Francis Brown, bm.

Brown, Jas. & Suckey Alvey, 10 Aug 1808; Jas. Denne, bm.

Brown, James & Suana Maner, 2 Jan 1817; John Grimsley, bm.

Brown, James & Patsy Johnson, 10 Dec 1817; Ambrose Johnson, bm.

Brown, James & Nancy Jarman, 16 March 1831; Rily Brown, bm.

Brown, James & Ann Corley, 6 Dec 1837; John E. Mastin, bm.

Brown, James T. & Polley Isbill, 25 March 1797; J. Stewart(?), bm.

Brown, Jeremiah & Milley McEwen, 15 March 1807; John N. Greer, bm.

Brown, Jesse & Mary Sumerlin, 14 Dec 1841; John Brown, bm.

Brown, Jesse & Ann Jones, 25 Jan 1813; John Greer, bm.

Brown, Jesse & Polly Towell, 27 Jan 1820; Yrpts Maberry, bm.

Brown, Joel & Rebekah Kamp, 5 Nov. 1805; Joshua Souther, bm.

Brown, Joel & Rebecah Clark, 12 May 1830; William Brown, bm.

Brown, Joel & Mary Bicknell, 30 Aug 1852; Wesley Felts, bm.

Brown, John & Elizabeth Risdin, 18 Jan 1783; Benjamin Herndon, bm.

Brown, John & Susannah Allison, 12 Feb 1785; Wm. Hamby, bm.

Brown, John & Polley Miller, 12 Dec 1799; David Miller, bm.

Brown, John & Mary Mundy, 2 Oct 1813; Hartwell Hayes, bm.

Brown, John & Mary B. Gordan, 30 Dec 1813; Nathl. Groon, bm.

Brown, John & Nancy Fergerson, 22 July 1820; Lewis Johnson, bm.

Brown, John & Sidney Johnson, 28 Oct 1820; William R. Sparks, bm.

23

WILKES COUNTY MARRIAGES, 1778-1868

Brown, John & Mary Wellborn, 31 July 1822; Eli Brown, bm.

Brown, John & Violet Fortner, 18 Jan 1825; Enoch Chapman, bm.

Brown, John & Elizabeth Brown, 15 Sept 1828; Daniel Brown, bm.

Brown, John & ___, 10 April 1837; Anderson Ashly, Lewis Day, Wm Mastin, bm.

Brown, John & Marinda Stamper, 1 March 1842; Toliver Shumate, bm.

Brown, John & Frances Jennings, 9 Feb 1847; Alfred B. Absher, bm.

Brown, John & Martha Church, 14 Jan 1866; Calvin Shumate, bm; m 14 Jan 1866 by William Hall.

Brown, John A., son of Larkin & Tempey Brown, & Leeta J. Abshire, daughter of Wesley & Letta Brown, m 30 Sept 1867 by A. E. Myers.

Brown, John B. & Sally McNiel, 18 May 1833; Lewis D. Merryman, bm.

Brown, John J. & Elizabeth Harnold, 12 Feb 1856; Wm. H. Absher, bm; m 23 Feb 1856 by L. Sebastian, J. P.

Brown, John L. & Leathe W. Barnett, 17 Dec 1853; m 18 Dec 1853 by Thos. S. Wellborn, J. P.

Brown, John N. & Sarah Pratt, 5 Nov 1843; Solomon Sparks, bm.

Brown, John W. & Mary Crows, 25 Dec 1854; L. C. Brooks, bm; m 25 Dec 1854 by A. Parks.

Brown, Joseph & Ann Hagler, 30 Jan 1794; Isaac Hagler, bm.

Brown, Larken & Sally Edwards, 7 June 1830; James Handy, bm.

Brown, Larkin & Tempy Heral, 25 Sept 1820; Eli Brown, bm.

Brown, Manley & Salley Kerler, 19 March 1811; Sion Harrington, bm.

Brown, Martin & Susanna Randell, 17 Sept 1843; William T. Ferguson, bm; m 18 Sept 1853 by G. W. Hendrix, J. P.

Brown, Mason & Susana Vannoy, 31 Jan 1843; Adam Sheets, bm.

Brown, Micajah & Catharine McDow__, (no date, during admn. of Gov. Nathl. Alexander); Wm. Brown, bm.

Brown, Moses & Mary Hoppis, 20 Aug 1846; Alfred B. Absher, bm.

Brown, Nathaniel & Mary Broyhill, 26 Feb 1810; James Broyhill, bm.

Brown, Noah & Sineth Becknal, 18 April 1823; John Ferguson, bm.

Brown, Peter & Mary Buttry, 19 July 1826; James Brown, bm.

Brown, Presley & Elizabeth Vannoy, 12 Feb 1823; Enoch Vannoy, bm.

WILKES COUNTY MARRIAGES, 1778-1868

Brown, Presley & Rachael Kilby, 6 Dec 1838; Elijah Brown, bm.

Brown, Reuben & Mary Ann Higgins, 28 Jan 1859; m 30 Jan 1859 by L. Sebastian, J. P.

Brown, Richard & Sarah Laxton (Lanton?), 21 Sept 1820; Allen W. Parks, bm.

Brown, Riley & Elizabeth McNiel, 18 March 1833; Thos Brown, bm.

Brown, Rufus B. & Ruth Barns, 27 July 1842; Joel Brown, bm.

Brown, S. F. & Nancy E. Brooks, 1 Aug 1865; Jno. Brown, bm; m 4 Aug 1865 by Jno. M. Brown, J. P.

Brown, Samuel & Jane Denney, 17 Dec 1783; Geo. Denny, bm.

Brown, Saml & Rebecca Mikell, 1 May 1837; Danl. M. Wellborn, bm.

Brown, Solomon & Nancy Brown, 21 Nov 1838; Wm. F. Brown, bm.

Brown, Thomas & Elizabeth Kerly, 24 March 1810; John Russel, bm.

Brown, Thomas & Malinday Mayfield, 11 Sept 1821; Thomas Isbill, bm.

Brown, Thomas & Eliza Ann Walker, 3 Jan 1840; Overton G. Walker, bm.

Brown, Thomas J. & Myra Jinings, 14 Oct 1858; m 22 Oct 1858 by Elder Jas. McNiel.

Brown, Thornton & Eppy Hall, 24 March 1834; Reuben Hays, Junr., bm.

Brown, Thornton & Mary L. Lane, 25 March 1851; C. H. Afzmann, bm.

Brown, Volintine & Polley Ross, 25 Nov 1825; Noah Prewitt, bm.

Brown, W. B. & Sarah Brown, 9 Feb 1864; Wm. M. Harrold, bm; m 11 Feb 1864 by L. Sebastian, J. P.

Brown, Walter & Kisiah Abshire, 10 Aug 1826; Wesley Brown, bm.

Brown, Walter & Elizabeth Brown, 22 June 1848; John J. Owens, bm.

Brown, Wesly & Letes Ginness, 30 Jan 1816; ___, bm.

Brown, Wesley & Marthy Herrold, __ Nov 1857; m by P. Grimes.

Brown, William & Nancey Isbell, 6 Sept 1801; Ben Hubbard, bm.

Brown, William & Ruth Rash, 12 Aug 1819; Harris Standley, bm.

Brown, Wm. & Mira Stephenson, 12 April 1825; James Patton, bm.

Brown, William & Jane Cottrel, 30 Dec 1828; Benjamin Brown, bm.

Brown, William & Sucky Abshir, 12 Dec 1833; Robt Hall Jr., bm.

WILKES COUNTY MARRIAGES, 1778-1868

Brown, Wm., son of Eli & Sarah Carley, 2 Sept 1836; David Gray, bm.

Brown, Wm. & Sarah Sebastion, 8 Jan 1839; George Owen, bm.

Brown, William & Sarah Herald(?), 28 Nov 1858; Wesley Brown, bm.

Brown, Wm. H. & Mary Shepherd, 21 May 1865; C. F. Vannoy, bm; m 21 May 1865 by R. P. McGrady, J. P.

Brown, Wm. H & Pollie Absher, 2 Dec 1865; P. R. McGrady, bm.

Brown, Wm. W., son of Ezekiel & Sarah Brown, & Lorena Frances Crysel, daughter of James E. & Elizabeth Crysel, 18 Jan 1868; m 23 Jan 1868 by Henry Jinnings, J. P.

Brown, Yancy & Nancy Wooton, 13 April 1839; B. F. Boswell, bm; m April 1839.

Brown, Zekel (Ezekiel) & Rachel Harmon, 17 Jan 1800; John Fletcher, bm.

Broyhill, James & Clarisa Harlow, 28 June 1820; L. Johnson, bm.

Broyhill, James & Rody Hampton, 2 March 1835; David Grey, bm.

Broyhill, Johnson, son of Jas. & Roda Broyhill, & Rutha E. Clanton, daughter of William & Nellie Clanton, m 20 Dec 1868 by Eld. James Kerly.

Broyhill, John N. & Polly Davis, 15 Sept 1810; Joel Branham, bm.

Broyhill, William & Nancy Johnson, 22 March 1816; Isaiah Hampton, bm.

Broyhill, William & Annie Earp, 16 Nov 1848; Thomas S. Earp, bm.

Brier, Mordecai & Elisabeth Adams, 31 Oct 1810; Wm. Deboard, bm.

Bruce, Robert & Margaret Perlair, 22 May 1813; Jerrymiah Cryssel, bm.

Bryan, Anderson & Nancy Benge, 28 Jan 1803; John Martin, bm.

Bryan, Andrew & Philedelpha Jones, 4 Jan 1791; William Johnson, bm.

Bryan, Gideon & Mary Johnson, 5 Oct 1818; Abner Caudle, bm.

Bryan, Henry & Lucy Robins, 29 July 1790; Andrew Bryan, bm.

Bryan, J. J. & Nancy Hampton, 12 Oct 1845; J. E. Mastin, bm.

Bryan, James & Jain E. Laxton, 30 Nov 1855; m by E. B. Philips, J. P.

Bryan, John & Ann Robins, 4 Oct 1788; Robt. Gallaway, bm.

Bryan, Joseph T. & Francis Speer, 3 April 1843; John S. Johnson, bm.

Bryan, Thomas & Ann Duncan, 18 Nov 1778; Thomas Harbin, bm.

WILKES COUNTY MARRIAGES, 1778-1868

Bryant, Thomas & Nancy Baughuss, 27 July 1818; Saml Johnson, bm.

Bryon, S. F. & Nancey S. Laxton, 20 May 1858; m by E. B. Philips, J. P.

Buchan & Elizebeth Felts, 21 Dec 1819; Samuel Nickleson, bm.

Buchen, George & Cathrone Smith, 8 Nov 1780; John Walker, Lucus Hood, bm.

Buckner, Pascall & Cinthia Rash, 22 May 1830; George Shepherd, bm.

Buhson, J. B. & Martha Hufmon, 24 July 1839; Samuel Buhson, bm.

Buhson, Saml W. & Limera Teashill, 6 Oct 1842; James W. Nicholls, bm.

Bullis, David W. & Zibba Huffman, 4 Sept 1860; Thos J. Gilreath, bm; m 29 Dec 1860 by Rev. Jas. McNeil.

Bullis, John & Bettey Goins, 30 Oct 1799; James Bruce(?), bm.

Bullis, Benjamin & Betsey Griffey, 13 Nov 1830; Moseph Nichols, bm.

Bullis, James E. & Eliza Mcniel, 16 May 1866; W. A. McNeill, bm; m 16 May 1866 by A. A. Whittenton, J. P.

Bullis, John & Polly Bumgarner, 21 Nov 1821; James Crain, bm.

Bullison, Saml W., son of Benj. & Martha Bullis, & Nancey C. Bumgarner, daughter of Stephen & Rebecca Bumgarner, 23 Sept 1867; m 24 Sept 1867 by W. W. Adams.

Bullus, Benjamin & Bettey Adams, 6 Sept 1800; Jeremiah Crisal, bm.

Bullus, Jas. S. & Vilott Nicholls, 24 July 1851; m 24 July 1851 by A. A. Whittenton, J. P.

Bumgarner, A. B. & Sarah Miller, 11 Sept 1866; H. A. Brown, bm; m by C. R. Simpson, J. P.

Bumgarner, Adam L. & Polly Brown, 24 Dec 1861; Wm. H. Brown, bm; m 14 Dec 1861 by Wm. S. McNeil, J. P.

Bumgarner, Amos & Matilda Church, 25 March 1841; Robert B. Foster, bm.

Bumgarner, Daniel & Salley Kilbey, 25 Oct 1813; Michal Bumgarner, bm.

Bumgarner, Daniel & Catharine Laws, 24 Nov 1860; J. P. Walker, bm; m 25 Nov 1860 by J. W. Church.

Bumgarner, Daniel Junr. & Elizabeth McNeal, 16 Aug 1837; John E. Mastin, bm.

Bumgarner, David & Dolly Lindermon, 2 July 1839; Samuel Linderman, bm.

WILKES COUNTY MARRIAGES, 1778-1868

Bumgarner, David & Cleary Miller, 26 March 1856; Alfred Parsons, bm; m 26 March 1856 by A. A. Whittenton, J. P.

Bumgarner, Eli H. & Elisabeth A. Hutson, 6 Sept 1866; Joseph A. Bumgarner, bm; m 6 Sept 1856 by A. A. Whittenton, J. P.

Bumgarner, Henry & Phebe Kilby, 3 Dec 1818; Daniel Bumgarner, bm.

Bumgarner, Henry & Amelia Church, 15 Feb 1843; James W. Nichols, bm.

Bumgarner, J. C. & Bethany Church, 1 June 1867.

Bumgarner, James L. & Phebe An Hinchey, 6 March 1854; Patterson Hinchey, bm; m by A. A. Whittenton, 6 March 1854.

Bumgarner, John & Mary Bumgarner, 4 Feb 1840; Samuel Lenderman, bm.

Bumgarner, John & Emeline Church, 16 Dec 1847; Wesley Bullis, bm.

Bumgarner, John H. & Mary An Laws, 3 Jan 1862; m 30 Jan 1862 by J. W. Church.

Bumgarner, John Wesley, son of John & Emeline Bumgarner, & Martha Adams, daughter of Solomon and Franky Adams, 13 Feb 1868; m 13 Feb 1868 by J. W. Church, J. P.

Bumgarner, Michael & Betsey Church, 30 Nov 1813; Elijah Church, bm.

Bumgarner, S. A., son of Stephen & Rebecca Bumgarner, & Sofie M. Hays, daughter of Bettie Hays, m 4 Aug 1867 by Henry Jinnings, J. P.

Bumgarner, Simeon & Susannah Osburn, 28 Aug 1828; Joseph Osbern, bm.

Bumgarner, Simeon A., son of Simeon & Susan Bumgarner & Elisabeth Bishop, daughter of John and Elisabeth Bishop, 28 Sept 1867.

Bumgarner, Stephen & Rebecca Nicholds, 5 Jan 1831; Joseph Nichols, bm.

Bumgarner, Wm. E. & Lewiza Hines, 28 Dec 1854; W. R. Whittington, bm; m 28 Dec 1854 by A. A. Whittenton, J. P.

Bunton, James & Keziah Sweeten, 2 Sept 1797; Edward Tugman, bm.

Bunton, Samuel & Tabitha Bishop, 7 Sept 1819; Robt. Church, bm.

Burch, William S. & Lucinda Barlton, 18 Nov 1826; James Burch, bm.

Burcham, John D. & Catharine Gentry, 5 Feb 1862; Nathan J. Walls, bm; m 5 Feb 1862 by J. M. Gambill, J. P.

Burcham, Levi D. & Elizabeth Guthey, 21 Dec 1859.

WILKES COUNTY MARRIAGES, 1778-1868

Burcham, S. W. & Mary E. Couch, 15 Jan 1862; B. F. Norman, bm; m 16 Jan 1862 by Wm. H. Pardew, Min.

Burcham, William C. & Mahuldah J. Carter, 27 Jan 1861; J. W. Fields, bm; m 27 Jan 1861 by J. M. Gambill, J. P.

Burcham, William & Pheny Lion, 17 Dec 1852.

Burchet, Harvey & Mahala Creed, 15 Oct 1830; Geo. Higgins, bm.

Burchet, Jno. & Kiziah Dickerson, 25 Jan 1826; William Fyffe, bm.

Burchet, William, son of Isaac & Nancy Burchet, and Merica Rhods, daughter of Bengaman and Mary Rhods, 7 Jan 1868; m 8 ___ 1868 by A. Wiles, J. P.

Burchett, Isaac & Peggy Wood, 8 July 1861

Burchett, James & Salley Wood, 7 April 1831; John Byrd, bm.

Burchett, Leonard & Alcey Phillips, 12 Dec 1816; John Fyffe, bm.

Burchit, Isaack & Emeline Hawkins, 22 Jan 1860; 22 Jan 1860, by Wm. Hall, minister.

Burchfield, Adam & Nancy Tolbey, 20 Aug 1808; John Burchfield, bm.

Burchfield, Thos. & Susannah Wiles, 14 Nov 1821; William Wiles, bm.

Burgay, William & Lucy Franklin, 17 Feb 1811; James Franklin, bm.

Burgess, Jonas & Metilda Holbrook, 5 Sept 1866; Wm. H. Walker, bm; m 6 Sept 1866 by Wilson Walker.

Burk, John & Ailse Sebastin, 6 June 1781; Henry Carter, bm.

Burn, David & Nancy Keland, 27 Jan 1781; Elisha Reynolds, bm.

Burnes, Samuel & Ann Duggar, 12 Feb 1791; Benja. Duggar, bm.

Burns, Alexander & Mary Roach, 7 Sept 1779; Robert Obarr, Francis Vannoy, bm.

Busey, Charles & Martha McBride, 31 Jan 1803; Zebediah Baker, bm.

Bussel, Tillis & Sarah Harris, 22 Dec 1865; G. B. Parker, bm; m 24 Dec 1866 by G. B. Parker, J. P.

Busel, Pressley & Mary Martin, 2 Oct 1813; Joshua Souther, bm.

Bussell, Pressley S. & Olly Fletcher, 19 Nov 1866; H. E. Kemp, bm.

Bussell, William & Abegail Cast, 1 Nov 1817; Hartwell Hayes, bm.

Butrum, Andrew & Tabias Katon, 30 July 1798; John Butrum, bm.

Butrum, William & Rachael Kidwell, 6 May 1802; Nicodemus Butrum, bm.

WILKES COUNTY MARRIAGES, 1778-1868

Byers, Cernelias & Suana Cuech, 25 Aug 181_; Hugh Hayes, bm.

Byers, James & Sarah Ann Maberry, 9 April 1867; m 10 April 1867 by M. A. Parks, J. P.

Byers, James J. & Marthaan Milum, 6 Jan 1866; George Minton, bm; m 7 Jan 1866 by Thos. Walsh, J. P.

Byers, Jas. S. & Emelen Sumerlin, 3 April 1852; Nelson Billings, bm; m 2 May 1852 by Amos Church, J. P.

Byrd, Braxton & Jean Wood, 23 Dec 1807; William Byrd, bm.

Byrd, George & Maryann Simmons, 4 Sept 1864; Esquire Dickerson, bm.

Byrd, James & Sarah Brooks, 5 Sept 1816; John Brooks, bm.

Byrd, James & ___, 3 Jan 1843; Josiah Byrd, bm.

Byrd, Jones & O. C. Bryan, 10 Aug 1853; L. E. Carmichael, bm; m 10 Aug 1853 by W. F. Adams, Baptist minister.

Byrd, James F. & Mary R. A. Wooton, 24 Jan 1867; M. F. Mitchell, bm; m 31 Jan 1867 by J. F. Somers, J. P.

Byrd, John & Nelly Johnson, 23 Sept 1831; Nathl. Barker, bm.

Byrd, John & Nancy Howard, 14 Nov 1839; Thomas Myers, bm; m 21 Nov 1839 by Thomas Roberts, J. P.

Byrd, John & Eliza Cockrem, 29 Nov 1857; m 29 Nov 1857 by J. M. Gambill, J. P.

Byrd, Josiah & Matilda Jones, 16 July 1836; Abraham Buttrey, bm.

Byrd, L. C. & Elizabeth J. Parker, 8 Nov 1864; Esley Staly, bm; m 15 Dec 1864 by Rev. R. W. Wooton.

Byrd, M. C., son of John & Elender Byrd, & Perlina G. Walker, daughter of Robert & Diana Walker, 14 Jan 1868; m 16 Jan 1868 by W. Joines, J. P.

Byrd, Solomon & Nancy McCrary, 24 Sept 1840; John Buttrey, bm.

Byrd, William & Dorchas Herben, 17 __ 1808; Braxton Byrd, bm.

Byrd, William F. & Merideth Thornton, 30 Jan 1867; Merideth Thornton, bm; m 6 Feb 1867 by J. K. Rose, Baptist minister.

Byrd, Wm. H. H. & R. Minda Brown, 7 Feb 1861; John M. Welborn, bm.

Byrd, Wm. J. & Marth Holeway, 13 July 1863; m by Eli Grimes, L. D. of M. E. C. S.

Byrd, William & Elizabeth Fletcher, 20 May 1847; John Bauguess, bm.

Cacy, James & Elizebeth Oldridge, 25 Nov 1852; Richard Sidden, bm; m 25 Nov 1852 by Ansel Parks.

WILKES COUNTY MARRIAGES, 1778-1868

Cacy, T. J. & Sealy Bauguess, 28 Dec 1855; A. J. Bauguess, bm; m 28 Dec 1855 by Ansel Parks.

Cacy, William & C. H. Baugus, 3 April 1863; Henry Cacy, bm; m 5 April 1863, by Rev. Wm. J. Combs.

Caler, John & Elizabeth Carel, 10 Dec 1814; Benjamin Carrel, bm.

Call, David H. & Susanah Miller, 12 Oct 1853; m 13 Oct 1853 by S. P. Smith.

Call, David D. & Nancy Sebastine, 16 Dec 1822; Isaac Call, bm.

Call, Isaac S. & Martha C. Mastin, 26 July 1854; m 26 July 1854 by R. W. Barber.

Call, William & Nancy Call, 18 March 1842; Wyatt Hendrin, bm; Wm Mastin, wit.

Call, William Jr., son of William & Nancy Call, & Nancy Elizabeth Foots, daughter of Auston & Elizabeth Foots, 22 Jan 1868; m 23 Jan 1868 by James M. Call, J. P.

Callaway, Joseph & Nancy Howard, 24 Feb 1807; Wm Allison, bm.

Calloway, Cary & Prudence Howard, 19 March 1826; Cornelius Howard, bm; W. Davenport, wit.

Calloway, James & M. L. Carmichael, 25 June 1835; J. J. Bryan, bm.

Calloway, James & Annie P. Yeakle, 5 May 1852; m 6 May 1852 by R. W. Barber, minister of the P. E. C.

Calloway, Thomas S. & Perliney E. Cleaveland, 16 April 1865; E. C. Hartzog, bm; m 16 April 1865 by Wm. Parks, J. P.

Calton, David & Amely Petty, 26 Dec 1814; Thornton Pettey, bm.

Camp, Wm. B. & Elizabeth Anthoney, 21 July 1827; Richard J. Cook, bm.

Campbell, Cyrus Franklin & Marthy Emily Allen, ___ 1846; Linvil Land, bm.

Campbell, David & Elisabeth Day, 19 March 1813; Hugh Day, bm; Darby Hendrix, wit.

Campbell, John & __ , 5 Nov 1823; Isaiah Hampton, bm.

Campbell, Peter & Sarah Landsdown, 26 Aug 1790, David Elston, bm.

Campbell, William & Amelia Clanton, 18 Aug 1818; Wesley Reynolds, bm.

Campbell, William & Elizabeth Wiett, 24 Feb 1844; Thomas Pipes, bm.

Campbell, Hugh & Elizh. Bu___, 27 Dec 1796; Isaac Russel, bm.

Canaday, N. C. & Polley N. Tucker, 2 Sept 1848.

Canaday, Saml & ___, 12 July 1792; Aaron Canaday, bm.

WILKES COUNTY MARRIAGES, 1778-1868

Canady, Aron & Polly Caudle, 11 Nov 1821; James Wals, bm.

Cane, Anderson, son of Abel & Malinda Cane, & Martha Hendren, daughter of Jehu & Cinda Hendren, 13 Nov 1867; m by Anderson Winkley.

Cannon, Newton & Rachal S. Wellborn, 25 Aug 1818; John Starnes, bm.

Cansler, Alex. J. & Mary A. Martin, 7 Sept 1847; J. M. Conly, bm.

Canter, George W. & Marthy Whittenton, 9 Aug 1864; W. W. Vannoy, bm; m 9 Aug 1864 by A. A. Whittenton, J. P.

Canter, Jonathan & Amelia Steelmon, 17 Dec 1844; James M. Canter, bm.

Canter, Stephen & Marthyan Sother, 24 Dec 1853; William Watson, bm; m 24 Dec 1853 by Wm. Church.

Canter, William & H. D. Steelman, 24 Oct 1855; Charles Hickerson, bm.

Cardwell, Franklin & Margaret Church, 14 Sept 1843; John Pearce (Pierce), bm.

Cardwell, J. H. & Cinthy M. McGee, 4 Jan 1866; Wm. A. Fairchild, bm; m 5 Jan 1866 by Rev. Jas. McNeil.

Cardwell, Jas. H. & Malissa Parisice Minter, 23 March 1866; m by Rev. Jas. McNeil, 25 March 1866.

Cardwell, Nathan & Rachel Crows, 4 June 1811; Peter Cardwell, bm.

Cardwell, Nathan P. & Martha Dockery, 7 March 1841; John S. Dockery, bm.

Cardwell, Peter & Elizabeth Harris, 24 Feb 1808; Braxton McQuin, bm.

Careley, Solomon & Mary Laws, 21 Oct 1833; John Greer, bm.

Cargile, Charles & Sarah Curry, 29 Oct 1805; John Chambers, bm.

Cargile, James & Sary Martin, 17 Nov 1812; John Chambers, bm.

Cargile, John & Nancy Grey, 22 May 1811; John Hart, bm.

Carinder, G. Thomas & Martha Sparks, 2 Jan 1861; J. B. Walker, bm.

Carinder, Jas. L. & Susanah Walker, 16 March 1861; Jas. O. Martin, bm; m 17 March 1861 by M. A. Parks, J. P.

Carley, Absalom & Elizabeth Teague, 16 Aug 1806; Dread Fortner, bm.

Carley, Larkin & Mary Barns, 4 Feb 1800; Wm. Isbell, bm.

Carley, Larkin & Susannah Morriss, 14 Nov 1809; Archd. McEwin, bm.

WILKES COUNTY MARRIAGES, 1778-1868

Carley, Larkin & Elizabeth Carley, 25 Feb 1814; John S. Curry, bm.

Carlton, Alfred & Polly Allison, 15 March 1825; Pierce Noland, bm.

Carlton, Allen B. & Nancy Swam, 23 Oct 1839; Wilson Laxton, bm.

Carlton, Ambrose & Prudence Isbell, 21 Nov 1805; George Howard, bm.

Carlton, Ambrose & Lucinda Foster, 9 Nov 1824; John Dula, bm.

Carlton, Calvin & Rebecca Land, 30 Oct 1850; Linvill Land, bm; m 1851 by Baptist minister.

Carlton, Charles & Sarah Saymer, 15 Nov 1841; John Carlton, bm.

Carlton, Dennis & Jane Livingston, 14 Dec 1829; John Carlton, bm.

Carlton, Henry & Prudence Brookshire, 2 Dec 1805; John Carlton, bm.

Carlton, John & Elizabeth Barlow, 14 Aug 1802; Thos. Carlton, bm.

Carlton, John & Elisabeth Burch, 18 Sept 1810; Thos Carlton, bm.

Carlton, John & Susanna Smyth, 30 April 1813; Eli B May(?), bm.

Carlton, John & Frances Gold, 15 March 1851; James Hamty(?), bm; m 1851 by A. Lipford, Baptist minister.

Carlton, L. T. & Jane A. Yrpleth, 15 Jan 1861; m 15 Jan 1861 by Pickens Carlton, J. P.

Carlton, Lewis & Elizabeth Eve, 13 Jan 1781; William Hitchcock, John Carlton, bm.

Carlton, Lewis & Nancy Crouch, 14 Dec 1805; Ambrose Carlton, bm.

Carlton, Lewis & Kissia Burch, 30 Dec 1813; Smith Ferguson, bm.

Carlton, Lewis & Lettice Land, 23 Nov 1825; Benjamin Burch, bm.

Carlton, Livingston & Elizabeth Triplet, 1 March 1823; Francis Brown, bm.

Carlton, Thos. & Catharine Livingston, 6 Feb 1799; Lewis Carlton, bm.

Carlton, Thomas & Ruth Burch, 31 July 1809; Lewis Carlton, bm.

Carlton, Thomas & Jenney Merryman, 26 March 1813; George Croach, bm.

Carlton, Thomas & Elizebeth Land, 23 Nov 1822; Charles Main, bm.

Carlton, Thomas C. & S. M. Triplett, 15 Sept 1856; m 16 Sept 1856 by Charles Carlton, J. P.

WILKES COUNTY MARRIAGES, 1778-1868

Carlton, Wyatt & Nancy Livingston, 11 Dec 1823; Orril Livingston, bm.

Carmichael, Abner & Fanny Bryan, 17 Nov 1814; R. Allen, bm.

Carney, Andrew & Patty Smith, 1 Nov 1825; Thomas Bryan, bm.

Carpenter, Wm & Arrittey Smith, 24 Nov 1858; Samuel Sprinkle, bm; m 25 Nov 1858 by J. M. Gambill, J. P.

Carrander, William, son of Joseph and Tirza Carrander, & Eliza C. Curry, daughter of George and Elisabeth Curry, m 23 Jan 1868 by W. S. Adams, Baptist minister.

Carrel, Archibald & Suana Bell, 19 Nov 1814; Wesley Swanson, bm.

Carrel, John & Mary Farguson, 18 Oct 1800; John Parker, bm.

Carrel, Samuel & Sally Kaylor, 2 April 1806; John Parker, bm.

Carrell, James & Sarah Noland, 23 Jan 1793; John Parker, bm.

Carrell, James & Sally Parkes, 23 Dec 1805; Richard Parks, bm.

Carrol, Samson & Nancy Livingston, 23 Nov 1807; John Livingston, bm.

Carstephens, Thomas & Peggy B. Tilley, 15 June 1792; Edmond Tilley, bm.

Carter, Benjamin F. & Martha Crows, 31 Dec 1856; Benjamin F. Norman, bm.

Carter, Benjamin & Zepha Napier, 29 July 1852; Joshua Carter, bm; m 29 July 1852 by B. F. Johnson, J. P.

Carter, Caleb W. & Mary E. Burcham, 17 April 1867; Wm. M. Carter, bm.

Carter, Charles & Elizabeth Cash, 15 Oct 1782; David Cash, bm.

Carter, Columbus F., son of Benjamin & Mary Carter, & Laurah Tulburt, daughter of Levi & Cintha Tulburt, 22 Nov 1867; m 24 Nov 1867 by John K. Rose, minister.

Carter, Daniel & Nancy Cobb, 22 Feb 1782; Elijah Stinson, bm.

Carter, Daniel & Susannah Canaday, 29 Feb 1816; Jno Carter, bm.

Carter, Ephraim & Sarah Finney, 30 Jan 1838; James J. Field, bm.

Carter, Fielding & Delphia Turnbill, 22 Aug 1830; Thomas W. Mitchel, bm.

Carter, Henry & Martha Parham, 11 Oct 1797; Wm Parham, bm.

Carter, Jno. & Fanney Canaday, 29 Feb 1816; Daniel Carter, bm.

Carter, Joshua & Matilday Blackburn, 27 Dec 1851; Littleton Carter, bm.

Carter, Levi, son of Caleb & Mary Carter, & Lucinda Money, daughter of Howel Money, 10 Sept 1867, by J. J. Parks.

WILKES COUNTY MARRIAGES, 1778-1868

Carter, Meradeth & Miss Gemima J. Couch, 19 July 1865; m by J. K. Rose.

Carter, Reuben A. & Elizabeth Harrald, 21 Feb 1803; Randy Carter, bm; William B. Lenoir, wit.

Carter, Samuel & Jane Simmons, 9 Jan 1836; Wilson Lufmon, bm.

Cash, Larkin & Sally Pumphry, 12 Sept 1806; Henry Pumphry, bm.

Cash, William & Polly McQuerry, 14 April 1808; Wm McQuerry, bm.

Cass, B. W. & Lu Annie T. Roberts, 10 Jan 1839; D. R. Bess, bm.

Cass, Ezekell & Ann Mitchell, 29 July 1820; William Nickleson, bm.

Cass(?), Henry B. & F. E. ___, 29 Jan 1862; D. H. Hollawang, bm.

Cass, James & Susannah Mabery, 11 Dec 1824; Charles Rash, bm.

Cass, Leander H. & Mary E. Wilborn, 29 Nov 1861; Gabriel E. Kemp, bm; m 1 Dec 1861 by R. W. Wooton, baptist minister.

Cass, Moses M. & Mahaley McCoy, 13 Sept 1858; m 13 Sept 1858 by Thos. Roberts, J. P.

Cass, Samuel & Sary Getts, 15 Oct 1816; James Nickleson, bm.

Cass, William & Malsia Lunsfords, 7 April 1827; Aaron Chambers, bm.

Cast, Moses & Lucy Jones, 15 July 1805; Wm. Hampton, bm.

Castle, Samuel & Nancy Tugman, 28 June 1840; Samuel Walsh, bm; m in January 1840 by Saml Walsh, J. P.

Caudell, Abner & Nancy Abshire, m 13 Feb 1867 by H. C. Sebastian, J. P.

Caudell, Stephen & Elizabeth Smith, 24 May 1817; Benjamin Caudell, bm.

Caudell, Daniel & ___, ___ 182_; Robert Walker, bm.

Caudell, Jesse & Sary Roberds, 11 Oct 1817; Caleb Holbrook, bm.

Caudill, John J., son of Daniel & Winnie Caudill, & Nancy E. Rash, daughter of William and Margret Rash, m 5 July 1868 by Henry Ginnings, J. P.

Caudill, Sanford, son of Jackson J. & Polly Caudill, and Nancy E. Wyatt, daughter of Vicrey & Sally Wyatt, m 11 April 1868 by Henry Jinnings, J. P.

Caudill, Stephen & Hulda Adams, 28 July 1832; Ralph Holbrook, bm.

Caudill, Steven & Jane Dehart, 3 April 1784; Thomas Caudill, bm.

Caudill, Thomas & Matilda Hallaway, 9 June 1858; Jesse Caudill, bm.

WILKES COUNTY MARRIAGES, 1778-1868

Caudill, Thomas B. & Martha Joines, 15 Feb 1864; S. F. Joines, bm; Frances Caudill, wit.

Caudill, William & Rachel Joines, 26 Oct 1811; Thos Joines, bm.

Caudill, William M. & Frances McGrady, 21 Dec 1848; Hugh M. Stokes, bm.

Caudle, David & Caroline Hall, 8 Dec 1865; Johnson Caudle, bm; m 29 Dec 1865 by Wilson Walker, J. P.

Caudle, Jesse & Elizabeth Whitty, 14 April 1842; Wm Niell, bm.

Caudle, John & Elizabeth Caudle, 30 Aug 1827; Coleby Alexander, bm.

Cauthin, W. R. & Sarah Bowges, 26 June 1863; Eli M. Cheek, bm.

Cauthin, William & Polly Roads, 5 Feb 1823; Willis Childers, bm.

Cauthron, Wm. P. E. & Martha Combs, 27 July 1860; m 27 July 1860 by A. B. Dancy, J. P.

Cavniss, Benj. & Polly Fur(?), 29 Oct 1836; John Brewer, bm.

Cearley, Elisha & Elizabeth Foster, 31 July 1821; Absolem Cerley, bm.

Ceaten, William & Bettey Fletchor, 19 Feb 1801; Samuel Wilson, bm.

Cecill, Robert & Francis Warren, 26 Aug 1833; Allen Cecill, bm.

Cerley, Jonathan & Rebecka Roberts, 1 April 1822; Larkin Cerley, bm.

Cerley, Wm. & Darkes Fortunar, 5 Oct 1807; Felix Fortner, bm.

Certain, James & Nancy Robins, 10 April 1786; James Sheppard, bm.

Ceus, Urias & Meley Parsons, 13 Feb 1855; m 13 Feb 1855 by E. B. Philips, J. P.

Chambers, Aaron & Lois Porter, 21 July 1818; Jno Curry, bm.

Chambers, Aaron & Polly Dowell, 26 Aug 1822; Reuben Stanley, bm.

Chambers, Elijah & Rebeckah Moore, 18 Nov 1796; Jesse Moore, Ambrose Coffey, bm.

Chambers, Enoch & Marget Brown, 18 Dec 1798; John Brown, bm.

Chambers, George & Bilenda Sparks, 6 June 1833; Henry Chambers, bm.

Chambers, Henry & Mary Adelaide Stokes, 22 June 1813; Max: Chambers, Alexr Long, bm.

Chambers, Henry R. & Tildey Martin, 8 Jan 1861; Noah Triplet, bm.

WILKES COUNTY MARRIAGES, 1778-1868

Chambers, James & Letty Hambey(?), 21 June 1832; Joel Hambey(?), bm.

Chambers, Samuel & Prissilla Curry, 15 Oct 1807; Thos Roberts, bm.

Chambers, Suth & Carlina Mabury, 2 July 1848; Noah Jarves, bm.

Chambers, William & Randay Hardin, 1 April 1851; James Redding, bm.

Chambers, John & Martha Ann Dunn, 1 Nov 1845; Randolph Mabery, bm; m 11 Nov 1845 by J. Roberts, J. P.

Chandler, Josiah & Sarah Edwins, 21 Aug 1784; Bailey Chandler, bm.

Chang (one of the Siamese twins) & Adalade Yates, 13 April 1843; Jesse Yeates, bm.

Chapel, G. C., son of Wm. J. & Mary Chapel, & Martha Gaulteny, daughter of Cyrus & Leviny Gaultny, m 17 Nov 1867 by Seth Chambers, J. P.

Chapel, Solomon C. & Sarah M. Brotherlin, 12 Feb 1866; Wm. J. Chapel, bm; m 15 Feb 1866 by H. Heyes, J. P.

Chapel, Wm. C. & Mary Thomas, 6 Feb 1865; J. C. Perkins, bm; m 6 Feb 1865 by Rev. J. C. Perkins.

Chapman, Elisha & Saly Deel, 2 April 1837; Lewis Little, bm.

Chapman, Enoch & Mary Barnet, 18 Dec 1780; John Chapman Junr., bm. (Any or all of these may be "late of Burke County").

Chapman, Enoch & Cloe Garland, 31 Jan 1815; Manley Barnet(?), bm.

Chapman, George & Sarah Brown, 14 Feb 1831; Enoch Chapman, bm; Peter Barnes, J. P., wit.

Chapman, John & Mary Matherly, 27 July 1806; John Chapman, bm.

Chapman, Richard & Judy Brown, 16 Sept 1832; Enoch Chapman, bm.

Chapman, Soloman & Mary A. Odom, 20 Sept 1836; Richard Chapman, bm.

Chapman, William & Ruth Barnes, 9 March 1807; John Chapman, bm.

Chapple, Silas E. & Amanda Parker, 10 March 1859; m 15 March 1859 by H. Hayes, J. P.

Chatham, Wyatt & Hellen Adams, 3 Jan 1856; Jesse H. Vickers, bm.

Cheatham, Martin & Elizabeth Cass, 20 July 1829; George B. Tate, bm.

Cheatham, Robert & Elizabeth Turnbill, 21 Feb 1832; Jeremiah Crisel (Crysel), bm.

Cheatwood, Wm & Amelia Kennedy, 16 April 1856; Norwood Kennedy, bm; m 16 April 1856 by A. Parks.

WILKES COUNTY MARRIAGES, 1778-1868

Cheek, Henderson & Juda Anne Bagley, 29 Sept 1827; Jonathan Osburn, bm.

Cheek, William & Lucinday Woodruf, 17 May 1842; Elmore Cheek, bm.

Chersser, Tenneson & Mary Gray, ___ 1800; Benjamin Johnson, bm.

Childers, Henry & Elizabeth Johnson, 23 Oct 1833; Hamilton Childers, bm.

Childers, Herbert & Nancy Gregory, 10 Oct 1827; Wm Billings, bm.

Childers, James & Milia Alexander, 13 June 1852; Willis Childers, bm; m 13 June 1852 by Wm. L. Adams, Baptist minister.

Childers, John & Nancy Brooks, 2 Jan 1822; David Wilkins, bm.

Childers, John E. & Lucy Joines, 17 April 1859; J. T. Billings, bm; m 17 April 1859 by John Brewer, Esqr.

Childers, John E., son of Willis & Carolina Childers, & Phebe Darnall, daughter of Wade & Nancy Darnall, m 22 Dec 1867 by W. F. Adams, Baptist minister.

Childers, William & Leuisia Mastin, 24 April 1856; Hamilton Childers, bm.

Childers, William & Marey Masteon, 15 April 1849; B. O. H. P. Martin, bm; William Masteon, wit.

Childres, Willis & Salley Fields, 21 Feb 1820; David Wilkins, bm.

Childress, Wiley & Sally Childress, 13 Dec 1832; William Billings, bm.

Church, Alexander & Mary Allen, 28 Feb 1825; Aaron Church, bm.

Church, Alfort B. & Mary McMillion, 20 Sept 1866.

Church, Allen & Nancy Mitchel, 12 Oct 1819; Wm Bingham, bm.

Church, Amos & Ally Billin, 13 Jan 1820; John Church, bm.

Church, Amos Jr. & Vicey Minton, 30 Jan 1834; Hiram Billings, bm.

Church, Amos Sr. & Rebeca Davis, 2 July 1835; David Gray, bm.

Church, Calvin & Susanah Curtis, 24 Feb 1859; m 24 Feb 1859 by Amos Church, J. P.

Church, Calvin A. & Newnicy Edmisten, 18 Feb 1851; David C. Allen, bm; H. P. Waugh, wit.

Church, David & Elizabeth Crain, 25 July 1836; John Church, bm.

Church, Elija & Ann Blanton, 10 Oct 1815; John Crain, bm.

Church, Esquire A., son of Joel & Rhoda Church, & Celah L. Church, daughter of William and Saraha Church, 16 Jan 1868.

WILKES COUNTY MARRIAGES, 1778-1868

Church, Gabrial & Nancy E. Foster, 1 June 1838; Wm. Hamby, bm.

Church, Gabril & Mary Brown, 22 April 1839; Aaron Church, bm.

Church, Gabril & Fanny Adams, 22 Oct 1858; Jesse C. Summerlin, bm; m 26 Nov 1858 by G. Lewelin(?), J. P.

Church, J. M. & Nancy Bullis, 7 May 1852; m 7 May 1852 by S. C. Wellborn, J. P.

Church, Hamilton B. & Ann Joines, 3 Aug 1847; John Bumgarner, bm.

Church, Hiram & Martha J. Pain, 6 April 1854; m by A. M. Fort, J. P.

Church, J. Calvin & Marthy Watson, 9 March 1853; William Watson, bm.

Church, James B. & Mary M. Bullis, 20 Sept 1860; George F. Brown, bm; m 15 Dec 1860 by Rev. Jas. McNeill.

Church, James G. & Merah Bullis, 15 Dec 1859; m 15 Dec 1859 by G. Sumerlin, J. P.

Church, Jesse F. & Sarah Adalaide Miller, 6 Oct 1848; Peter McNiell, bm; m 7 Oct 1848 by Wm. Church.

Church, Joel & Catherine Pain, 29 Sept 1844; Uriah Payne, bm.

Church, Joel L. & Margarett Edmisten, 28 Feb 1854; m 28 Feb 1854 by M. S. Stokes, J. P.

Church, John & Salley Billings, 29 Oct 1811; John Vannoy, bm.

Church, John A. & Bibba Bullis, 30 July 1866; Stephen Huffman, bm; m 2 Aug 1866 by Rev. Jas. McNeil.

Church, John W. & Nancy Jane Tomlinson, 16 Nov 1848; Jesse Miller, bm.

Church, John W. & Hily Bunting, 27 Jan 1855; Elisha White, bm.

Church, Jordan & Malindy Payne, 24 Jan 1852; Joel Church, bm.

Church, Larkin & Ann Wyatt, 20 Nov 1832; George Shepherd, bm.

Church, Leander & Mary Eller, 4 Jan 1861; Wm. H. McNeil, bm; m 22 Jan 1861 by Rev. Jas. McNeill.

Church, Levi & Caroline Miller, 2 Dec 1864; W. W. Brown, bm; m 2 Dec 1864 by John Hall, J. P.

Church, Robert & Rebecka Gordan, 26 Sept 1816; Saml. A. Chesten, bm.

Church, Thos. J. & Mary Bumgarner, 29 Jan 1846; Absalom Bullis, bm.

Church, Wesley & Caroline Adams, 6 June 1844; Alfred Minton, bm.

Church, William & ___, (no date); William Wilson, bm.

WILKES COUNTY MARRIAGES, 1778-1868

Church, William & Sally Lenderman, 22 Dec 1825; Nathaniel Church, bm; consent from Leonard Lenderman.

Church, William & Rebecca Welch, 26 Dec 1849; Hiram Church, bm.

Church, Wm. F. & Elisabeth Castel, 26 Feb 1861; m 1 March 1861 by J. W. Church.

Church, William F. & Cenith Lipps, m 4 Oct 1866 by J. W. Church, J. P.

Church, William H. & M. A. McKee, 18 Aug 1866; James H. Foster, bm; m 21 Aug 1866 by John W. Church.

Church, Winston & Sarah Kees, 13 Dec 1854; Johnston Philips, bm.

Clanton, John & Elizabeth Bowls, 19 Feb 1861; m 19 Feb 1861 by J. D. Hubbard, J. P.

Clanton, William & Elender Lain, 23 Jan 1828; Joshua Lewis, bm.

Clark, Thomas & Betsey McBride, 1 May 1800; John Fletcher, bm.

Clark, Thos. & Polley Coleman, 26 March 1826; Thos Clark, bm.

Clary, Benjamin & Madelphia Barnard, 20 April 1820; Thos. Witherspoon, bm.

Cleveland, Absolem & Pattie Hanson, 14 Nov 1782; Benja. Cleveland, bm.

Cleveland, John & Caty Mungumry, 9 June 1781; William Reynolds, bm.

Cleveland, John & Comfort Gilbert, 12 Dec 1783; Isaac Garrison, bm.

Cleveland, John & Amelia Martin, 24 July 1805; Robert Martin, Esqr., bm.

Clifton, Samuel & Betsy Swanson, 15 Jan 1816; James Gray, bm.

Coats, Hennery & Salley Bussell, 23 March 1811; John Bussell, bm.

Cockerham, David & Elisabeth Palmer, 3 Oct 1810; John London, bm.

Cockerham, George & Elizabeth Pardew, 10 Sept 1803; Franklin Cockerham, bm.

Cockerham, Henry & Fanny Greenwilt, 8 Jan 1831; Nathl. Barker, bm.

Cockerham, Irvin & Caroline Darnall, 23 June 1856; James P. Cockerham, bm; m 29 June 1856 by J. M. Gambill, J. P.

Cockerham, James & Rhoda W. Cann, 22 Nov 1823; Reuben Suttle Junr., bm.

Cockerham, Jno & Fanny Wades, 3 Oct 1814; Wm. Persons, bm.

WILKES COUNTY MARRIAGES, 1778-1868

Cockerham, Martin & Lidda Baugus, 14 Nov 1829; John Durham, bm.

Cockerham, Moses H. & S. D. A. Higgins, 23 Feb 1863; Wm. L. Higgins, bm.

Cockerham, W. F., son of James & Roda Cockerham, & Jane Hanks, daughter of Wm. & Nancy Hanks, m 14 Dec 1867 by John Hughes, Baptist minister.

Cockerham, Wm & Elizabeth Hill, 29 March 1821; Samuel Parsons, bm.

Cochrane, Wm & Nancy Brock, 27 Dec 1839; James Crysel, bm.

Cocks, Brandon & Oriller Hall, 12 Sept 1848; James Kindle(?), bm.

Cocrum, Chesley & Peggie Martin, 17 Aug 1782; Giles Martin, bm.

Coffey, Austin & Sally Hawkins, 24 Oct 1822; Thomas W. A. Sumpter, bm; Mary Davenport, wit.

Coffey, Bengiman & Sally Ferguson, 5 Feb 1805; Benet Coffey, bm; Thos Norman, wit.

Coffey, Cleveland & Matilda Tilley, 15 May 1830; Reuben Fields, bm.

Coffey, Cleavland & Jane Witherspoon, 11 Feb 1794; Tho Coffey, bm.

Coffey, Elijah & Betsey Robins, 1 June 1831; James Lewis, bm.

Coffey, James & Sarah Coffey, 30 Aug 1794; George Hays, bm.

Coffey, James & Liley Farguson, 31 Aug 1799; Moses Farguson, bm.

Coffey, Jesse & Winneford Crumpton, 22 Dec 1821; Larkin Coffey, bm.

Coffey, Joel & Jane Coffey, ___ Aug 1793; Benjamin Coffey, bm.

Coffey, John & Hannah Wilson, 3 Oct 1796; Eli Coffey, bm.

Coffey, Joshua & Rebbecca Shepherd, 1 Nov 1842; John F. Shepherd, bm.

Coffey, Larken & Libby Wyatt, 28 Nov 1853; Linvill Barlow, bm.

Coffey, Larkin & Catherine H. Wilson, 9 Jan 1826; Lewis Coffey, bm; Mary Davenport, wit.

Coffey, Levi & Dolley Edmundson, 17 Aug 1799; Wm Edmisten, bm.

Coffey, Lewis & Bidunt Moore, 10 Dec 1795; Ambrose Coffey, bm.

Coffey, Thomas Junr. & Nancey Barlow, 22 Sept 1823; Lewis Coffey, bm.

Coffey, Wellborn & Sarah Cottrell, 2 Jan 1832; Filliam Coffey, bm.

WILKES COUNTY MARRIAGES, 1778-1868

Coffey, Wm. C. & Carrie L. Curtis, 10 May 1866; A. J. Curtis, bm; m 10 May 1866 by Rev. Jas. McNeil.

Coffey, William & Polley Coffey, 3 July 1796; Benjamin Coffey, bm.

Coffey, William & Margret Robins, 15 Aug 1829; John Robins, bm.

Coffhen, Thomas & Mary Combs, 8 Sept 1818; Jacob Hoots, bm.

Cokerham, Wm & Mary Henderson, 17 March 1781; William Lansdown, bm.

Colbert, Henry & Viney Garres, 5 April 1864; J. H. Alexander, bm.

Cole, Leven & Sarah Francis, 13 Nov 1783; Randolph Walker, bm.

Coleman, Beverly & Rebekah Nickelson, 20 Dec 1808; Lazarus Nichelson, bm.

Coleman, Bevily & Nancey Norman, 7 Dec 1851; Ameus Rash, bm; m 7 Dec 1851 by Alfred Warren, J. P.

Coleman, John & Susannah Felts, 26 Dec 1818; Charles Rash, bm; Amelia Martin, wit.

Coleman, Robert & Betsey Rash, 2 June 1803; Asa Rash, bm.

Collett, Abram & Mary Stuart, 31 July 1823; Samuel Stuart, bm.

Collett, James & Jane Stuart, 15 Dec 1829; Samuel Stuart or James Stewart, bm.

Collyer, Mereday & Elizabeth Night, 21 Dec 1806; Marel Collier, bm.

Collins, Riah (Rie) & Anna Silcock, 23 May 183?; Andrew Silcock, bm.

Colman, Campbell (Camel) & Charity Lowe(?), 25 March 1851; John Chambers, bm.

Colman, John B. & Rebecca Brown, 14 Aug 1828; William Dowell, bm.

Colman, Robert & Marryann Joines, 29 Sept 1845; Seth Chambers, bm.

Colvard, Jesse & Nancy Merriman, 12 Nov 1834; Thornton Kilby, bm.

Colvard, Rufus W. & Nancy E. Whittington, 16 Feb 1867; L. C. Whittington, bm; m 17 Feb 1867 by Calvin Plyler.

Colvard, Wade & Phoebe Vannoy, 29 Oct 1831; Thornton Kilby, bm.

Comes (Combes), Thomas & Lucy Combes, 15 Dec 1813; William Beall, bm.

Combes, William & Mitilday Luis, 18 Feb 1854; Hicks Combes, bm.

Comes, Eli & Alcy Waddle, 28 March 1864; Wm. R. Adams, bm; m 29 March 1864 by Jno. W. Brown, J. P.

WILKES COUNTY MARRIAGES, 1778-1868

Combs, Frederick & Mary Nott, 13 Sept 1805; Ephraim Nott, bm.

Combs, George & Salley Wallace, 24 Jan 1820; Phillip Glass, bm.

Combs, Henry & Elizabeth Chambers, 14 Nov 1805; John Chambers, bm.

Combs, Hickes & Elizabeth Lewis, 9 Oct 1840; Wesley Anderson, bm.

Combs, Hickes & Janey Browan, 16 March 1858; Archaful Bell, bm; m 25 March 1859 by Thos. H. Saintclaw, J. P.

Combs, Hicks & Keziah Hays, 3 Feb 1801; Henry Hayes, bm.

Combs, Jessey & Polley Price, 8 Jan 1801; Jonathan Hayes, bm.

Combs, John & Biddy Nance, 31 May 1779; Jos. Porter, bm.

Combs, John & Elizabeth Bell, 10 Feb 1814; David Parker, bm.

Combs, John & Elisath (sic) Phillips, 2 Oct 1833; Henry Childers, bm.

Combs, John W. & Nancey Lewis, 1 Jan 1867; A. M. Anderson, bm; m 3 Jan 1867 by G. W. Hayes, J. P.

Combs, Levi & Sary Arrington, 27 July 1817; John Arrington, bm.

Combs, Levi & Mary Moore, 26 Aug 1856; Levi Dowell, bm.

Combs, Stephen & Melinda Caudile, 15 Aug 1844; John M. Combs, bm.

Combs, Wiley & Lucy Estep, 28 July 1831; Robert Walker, bm.

Combs, William & Hannah Tomsson(?), 8 Dec 1780; John Combs, bm.

Combs, William & Ascena Ellis, 8 Jan 1822; Hix Combs, bm.

Combs, William & Cintha Elizabeth Moore, 9 Jan 1866; Rily Moore, bm; m 10 Jan 1867 by G. W. Hayes, J. P.

Comer, John & Ann Mcfactridge, 6 Aug 1818; James Gywn Junr., bm.

Comes, Frankling & Elizabeth Johnson, 8 June 1851; m 8 June 1867 by Eli Grimes, L. D. of M E. Ch South.

Comer, William & Elizabeth Marlow, 17 Dec 1813; John Parker, bm

Compton, Jesse & Eleanor Coffey, 10 Feb 1819; Thos Compton, bm.

Conley, J. Mortimer & Emily A. Parks, 22 March 1848; Walter W. Lenoir, bm.

Coock, James & Leety Pety, 14 March 1860; James M. Beng, bm.

Cook, Aaron & Patsy Denney, 11 March 1807; Richard Cook, bm.

Cook, Abraham & Elizabeth Cass, 17 July 1781; Randall Mabry, bm.

Cook, Ambrose & Alcy Bell, 16 Oct 1828; Jesse Walker, bm.

43

WILKES COUNTY MARRIAGES, 1778-1868

Cook, Aron & Temperounce Brown(?), 20 Oct 1812; James De___, bm.

Cook, C. L. & Mary S. Brown, 21 March 1858; m by Brown, J. P., 21 March 1858.

Cook, Calvin & Sally Barker, 7 June 1834; Jas. Marlow, bm.

Cook, Ephrem & Viney Marlow, 26 March 1819; Quiller Williams, bm.

Cook, Henry & Nancy Gibs, 6 May 1820; Johnson Cook, bm.

Cook, Isaac & Salley Crickmore, 25 Oct 1832; Mark Cook, bm.

Cook, Johnson & Barbary Clark, 7 Oct 1819; Tillous Russell (Bussell?), bm.

Cook, Richard & Rhoda Gilreath, 8 Nov 1806; James Martin, bm.

Cook, Richard & Rebeccah Cheek, 11 May 1811; Micajah Jackson, bm.

Cook, Richard J. or I. & Rebeccah Brooks, 21 Feb 1831; Levi Chappel, bm.

Cook, Richmond & Sarah Cook, 3 March 1851; William R. Cook, bm; m 3 March 1851 by A. Gilreath, J. P.

Cook, Thomas & Charlot Anderson, ___ 1803; Benj. Martin, bm.

Cook, Wm. R. & Adaline M. Young, 25 Jan 1853.

Cooper, C. A. & Francis A. McDaniel, 28 Feb 1855; J. O. Shue, bm; m 1 March 1855 by Eli Johnson, J. P.

Cooper, Enoch & Caroline McGlemry, 19 May 1847; Jas. Edmonson, bm.

Cooper, Jas. & Elizabeth Griffen, 2 April 1866; L. B. Griffen, bm; m 8 April 1866.

Cooper, John A. & Amelia F. Adams, 20 Feb 1855; m 6 March 1855 by S. P. Smith, Minister.

Cooper, Nathan M. & Sarah Cammell, m 13 Aug 1860 by A. W. Vannoy.

Cooper, Samuel & Ellen Shelly, 12 Oct 1850; Laben Hartzog, bm.

Cope, Henry & Mary Decker, 24 Nov 1831; Phillip G. Bumgarner, bm.

Cordall, Wm. R. & Sarah Smith, 6 Jan 1853; Eli Norman, bm; m 6 Jan 1853 by Ansel Parks.

Cordel, Jno: & Levici Smith, 17 Dec 1825; James Smith, bm.

Cordell, William & Susanna Creed, 1 Nov 1828; George W. Thomson, bm.

Cordill, James & Sarah M. Philips, 9 Aug 1854; A. Parks, bm; m 9 Aug 1854 by Ansel Parks.

Cornell, Jesse & Salley Johnson, 27 Nov 1820; James Jonson, bm.

WILKES COUNTY MARRIAGES, 1778-1868

Cornwell, John & Nancy Porter, 6 Aug 1800; William Johnson, bm.

Copening, D. J. & Jane C. Horton, 6 June 1843; Leander Horton, bm.

Caudle, Jeremiah & Elizabeth Riggins, 28 June 1828; John W. Beaty, bm.

Cothran, Leander D. & L. Joyner, 2 Feb 1847; Jesse Billings, bm.

Cotterell, William W. & Fanny E. Dula, 24 April 1858; Edmund Curtis, bm; m 11 May 1858 by P. ___.

Cottrel, Wm & Lucy Day, 14 April 1804; Hugh Day, bm.

Cottrell, J. E. & Miss N. W. Hindrix, 23 April 1865; m 27 April 1865 by Larkin Pipes, minister.

Cottrell, Thomas C. & Miry E. Cottrell, 28 Oct 1865; m 1 Nov 1865 by Larkin Pipes, minister.

Couch, Meshack & Mary Bryan, 8 Jan 1850; Jonathan G. Atkins, bm.

Couler, Rufus G. & Frances C. Bumgarner, 9 Nov 1859; Wm. J. Milam, bm; m by Wm. S. McNeil, J. P.

Counsill, Matthew & Margret Farguson, 8 Jan 1799; John Farguson, bm; consent from John Faugerson, father of Marget, 8 Jan 1799.

Couthner, Alfred & Elizabeth Edwer, 20 Nov 1835; Austin Yeats, bm.

Cox, Ambrose & Polly Kirby, 27 Dec 1827; Thomas Storie(?), bm.

Cox, Andrew & Nancy Addames, 27 March 1823; John Elledge, bm.

Cox, Braxton & Nancy Ellison, 22 Oct 1798; Wm Ellison, bm.

Cox, Isaac & Sealy Williams, 8 July 1815; Thomas Stanley, bm.

Cox, Jesse & Thursey Harper, 27 July 1815; Payton Colvard, bm.

Cox, Joel & Nancy Adkins, 11 Feb 1843; Charles Hix, bm.

Cox, Montgomery & Jane Amanda Waters, 1 Aug 1849; Phineas Horton, bm.

Cox, Montgomery & Elizabeth Lipps, 3 July 1858, John H. Ferguson, bm.

Cox, Reuben & Susy Pajet, 10 Dec 1805; James Parker, bm.

Cox, Silas & Isabella Kerby, 20 Jan 1829; Ambrose Cox, bm.

Cox, Smith & Malinda West, 2 Jan 1856; Montgomery Cox, bm.

Cox, Walton & Caroline Kindall, 3 Jan 1848; James Kindell, bm.

Cox, William & Nancy Anderson, 21 Jan 1826; Reuben Standly, bm.

Crab, William & Polley Massey, 1 Nov 1820; Williford Pruitt, bm.

WILKES COUNTY MARRIAGES, 1778-1868

Crabe, James & Nance Fletcher, 4 Dec 1851; Winsten Mason, bm; m by R. W. Wooton.

Crafferd, Samuel & Elizabeth Roye, 30 June 1783; Charles Bond, bm.

Craft, Archelus & Elizabeth Adams, 1 Dec 1785; Jacob Addams, bm.

Craig, James & Nancy Tilley, 21 Sept 1835; William Watts, bm.

Crain, James Jr. & Nancy Bishop, 29 March 1834; Andrew McGrady, bm.

Crain, Jefferson & Rosanna Bishop, 16 Oct 1829; Wm. Hamby, bm.

Crane, James & Mary Church, 24 July 1812; John Parlier, bm.

Crane, John & Biddy Cardwell, 18 Nov 1828; Andrew Hufman, bm.

Crane, William & Polly Bullison, 23 Dec 1852; Wm. N. Parsons, bm; m 23 Dec 1852 by Amos Church, J. P.

Cranford, J. M. & Huldah J. Poplin, 19 Oct 1859; Miles G. Lyon, bm.

Crawley, William & Elizabeth Lovelace, 9 Sept 1799; Geo. Lovelace, bm.

Creed, John & Nancy Walls, 24 Jan 1831; James Darnall, bm.

Creekmore, J. C. & Sary Brown, 24 Feb 1865; Berton Cook, bm.

Crickmore, Thos & Lidda Alvey, 9 March 1827; Jesse Willcoxson, bm.

Crisp, Chesley & Barbary Bates, 2 April 1796; Robt Epperson, bm.

Crisp, John & Cassey Coffey, 25 July 1818; Abel Crisp, bm.

Cross, John & Nancy Riley, 11 March 1783; Michael Childress, bm.

Crets, Nathaniel & Permealy Nicholls, 17 March 1864; John Edmuston, bm.

Crouch, John & Abigal Hampton, 22 Oct 1817; Jacob Crouch, bm.

Crouch, John & Patsey ___, 24 March 1825; George Parsuns, bm.

Crouch, Loveson & Sarah E. Ferguson, 24 Sept 1860; m 27 Sept 1860 by E. B. Philips, J. P.

Crouch, Richard & Charity Adams, 18 May 1803; Isaac Hayes, bm.

Crouse, Henry, son of John and Nancy Crouse, & Sulila Smith, daughter of Elisha & Elizabeth Smith, m 8 March 1868 at the house of Micajah Phillips, by J. I. Parks, J. P.

Crows, David & Mary Hollaway, 2 June 1818; John Hollaway, bm.

Crowse, D. M. & Mary Norman, 26 Sept 1866; Hiram Crowse, bm; m 26 Sept 1866 by Rev. William P. Combs.

WILKES COUNTY MARRIAGES, 1778-1868

Crowse, William & Sally Rose, 16 Nov 1816; Sterling Rose, bm.

Crysel, Columbus A. & Mary Eveline Walker, 28 Nov 1859; William Walker, bm.

Crysel, James E. & Elizabeth Sparkes, 5 June 1843; John Lan, bm.

Crysel, John B. & Nancy G. Lane, 20 Oct 1813; Thomas Lane, bm.

Culler, John B. & ___, 28 Jan 1841; Wm. W. Crysel, bm.

Cunningham, Benj. & Lucy Lenoir, 14 Sept 1809; Thomas Martin, bm.

Cunningham, John & Mary Louisa Jones, 22 Dec 1830; Wm. A. Lenoir, bm.

Cunningham, Langston & Nancy Robins, 23 April 1805; John Robins, bm.

Cunningham, Richd. & Patsey Bagbey, 23 Nov 1801; Thomas Martin, bm.

Curbey, Squire & Mary Beach, 18 April 1834; William W. Merriman, bm.

Curry, George & Elizabeth Gray, 27 Feb 1817; Wm. Gray, bm.

Curry, Joseph & Ebey Ellis, 22 Aug 1815; John Brooks, bm.

Carter, Joshua & ___, 7 July 1794; Samuel Baker, Lewis Stevens, bm; Susanna Baird, Ezekiel Baird, wit.

Curtis, H. W. & Eliza Curtis, 13 March 1867; J. C. Welch, bm.

Curtis, Samuel & Alpha E. Church, 22 Jan 1856; Calvin Church, bm; m 22 Jan 1856 by M. S. Stokes, J. P.

Curtis, James & Nancy Hagler, 6 March 1818; Thomas Holdman, bm.

Curtis, William & Elizabeth Jane Bumgarner, 5 July 1866; W. W. Carmichael, bm; m 6 July 1866 by J. W. Church, J. P.

Curtiss, John & Sarah Simons, 15 April 1824; Thomas Cottrell, bm.

Curtiss, Samuel & Susanna Cottrell, 11 March 1788; Thos Farguson, bm.

Dacons, Sires & Sarah Howard, 13 June 1850; W. J. Chapple, bm.

Dancy, Alexander B. & Susanah Jinnings, 29 March 1855; Levi Jinnings, bm; m 29 March 1855 by A. A. Whittenton, J. P.

Dancy, Edward J. & Nancy McNeil, 7 Feb 1836; Wm. Martin, bm.

Dancey, Isam & Rachell Church, 28 July 1831; George Shepherd, bm.

Dancy, Abraham J. & Sarah Ann Brown, 14 Oct 1845; Thornton Kilby, bm.

WILKES COUNTY MARRIAGES, 1778-1868

Dancy, Edward & Milley Vannoy, 8 July 1802; Francis Vannoy, bm.

Dancy, Jesse J. & Rebecca Davis, 9 Dec 1831; John Dancy, bm.

Dancy, John & Rachel Johnson, 15 Oct 1816; Thomas Griffy, bm.

Dancy, John & Faney Kilby, 30 May 1835; Noah Dancy, bm.

Dancy, John M. & Susanah Brown, 26 Feb 1855; Ezekael Brown, bm.

Dancy, Joseph H. & Harriet Wilcoxson, 23 Jan 1853.

Dancy, Joseph E. & C. E. Vannoy, 2 April 1865; C. F. Vannoy, bm; m 2 April 1865 by Wm. Hall.

Dancy, Neil & Reley Cockes, 6 Aug 1846; Wm. S. Kilby, bm.

Dancy, Noah & Albey Kilby, 23 Feb 1835; Tarlton Wilson, bm.

Dancy, Obidier D. & Alcey Shepherd, 5 March 1865; J. E. Dancy, bm; m 5 March 1865 by A. A. Whittenton, J. P.

Daniel, Allen & Nancy Barns, 25 Aug 1828; Richard Harris, bm.

Daniels, John Westley & Minday Mabery, 17 Dec 1850; Franklin Gregory, bm.

Danold, Henry M. & Sophia Deaton, 23 Dec 1809; Michael Keelan, bm.

Dansy, David C., son of Obediah & Elizabeth Dansy, & Mansy B. Kilby, daughter of R. W. & Elizabeth Kilby, 7 March 1867; m 8 March 1867 by William Hall.

Darnel, Benjamin & Faney Vier, 23 May 1802; Stephen Shepard, bm.

Darnla, John & Jain Absher, 26 Feb 1849; Leonard Wyatt, bm.

Darnall, Peter & Sarah Couch, 31 May 1857; Allen Lion, bm.

Darnall, Ancel & Pheba Cockerham, 1 Dec 1864; Nathan J. Walls, bm; m 1 Dec 1864 by James M. Gambill, J. P.

Darnall, Ansel & Elizebeth Johnson, 21 Aug 1856; L. C. Brooks, bm.

Darnall, James & Mary Walls, 12 Dec 1859; N. J. Walls, bm; m 15 Dec 1859 by J. M. Gambill, J. P.

Darnall, John & Nancy Parks, 1 Nov 1800; Jonathan Parkes, bm.

Darnall, John & Martha Fields, 30 Jan 1830; Joseph Walls, bm.

Darnall, Jonathan & Elizabeth Auntney, 7 Sept 1866; N. J. Walls, bm.

Darnall, Joseph M. & Nancey Darnell, 9 Dec 1865; Wm. F. Byrd, bm; m 17 Dec 1865 by J. M. Rose, Baptist minister.

Darnall, Thomas & Sarah Saunders, 19 Sept 1809; Isaac Teague, bm.

WILKES COUNTY MARRIAGES, 1778-1868

Darnall, William & Elisabeth Gentry, 8 Jan 1827; John Darnall Junr., bm.

Darnall, William P. & Nancy Lomack, 19 May 1856; Wm. S. Edwards, bm; m 20 May 1856 by J. M. Gambill, J. P.

Darnel, Nathan & Elisabeth Wingler, 22 Dec 1866; Daniel Sheats, bm.

Darnel, Roley & Martha An Tucker, 17 Jan 1854; James Darnel, bm; m 18 Jan 1854 by Wm. Burcham, J. P.

Darnell, son of Wm. & Elizabeth Darnell, & Laura Tucker, daughter of Washington & Sallie Tucker, 19 Aug 1868; m 20 Aug 1868 by John K. Rose, Baptist minister.

Darnold, James & Salley Burchfield, 24 Dec 1811; John Burchfield, bm.

Daughrity, John & Milley Ball, 23 Dec 1799; W. Gilreath, bm.

Daughtry, George K. & Tempy Dunken, 11 Nov 1820; James Smith, Joseph James, bm.

Dalton, Joshua & Powel Poe, 26 March 1852; William L. Franklin, bm; m 26 March 1852 by Ansel Parks.

Dauson, James & Milley Persons, 10 Nov 1808; Geo. G. Parsons, bm.

Davenport, John & Ann Lewis, 29 July 1822; Robert Slone, bm.

Davenport, Wm & Mary Gordon, 12 Oct 1802; Edm: Jones, bm.

Davison, James & Nancey Isbell, 14 April 1800; A. Parks, bm.

Davidson, Jas. & Salley Whittenton, 23 June 1807; Thos Robins, bm.

Davidson, Richard & Elizabeth Williams, 22 Aug 1824; Silas Ball, bm.

Davis, Alexander & Leoiny Prewett, 24 Dec 1857; m 24 Dec 1857 by William Goforth, minister.

Davis, Alfred M. & Matilda Nichols, 8 Dec 1853; m 8 Dec 1853; m 8 Dec 1853 by S. C. Wellborn, J. P.

David, Allexander & Mary Fougar, 23 Jan 1816; James Marlow, bm.

Davis, E. J. & Elizabeth J. Ausbon, 14 Nov 1864; no bm; m 14 Nov 1864 by Eli Grimes, L. D. of M. E. C. S.

Davis, Ephraim & Suzanna Dockery, 3 Oct 1848; John Jones, bm.

Davis, Ephraim & Annis Foster, 27 Sept 1826; David Watson, bm.

Davis, Franklin & Jane Andrew, 25 March 1845; Lewis Russell, bm.

Davis, Henry & Nancy Kendoll, 28 Oct 1848; Jestus Davis, bm.

Davis, Isaac & Elizabeth Bever, 3 Nov 1796; Adam Hall, bm.

WILKES COUNTY MARRIAGES, 1778-1868

Davis, Jacob & Lizzey Sparks, 21 May 1782; Benjamin Allen, bm.

Davis, James & Prissilla Harris, 28 Oct 1782; John Walker, bm.

Davis, James & Fanny Bryant, 6 May 1828; Isaac Bever, bm.

Davis, James H. & Matilda Roberson, 4 April 1842; John W. Jones, bm.

Davis, Jestus & Mary Ginnon, 21 Jan 1834; Charles Garmon, bm.

Davis, John A. & Bethany Church, 9 April 1846; Hamilton B. Church, bm.

Davis, John B. & Frances Bethenia Nicholds, 11 Jan 1849; Thomas S. Davis, bm.

Davis, John N. & Jane Steelmon, 1 Jan 1842; Alexander W. Williamson, bm.

Davis, John W., son of John N. & Jane Davis, & Margaret E. Ray, daughter of Joseph & Elizabeth Ray, 8 May 1868; m by Wm. J. Chapel.

Davis, Joseph & Nancy C. Johnson, 7 Dec 1863; E. C. Temple, bm; m 11 Dec 1863 by A. L. Rousseu, J. P.

Davis, Joshua & Kisiah Stanfield, 8 Sept 1832; David Hanks, bm.

Davis, Philip & Elizabeth Forguson, 9 March 1791; Nebuzaradan Coffey, bm.

Davis, Solomon & Elizabeth Gidong, 16 May 1815; John Shoemaker, bm.

Davis, Solomon & Irina Hendrix(?), 2 Nov 1839; Wm. D. Philips, bm.

Davis, Thomas & Frances Robins, 17 June 1805; Jordan Phipps, bm.

Davis, Thomas & Sary Mize, 18 Sept 1817; William Davis, bm.

Davis, Thos & Rebecca Foster, 3 Aug 1824; Joseph M. Bogle, bm.

Davis, Thomas K. & Clarisa Buship, 6 Jan 1848; Jesse Caudell, bm.

Davis, William & Anne Loving, 10 Nov 1780; Gabriel Loving, bm.

Davis, William & Delilah Noland, 6 July 1792; Luke Carrel, bm.

Davis, William & Rachel Oings, 8 Aug 1812; Wm. R. Padget, bm.

Davison, Alfred & Martha Earp, 26 Aug 1822; Benj. Grayson, bm.

Dawson, William & Susanah Durham, 20 Feb 1803; Thomas Durham, bm.

Day, Alvearan & Sareyan Harris, 1 April 1844; Joel Perdue, bm.

Day, Edward & Susannah Welch, 10 April 1797; Laban Day, bm.

WILKES COUNTY MARRIAGES, 1778-1868

Day, Elias & Lewesy Dun, 25 Nov 1852; Rufus Hampton, bm; m 29 Nov 1852 by William Goforth, minister of the gospel.

Day, Hugh & Polley Hodge, 22 Sept 1825; Hugh Nelson, bm.

Day, James & Emeline Curry, 29 Sept 1852.

Day, John & Mary Stallings, 27 March 1779; Moses Guest, Abraham Stallings, bm.

Day, John & Sussanna Pipes, 6 Oct 1857; Thos. Day, bm. m 11 Oct 1857 by G. W. Hendrix, J. P.

Day, Labon & Mary McKensey, 20 July 1793; Benjamin Coffey, bm.

Day, Lewis & Betsy Grason, 2 Dec 1815; Benj. Grason, bm.

Day, Samuel & Rebecca Pipes, 13 Nov 1851; Ezekiah Holder, bm; m 3 Feb 1852 by G. W. Hendrix, J. P.

Day, William & Elender Perdue, 2 Jan 1844; David Hampton, bm.

Deboard, Adna & Emela Patterson, 19 July 1827; William Cawthin, bm.

Deboard, Ira & Ann Midleton, 18 June 1827; William Cauthin, bm.

Deboard, Benjamin & Nancy Summers, 25 Sept 1809; William Debord, bm.

Debord, Gideon & Lotta Dickerson, 21 Oct 1840; Thomas Money, bm.

Debord, Jephthat & Nancy Middleton, 31 March 1827; Gedion Deboard, bm.

Debord, John & Jean Kilbe, 19 April 1804; William Debord, bm.

Deborde, Ezra & Mary C. Boaze, 27 ___ 1849; William Luffman, bm.

Deborde, Gideon & Salley Pigg, 12 March 1822; Joseph Deboard, bm.

Deborde, Gedion & Polly Cothern, 6 March 1824; Wm. Parsons, bm.

Deass, Jesse & Mary Bross, 15 Feb 1795; George Brown, bm.

Demoss, Thomas & Ann Greer, 11 Sept 1798; Job Cole, bm.

Deney, Ely & Polley Johnson, 29 Sept 1817; John Johnston, bm.

Denman, James & Claranner Welborn, 12 July 1785; Isaac Welborn, bm.

Denney, George & Mary Brown, 13 Oct 1783; Charles Brown, bm.

Denney, James & Hannah Sparks, 23 Nov 1784; Geo: Denney, bm.

Denney, James & Elisabeth Cockerham, 21 Aug 1807; John Denney, bm.

Denney, Solomon & Elizabeth Chambers, 29 April 1842; Henry Chambers, bm.

WILKES COUNTY MARRIAGES, 1778-1868

Denny, Anderson & Caroline Calloway, 26 Jan 1867; G. H. Brown, bm; m 26 Jan 1867 by C. E. S. Simpson, J. P.

Denny, James & Emily Jenkins, 30 Oct 1854; Joseph James, bm; m 30 Oct 1854 by L. J. Bicknell, J. P.

Denny, Solomon & Sarah Ann Segroves, 13 March 1852; m by Wm. S. McNeil, J. P.

Deshmon, Jesse & Theny Hollow, 13 April 1837; Andrew J. Souther, bm.

Deshmon, Lewis & Nelly Bell, 30 Jan 1839; Milos Nance, bm.

Deshmon, Wesly & Betsey Vest, 3 Jan 1834; Wm. Duncan, bm.

Dick, Koonrod & Charlotte Harrald, 26 April 1806; John Harrald, bm.

Dickens, James & Sarah Hather, 23 Jan 1800; John Chambers, bm.

Dickens, Richard & Charity Williams, 29 Feb 1800; James Dickens, bm.

Dickinson, James & Julia Thurmond, 27 Dec 1828; Hugh Gwyn, bm; power of attorney dated 25 Dec 1828 from James Dickenson to Hugh Gwyn to obtain bond, wit by Thos. J. Thurmond.

Dickerson, Davd. & Sabia Shoud, 3 Nov 1795; Cabiat Chout, William Ellison, bm.

Dickerson, Isaac & Polley Pratt, 9 Feb 1822; Hiram Suttle, bm.

Dickerson, Isaac & Leweretia Wall, 26 July 1851; m 15 Aug 1851 by Danl. Fields, J. P.

Dickerson, Isham & Polley Harris, 16 Feb 1822; John Durham, bm.

Dickerson, Isam L. & Jane Dimett, 25 Feb 1854; m 4 March 1854 by James Milam(?), J. P.

Dickerson, James & Linday Sanders, 26 Jan 1850; Isom Bichill, bm.

Dickerson, Squire & Marth Wall, 4 Jan 1854; William Harris, bm.

Dickson, James D. & Mary M. Bumgarner, 2 April 1866; James C. Bumgarner, bm; m 2 April 1866 by Rev. Jas. McNeil.

Dickson, Joseph & Mary Murphey, 25 July 1798; Paul Poulson, bm.

Dier, Hezakiah & Ann Kelly, 4 Juen 1782; Isaac Elledge, bm.

Dier, John & Betsey Cotton, 4 Aug 1779; James Dier, bm.

Dillaird, Thos & Ruth McBride, 27 Dec 1810; Levi Rash, bm.

Dimit, Willis & Susan Mastion, 6 Jan 1847; Alexander Mastin, bm.

Dimmet, Paten & Marthia Duram, 1 Feb 1855; m by John Brewer, Esqr.

WILKES COUNTY MARRIAGES, 1778-1868

Dimmit, James & Elisabeth Ellis, 4 July 1824; Tyrel Gray, bm.

Demmett, Joel & Mahala Parks, 15 May 1830; John B. Demmett, bm.

Dimmitt, Joel & Rebecca Sprinkle, 1 Jan 1852; Willis Dimmitt, bm; m 1 Jan 1852 by Wm. F. Adams, Baptist minister.

Dinkins, Joshua E. & Sally Dula, 12 Feb 1833; Elam Caldwell, bm.

Dishman, James & Polly Nance, 1 June 1832; Jerome Souther, bm.

Dishman, Jefferson & Peggy Spice, 5 Oct 1835; John Marlow, bm.

Dishmond, Martin & Jane Hardin, 3 May 1862; Elknah Rupard(?), bm; m 4 May 1862 by Elder R. W. Wooton.

Dobson, James & Fanny Lunceford, 14 Sept 1811; Joel Lunceford, bm.

Dobson, John H. & Elizabeth Martin, 15 Aug 1840; Thomas D. Kelly, bm.

Dockery, Elijah W. & Eveline Gowforth, 6 Jan 1841; John S. Dockery, bm.

Dockery, John S. & Delphy Roberds, 21 Dec 1831; Benjamin Walker, bm.

Dodd, William & ___, (no date, during admn. of Gov. Alexander Martin); William Cocorum, bm.

Dogan, Samuel & Sarah Handon, 10 June 1790; John Robins, bm.

Donathan, Hawkins & Mary Frost, 31 March 1779; Isaac Elledge, bm.

Done, Isaac & Sally Hays, 10 Nov 1832; John Grasty, bm.

Donnelly, Robt & Frankey Adkins, 17 Aug 1807; Joseph Brown, bm.

Dornbush, Thos & Prissy Wallace, 16 March 1816; Micajah Lunsford, bm.

Dorrity, Michel & Hanner Shelley, 20 Sept 1854; W. R. Whittington, bm; m 21 Sept 1854 by A. A. Whittenton, J. P.

Doss, Lemuel & Elizabeth Miller, 20 Dec 1820; Ambrose Foster, bm.

Doss, Lemuel & Martha Laws, 17 June 1824; William Todd, bm.

Doss, Solomon & Ann ___, (date torn off).

Dotson, Joel & Franky Land, 18 Oct 1806; Aaron Parks, bm.

Doughethee, John & Jamima Sale, 18 Oct 1837; James Sale, bm.

Douglass, William Senr. & Elizabeth Hanks, 9 March 1824; Jas. Martin, bm.

Doughten, Flinn S. & Delia A. Petty, 2 Oct 1866; S. A. Parks, bm; m 23 Oct 1866 by Ira T. Wyche, minister.

WILKES COUNTY MARRIAGES, 1778-1868

Dougle, John S. & ___, 10 Feb 1849; Jonathan Gentry, bm.

Douthit, Uriah & Sarah Smith, 16 Aug 1851; R. M. Smith, bm; m 1 Nov 1851 by Z. B. Adams, Minister.

Douthit, Columbus & Isabella McBride, 5 Apr 1860; James Gray, bm.

Dowdy, John & Ellender Staley, 11 Feb 1815; Saml Sullivan, bm.

Dowdy, Orren & Zilpah York, 21 Sept 1822; Frederick Tiser, bm.

Dowel, Francis & Elizabeth Mahaffey, 11 Dec 1856; William Mahaffey, bm.

Dowel, Lovy & Margaret Jones, 1 Nov 1841; m 1 Nov 1841 by Thomas Roberts, J. P.

Dowell, Almon & America Cowles, 8 Dec 1855; John F. Mahaffy, bm.

Dowell, Emeral & Rhoda Broyhill, 5 Sept 1860; m 5 Sept 1860 by S. J. Ginnings, J. P.

Dowell, Hanon & Emaline Johnson, 2 Jan 1856; S. J. Forester, bm; m by John Brewer, Esqr.

Dowell, Henderson & Nancy Hickerson, 26 Aug 1865; R. F. Hackett, bm; m 27 Aug 1865 by W. B. Woodruff, M. G.

Dowell, James & Patsy Coffee, 5 Sept 1807; Reuben Coffey, bm.

Dowell, John & Sarah Hickman, 23 Sept 1797; Eli Coffey, bm.

Dowell, John & Sarah Shores, 30 Oct 1814; Ambrose Johnson, bm.

Dowell, Joshua & Dicey Wadkins, 7 July 1845; Alfred Warren, bm.

Dowell, Nelson & Mahaley Corthon, 7 Feb 1857; Amon Dowel, bm.

Downs, Saml. & Eliza L. Jones, 13 July 1819; W. R. Lenoir, bm.

Driver, John & Jelico Scisk, 23 Nov 1866; Isaac Austill, bm.

Dudley, James & Jane Tyra, 17 Feb 1856; m by N. Church, J. P.

Dula, Bennet & Adaline Brown, 30 Oct 1840; Thomas Dula, bm.

Dula, James & Anna Hendrix, 20 Sept 1858; Sanford Dula, bm; m by G. W. Hendrix, J. P., 30 Aug 1858.

Dula, John & Mary Prewit, 20 Sept 1827; Jefferson Dula, bm.

Dula, John Jr. & Mary Prewit, 12 March 1824; William Ray, bm.

Dula, Lee & Gilley Mitchell, 22 June 1839; David Watson, bm; m by Saml Walsh, J. P.

Dula, Louceny, son of Jefferson & Ally Dula, & Martha Jane Harris, daughter of John and Catharine Harris, 21 Jan 1868; m 23 Jan 1868.

Dula, Rily & Susannah Thornton, 1 March 1841; John Hix, bm.

WILKES COUNTY MARRIAGES, 1778-1868

Dula, Sampson, son of James & Peggy Dula, & Elizabeth Triplett, daughter of Asa and Balinda Triplett, 7 Jan 1868; m 8 Jan 1868 by E. B. Phillips, J. P.

Dula, Sylvannis & Carline Holder, 17 June 1855; William L. Dula, bm.

Dula, Thomas & Elizabeth Hulme, 23 Feb 1803; Wm Dula, bm.

Dula, Thomas & Mary Keeton, 9 Feb 1822; John Orr, bm.

Dula, Thomas & Mary Keton, 30 Sept 1822; John Dula, bm.

Dula, Thomas & Elizabeth Foster, 20 Nov 1823; John Dula, bm.

Dula, Thomas & Anny Triplett, 23 May 1844; Reubin Hamby, bm.

Dula, Thomas B. & Amanda C. Jones, 30 April 1829; William H. Dula, bm.

Dula, Wm & Rebeckah McKinney, 30 Dec 1801; James Ray, bm.

Dula, William C. & Cordelia Ann Jones, 6 Oct 1865; George B. Walsh, bm.

Dula, William & Mary Fogerson, 31 Aug 1816; Peter Ray, bm.

Dula, William H. & Sarah Witherspoon, 3 Nov 1828; Larkin Coffey, bm.

Dula, William L. & Ladosia Pryor, 24 May 1858; Harry Dula, bm; m 25 May 1858 by A. M. Foster, J. P.

Duley, Bennet & Anna Stoe, 10 April 1791; William Duley, bm.

Duley, William & Docia McMullen, 5 April 1790; Jesse Lay, bm.

Duncan, Chapman & Nancy Hampton, 8 Dec 1833; Archibald Tomlinson, bm.

Duncan, James W. & Elizabeth A. Joines, 14 Jan 1867; James L. Steelman, bm; m 14 Jan 1867 by H. Hayes, J. P.

Duncan, Henry & Matilda Odom(?), 18 April 1839; John Rains, bm.

Duncan, James & Rebecca Hampton, 11 Aug 1838; James Broyhill, bm.

Duncan, Jonathan & Tempey Harris, 4 Nov 1829; William Duncan, bm.

Duncan, Thomas & Lidy Grayham, 15 Aug 1787; Thos Isbell, bm.

Duncan, William & Mary Ann Harris, 22 March 1832; W. C. Emmit, bm.

Duncan, Wm & Sarah McAlroy, 1 May 1834; Wm. French, bm.

Duncan, William & Elizabeth Scott, 11 Aug 1838; John Dunkin, bm.

Dunker, Benjamin & Delphia Cook, 25 Dec 1827; William Dunker, bm.

WILKES COUNTY MARRIAGES, 1778-1868

Dunkin, G. W. & Sarah Shewmaker, 16 Aug 1860; m 19 Aug 1860 by Israel Holo, Baptist minister.

Dunkin, John & Elizabeth Brooks, 26 March 1811; William Martin, bm.

Dunkin, Jonathan & Sally Shin, 5 March 1811; Hugh Campbell, bm.

Dunlap, Alexander & Margaret Stuart, 14 Sept 1819; James M. Lee, bm.

Dunlap, John & Polley B. Gordon, 21 Sept 1820; William Davenport, bm.

Dunn, Edmund & Sarah Jane Lipford, 17 Dec 1864; John J. Foster, bm.

Dunsmore, Wm & Zevirah Standsberry, 20 Jan 1801; Wm. Hulme, bm.

Duram, Wm & Eleanor S. Shumate, 19 Nov 1855; m 19 Nov 1855 by P. R. McGrady, J. P.

Durham, Barton R. & Sarah Greenwell, 4 March 1861; m 4 March 1861 by J. M. Gambill, J. P.

Durham, Calvin J. & Mary Billings, 17 July 1866; R. B. Bryan, bm; m 19 July 1866 by J. M. Rose, Baptist minister.

Durham, James & Patsey Ryans, 10 Oct 1814; Saml Sullivan, bm.

Durham, James & Mity Sparks, 15 Aug 1846; Meredith Lyon, bm.

Durham, John & Keziah Ryon, 11 Jan 1819; John Thornton, bm.

Durham, John & Mary Ann Pratt, 4 April 1842; Martin Cockerham, bm.

Durham, John & Sally Sparks, 20 Nov 1851; James Durham, bm; m 21 Dec 1851 by James Milam, J. P.

Durham, Mathew & Mary Sparkes, 28 Dec 1801; Cahles Sparkes, bm.

Durham, Thomas & Polley Hooper, 13 July 1807; Williford Prewit, bm.

Dyer--See also Dier

Dyer, Benjamin & Matha Pague, 18 May 182_; Thos Isbell, bm.

Dyer, Elijah & Polley Foster, (no date, during admn. of Gov. Samuel Ashe); Robert Foster, bm.

Dyer, Elijah & Matilda Church, 2 July 1854; m 2 July 1854 by A. M. Foster, J. P.

Dyer, H. T. & Mary Ann Foster, 5 Nov 1851; Wm S. Kilby, bm; m 10 Nov 1851 by A. Church, J. P.

Dyer, Joel & Sarah Triplet, 18 Dec 1820; John Ferguson, bm.

Dyer, John W. & Susah. Mitchell, 13 Oct 1831; Wm. Dyer, bm.

Dyer, Josiah & Sarah Whittenton, 24 July 1786; John Whittenton, bm.

WILKES COUNTY MARRIAGES, 1778-1868

Dyer, Manoah & Rebekah Treble, 26 Oct 1791; Shadrach Treble, bm.

Dyer, William & Nancy Furguson, 4 Aug 1840; Thos Harry Foster, bm.

Dyson, Jackson & Amelia Mattba, 17 Oct 1843; Nimrod Land, bm.

Earnest, David & Elizabeth Evelina Jones, 10 April 1825; William F. Thomas of Iredell Co., bm.

Earp, Benjamin & Nancy Gray, 14 Feb 1817; Benjamin Gray, bm.

Earp, Caleb & Maria Watts, 24 Dec 1825; Benj. Earp, bm.

Earp, George R. & Nancy C. Marley, 23 March 1854; m by C. Carlton, J. P.

Earp, Obednego & Susannah Montgomory, 2 Sept 1828; William S. Kilbey, bm.

Earp, Thomas & Nancy Wilson, 20 ___ 1866; Thos W. Malloy, bm.

Earp, Thomas S. & Ellenar Person, 13 March 1850; L. H. Pearson, bm.

Earp, Wilson H., son of Caleb Earp, & Mary Ferguson, daughter of Chapman & Elizabeth Ferguson, 13 July 1867; m 17 July 1867 by Smith Ferguson, minister.

Earp, Wright & Susan Wellborn, 17 Dec 1833; Thos Earp, bm.

Earpe (Harp) Thomas & Ann Land, 19 Feb 1816; John Gray, bm.

East, Seaton & Anney Crickmore, 24 Oct 1841; Thomas C. Greenwood, bm.

Eastep, Doctor C. & Manda Duncan, 23 Feb 1858; m 25 Feb 1858 by H. Hayes, J. P.

Eastep, Samuel & Tempy Marlow, 5 March 1850; Harrel Hayes, bm.

Eavens, John & Louisa Dickens, 21 Jan 1862; Wm. Pearson, bm; m 26 Jan 1862 by Thos H. Saintclair, J. P.

Edds, Gilpin & Patsey Vest, 27 Feb 1834; Wm. Duncan, bm.

Edmisten, James & Mary Cooper, 18 Oct 1849; Wm. Whittington, bm.

Edmisten, Jas. & Elenor Minton, 23 July 1853; m by Amos Church, J. P.

Edmisten, John T. & Matilda Minton, 5 Feb 1843; David Ellen, bm.

Edmisten, John T. & Susan Nicholl, 16 April 1862; Jos. W. Nicholls, bm; m 16 April 1862 by A. A. Whittenton, J. P.

Edmondson, Gilford & Polley Denney, 15 Aug 1825; Thos Gilliam, bm.

Edmundson, Robert & Catey Israel, (no date, during admn. of Gov. Samuel Ashe); Michael Israel, bm.

WILKES COUNTY MARRIAGES, 1778-1868

Edwards, David A. & Poulena Gentry, 11 July 1854.

Edwards, David A. & Elizabeth J. Caudell, 19 May 1858; James Mastin, bm; m 20 May 1858 by W. F. Adams, Baptist minister.

Edwards, Jesse R. & Elizabeth Cuningham, 5 Nov 1817; Thomas Martin, bm.

Edwards, Nathaniel, son of William & Nancy Edwards, & Nancy Sprinkle, daughter of Harrison and Susanah Chapell, 5 Aug 1867; m 11 Aug 1867 by B. J. Wall, J. P.

Edwards, Wm. S. & Diana L. H. Smith, 11 Sept 1848; Chas. Hickerson, bm.

Eggerton, James & Elisabeth Chambers, 17 Sept 1814; Jas. Mathis, bm.

Eldredg, James W. & Roxann Tolbert, 14 July 1862; Robert Spensar, bm; m 17 July 1862 by J. M. Gambill, J. P.

Elet, John & Elisabeth Rash, 18 January 1867; J. E. Henderson, bm; m 20 Jan 1867 by Alfred Warren, J. P.

Elledge, James & Sarah Ann Sebastin, 25 Feb 1867; Alfred Elledge, bm.

Elledge, Jacob & Dice Ward, 17 March 1807; John Elledge, bm.

Elledge, John & Susanna Elrod, 16 Aug 1779; Devereux Ballard, bm.

Elledge, John & Rebeca M. Brown(?), 24 June 1850; Washington Hawkins, bm.

Elledge, Joseph & Nancy McGill, 3 Dec 1799; Joshua Mitchell, bm.

Elledge, Joseph & Elizabeth Hawkins, 3 Oct 1843; Ezekiel Hawkins, bm.

Elledge, Joseph A. & Margerett Roberts, 20 Dec 1822; Thos Roberts, bm.

Elledge, Joshua & Mary Parsons, 6 April 1794; Jeremiah Gilbert, bm.

Elledge, Whitfield, & ___, 29 Oct 1792; Thos Bradburn, bm.

Elledge, William & Sarah M. Hayse, 19 Sept 1845; Robt Hayse, bm.

Eller, A. P. & N. J. Sout, 6 May 1867; T. S. Shinn, bm.

Eller, Absalom & Sally Reynolds, 28 Feb 1824; John McNeil, bm.

Eller, Anderson & Alvy J. McNeill, 28 Jan 1854; m by Jas. McNeil, an Elder of the BP.

Eller, B. F. & Mary A. Brookshire, 13 Sept 1858; James R. Whittenton, bm; m 20 Sept 1858 by J. H. Brown.

Eller, Conrod & Eliza Laws, 26 Aug 1844; Saml. Steelman, bm.

WILKES COUNTY MARRIAGES, 1778-1868

Eller, David & Talitha Judd, 17 Oct 1818; John Judd, bm.

Eller, David & Mary McNiel, 31 Jan 1854; m 7 Feb 1854 by Jas. McNeil, an Elder of the BP.

Eller, David & Anna Eller(?), 11 April 1855; m by Saml Walsh, J. P.

Eller, Elsey & Ann Holeman, 25 May 1849; Anderson Vannoy, bm.

Eller, Francis & Mary L. Foster, 1 Oct 1860; m by J. H. Brown.

Eller, George & Mary Minton, 24 July 1845; George Minton, bm.

Eller, H. G. & V. C. Fairchild, 6 Aug 1860; William T. Griffey, bm; m 6 Aug 1860 by A. W. Vannoy.

Eller, H. H. & Martha C. Brown, 21 Nov 1866; Peter Eller, bm; m 22 Nov 1866 by Rev. Jas. McNeill.

Eller, Harvy & Caroline Vannoy, 17 Nov 1841; Wm. H. McNeil, bm.

Eller, Henry & Margret Alby, 4 April 1832; John Jacobs, bm.

Eller, Henry & Edn Grimes 20 Sept 1851; m by Wm. H. Hubbard.

Eller, Henry C. & Martha Huffman, 14 Feb 1855; m 22 Feb 1855 by Jas. McNeil, an Elder of the BP.

Eller, Jacob & Maran Secres, 16 Oct 1833; Eli Forester, bm.

Eller, James & Maryan Carlton, 6 Oct 1849; Franklin F. Ferguson, bm.

Eller, J. M. & Elizabeth Walsh, 19 Dec 1865; Benjamin Huffman, bm; m 31 Dec 1865 by James McNeil.

Eller, J. M. & E. C. Robison, 6 Nov 1865; M. C. Brown, bm; m 8 Nov 1865 by Jas. McNeil.

Eller, James F. & Delila Minton, 27 Dec 1861; Hugh Bolin, bm; m 1 Jan 1862 by Amos Church, J. P.

Eller, Jesse F. & Mary A. Laxton, 26 April 1858; m 28 April 1858 by Jas. McNeil, M. G.

Eller, Jesse H. & Mary C. Wilcoxon, 10 Jan 1850; James C. McNiel, bm.

Eller, John & Elizabeth Vannoy, 20 April 1820; Peter Eller, bm.

Eller, John Jr. & Jane Montgomery, 13 Feb 1845; W. G. Johnson, bm.

Eller, John A. & Bethany Fairchild, 27 Oct 1852.

Eller, Lafaytt, son of Nancy Eller, & Sarah Carline Vannoy, daughter of Abram & Aly Vannoy, 16 Oct 1868; m by Eld. James Kerby, 25 Oct 1868.

Eller, Leander & Lodemma Nicholls, 21 March 1865; Lafayette Eller, bm; m 21 March 1865 by Rev. Jas. McNeil.

WILKES COUNTY MARRIAGES, 1778-1868

Eller, Levi & Elizabeth Davis, 2 Jan 1860; m 2 Jan 1860 by Wm. H. Hubbard, J. P.

Eller, Peter & Louisa Church, 15 Nov 1863; A. G. Whittington, bm; m by A. W. Vannoy.

Eller, Rufus F., son of Peter Eller, & Alph C. Church, daughter of Gabril Church, m 12 Sept 1867 by R. Jacks, minister.

Eller, Simeon & Fany McNiel, 16 April 1817; Amos Harmon, bm.

Eller, William & Cathrine Pernell, 20 Dec 1845; John A. Eller, bm.

Eller, Wm & Emila Holbrook, 26 Dec 1860; m 26 Dec 1860 by Philip Grimes(?).

Eller, Wm. H. & Martha Vannoy, 22 Feb 1864; Jesse Yates, bm.

Ellern, Hugh M. & N. Barker, 15 Aug 1850; Henry A. Eller, bm.

Ellis, Benjamin & Mary Anderson, 14 Jan 1817; Enos Anderson, bm.

Ellis, Enoch & Lydia Roberson, 8 April 1847; John Smith, bm.

Ellis, Evan & Dicy Cook, 23 Nov 1825; Daniel Call, bm.

Ellis, Evan & Mary Call, 11 Dec 1860.

Ellis, Henry & Phebe Roberts, 26 Aug 1850; John Reeves, bm.

Ellis, J. E. & M. A. C. Corthen, 4 Aug 1862; m 5 Aug 1862 by A. B. Dancey, J. P.

Ellis, James D. & Nancy C. Higgins, ___ 1861; m 27 Feb 1861 by A. B. Dancey, J. P.

Ellis, Joel & Mary Ellis, 13 Aug 1813; Henry Gilreath, bm.

Ellis, Wm & Nancy Rhoads, 18 March 1826; William Wildes, bm.

Ellis, William & Delphia Hall, 16 Oct 1851; Willis Hall, bm; m 30 Dec 1852 by L. Sebastian, J. P.

Ellis, William & Susanah Fuget, 10 Nov 1856; John D. Jinnings, bm; m 11 Nov 1856 by L. Sebastian, J. P.

Ellison, Ephraim & Elizabeth Coffey, 18 Dec 1799; Thomas Cole, bm.

Ellison, James & Charity Dickerson, 6 Feb 1799; Robert Foster, bm.

Ellison, Thomas & Ama Murphey, 28 Feb 1791; Thomas Cottrell, bm.

Ellison, Wm & Elizabeth Rousseau, freed people, 10 Jan 1867; m 27 Jan 1867 by C. H. Simpson, J. P.

Elmore, George W. & Miss Marinda Myers, 17 July 1865; m 20 July 1865 by Henry Chambers, J. P.

Elmore, William & Sary Collens, 2 Aug 1856; Watson Chambers, bm.

WILKES COUNTY MARRIAGES, 1778-1868

Elrod, Adam & Nancy Philips, 9 April 1806; Peter Elrod, bm.

Elrod, Calloway & H. L. Jones, 16 May 1840; A. J. Jones, bm.

Elrod, Henry & Sarah Brookshire, 25 Jan 1843; Thos Brookshire, bm.

Elrod, John & Elizabeth Brookshire, 12 April 1854; Elisha Brookshire, bm.

Emmit, William C. & Rebecca C. Stokes, 21 June 1820; Saml. F. Patterson, bm.

Eng (one of the Siamese twins) & Sarah Yates, 13 April 1843; Jesse Yeats, bm.

England, Ezekiel & Charlotte Councill, 17 Feb 1789; Jesse Council, bm; Elisha Dyer, John England, wit.

Epperson, James & Kezia Powers, 5 June 1790, Robert Epperson, bm.

Epperson, Joel & Salley Brassfield, 6 Nov 1794; Thomas Brassfield of Burke Co., bm.

Erwin, Andrew & Jane Patton, 19 March 1794; Charles Gordon Junr., bm.

Erwin, Arthur & Phebe Franklin, 11 March 1819; Samuel Stallings, bm.

Erwin, James M. & Elisay J. Bryan, 10 March 1829; Jno. J. Bryan, bm.

Erwin, John & Tempy Colbert, 15 May 1806; John Chambers, bm.

Esteep, Rudey & Sarah A. Johnson, 21 June 1852; m by W. W. Wright, J. P.

Estep, G. R. & Elvira Smithy, 10 Oct 1838; Joseph Y. Stanly, bm.

Estridge, Efferom & Betsey Chapel, 18 Feb 1802; Nathan Estridge, bm.

Evans, John & Milley Phillips, 17 Aug 1824; John Phillips, bm; consent from Stephen Philips, 17 Aug 1824.

Eversol & Patty Jones, __ March 1803; Rasmus Jones, bm.

Eversold, John & Elisebeth Judd, 5 Oct 1805; William Judd, bm.

Evins, John & Delina Harris, 24 Nov 1842; John Anderson, bm.

Evridy, Edmun & Elizabeth Summers, 29 July 1851; Alfred Warren, bm.

Fagerson, William & Elizabeth Holderfield, 4 March 1819; Wm Noland, bm.

Fairchild, Abijah & Vilet Gullet, 17 March 1795; David Shay, bm.

Fairchild, Abijah & Katherine Vannoy, 30 Nov 1831; Joel Vannoy, bm.

WILKES COUNTY MARRIAGES, 1778-1868

Fairchild, Wm. A. & Martha L. Mead McGee, 24 Oct 1855; m 24 Oct 1855 by Saml Walsh, J. P.

Fairchild, Wilson F. & Elizabeth Triplet, 21 Jan 1829; Abijah Fairchild, bm.

Farrington, James & Temperance Brewer, 27 May 1856; A. G. Whittington, bm; m 29 May 1856 by A. A. Whittenton, J. P.

Falls, William & Rebecca Amanda Saintclair, 28 April 1828; James Todd, bm.

Ferguson, Jeremiah & Frances Triplet, 17 March 1787; Saml Sloan, bm.

Ferguson, Jeremiah & Alce Rathbone, 14 June 1794; George Hulme, bm.

Ferguson, Moses & Mourning See, 20 July 1802; James Coffey, bm.

Ferguson, Richard & ___, (no date); Thomas Holeman, bm.

Farington, Hughey & Aly Bear, 6 Jan 1855; William Bear, bm; m 7 Jan 1855 by A. A. Whittenton, J. P.

Farmer, James & Tamer Castle, 22 Oct 1799; John Fargason, bm.

Farmer, Thomas & Mary Farchild, 16 May 1800; Peter Regan, bm.

Farmer, Thomas & Nancy Hubbard, 30 March 1819; Wesley Reynolds, bm.

Farrow, Clement & Ann Hoover, 4 June 1825; Robert Spear, bm.

Fauguson, John & Priscilla Triplet, 19 Dec 1804; Benjamin Hagler, bm.

Fauguson, Micajah & Frances Isbell, 20 Jan 1809; A. G. McKenzie, bm.

Faw, Absalom & Caroline Whitington, 6 Sept 1837; Allen A. Whittenton, bm.

Faw, Alexander J. & Emeline C. Vannoy, 28 Aug 1865; Adam Staley, bm; m 29 Oct 1865 by Rev. Jas. McNeil.

Faw, James L. & Sarah A. Rash, 5 Aug 1866; John A. Fair, bm; m 6 Aug 1866 by A. A. Whittenton, J. P.

Faw, Jonathan & Lucy McQuerry, 27 Oct 1813; Jaremiah Creech, bm.

Faw, Martin & Nancy M. Kilby, 20 Jan 1845; James Calloway, bm.

Faw, Wm. H. & Mary Jane Hinshaw, 21 Sept 1865; Wm. W. Roberson, bm; m 21 Sept 1865 by Henry Evans.

Felps, John & Elizabeth Monday, 30 Oct 1806; Nathaniel Hooper, bm.

Felts, A. W. & Elizabeth Reynolds, 15 Dec 1863; T. D. Mills, bm.

Felts, Aaron & Rebecah Felps, 14 Aug 1827; John Jinings, bm.

Felts, Elija & Alcey Ball, 26 Feb 1833; Amos Ladd, bm.

WILKES COUNTY MARRIAGES, 1778-1868

Felts, Elisha & Salley Martin, 13 Dec 1817; Isom Felts, bm.

Felts, Elsey, son of John L. & Ruthy Felts, & Marthey McBride, daughter of Daniel & Clary McBride, 25 Aug 1868; m 27 Aug 1868 by R. Sprinkle, J. P.

Felts, George & Casander Robbins, 22 Nov 1849; C. L. Cook, bm.

Felts, Isom & Susannah Brown, 16 Aug 1817; Jesse Walker, bm.

Felts, James & Nancy E. Sales, 28 Aug 1858; John Pertoll, bm; m 1 Sept 1858 by W. F. Adams, Baptist minister.

Felts, Jesse & Jane Westlock, 24 Aug 1809; John Felts, bm.

Felts, Joel & Elizabeth Normon, 21 Nov 1835; Charles Jinnings, bm.

Felts, John & Mary Walker, 20 Sept 1826; Hardy Wells, bm.

Felts, John W. & Martha E. Woodruff, m 4 Nov 1857 by S. D. Swann, Baptist minister.

Felts, Lindsey & Ruth Sprinkle, 20 Jan 1830; Jinkins Felts, bm.

Felts, William & Sarah Jackson, 16 March 1824; Wilie Felts, bm.

Felts, William & Aan Swaling, 5 April 1844; Lindsey Felts, bm.

Fergson, James & Mary Castevens, 29 Nov 1821; John Ferguson, bm.

Ferguson, Anderson & Lucinda Grimes, 26 Dec 1839; John Anderson, bm.

Ferguson, Bartlet & Marthy Watson, 6 Oct 1852; James Harrison Brown, bm.

Ferguson, Isaac & Clarasa Wadkins, 10 Feb 1847; John Anderson, bm.

Ferguson, James H. & Nancy M. Howell, 26 June 1847; Caleb Minton, bm.

Ferguson, Jeremiah & Louisa McGee, 10 Feb 1836; Jeremiah Lane, bm.

Ferguson, Jesse & Polly Brown, 25 Feb 1830; Allison Foster, bm.

Ferguson, John & Nancy Morgan, 23 Jan 1807; Joel Branham, bm.

Ferguson, Nimrod & Elizabeth Isbel, 9 Oct 1818; John Ferguson, bm.

Ferguson, Samuel S. & Lusean M. Roberts, m 30 Dec 1858 by E. B. Philips, J. P.

Ferguson, Smith & Sally Cox, 28 March 1821; Reuben Cox, bm.

Ferguson, Smith & Martha Parsons, 25 Sept 1861; m 25 Oct 1861 by Pickens Carlton, J. P.

Ferguson, Thos. & Edia Foster, 8 March 1785; William Cargill, bm.

WILKES COUNTY MARRIAGES, 1778-1868

Ferguson, Warren & Mary Crouch, 19 Dec 1827; Thomas Fields, bm.

Ferguson, William & Betty Settles, 15 Aug 1782; John Robinson, bm.

Ferrington (Pheranton), Alexander & Peggy Love, 8 May 1821; John Joiner, bm.

Ferrington, Saml. & Polley Saunders, 3 Jan 1824; Alexr. Ferrington, bm.

Feurgueson, James M. & Elizabeth Hubbard, 4 June 1819; J. Hubbard, bm.

Fields, Daniel & Leusia Haris, 16 Feb 1816; William Haris, bm.

Fields, John W. & Elizebeth M. Walls, 4 Jan 1851; John D. Perdue, bm.

Fields, John W. & Charty Dickerson, 2 Aug 1857; Samuel Hanks, bm.

Fields, Joseph & Maret Harris, 1 Feb 1820; Squire Harris, bm.

Fields, Morgan & Catherine Humphrey, 5 Jan 1819; William Pendley, bm.

Fields, Reuben & Susy See, 14 Feb 1797; Owen Humphry, bm.

Fields, Reuben & Leanah Penley, 17 Dec 1800; Owen Humphrey, bm.

Fields, Reuben Jr. & Elizabeth James, 13 March 1833; Thomas Fields, bm.

Fields, Thomas & Susanna Humphrey, 20 May 1824; David Earnest, bm.

Fields, William & Rachel Humphrey, 13 June 1831; Thomas Fields, bm.

Fiffe, John & Ann Alford, 6 Feb 1829; John Darnall, bm.

Finley, A. W. & M. L. Gordon, 30 March 1842; J. F. Finley, bm.

Finley, John T. & Sarah A. Gordon, 22 July 1846; L. B. Carmichall, bm.

Flannagan, John & Betty Cardwell, 25 Oct 1784; William Cargill, bm.

Fletcher, B. F. & L. A. Yates, 23 Sept 1865; m 24 Dec 1865 by J. W. Church, J. P.; W. C. Fletcher, bm.

Fletcher, Elias & Nancy Wilson, 15 June 1811; James Wilson, bm.

Fletcher, Enock & Polley Shumate, 26 Dec 1799; John Jones, bm.

Fletcher, Enoch H. & Sarah M. Nàris (Noris?), 3 Oct 1860; Frederick Micheal, bm; m 4 Oct 1860 by J. W. Church.

Fletcher, James Calaway & Marian Robberts, 31 March 1867; m 5 April 1867 by Thos Walsh, J. P.

WILKES COUNTY MARRIAGES, 1778-1868

Fletcher, James F. & Nancey Profett, 10 Oct 1799; John Fletcher, bm.

Fletcher, James & Nancy Shoemaker, 12 Dec 1811; Braxton Burd, bm.

Fletcher, John & Hanner Judd, 19 Jan 1822; John Kilby, bm.

Fletcher, John & Betty Horton, 17 Oct 1799; James F. Fletcher, bm.

Fletcher, Matthew & May Adlaid Haney, 2 April 1866; J. C. Tumlin, bm; m 4 April 1866 by Thos. Walsh, J. P.

Fletcher, Mathew, son of Hiram & Hanny Fletcher & Elza Ginter, daughter of Chapman & Elizabeth Dunkin, m 6 Dec 1868 by Rev. Jas. McNeil.

Fletcher, Joshua & Margaret Law, 12 April 1845; Joseph Wood, bm.

Fletcher, Reubin & Mary Gray, 2 Oct 1778; Cornelius Sale, bm.

Fletcher, Siles & Elizabeth Luncford, 28 May 1818; Joel Lunceford, bm.

Fletcher, Spencer & Theney Carter, 17 Feb 1838; J. E. Mastin, bm.

Fletcher, Thomas & Sarah Dogen, 2 Dec 1802; Jas. Fletcher, bm.

Fletcher, Wesly R. & Mary Vannoy, 11 Nov 1833; Eli Forrester, bm.

Fletcher, William & Peggy Cargile, 6 Oct 1779; Wm. Gilreath, bm.

Fletcher, Wm & Meriah Pratt, 12 Aug 1811; Moses Cart, bm.

Fletcher, William & Levina Tucker, 15 Aug 1817; William Wilson, bm.

Fletcher, William & Elizabeth Kilby, 10 Oct 1818; William Gryr(?), bm.

Fletcher, William & Luisa Vest, 5 Aug 1845; G. W. Hayes, bm.

Fletcher, William F. & Sarah C. Dula, 15 April 1850; Phineas Horton, bm.

Fletcher, Wm. C. & Alpha J. Eller, 15 Aug 1861.

Fletcher, Windfield Taylor, son of Spencer & Barthenia Fletcher, & Mary Elizabeth Joines daughter of Eli & ___ Joines, m 22 Dec 1867 by Jno. Parlin, J. P.

Fondling, John Washington & Elizabeth Aidey, 13 Sept 1832; William Mastin, bm.

Fondren, Wm & Crotia McCollister, 26 Dec 1832; John W. Fondren, bm.

Foote, James H. & Cynisca Hunt, 29 June 1858; Hezekiah Curtis, bm; Isaac S. Call, wit; m 30 June 1858 by Edwin Martin.

WILKES COUNTY MARRIAGES, 1778-1868

Forbush, Eli & Fanney Estridge, 7 Dec 1819; John Barnard, bm.

Forbush, George & Nancy Mason, 11 Dec 1830; Wm. Forbush, bm.

Ford, John R. & Elizabeth Curry, 16 Oct 1844; Hugh Jones, bm.

Ford, Mathew & Mary Parsons, 1 July 1845; James Calloway, bm.

Forester, Jonathan & ___, 20 Aug 1803; William Forester, bm.

Forester, Wm. M. & Fanny Minton, 27 Jan 1830; A. M. Cleveland, bm.

Forguson, William & Sary Dula, 1 Nov 1814; Jno Dula, bm.

Forguson, Coleman & Polly Prophett, 3 Nov 1811; David Roussau, bm.

Forguson, Thomas & Eliza Dula, 13 Oct 1829; Benj. W. Cass, bm.

Forkner, Flood & Nancy Russel, 15 Aug 1801; George Brown, bm.

Forrester, Arthur & Sarah Musgrove, 4 Jan 1834; Eli Forrester, bm.

Forrester, John & Milley Forrester, 13 April 1816; Fielding Forrister, bm.

Forrester, William & Mary Tilley, 11 Feb 1800; Thomas Castevens, bm.

Fortner, Aaron & Elenor Sharpe McEwen, 1 Dec 1808; William Kertee Junr., bm.

Fortner, Aaron & Sarah Orand, 13 Feb 1831; Jacob Orren, bm.

Fortner, Aaron & Judy Phillips, 25 April 1831; Elijah Webster, bm.

Fortner, Cager & Elisabeth Barns, 5 Feb 1807; Flud Fortner, bm.

Fortner, Daniel & Nancy Howel, 31 Dec 1831; Aaron Fortner, bm.

Fortner, Emanuel & Nancy Strickland, 29 April 1824; Thomas Bumgarner, bm.

Fortner, Ford & Bettie Mangum, 20 Dec 1783; James Meadows, bm.

Fortner, Jacob & Rachel Ingmon, 13 March 1824; William Borffet, bm.

Fortner, John & Elizabeth Highfield, 26 Oct 1816; ___, bm.

Fortner, Levi & Salley Grear, 9 March 1824; William Russel, bm.

Fortner, Newel & Ruth Barnes, 16 Sept 1812; Archd. S. McLie, bm.

Forton, William & Hiley Ball, 31 Aug 1822; Sampson Ball, bm.

Foster, A. E. & Delpha A. Rose, 27 May 1859; E. W. Foster, bm; m 30 May 1859 by A. M. Foster, J. P.

Foster, Akilles & Lavina Goforth, 12 June 1830; John Foster, bm.

WILKES COUNTY MARRIAGES, 1778-1868

Foster, A. M. & Elizabeth Foster, 21 Jan 1843; Wm. E. Reynolds, bm.

Foster, Allison & Mary Blackburn, 31 Oct 1832; Eli Forrester, bm.

Foster, Ambrose & Fanny Jones, 27 Oct 1814; John Foster, bm.

Foster, Ambrose & Mary Miller, 16 Dec 1816; Akilles Foster, bm.

Foster, Anthony & Lucy Goforth, 30 April 1813; William Goforth, bm.

Foster, Anthony & Rachel M. Curry, 7 Feb 1850; Thos M. Foster, bm.

Foster, Benjamin & Phebe Case, 4 Dec 1816; Ambros Foster, bm.

Foster, Benjamin F. & Sarah Forester, 12 Feb 1862; James P. Warren, bm; m 14 Feb 1862 by J. N. Haynes, J. P.

Foster, Edmon W. & Jane Eller, 9 Dec 1854; William S. Ferguson, bm; m 17 Dec 1854 by Jas. McNeil, Elder of the BP.

Foster, George & Amey Gray, 21 June 1800; William Gray, bm.

Foster, James H. & Elizabeth A. Church, 7 Jan 1867; H. B. Church, bm; m 9 Jan 1867 by J. W. Church, J. P.

Foster, James H. & Lurany Eller, 24 July 1854; m by Wm. S. McNiel.

Foster, John J. & Sarah Ann Foster, 20 Dec 1848; Ambrose Foster, bm.

Foster, John S. & N. E. Johnson, 30 Jan 1866; John A. Ward, bm; m 1 Feb 1865 by W. F. Adams, Baptist minister.

Foster, John T., son of Killis & Lavina Foster, & Marthe Adkins, daughter of Lewis & Sarah Adkins, 20 Nov 1867; m 20 ___ 1867 by Jonathan Stout, J. P.

Foster, Joseph & Martha Scott, 9 March 1867; John Scott, bm; m 9 March 1867 by J. K. Hendrix, J. P.

Foster, Robert & Mary Allison, 1 March 1799; Andrew Erwin, bm.

Foster, Robert B. & Mary Church, 19 Oct 1843; J. A. Davie, bm.

Foster, Ruphus M. & Rachael A. Church, 20 July 1852; m 20 July 1852 by M. A. Stokes, J. P.

Foster, Thomas Jr. & Barborah Fyppe, 3 Nov 1835.

Foster, Thos N. & Amelia Mastin, 21 March 1843; Anthony Foster, bm.

Foster, Thomas H. & Martha J. Church, 21 Sept 1858; m 23 Sept 1858 by Amos Church, J. P.

Foster, William & Mary A. Joines (Jones?), 24 Oct 1840; Calloway Elrod, bm.

WILKES COUNTY MARRIAGES, 1778-1868

Foster, Wilson & Martha Bowman, 9 Feb 1842; Larkin Hamby, bm.

Fox, Francis & Catherine Harper, 2 June 1818; John Minton, bm.

Fox, John & Elizabeth Loving, 19 July 1781; Wm. Loving, bm.

Fox, Lindsey, son of Francis & Bridget Fox, & Eliza Hutson, daughter of Joseph & Elizabeth Hutson, 26 July 1867; m 28 July 1867 by E. B. Phillips, J. P.

Fox, Linvel & Hiley Hamby, m 17 June 1860 by E. B. Philips, J. P.

Fox, Thos & Susan M. Dockery, 10 Oct 1848; John S. Dockery, bm.

Fox, Titus & Elizabeth Wright, 18 Aug 1780; James Fox, bm.

Fox, William & Mourning Ayres, 13 Feb 1832; Joseph R. Laws, bm.

Frances, James & Nancy Hamby, 27 May 1812; Jesse Gullett, bm.

Franklin, Barnabas & Rebecca M. Wellborn, 25 Oct 1824; Benj. J. Parkes, bm.

Frances, Barnard & Susanner Fletcher, 21 Feb 1807; Robt Cleveland, bm.

Franklin, Eli & Anne Collins, 14 April 1831; William Edmiston, bm.

Franklin, James & Nancy Burgus, 17 ___ 1811; Ambrose Burguss, bm.

Franklin, Robert & Sidney Kerba, 17 March 1829; John Pennell, bm.

Franklin, Wm & Nancy Grimsly, 28 Dec 1818; Littleton Grimsley, bm.

Franklin, Wm Lewis & Peggy Grimsly, 16 Jan 1814; James Grimsly, bm.

Frasier, William & Temperance Sparks, 4 Feb 1832; Peter Dowell, bm.

Frasier, Alexander & Mary Tomson, 1 Oct 1860; m 1 Oct 1860 by Jno Pardew, J. P.

Frazer, A. D. & Sarah Joines, 6 Dec 1841; W. G. Johnson, bm.

Freeman, Hutson & Polly Ferguson, 28 Nov 1827; Th. W. Wilson, bm.

Frynck, William & Mary Hampton, 27 Dec 1827; Isaiah Hampton, bm.

Fuget, John & Nancy Ivey, 25 Jan 1820; Thos Gilliam, bm.

Fuget, William & Winey Ivey, 7 Feb 1821; William Sales, bm.

Fugit, Esom & Margaret Macrare, 9 Nov 1849; Jacob J. Lyon, bm.

WILKES COUNTY MARRIAGES, 1778-1868

Fugit, John & Elisabeth Ivey, 24 March 1827; Ruffin Ivey, bm.

Fuguet, John & Patsey Johnson, 8 May 1823; Wm Sale, bm.

Fuller, Alexander & Jenny ___der, 5 Aug 1794; George Brown, bm.

Fyfe, Samuel & Winne Johnson, 1 Nov 1796; William Johnson, bm.

Gambill, Henry & Elisabeth Holbrook, ___ Jan 1816; Benjamin Gambil, bm.

Gambill, Henry & Charity Morgan, 6 Oct 1778; Thos Gambill, bm.

Gambill, Henry W. & Frances Gentry, 7 Nov 1848; James M. Gambill, bm.

Gambill, Jas. & Ailes Morgan, 24 July 1785; Dennis Philips, bm.

Gambill, James M. & Nancy P. Walls, 5 Jan 1848; Henry W. Gambill, bm.

Gambill, John & Mary Brown, 9 Sept 1822; Goen Abshir, bm; consent from Ezekel Brown, wit. by John Asbher.

Gambill, Thos & Suckey Brewer, 8 April 1780; Wm Gambill, Samuel Johnson, bm.

Gambill, William & Sinthay Cox, (no date, during admn. of Gov. William R. Davie); John Cox, bm.

Gambill, Wm. & Elisabeth Allexander, 14 March 1822; Henry Gambill, bm.

Gares, L. W. & Mary Hoots, 19 Dec 1865; John A. Rhoades, bm.

Gargess, Jobe & Susannah Caton, 2 March 1820; Edwards Wallace, bm.

Garland, Alford & Lucinda Church, 22 March 1862; Wesley Fletcher, bm; m 22 March 1862 by J. W. Church, J. P.

Garland, Harper & Betsey Minton, 17 Jan 1799; Moses Adams, bm.

Garmon, Charles & Elizabeth Brown, 29 Sept 1834; Thomas Brown, bm.

Garmon, Wellborn & Jane Ingmon, 26 Nov 1834; David Gray, bm.

Garner, H. T. & July Ann Gray, 28 Dec 1857; m 2 Jan 1858 by Wm. J. Chappel, Minister.

Garner, Isaac L. M. N. & Adlaid Caudill, 15 Jan 1866; Wm. D. Garner, bm; m 18 Jan 1866 by A. E. Myers.

Garrass, Charles & Sally Massey, 1 Sept 1813; Williford Pruett, bm.

Garris, John J. & Sary Adaline Billings, 16 Feb 1856; Wiley Garris, bm; m by John Brewer, Esqr.

Garris, Wiley & Rebeca Brown, 25 Aug 1855; John Billings, bm.

Gautney, Howel L. & Alsey Hendren, 20 Feb 1830; Wm. Hendren, bm.

WILKES COUNTY MARRIAGES, 1778-1868

Gaultney, W. R. & A. E. Staley, 8 Jan 1866; Wm. McNiel, bm; m 30 Jan 1866 by Rev. Jas. McNeil.

Gearmon, James & Nancy McGinnes, 9 Nov 1839; Willis McGinnis, bm.

Gearmon, Thomas & Rebecca Brown, 7 Sept 1829; Jesse Ferguson, bm.

Gentle, Stephen & Dolley Maston, 24 July 1815; Thomas Mastin, bm.

Gentle, Thomas J. & Eliza Jane Duncan, 31 Dec 1860; m 1 Jan 1861 by Wm. H. Hubbard, J. P.

Gentle, W. P. & Mary C. Ray, 20 Dec 1861; Harper Adams, bm; m 21 Dec 1861 by H. Hayes, J. P.

Gentrey, John & Elizebeth Lyon, 17 Dec 1821; James Lyon, bm.

Gentrey, Wiley & Matilda Sparks, 12 Dec 1825; William R. Sparks, bm.

Gentry, Artha & Rachel Lions, 18 Feb 1817; James Lion, bm.

Gentry, James & Pheba D. Atkins, 20 Aug 1862; Felix Lambill, bm; m 21 Aug 1862 by James M. Gambill, J. P.

Gentry, Jerdan & Susan Fields, 7 Aug 1865; Gilbert Gentry, bm.

Gentry, Jonathan & Gemima Spicer, 1 March 1832; Harden Spicer, bm.

Gentry, Nathan & Rebecka Passmore, 4 May 1831; James Lyon, bm.

Gentry, Stanley & Janelese Bircham, 30 April 1854; m 5 May 1854 by C. Sparks.

German, Levi & Rachel Booth, 29 Dec 1829; Elisha Cerly, bm.

Gibbs, John W. & Marthey J. Triplet, 29 Sept 1852; m 29 Sept 1852 by C. Carlton, J. P.

Gibbs, Nathan & Martha Church, 20 Sept 1814; J. Gibbs, bm.

Gibbs, Nathan & Nancy Lips, 26 July 1815; Fielding Forrister, bm.

Gibbs, R. J. & S. M. Carlton, 4 Sept 1865; A. L. Triplett, bm.

Gibbs, Thomas & Elizabeth Howel, m 5 July 1858 by Charles Carlton, J. P.

Gibson, G. W. & Nancy McKinzy, 6 Nov 1840; Wm. S. Kilby, bm.

Gibson, Wm & Margaret Sparks, 29 April 1782; William Wilcockson, bm.

Giddins, James & Martha Mills, 1 Feb 1787; Stephen Carpenter, bm.

Gilbert, George & Elviny Parsons, 19 Sept 1842; Wm. W. Gilbert, bm.

WILKES COUNTY MARRIAGES, 1778-1868

Gilbert, Gideon & Bicy Walker, 2 Oct 1815; Samuel Millinde, bm.

Gilbert, James & Peggy Hall, 28 Jan 1830; Josiah Presnell, bm.

Gilbert, Jeremiah & Polly Lane, 5 Nov 1821; Jesse Allison, bm.

Gilbert, Jesse & Elizabeth Walsh, 10 Feb 1867; Wm. C. Dula, bm; m 18 Feb 1867 by J. K. Hendrix, J. P.

Gilbert, John & Elizabeth Ray, 7 July 1823; John Hawkins, bm.

Gilbert, John & Ann Walker, 20 Dec 1831; John Walker, bm.

Gilbert, John & Eliza Triplett, 16 May 1859; William L. Dula, bm.

Gilbert, Johnson & Delily Barnet, 15 Sept 1853; Wm. T. Ferguson, bm; m 18 Sept 1853 by G. W. Hendrix, J. P.

Gilbert, Johnson & Dovey Merriman, 11 Jan 1859; J. L. Tugman, bm; m 11 Jan 1858 by J. F. Tugman, J. P.

Gilbert, Joseph H. & Elizabeth Evaline Walsh, 19 Oct 1865; m 29 Oct by J. H. Brown.

Gilbert, Joseph & Bedy Hamby, 29 July 1830; Martin Hamby, bm.

Gilbert, Joseph & Amelia Kerby, 28 Oct 1835; Calvin Bradley, bm.

Gilbert, Thomas & Nancy Gilbert, 18 Oct 1858; John Gilbert, bm.

Gilliam, Andrew J. & Saron McBride, 17 Feb 1854; Hiram Redding, bm; m 22 Feb 1854 by S. D. Swaim, Baptist minister.

Gilliam, Ephraim & Martha Addams, 23 Jan 1854; Rufus Hampton, bm; m 2 Feb 1854 by S. D. Swaim, Baptist minister.

Gilliam, John & Nancy Kennaday, 5 Oct 1807; John Kennaday, bm.

Gilliam, John & Nancy Adams, 28 Feb 1843; Jacob Delinger, bm.

Gilliam, Richard & Rosannah Powell, 16 Oct 1820; Thomas Gilliam, bm.

Gilliam, Thos & Mary Demmit, 22 Feb 18__; Wm. Gilliam, bm.

Gilliam, Thomas J. & Elvira Studavent, 3 Jan 1866; J. W. Gilliam, bm; m by Thomas Howell, 4 Jan 1866.

Gilliam, William & Elisabeth Walker, 18 Dec 1810; William Demit, bm.

Gilreath, Alexander & Elizabeth Souther, 7 June 1781; Richd. Allen, bm.

Gilreath, Alexander Jr. & Sarah Perleir, 27 Sept 1836; John N. Davis, bm.

Gilreath, G. A. & Rebecca Duncan, 3 Jan 1843; Joseph Marlow, bm.

Gilreath, George & Salley A. Wallin, 7 Aug 1807; Jeremiah Gilreath, bm.

WILKES COUNTY MARRIAGES, 1778-1868

Gilreath, Henry & Levenah Parkes, 16 Nov 1802; William Gilreath, bm.

Gilreath, James P. & Eliza Louisa Duncan, 24 June 1861; T. J. Gilreath, bm; m 26 June 1861 by Wm. H. Hubbard, J. P.

Gilreath, Jesse & Charlot Howson, 14 May 1817; Gideon Gilreath, bm.

Gilreath, Luke & Caroline Grenter, 30 Dec 1865; Henry Holder, bm.

Gilreath, William & Peggey Allen, 25 March 1800; Henry Gilreath, bm.

Gilreath, Noah & Aly Nance, 6 Feb 1862; John Parker, bm; m 6 Feb 1862 by Wm. Tedder, Baptist minister.

Gilreath, William & Pissila Parks, 25 March 1802; Uriah Parks, bm.

Ginings, Daniel & Rebecca Powell, 27 Feb 1822; Elijah Ginnings, bm.

Ginings, Luke & Betsey Bulliss, 21 Dec 1822; Wm. H. Adams, bm.

Gittins, Reuben & Nancy Strutton, 4 Nov 1797; George Hayes, bm.

Glass, Henry Jr. & Elizabeth M. Johnson, 16 March 1852; Jas. M. W. Johnson, bm; m 21 March 1852 by Con. Gray, J. P.

Glass, John & Hessa Shew, 12 July 1827; Joel Shew, bm.

Glass, John & Elizabeth King, 5 Sept 1866; A. Porter, bm; m 6 Sept 1866 by Wm. J. Chapel.

Glass, Philip & Elizabeth Anderson, 3 Sept 1846; Simon Glass, bm.

Glass, Simon & Sarah Shoe, 5 Sept 1838; Absolom Shatterby, bm.

Glass, Wm. D. & Sary Shepwash, 18 March 1865; William Byrd, bm.

Glass, William R. & Leusindy Riddle, 30 June 1853; m 30 June 1853 by C. Johnson, J. P.

Glover, James & Hanah King, 28 May 1782; Edmond Carothers, bm.

Goforth, J. T. & Hanah Louisa Phillips, 29 Jan 1862; A. E. Foster, bm; m 2 Feb 1862 by A. W. Vannoy.

Goforth, John & Rody Parsons, 10 April 1818; Jesse Gullett, bm.

Goforth, John & Elizabeth Kendell, 10 March 1835; James Martin, bm.

Goforth, John W. & Temperance Wooton, 27 Feb 1839; Yancy Brown, bm; m 28 Feb 1839 by Thomas Roberts, J. P.

Goforth, Joseph N. & Mary Sparks, 21 Oct 1852; Samuel S. Goforth, bm.

WILKES COUNTY MARRIAGES, 1778-1868

Goforth, Samuel S. & Janey Walker, 12 Dec 1856; Charles Walker, bm.

Goforth, William & Sally Foster, 16 July 1813; Russel B___, bm.

Gold, Jackson & Selah L. Hamby, 31 March 1857; James S. Hamby, bm.

Gold, John & Nancy Minton, 4 March 1823; Timothey Laws, bm.

Golson, Sanders & Susanah Suite, 28 Sept 1824; Stephen Seamans, bm.

Goode, Thomas & Elizabeth Bolings, 18 Feb 1819; Isam Hall, bm.

Gooden, Bartlett & Nancy L. Brotherton, 3 April 1841; Hugh Brotherton, bm.

Gordon, Alexr & Susanna Terrel, 30 Aug 1780; Joel Lewis, bm.

Gordon, Charles Jr. & Mary Lenoir, 20 Jan 1790; Jos. Herndon, bm.

Gordon, James H. & Caroline M. Gwyn, 14 Sept 1823; James Gwyn Jr., bm.

Gordon, John & Philadelpha Herendon, 24 Sept 1800; Thos Robins, bm.

Gordon, John & Mary Grinton, 6 Oct 1866; J. S. Call, bm.

Gordon, John W. & Nancy Robinett, 22 April 1808; Wm. P. Waugh, bm.

Gordon, Nathaniel & Nancy Gordon (no date, during admn. of Gov. Samuel Ashe); G. Jones, bm.

Gordon, Nathl. & Sarah Gwyn, 30 March 1820; Thos Witherspoon, bm.

Gordon, Richmond & Elizebeth Fletcher, 15 Jan 1818; Bartlett Shipp, bm.

Gordon, Robert & Isabel Gordon, 19 Dec 1815; Hugh Gordon, bm.

Gordon, Thos A. & Louisa Garland, 16 March 1815; W. Gordon, bm.

Gore, Michael & Betsey Grantum, 17 April 1798; James Gray, bm.

Gortney, Nathan, son of Siras & Vina Gortney, & Matilda McBride, daughter of Daniel & Clary McBride, m 13 Sept 1868 by W. F. Adams, Baptist minister.

Goss, J. B. & Eveline Buttry, 27 Feb 1866; m 27 Feb 1866 by Wilson Walker, J. P.

Goss, Jackson & Sarha Walker, 6 June 1858; James Burches, bm.

Gouge, William & Milley Poe, 1 Aug 1797; Stephen Philips, bm.

Graham, Allen & Elizabeth Bass, 13 Feb 1817; Moses Graham, bm.

Graham, James & Marry Parson, 1 Nov 1822; James Allison, bm.

WILKES COUNTY MARRIAGES, 1778-1868

Grant, John & Margaret Sail, 13 April 1784; Wm. Allen, bm.

Grasty, John & Sarah Gentle, 13 Oct 1828; Thomas Gentle, bm.

Gray, Constant & Ginsey Sale, 18 Jan 1828; Wm Gray, bm.

Gray, David & Sarah W. Mastin, 27 July 1837; John E. Mastin, bm.

Gray, E. G. & Mary Ann Foster, 27 Jan 1866; R. F. Amefield, bm.

Gray, Harrison & Leacia Ellis, 31 May 1822; Warren Powell, bm.

Gray, James & Peggay Parkes, 2 Dec 1790; Ambrose Parks, bm.

Gray, James & Elcy Swanson, 8 Oct 1796; William Laws, bm.

Gray, James & Lucinda C. Pardew, 17 March 1863; John Sale, bm; m 22 March 1863 by J. P. Adams, J. P.

Gray, James Jr. & Elizabeth Green, 4 Dec 1839; John McBride, bm; m 14 Dec 1839 by Thomas Roberts, J. P.

Gray, James W. & Winna Johnson, 29 Dec 1848; John Byrd, bm.

Gray, John & Susanny Land, 31 Jan 1811; George Foster, bm.

Gray, Pary & Liday Champton, freed people, 8 Feb 1867; Ames Hampton, bm.

Gray, Riley & Rebecca Gray, 8 Sept 1866; W. G. Hix, bm; m 8 Sept 1866 by G. B. Parks, J. P.

Gray, Thos & Jane Caul, 20 July 1820; Jesse Walker, Wm. B. Sawyers, bm.

Gray, Thomas & Carline Day, m 24 Dec 1866 by Seth Chambry, J. P.

Gray, Thos & Elisabeth Curry, 5 March 1821; Wm. Gray, bm.

Gray, William & Frankey Land, 13 Dec 1802; Newton Coffey, bm.

Gray, William & Rachel Curry, 13 Feb 1810; Jas. Andrew, bm.

Grayson, Benjamin & Elizabeth Kilby, 12 April 1817; J. Hubbard, bm.

Grayson, Joseph & Dicy Dyer, 10 Sept 1818; Benj. Grayson, bm.

Grayson, Wm. E. & Lucinda Baits, 4 Dec 1845; Richmond Anderson, bm.

Green, Bartlet & Malinda Hamby, 17 May 1858; Wm. W. Payne, bm; m 17 May 1858 by W. Fletcher, J. P.

Green, Bartlett & Mandy Watson, 2 June 1849; Larkin Green, bm.

Green, David & Tempy Ates, 30 Jan 1832; Wm. Ates, bm.

Green, Eliazer & Susanna Simmons, 21 Sept 1850; James Keer, bm.

Green, Hiram & Nancy V. Broosher, 29 Sept 1845; Thos. W. Brookshire, bm.

WILKES COUNTY MARRIAGES, 1778-1868

Green, John & Sarah Gilliam, 4 Oct 1821; William Green, Martin Green, bm.

Green, John Wriley & Malinda Watson, 7 Oct 1844; Linvel Land, bm.

Green, Larkin & Lucindy Tribet, 11 Sept 1843; C. D. Elrod, bm.

Green, Levi & Elizabeth Merrimon, 14 Feb 1830; Owen Merrimon, bm.

Green, Martin & Martha Martin, 27 May 1818; John Green, bm.

Green, Solomon & Elsy Triplett, 28 Dec 1848; Thomas Triplett, bm.

Green, Thomas & Elizabeth Sale, 30 Sept 1844; Alfred Forester, bm.

Green, William & Nancy Younger, 24 April 1809; John Martin, bm.

Green, William & Rachael Story, 4 March 1824; Thomas Story, bm.

Green, William & Fanney Canadey, 4 July 1846; David Shorse, bm.

Green, William C. & Laura Gray, 30 June 1865; m 18 July 1865 by E. Martin.

Greenstreet, Jesse & Rebecca Hart, 25 Feb 1806; John Chambers, bm.

Grenville, Elias Wilson & Sally Tucker, 3 Oct 1834; John Pratt, bm.

Greenway, Joshua & Christeen Right, 21 Dec 1843; John Dula Kindall, bm.

Greenwell, Henry & Rachel Parkes, 26 Sept 1827; Alfred Parkes, bm.

Greenwell, Henry & Serey Perdue, 9 Jan 1840; Clavin Parkes, bm.

Greenwell, Wilson & Pharaby Wolf, 6 March 1857; James Harris, bm.

Greenwood, James H. & Roxann Thompson, 10 May 1862; Osburn Bauguss, bm; m 10 May 1862 by Rev. Wm. J. Combs.

Greer, Benjamin & Sarah Jones, 26 April 1791; James Jones, bm.

Greer, Benjamin & Leah Waters, 31 Jan 1822; Lewis Waters, bm.

Greer, Edmond J. & Sarah Ann Gibbs, 23 Nov 1852; Wm. F. Hagler, bm; m 24 Nov 1852 by Wm. H. Hubbard, J. P.

Greer, Edwin & Elizabeth Ceareley, 29 July 1834; Hiram Cerley, bm.

Greer, Jesse & Judah Hampton, 14 Aug 1779; Francis Hardgrave, Aquila Greer, bm.

Greer, John B. & Franky Kilby, 26 Aug 1835; Edwin B. Greer, bm.

WILKES COUNTY MARRIAGES, 1778-1868

Greer, Joshua & Nancy Cerby, 23 Sept 1822; John N. Greer, bm.

Greer, Newton & Elizabeth Wheler, 25 Oct 1863; m 29 Oct 1863 by Larkin Pipes, minister.

Greer, Vinson & Susannar Sails (no date, during admn. of Gov. Benjamin Williams); Joseph Hickeson, bm.

Greer, Whily & Francis Watson, 31 March 1849; Bartlet Green, bm.

Gregga, Joseph & Locky Blackburn, 3 March 1850; Jas Manor, bm.

Gregory, George A. & Malinda Welborn, 24 Jan 1866; John W. Sturdivant, bm; m 28 Jan 1866 by J. F. Somers, J. P.

Gregory, J. &. & Sarah Kemp, 24 July 1865; Austion Money, bm; m 27 July 1865 by Henry Chambers, J. P.

Gregory, James & Mary Rash, 15 Oct 1854; William S. Coleman, bm; m 21 Oct 1854 by Alfred Warren, J. P.

Gregory, James & Salley Gray, 29 March 1828; Leonard Walker, bm.

Gregory, James & Linday Curry, 3 Sept 1830; Samuel P. Smith, bm.

Gregory, John & Nancy Hawkins, 6 Nov 1827; William Gregory, bm.

Gregory, John N. & Salley Reddings, 18 Sept 1845; James Brown, bm.

Gregory, Miles N. & Tobitha Ball, m 22 March 1866 by J. F. Somers, J. P.

Gregory, William & Lotty Walker, 14 Aug 1823; James Andrew, bm.

Grier, Jesse F. & Martha E. Carlton, 10 Dec 1847; Edwin B. Grier, bm.

Grier, Solomon & Hannah Low, 1 Jan 1786; Jesse Greer, bm.

Griffin, Larkin & Malinda Waters, 25 Dec 1867; m 26 Dec 1867 by William Church, minister.

Griffey, Barnet & Elizabeth Cardwell, 24 Feb 1840; Mathew P. Cardwell, bm.

Griffin, John H. & Nancy J. Laws, 1 May 1853; m 1st May 1853 by Wm. S. McNeil, J. P.

Griffin, Joseph & Delpha Forrester, 1 Dec 1787; Lewis Sabastin, bm.

Griffith, Samuel & Nancy Wiet, 26 Sept 1812; Thomas Griffeth, bm.

Griffith, William & Sarah Reynolds, 18 Sept 1815; Thomas L. Bennet, bm.

Grigory, Joseph & Elizabeth M'Dowel, 1 March 1864; W. F. Hawkins, bm; m 1 March 1864 by Eli Grimes, L. D. M. E. C. S.

WILKES COUNTY MARRIAGES, 1778-1868

Grigsby, William & Rachael Parlier, 24 Aug 1799; John Parlier, bm.

Grimes, A. F. & Anne Merier Cooper, 14 Oct 1866; Lafat Wood, bm; m 14 Oct 1866 by Wilson Walker.

Grimes, Alfred & Ibby Ferguson, 12 March 1842; Anderson Ferguson, bm.

Grimes, Edmund & Rachel Underwood, 10 Aug 1827; Jesse Bass, bm.

Grimes, Eli & Martha E. McDowel, 15 Jan 1839; William Walker, bm.

Grimes, Eli P. & Elizebeth M. Byrd, 11 Aug 1866; Joseph Johnson, bm; m 12 Aug 1866 by Wilson Walker, J. P.

Grimes, George & Sarah Scoott, 1 April 1847; John Anderson, bm.

Grimes, James M. & Mary Coopper, 29 July 1858; m 29 July 1858 by Eli Grimes, M. E. Ch. S.

Grimes, Moses & Elitha Gibbs, 3 Nov 181_; Thomas G. Love, bm.

Grimes, Philip & Eliza Childers, 12 Sept 1829; Elza Johnson, bm.

Grimes, Solomon & Adelphia Johnson, 29 Dec 1828; Alsey Johnson, bm.

Grinton, Allen & Nancy Roland, 7 Oct 1841; J. J. Bryan, bm.

Gross, John & Polley Higgins, 17 Sept 1831; Elza Johnson, bm.

Gross, Thos & Lidia Bird, 27 Dec 1831; Calvin Slone, bm.

Guartney, Wm & Phoeba Mabery, 11 Nov 1808; Randol Mabery, bm.

Guest, Benjamin & Mary Isaacs, 24 June 1782; John Beverly, bm.

Guest, William & Ann Allen, 23 July 1779; John Bevely, bm; Ann Lenoir, wit.

Gullet, Jesse & Elizabeth Roberts, 3 Aug 1778; John Byars, Joseph Sewell, bm; consent from William Robarts, father of Elizabeth, 1 Aug.

Gullet, John & Polley Hansley, 16 ___ 1811; Mathew Adams, bm.

Gullett, Wm & Tempy Hopper, 26 Feb 1813; Mathew Davis, bm.

Gunter, Jesse & Ann Manton, 18 Feb 1792; James Passons, bm; Wm. Johnson, wit.

Gwyn, Charles & Patsie Hickerson, freed people, 26 Dec 1866; Enoch N. Gwyn, bm; m 27 Dec 1866 by Enoch N. Gwyn, minister.

Gwyn, Humprey R. & Salley Thurmond, 28 Feb 1800; Harrison Thurmond, bm.

Gwyn, James Jr. & Maryan Lenoir, 28 May 1839; Wm. Martin, bm.

Gwyn, Sandy W. & Eliza Hickerson, 21 Feb 1866; R. L. D. Pardew, bm; m 4 March 1866 by James Minish.

WILKES COUNTY MARRIAGES, 1778-1868

Gwyn, Thomas, son of Jackson & Nancy Lenoir, & Silva Gwyn, daughter of Isaac Marsh & Tennessee Gwyn, 30 March 1868; m 5 April 1868 at Maple Spring Church, by F. A. Harris, J. P.

Hackett, James & Polly Herndon, 7 Aug 1805; Jas. Patton Jr., bm.

Hackett, John G., son of Heigh & Hanner Hackett & Lucey Ann Green, daughter of Irvis(?) Green, m 18 Aug 1867 by C. Plyler.

Hackett, Joseph & Sarah Stokes, 4 Sept 1833; David E. Moore, bm.

Hackney, B. A. & Laura J. Mastin, 26 Oct 1863; M. W. Vannoy, bm; m 27 Oct 1863 by R. J. N. Stephenson, M. G.

Haddon, Massy & Elizebeth Allerson, 5 Oct 1818; Jesse Caudle(?), bm.

Hadon, George & Mary Allerson, 3 March 1818; James Alison, bm.

Hagans, Hiram & Nancy Adams, 5 Dec 1852; m 5 Dec 1862 by Eli Grimes, L. D. of M. E. C. S.

Hagans, Isaac & Amanda C. Dancey, 2 Sept 1865; Adam Staley, bm; m 3 Sept 1865 by H. Sebastian, J. P.

Hagen, H. N., son of Susy Hagens & Eline Cheeks, daughter of William & Elizabeth Cheeks, m 25 April 1868 by N. Haynes, minister.

Hagins, Willis & Nancy Billings, 4 Sept 1853; m by Eli Grimes, L. D. of M. E. C. S.

Haglar, Jacob & Frances Robins, 7 July 1786; Hans Hagler (German signature), bm.

Hagler, Abraham & Easter Nathery, 16 March 1787; John Hagler, bm.

Hagler, Isaac & Susannah McGee, 7 Nov 1797; Jacob Hagler, bm.

Hagler, John & Edith Triplett, 11 Oct 1829; Skelton Hagler, bm.

Hagler, William & Elizabeth Mullins, 29 April 1800; Benjamin Hagler, bm.

Hagler, William W. & Milley Triplett, 26 Jan 1828; John Hagler, bm.

Haines, Harrison & Rebecca Carter, 27 Dec 1845; Wm. Harris, bm.

Hains, Abraham & Alic Canaday, 3 Nov 1800; William Canaday, bm.

Hains, Joseph & Rosie Burgin, 17 Dec 1783; Wm Spicer, bm.

Hais, James & Susanna Hopper, 12 Sept 1781; Thos Hopper, bm.

Haise, Jesey & Nanney Dickerson, 9 July 1782; Joseph Tanner, bm.

Hall, Benjamin & Sarah Sparks, 16 Jan 1828; Daniel Brown, bm.

WILKES COUNTY MARRIAGES, 1778-1868

Hall, C. R. & Mary Fry, 5 March 1865; m 6 March 1865 by A. C. Dancey, J. P.

Hall, D. M. & Fanney E. Absher, 7 Sept 1859; m 8 Sept 1859 by William Hall, minister.

Hall, David & Patsey Wood, 5 Sept 1824; Lewis Keller, bm.

Hall, Ephraim & Viney Gregory, 7 Feb 1826; Thos Wood, bm.

Hall, Felix & Mary M. Hall, 7 April 1858; Nathaniel Brewer, bm; m 7 April 1858 by John Brewer, J. P.

Hall, Gedian & Sophina Chandler, 1 March 18__; William Stamper, bm.

Hall, Hiram & Suca Sloan, 10 Oct 1834; Owen Hall, bm.

Hall, Isam & Tabitha Handy, 30 March 1820; Asey Mitchell, bm.

Hall, J. H. & Jinney Simmons, m 20 April 1865 by Larkin Pipes, M. G.

Hall, J. P. & Lindy Burchett, 29 Nov 1865; W. Mastin, bm; m 30 Nov 1865 by A. B. Dancey, J. P.

Hall, James C. & Margaret Richardson, 2 Dec 1855; Jesse F. Owen, bm; m 2 Dec 1855 by John Owens, D. D.

Hall, James E. & Caroline Shumate, 26 Aug 1865; Henry L. Brewer, bm; m 27 Aug 1866 by A. Wiles, J. P.

Hall, Jessey & Mary Nicholas, 10 Jan 1786; William Laws, bm.

Hall, John & Barsheba Hall, 9 Nov 1784; James Mulkie, bm.

Hall, John & Polly Holeman, 19 July 1806; Eli Brown, bm.

Hall, John & Nancy Stamper, 24 Sept 1834; Jesse Hays, bm.

Hall, John & Martha Shumate, 11 March 1835; Owen Hall Jr., bm.

Hall, Joseph & Cynthia Lunsford, 27 Dec 1827; Andrew Wadkins, bm.

Hall, L. G. & Nancy Childers, 15 March 1858; m 15 March 1858 by A. Pertor, J. P.

Hall, Larkin & Polly Tire, 20 June 1835; Jesse Hayes, bm.

Hall, Martin & Mary Bolling, 31 March 1820; Thomas Good, bm.

Hall, Nathaniel & Hila Owens, 21 Oct 1865; Jesse Hall, bm; m 22 Oct 1865 by A. B. Dancey, J. P.

Hall, Owin & Juda James, 3 Jan 1818; Asa Mitchell, bm.

Hall, Reubin R. & Milly Yeats, 25 Dec 1851; Alston Yeats, bm; m 26 Dec 1851 by L. Sebastian, J. P.

Hall, Robert & Nancy Jane Warren, 20 Jan 1867; m by W. Joines, J. P.

Hall, R. D. & Franky Eller, 22 Feb 1867; m by J. W. Church.

WILKES COUNTY MARRIAGES, 1778-1868

Hall, Thomas & Elizabeth Hampton, 24 Oct 1827; Jesse Triplett, bm.

Hall, Thomas & Mirah Holder, 13 Aug 1855; James Robberson, bm.

Hall, William & Mary Land, 8 Jan 1859; m 9 Jan 1859 by Elder Jas. McNiel.

Hall, William, son of Aly Hall, & Aly Walter, daughter of Joel & Rebecca Walter, m 8 Sept 1867 by L. Land, minister.

Hall, William P. & Mary Joinnel, 10 Feb 1842; Merry W. Walsh, bm.

Hallaway, John & Celia Mahaffey, 29 April 1833; Thomas Mahiffey, bm.

Hambey, James M. & Polly Dyer, 24 March 1832; Wm. Dyer, bm.

Hamby, Allen & Polly Hubbard, 29 Nov 1828; Wm. Olliver, bm.

Hamby, Allen & Nancy Hamby, 2 Feb 1843; Thomas Pipes, bm.

Hamby, Andrew & Miry Profit, 8 Sept 1831; Martin Cheatham, bm.

Hamby, Benjamin N. & Martha Minton, 5 July 1856; m 5 July 1856 by Saml Walsh, J. P.

Hamby, Edom M. & Edny E. Davidson, 10 June 1836; John S. Dockery, bm.

Hamby, Edom M. & Emmeline Daveson, 15 June 1836; Jesse F. Davis, bm.

Hamby, Ely & Sary Lewis, 27 Feb 1816; Paul F. Summers, bm.

Hamby, Ezekiel & Elizabeth ___, 14 Oct 1812. (torn).

Hamby, Franklin & Mary Lewis, 30 Dec 1846; Aaron Saunders, bm.

Hamby, Henry & Sary Cross, 27 Nov 1810; Zekel Hamby, bm.

Hamby, Henry & Elizabeth Better, 11 Jan 1859; S. H. Green, bm; m 11 Jan 1859 by William Church.

Hamby, Hugh & Elizabeth Ates, 6 Aug 1842; Hugh Ates, bm.

Hamby, Hugh & Elizabeth Hutson, 12 Aug 1845; Thomas Hamby, bm.

Hamby, James & Sarah Summerlin, 28 March 1842; Samuel Walsh, bm.

Hamby, James & Sarah Gold, 27 Nov 1848; Asa T. Ferguson, bm; m 29 Nov 1848 by Saml Walsh, J. P.

Hamby, Jerden & Susaner Sanders, 25 Jan 1833; Joel Hamby, bm.

Hamby, John & Ede Webb, 1 Nov 1803; John Stephens, bm.

Hamby, John & Sarah Ates, 15 Aug 1823; Reubin Hamby, Thomas Davis, bm.

Hamby, John & Eliza Watson, m 22 Sept 1867 by Chas: Walker, J. P.

WILKES COUNTY MARRIAGES, 1778-1868

Hamby, John C. & Nancy Wilcox, 9 June 1826; M. C. Hill, bm.

Hamby, John H. & Selenia Davis, 5 May 1866; Wm. Edmisten, bm; m 5 May 1866 by D. M. Wellborn, minister.

Hamby, Larkington & Nancy Foster, 2 Feb 1836; Riley Hamby, bm.

Hamby, Larkin & Eliza Hampton, 22 Feb 1842; W. G. Johnson, bm.

Hamby, Levi & Sally Norris, 29 Aug 1826; Jno Hamby, bm.

Hamby, Lewis & Alsa J. Johnson, 23 Feb 1861; m 26 Feb 1861 by William Tedder, Baptist minister.

Hamby, Lindsey & Sarah Emeline Crouce, 20 Oct 1855; T. T. Ferguson, bm; m 20 Oct 1855 by Saml Walsh, J. P.

Hamby, Martin & Elizabeth Wells, 9 Aug 1832; John Robins, bm.

Hamby, Needham & Ferebe Roberts, 2 May 1820; Amos Harmon, bm.

Hamby, Reubin & Rebecca Watson, 16 Dec 1847; John Jones, bm.

Hamby, Samuel & Susan Blankenship, 12 April 1857; Thos Lane, bm.

Hamby, Simson & Elizabeth Watson, 13 Jan 1805; Samuel Hamby, bm.

Hamby, Stephen & Fanny Cloud, 25 Feb 1805; Benjamin Hagler, bm.

Hamby, Thomas & Mary Hutson, 14 March 1844; Lewis Watson, bm.

Hamby, Wesly & Sarah Crows, 16 Nov 1835; Asa Hamby, bm.

Hamby, Wiley & Rachal Hamby, __ Feb 1814; Manoah ___, bm.

Hamby, William & Sealica Lanthford, 21 Feb 1810; Henry Hamby, bm.

Hamby, Wm & Nelly Jones, 7 Dec 1812; James Bowman, bm.

Hamby, William & Nancy Miller, 16 Sept 1831; Shad. Callaway, bm.

Hamby, Wm. N. & Elizabeth Davidson, 6 July 1837; Gabriel Church, bm.

Hamby, William & Adaline Haly, 23 July 1850; James Hamby, bm.

Hammons, John & Polley Denney, 3 Sept 1782; Wm. Holebrooks, bm.

Hammon, Jeremiah & Suanah Hays, 11 Nov 1823; Henry Hays, bm.

Hammon, Wm. & Sally Hammon, 5 Nov 1825; Jeremiah Hammon, bm.

Hampton, Abijah & Sarah Souther, 1 Feb 1803; Jesse Gunter, bm.

Hampton, Bartlet & Lucindy Watson, 20 April 1842; David Watson, bm.

Hampton, Elijah & Francis Broyhill, 12 Oct 1813; Josiah Hampton, bm.

WILKES COUNTY MARRIAGES, 1778-1868

Hampton, Harris, son of Harris & Mim Hampton & Ann Grinton, daughter of Phebe Grinton, all colored, m 29 Nov 1867 by C. L. S. Simpson, J. P.

Hampton, Isaiah & Sary Broyhill, 23 Sept 1815; Gipson Adams, bm.

Hampton, Jacob & Catey Laws, 20 June 1806; Owen Umphrey, bm.

Hampton, James & Elisabeth Miller, 3 Feb 1814; Welcome W. Hampton, bm.

Hampton, James & Elizabeth L. Harp, 12 Oct 1838; Wm. S. Kilby, bm.

Hampton, Jeremiah & Molly Waters, 1 Feb 1803; Welcome W. Hampton, bm.

Hampton, Jeremiah & Sela Laws, 1 Jan 1829; John Mitchell, bm.

Hampton, John & Lewcreasey Speakes, 20 Jan 1848; John N. Grigory, bm.

Hampton, Johnson & Elizabeth Pearson, 1 Nov 1832; Jeremiah Crysel, bm.

Hampton, Johnson & Adline Gentle, 1 July 1840; N. G. Lane, bm.

Hampton, Julius & Harret Forrester, 26 Aug 1865; James Calloway, bm.

Hampton, Levingston & Feby Boman, 15 Jan 1806; William Petty, bm.

Hampton, Micajah & Hannah Michal, 1 Dec 1813; Elijah Hampton, bm.

Hampton, Noah & Nancey E. Welborn, 6 Oct 1845; William Redding, bm.

Hampton, Rufus & Sary Ann Grigery, 30 Oct 1854; John Hampton, bm.

Hampton, Silas & Marey Brown, 11 Jan 1851; Talport Tripplett, bm.

Hampton, Wm & Susannah Grayson, 12 Feb 1825; Caleb Earp, bm.

Hamrick, Robert & Hanner Hubbard, 8 Dec 1779; William Fletcher, Isaac Elledge, bm.

Handey, James & Polly Parsons, 18 March 1833; Noel Richerson, bm.

Handey, Saml & Mahaly Shoemate, 17 Aug 1831; William Shoemate, bm.

Handy, John & Peggy Stamper, 23 Dec 1818; Wm. Barker, bm.

Handy, John & Peggey Richerson, 22 Nov 1828; Isaac Call, bm.

Handy, John & Priscilla Ellis, 28 March 1832; James Handy, bm.

Handy, John & Fanney Adams, 16 June 1836; John Rains, bm.

WILKES COUNTY MARRIAGES, 1778-1868

Handy, J. T. & Susan Absher, 3 May 1862; J. B. Handy, bm; m 3 May 1862 by R. P. McGrady, J. P.

Handy, Noel, son of Thos & Margrat Handy & Emily Gregory, daughter of Clabon & Sarah Waddell, m 6 Nov 1867 by L. D. Burcham, J. P.

Handy, Thomas & Mary Stamper, 24 Feb 1817; Jonathan Stamper, bm; Mary Martin, wit.

Handy, Thomas & Rachel Stamper, 25 July 1822; Peter Brown, bm.

Handy, Thomas Jr. & Mary Bauguess, 7 Feb 1855; Marion Handy, bm.

Handy, Thos & Mary Wyatt, 3 July 1864; James Reeves, bm; m 3 July 1864 by John Hall, J. P.

Handy, Thomas B. & Rachel Johnson, 5 Jan 1867; M. F. Richardson, bm.

Handy, Thos. B. & Celia A. Johnson, 5 Jan 1867; m by W. Joines, J. P.

Hanes, Daniel & Rhoda A. Luffmon, 12 Jan 1860; C. H. Harris, bm.

Hanes, John & Sarah Roberts, 2 Nov 1822; Thomas Roberts, bm.

Hanes, Simeon, son of Andrew & Mary Hanes, & Mary E. Hanes, daughter of Harrison & Rebeca Hanes, m 1 Nov 1867 by Rev. William J. Combs.

Hanks, Bedford & Nancy Lyon, 12 Dec 1865; M. G. Lynes, bm; m 14 Dec 1865 by Rev. R. Sparks, D. D.

Hanks, James & Lusinda Sparkes, 13 Jan 1838; Meredith Lyon, bm.

Hanks, Samuel & Lettice D. Cockerham, 12 Jan 1860; m 12 Jan 1860 by Rev. R. Sparks, D. D.

Hanks, William & Nancy McCan, 16 March 1845; Jacob Lyon, bm.

Hanoy, Wm., son of Samuel & Mahaly Hanoy, & Margret M. Reese, daughter of James Reese, m 13 Nov 1867 by R. C. Sebastian, J. P.

Harbin, James F. & Louisa Jones, 26 May 1835; Joseph Caldwell, bm.

Harbin, Thomas & Polley Witherspoon, 10 Oct 1787; James Witherspoon, bm.

Harden, Albert & Polly Shoemaker, 18 Sept 1858; Calep Rupord, bm.

Harden, Thomas & Caroline Laws, 5 July 1838; J. E. Mastin, bm.

Hardin, Adley & Sarah Woten, 14 Feb 1836; Francis Williams, bm.

Hardin, Thomas & Sarah Hubbard, 26 Dec 1833; Thomas Forguson Jr., bm.

Haris, Jacob & Virginia Grims, 11 Jan 1863; A. Baily, bm; m 11 Jan 1863 by H. H. Dent, J. P.

WILKES COUNTY MARRIAGES, 1778-1868

Haris, Jahue & Clarissy Chavis, 1 June 1821; John Haris, bm.

Haris, John W. & Salley M. Greenwell, 16 Jan 1849; James F. Adams, bm.

Harison, Daniel & Rachel Kerby, 17 Dec 1814; Skewer Bently, bm.

Harmon, Amos & Rebeca Sheppard, 2 June 1806; William Judd, bm.

Harp, James & Ann Gray, 19 Oct 1819; John Gray, bm.

Harp, Martin & Racheal Burnes, 3 Oct 1832; Ruben Watts, bm.

Harper, Jesse & Elizabeth Minton, 4 June 1834; Hugh Minton, bm.

Harrald, Emanuel & Martha Harrald, 29 March 1857; John Harrald, bm.

Harrald, John & Clary Walker, 22 Nov 1826; Turner Walker, bm.

Harrald, John M. & Matilda Sebastin, 8 April 1858.

Harrald, William & Elizabeth Hawkins, 23 Dec 1858; John Harrald, bm; m 2 Jan 1859 by L. Sebastian, J. P.

Harrald, Wm. M. & Candace Johnson, 14 Oct 1864; James Wiles, bm; m 15 Oct 1864 by Eli Grimes, L. D. of M. E. C. S.

Harrell, William & Pheby Brown, 16 Nov 1832; Lewis Sebastian, bm.

Harrill, Lawson & Carrie Carmichael, 16 Feb 1864; Stephen Johnson, bm; m 18 Feb 1864 by R. W. Barber.

Harrington, Sion & Rebecca Brown, 30 Oct 1804; James Watts, bm.

Harrington, Sion & Lydia Barnes, 5 Oct 1831; William Watts(?), bm.

Harris, Charles & Fanny Baugus, 31 Oct 1839; John Holbrook Jr., bm.

Harris, Edmund J. & Jane Pettijohn, 31 Dec 1853; Elisha Coleman, bm; m 1 Jan 1854 by Thos Roberts, J. P.

Harris, Edward & Catharine Jones, 12 April 1783; Thos Jones, bm.

Harris, George, son of George W. & Alsey Harris, & Adelia Martin, daughter of Perry & Sophah Martin, m 11 April 1868 by M. A. Parks, J. P.

Harris, Isaac & Icy Wotten, 22 Sept 1832; Montelion Wade, bm.

Harris, Isaac & Sarah Anderson, 26 March 1839; John Anderson, bm.

Harris, J. T. & Martha Carender, 12 Nov 1865; Martin G. McBride, bm.

Harris, Jack & Nancey Murrah, 28 Dec 1802; Joshua Murrah, bm.

Harris, Jacob & Lucy Lorance, 28 May 1823; Jesse Bass, bm.

WILKES COUNTY MARRIAGES, 1778-1868

Harris, Jacob & Jane Kannaday, 29 Aug 1827; Meredith Phillips, bm.

Harris, James & Francis Fields, 26 Aug 1820; Wesley Fields, bm.

Harris, James F. & Amelia Masten, 22 Sept 1855; John W. Wadkins, bm.

Harris, John & Julia Hanes, 30 Dec 1846; James Hanes, bm.

Harris, Joseph H., son of James & Nancy Harris, & Mary Ann Hines, daughter of Ann Hines, 19 Aug 1868; m 30 Aug 1868 by J. F. Keenans, minister.

Harris, John & Marey Lunsford, 3 Oct 1857; Wilie Jams(?), bm; m 15 Oct 1857 by Israel Hollar, Baptist minister.

Harris, Jorden & Rachal Grunton, 16 Oct 1846; Henry Scoott, bm.

Harris, Lewis & Elizabeth Gray, 23 Sept 1848; George Roberts, bm.

Harris, M. L. & S. E. Alexander, 28 July 1859; m by S. P. Smith.

Harris, O. J. & Mary Harbin, 1 May 1866; J. F. Harris, bm; m 3 May 1866 by C. Plyler.

Harris, Squire & Miriam Phillips, 26 Aug 1820; Larkin Maynard, bm.

Harris, W. C. & S. A. Crouder, 15 Feb 1867; O. J. Harris, bm; m 17 Feb 1867 by Calvin Plyler.

Harris, Wm. L. & Hannah Smith, 21 Dec 1826; Elza Walsh, bm.

Harrison, Bently & Elisabeth Bentley, 21 April 1820; Squire Bentley, bm.

Harrison, John & Elizabeth Durham, 1 Dec 1810; Joshua Davis, bm.

Harrison, Nathaniel & Christenah Phesler, 11 Sept 1783; James Davis, bm.

Harriss, James & Nancy Martin, 1 Nov 1824; Richard Gilliam, bm.

Harriss, John & Lucinda Perden, 3 Aug 1824; R. Gilliam, bm.

Harrold, Alexander & Polly Johnson, 21 Jan 1836; Mayland Johnson, bm.

Hart, Daniel & Nancy Curry, 23 Dec 1813; A. Tomlinson, bm.

Hart, Wm. & Elisabeth Hubbard, 21 Sept 1825; John McQuerry, bm.

Hart, Isham & Marthy J. Calaway, 27 Dec 1855; Wm. R. Whittington, bm.

Hartzog, Laban & Elizabeth Kilby, 26 Aug 1848; Alexr. G. Whittington, bm.

Hartzog, Philip & Marthy McGlomery, 8 Jan 1850; James Calloway, bm.

WILKES COUNTY MARRIAGES, 1778-1868

Harvil, James & Betsy Dickens, 27 Jan 1807; James Norman, bm.

Harvill, Isham & Metilder Cost, 5 March 1781; Thos. Newberry, bm.

Harville, William & Mary Crabtree, 29 Nov 1809; John Stanley, bm.

Hatcher, John & Nancy Boyd, 6 Sept 1819; Thos Royall, bm.

Hatchett, William & Gemima Mitchel, 30 Dec 18__.

Hatton, John & Peggey Galey, 15 Oct 1808; William Chambers, bm.

Havner, Jesse L. & Mary Ann Hall, 28 May 1867; J. U. Rhods, bm; m 31 Jan 1867 by Henry Jinnings, J. P.

Hawkins, Alexander & Susanah Hawkins, 16 Jan 1855; m 16 Jan 1855 by Eli Grimes, of M. E. Ch.

Hawkins, Charles & Deborah Adams, 16 Dec 1827; Wm. H. Adams, bm.

Hawkins, Ezekiel & Aggy Eles, 2 Jan 1858; Ezekel Hawkins, bm; m 2 Jan 1858 by L. Sebastian, J. P.

Hawkins, Henery & Sarah Gilbert, 13 Sept 1820; John Hawkins, bm.

Hawkins, James & Nancy Hawkins, 30 Jan 1867; S. E. Walker, bm; m 2 Feb 1867 by A. Wiles, J. P.

Hawkins, James W. & Dianah Smith, 4 Feb 1862; James H. Walker, bm; m 9 Feb 1862 by R. T. Wall, J. P.

Hawkins, Jesse & Melindy L. Fugit, 14 July 1856; m 14 July 1856 by S. J. Gambill Esqr.

Hawkins, Jesse D. & Sophier Hartly, 9 April 1852; m 13 April 1852 by Larkin Pipes, M. G.

Hawkins, John & Rachel Groce, 15 Oct 1827; Willis Wheatley, bm.

Hawkins, Joseph & Sarah Brown, 14 June 1864; C. F. Sebastian, bm; m by Eli Grimes, L. D. of M. E. C. S.

Hawkins, Ruben & Mira Hall, 2 Nov 1852; m 5 Nov 1852 by Eli Grimes, L. D. of M. E. C. S.

Hawkins, Samuel & Elisa Coffey, 14 Dec 1825; Larkin Coffey, bm.

Hawkins, Samuel & Americk Pollard, 20 Sept 1856; m 20 Sept 1856 by S. J. Gambill, J. P.

Hawkins, Thomas & Sary Howard, 19 Feb 1818; Joseph Howard, bm.

Hawkins, William & Nancy Adams, 13 Sept 1806; Henry Adams, bm.

Hawkins, William & Margarett Stilwell, 7 June 1814; W. Goodon, bm.

Hawkins, William & Mahaley Hawkins, 29 Nov 1832; John Hawkins, bm.

WILKES COUNTY MARRIAGES, 1778-1868

Hawkins, Wm & Elizabeth Blackman, 13 Sept 1857; m 13 Sept 1857 by Eli Grimes, L. D. of M. E. C. S.

Hawkins, Wm. L. & Nancy M. Havenor, 3 April 1848; Elexander Hawkins, bm.

Hayes, Charles & Aly Lewis, 31 July 1841; George Hayes, bm.

Hayes, George & Judah Mills, 14 May 1785; Benjamin Coffey, bm.

Hayes, George & ___, 5 May 1818; Ezecal Hays, bm.

Hayes, George & Polly Riddle, 28 Oct 1851; m 2 Nov 1851 by L. J. Bicknell, J. P.

Hayes, Harel & C___ Johnson, 20 Nov 1820; John Hayes, bm.

Hayes, Harrel & Gennetta Marlow, m 15 Jan 1858 by David

Hayes, Hartwell & Rebekah Brown, 5 Nov 1805; Jesse Combs, bm.

Hayes, Henry & Frances Johnson, 29 Dec 1818; Joshua Johnston, bm.

Hayes, James & Sally Polard, 16 April 1819; Joseph James, bm.

Hayes, Jefferson & Rebecca Tribble, 16 Nov 1833; Hugh Hays, bm.

Hayes, John & Elizabeth Holt, 8 Aug 1795; Ambrose Holt, bm.

Hayes, Thomas & Sally Rucker, 19 Sept 1807; John Coffey, bm.

Hays, Andrew J. & Nancy C. Curry, 29 July 1851; Isaac S. Call, bm; m 31 Aug 1851 by Wm. H. Hubbard, J. P.

Hays, David D. & Rebecka Roberds, 8 April 1820; Hugh Hays, bm.

Hays, Henry & Jane Addams, 18 Aug 1819; Joseph Hays, bm.

Hays, Henry H. & Emeline Cook, 1 Sept 1860; m 6 Sept 1860 by H. Hayes, J. P.

Hays, Jesse & Sarah Rhodes, 31 Aug 1819; John Rhodes, bm; Mary Martin, wit.

Hays, John & Elvira Gilreath, ___ 182_; John Smoot, bm.

Hays, John & Martha Hooper, 2 April 1829; Joshua Souther Jr., bm.

Hays, Jon'n & Rachel Mitchel, 30 Oct 1798; Henry Hays, bm.

Hays, Joseph & Mary Hammon, 17 Nov 1823; John Saintclair, bm.

Hays, Joseph & Mary Hays, 31 May 1816; William Adams, bm.

Hays, Olfin & Martha Harrison, 10 May 1828; Benjamin Harrison, bm.

Hays, Reubin Jr. & Hanah Owens, 31 March 1849; John Elledge, bm.

Hays, Robert & Nancy Noland, 3 Oct 1810; Peter Noland, bm.

WILKES COUNTY MARRIAGES, 1778-1868

Hays, W. Y., son of Y. W. & Anna Hays, & Mary C. Roberson, daughter of Walter & Nancy Roberson, m 9 Oct 1868 "at my house" by Richard Jacks.

Hays, William H. & Catherine Davis, 24 Oct 1866; Harrald S. Hayes, bm; m 25 Oct 1866 by H. Hayes, J. P.

Hays, William & Rachal Johnson, 3 Oct 1814; Lewis Johnson, bm.

Hayse, James H. & Elizabeth Eastep, 8 Feb 1843; Wilson Moore, bm.

Hayse, Jesse & Susana Adams, 14 April 1842; Robert Hayse Jr., bm.

Hayse, Reubin Jr. & Nancy Wheatly, 17 Dec 1845; Andrew Porter, bm.

Hayse, Robt & Milly Elledge, 27 Dec 1845; Jesse Hayse, bm.

Hayse, Wm. P. & Mary Moore, 14 Jan 1842; George W. Hays, bm.

Head, William O. & Catharine Norman, 3 Sept 1845; Eligan Norman, bm.

Heagins, Richard & Easter Seeden, 8 March 1809; Andrew Johnson, bm.

Heathman, Benja. & E. M. Martin, 15 Sept 1843; B. F. Pettey, bm.

Higgins, Wm. L. & Marth E. Cockerham, 12 Jan 1860; m 12 Jan 1860 by Rev. R. Sparks, D. D.

Higgins, William L. & Tennessee Woolf, 14 March 1856; James McCann, bm; m 14 March 1856 by Ansel Parks.

Henderson, Abener & Mary Ball, 17 Jan 1867; J. M. Templeton, bm; m 17 Jan 1867 by Alfred Warren, J. P.

Henderson, Charles & Edia Mongumry, 11 Nov 1782; Gilbird Cottrell, bm.

Henderson, James & Elizabeth Martin, 22 Dec 1832; William Redding, bm.

Henderson, M. J. & Rody Souther, 15 Jan 1867; J. W. Redding, bm; m 17 Jan 1867 by Israel Hollar, Baptist minister.

Henderson, Meredy & Clary Comes, 8 Jan 1856; John Myers, bm; m 10 Jan 1856 by William Goforth, Baptist minister.

Henderson, William A. & Martha Grey, 7 Oct 1865; m 23 Nov 1865 by J. F. Somers, J. P.

Hendren, Oliver & Martha Curry, 10 Oct 1861; m 10 Oct 1861 by Wm. L. Chapel, minister.

Hendron, Ambrose & Nancy Mitchel, 27 Jan 1824; Elijah Mitchel, bm.

Hendron(?), Eli & Elizabeth Gilreath, 3 Dec 1834; Joel J. Hendron, bm.

WILKES COUNTY MARRIAGES, 1778-1868

Hendren, Jabez & Nancy Combs, 3 March 1829; Wm. Hendren, bm.

Hendren, James W. & Mary Lewis, 8 Sept 1852; William W. Hendren, bm; m 9 Sept 1852 by L. J. Bicknell, J. P.

Hendren, Jehu & Elizabeth Combs, 9 Jan 1833; William Hendren, bm.

Hendren, Jesse & Rebecca E. Parlier, 5 June 1851; John F. Parlier, bm; m 5 June 1851 by A. Gilreath, J. P.

Hendren, John & Mary Davis, 12 Dec 1831; William Hendrin, bm.

Hendren, Josiah & Keziah Roberson, 23 Feb 1842; Jehu Hendren, bm.

Hendren, Oliver & Martha Curry, 10 Oct 1861; m 10 Oct 1861 by Rev. Wm. J. Chapel.

Hendren, Richard & Easter Brotherton, 21 Feb 1835; Solomon Hendren, bm.

Hendren, Solomon & Drucilla Williams, 7 Jan 1854; J. B. Gordon, bm; m 10 Jan 1854 by A. Gilreath, J. P.

Hendren, Stephen & Mary Cook, 14 Aug 1834; William Hendren, bm.

Hendren, William Y. & Martha Shumaker, 23 Oct 1858; Herrald Hays, bm; m 23 Oct 1858 by H. Hayes, J. P.

Hendren, Wyatt & Sarah Call, 1 Dec 1841; Oliver Hendren, bm.

Hendrex, Micajah & Locky Macguire, 1 March 1806; John Dula, bm.

Hendricks, James & Marthy Dula, 18 June 1830; Wm. P. Witherspoon, bm.

Hendrix, Alexander & Mary Hunneycut, 20 Feb 1851; Rufus Hampton, bm.

Hendrix, Gay & China Hendrix, 28 July 1860; m 30 July 1860 by Larkin Pipes, minister.

Hendrix, George & Milley Dula, 11 April 1837; Joshua Pennel, bm.

Hendrix, Gilson & Elizabeth Green(?), 1 Nov 1841; Charles Hatten, bm.

Hendrix, Hansel & Emma Mahafe, 12 Oct 1844; Albert P. Bruse, bm.

Hendrix, James K. & Anna A. Dula, 1 Jan 1859; m 2 Jan 1859 by P. Walsh, J. P.

Hendrix, Jesse H. & Eliza J. Thomas, 25 July 1865; Thomas Lewis, bm; m 27 July 1865 by Henry Chambers, J. P.

Hendrix, John & Sary Lewis, 5 Feb 1853; Rufus Hampton, bm.

Hendrix, Leander J. & Martha C. Land, 15 Oct 1866; Green Hendrix, bm; m 25 Oct 1866 by J. K. Hendrix, J. P.

Hendrix, Lowry & Miry L. Cottreal, 30 Dec 1857; James Tugman, bm; m 1 Jan 1858 by P. Walsh.

WILKES COUNTY MARRIAGES, 1778-1868

Hendrix, Luke & Frances Triplett, 14 April 1827; Nelson A. Strange, bm.

Hendrix, Micajah & Anna E. Dula, 20 Feb 1853; Martin Brown, bm; m 22 March 1853 by Burton Bradly.

Hendrix, Moses & Sebrah Greer, 27 Sept 1842; William Adkins, bm.

Hendrix, Sanferd & Addleine Triplett, 7 Nov 1865; m 9 Nov 1865 by Larkin Pipes, M. G.

Hendrix, Thomas, son of Hansle & Emily Hendrix, & Tilda Walker, daughter of Ismeal & Elizabeth Walker, m 7 Oct 1867 by Wilson Walker.

Hendrix, Vinson & Martha Walsh(?), 28 Sept 1861; A. B. West, bm; m 29 Nov 1861 by L. Land, minister.

Hendrix, Willson & Margaret West, 3 June 1849; William Triplett, bm.

Hendrixon, Josiah & Nancy Jones, 21 Aug 1805; Richard Robards, bm.

Hendry, James E. & Ann Eliza Jones, 25 June 1828; Larkin G. Jones, bm.

Herndon, Benja. & Sarah Chapman Gorden, 2 Oct 1804; Nathl. Gordon, bm.

Herrald, D. C. & Sara L. Grimes, 28 Feb 1864; m 28 Feb 1864 by H. Johnson.

Herrald, Wm & Matilda Wheatly, 3 Aug 1863; Calaway Hairld, bm; m by Eli Grimes, L. D. of M. E. C. S.

Hester, John & Rebecka Vannoy, 18 Dec 1803; Edward Dancey, bm.

Hester, William R. & Mary Bolin, 1 May 1850, John Bolin, bm.

Hickerson, David & Patsey Summerlin, 2 Nov 1809; John Adams, bm.

Hickerson, Joseph & Ann Greer, 24 Jan ___; Rowland Judd, Esqr., bm.

Hickerson, Joseph & Nancy Roussau, 7 Oct 1818; Chas. Hickerson, bm.

Hickerson, Little & Milley Gwyn, 17 Nov 1827; Winston Somers, bm.

Hickes, Wm & Salley Canler, 3 Oct 1817; Jas. Hickes, bm.

Hicks, Charles & Lotty Cass, 1 March 1837; Thomas Hicks, bm.

Hix, Thomas & Matilda Cox, 3 Sept 1840; William Howard, bm.

Hicks, Wm. & Catey Beakins, 9 Aug 1825; Micajah Hicks, bm.

Higgins, A. D. & Laura Pardue, m 15 July 1866 by J. N. Haynes.

Higgins, Argalos & Betsy Wood, 13 Dec 1834; Braxton Byrd, bm.

WILKES COUNTY MARRIAGES, 1778-1868

Higgins, George & Elizabeth Rhods, 31 Aug 1821; David Wilkins, bm.

Higgins, George & Frances Hall, 9 Oct 1845; Wm. Laws, bm.

Higgins, Henry & Hiley Higgins, 25 March 1853; Hiram Higgins, bm; m by John Brewer, J. P.

Higgins, John, son of Wilsson Higgins, & Sarah Sparks, daughter of William Sparks, __ Oct 1867; m 24 Dec 1867 by J. B. Spicer, J. P.

Higgins, Wm & Mary Roberds, 1 May 1827; Joseph Elledge, bm.

Higgins, Wm & Pegy Elledge, 24 July 1853; Willia Higgins, bm; m 24 July 1853 by L. Sebastian, J. P.

Hill, Francis & Ann Ballrip, 7 Sept 1779; Andrew Vannoy, bm.

Hill, James & Nancy Padget, 18 Dec 1811; Eli Pettey, bm.

Hill, James & Patsey Johnson, 2 Sept 1820; Eli Denney, bm.

Hill, William & Jane Juson, 13 Aug 1816; John Vicus, bm.

Hincher, Patterson & Rebecca Holderway, 28 April 1825; Moses Williams, bm.

Hinchey, Michel & Elisabeth L. Adams, 1 Sept 1857; Wm. D. Hinchey, bm; m 10 Sept 1857 by ___.

Hincher, Thomas J., son of William & Sharlott Hincher & Martha Shoemate, daughter of John & Nancy Shoemate, m 24 Oct 1868 at the house of John Shumates, by Henry Jinnings, J. P.

Hinchy, Wm. D. & Mary Adams, 23 Oct 1855; Abraham C. Nichols, bm; m 23 Oct 1855 by A. A. Whittenton, J. P.

Hinchey, George & Mary Crysel, 4 April 1839; John B. Kilby, bm.

Hindrine, Jehue & Jane Lucinda Nicholson, 6 May 1843; m 6 May 1843.

Hindrix, Floyed & Martha E. Triplett, 24 May 1863; D. A. Melon, bm; m 24 May 1863 by J. F. Tugman, J. P.

Hinds, Joseph & Sarah Poe, 26 July 1816; Joshua Tanner, bm.

Hinds, Joseph & Milley Phillips, 17 Sept 1816; John Sparks, bm.

Hinds, Saml & Polley Blackburn, 1 Feb 1808; Wm. Blackburn, bm.

Hinshaw, Jonathan & Ann McDanel, 5 Sept 1801; William Hinshaw, bm.

Hix, John, son of Pollie Hix, & Martha Combs, daughter of Clay Combs & Thoms Love, m 15 Oct 1867 by Seth Chambers.

Hockkings, Elisha & Izey Robberds, 8 Oct 1823; John Hockkings, bm.

Hodge, Isaac & Sarah Boring, 27 May 1825; John Bumgarner, bm.

WILKES COUNTY MARRIAGES, 1778-1868

Hodge, William & Frankey Hampton, 13 March 1831; Russel Triplett, bm.

Hodges, John R. & Permina Triplitt, 4 Oct 1844; A. W. Pendley, bm.

Hodges, William & Mary Mullins, 29 Dec 1800; John Hodges, bm.

Hodges, William & Nancy Triplett, 16 Dec 1848; Joel Blackborn, bm.

Hogstan, Archibald & Mary McCartay, 20 July 1790; John Kilby, bm.

Hogin, James & Jane Crisp, 8 Aug 1799; Jesse Bowman, Joel Crisp, bm.

Holaway, Martin & Susanah Hagnor, 13 Aug ___; Daniel Vannoy, bm.

Holbrook, John W. & Luisa Johnson, 19 Dec 1855; Joseph Spicer, bm.

Holbrooks, Ezecal & Suanah Grass, 1 March 1820; C. B. Holbrooks, bm.

Holbrook, Caleb & Phoebe Abshear, 17 July 1844; John Buttrey, bm.

Holbrook, H. S. & N. D. Bryan, 30 Dec 1856; John Q. A. Bryan, bm.

Holbrook, James M. & Elizabeth Spicer, 14 March 1861; H. J. Spicer, bm; m 17 March 1861 by Wm. Hall, D. D.

Holbrook, John & Nancy Abshire, 3 May 1822; Going Abshire, bm; consent from John Abshier father of Nancey; Going Asbheer, wit.

Holbrook, John & Jane Baugus, 5 Nov 1829; Ralph Pruitt, bm.

Holbrook, John T. & Luiza Woodey, 19 Nov 1865; Wm. T. Walker, bm; m 19 Nov 1865 by A. E. Myers.

Holbrook, J. S. & Fanny C. Alexander, 14 March 1866; Joshua Spicer, bm; m 18 March 1866 by Rev. William J. Combs.

Holbrook, Ralph & Nancy Spicer, 4 Feb 1834; James Spicer, bm.

Holbrook, William & Salley Spicer, 17 July 1814; Jesse Lyon, bm.

Holbrook, Willm & Sally Kenedy, 17 Feb 1826; Cally Alexander, bm.

Holbrook, Wm. J. & Susan Woody, 16 March 1854; m 16 March 1854 by S. J. Gambill, Esqr.

Holbrooks, Wm & Jane Esque, 28 June 1865; m by Eli Grimes, L. D. M. E. C. S.

Holdaway, John & Rebekah Cross, 14 Nov 1805; Benja. Bruce, bm.

Holder, Dempsey & Polly Barnet, 24 Sept 1825; David Horton, bm.

WILKES COUNTY MARRIAGES, 1778-1868

Holder, Elijah & Polley Simmons, 23 Feb 1826; James Holder, bm.

Holder, G. A. & Mary Poter, m 17 Dec 1865 by Wilson Walker, J.P.

Holder, Geore & Jane Powell, 22 Aug 1833; Wm. W. Paden, bm.

Holder, James & Betsey Pauley, 3 July 1823; Thomas Stapp, bm.

Holder, John & Amandy Nichols, 7 Jan 1859; Joel Roberts, bm; m 7 Jan 1859 by G. Sumerlin, J. P.

Holder, Nathan & Martha Livingston, 10 March 1840; Thomas E. Molba, bm.

Holder, William & Maryan Holder, 16 Jan 1855; Wm. West, bm; m 16 Jan 1855 by G. W. Hendrix, J. P.

Holder, William & Charity Church, 20 June 1833; James Crane, bm.

Holder, William & Lois Dula, 6 Dec 1865; m 6 Dec 1865 by J. H. Brown.

Holdeway, John & Adline Mathis, 23 April 1864; Chapman Duncan, bm; m 29 April 1864 by Wm. H. Hubbard, J. P.

Holderway, Jeremiah & Felicia Crowel, 2 Oct 1813; Jeremiah Crisel, bm.

Holderway, William & Elizabeth Forester, 21 July 1819; Edward Lam(?), bm.

Holdman, John & Charlotty Clawson, 3 Sept 1849; m 3 Sept 1849 by Saml Walsh, J. P.

Holebrook, John & Malinda J. Phillips, m 18 Feb 1858 by Rev. D. H. Davis.

Holebrooks, William & Aggia Collear, 10 Dec 1782; Jno Collear, bm.

Holeman, Asa & Almiah Boman, 14 Oct 1833; Wm. W. Peden, bm.

Holeman, Daniel & Salley Ferguson, 30 Jan 1810; William Tugman, bm.

Holeman, James & Rachel Welch, 25 Dec 1848; Elza Eller, bm.

Holeman, Thomas & Ailsey Tugman, 21 March 1791; Edmond Tugman, bm.

Holeyfield, Daniel & Elizabeth Allen, 22 Dec 1807; Wm. Noland, bm.

Holland, Azel & Saercy Coleman, 3 April 1845; Bevily Coleman, bm.

Holler, Isreal & Nancy Brown, 13 Oct 1842; John Dishmon, bm.

Hollaway, Hampton & Mary Sparkes, 1 Feb 1834; Wm. M. Forester, bm.

Hollaway, Isaac & Polley Pruett, 17 March 1828; Daniel Brown, bm.

WILKES COUNTY MARRIAGES, 1778-1868

Hollaway, John & Betsey Wheatly, 11 Jan 1818; Daniel Hollaway, bm.

Holleman, Axum & Elisa Coock, 3 March 1838; Isaac Cook, bm.

Holleman, John & Mary Armstrong, 27 Nov 1848; Bennet Holleman, bm.

Hollen, Enock & Irena Dishmon, 14 Aug 1865; Israel Hollar, bm; m 17 Aug 1865 by Israel Hollor, Baptist minister.

Holler, Ephraim, son of Isreal & Nancy Holler & Nansy M. Howard, daughter of Fily & Mary Howard, m 30 Jan 1868 by Israel Hollor, Baptist minister, at the house of Finley Howerd.

Holloway, Daniel & S. Jane Brock, 18 Dec 1860; m 20 Jan 1860 by Jas. M. Gambill.

Holman, Enoch & Caroline Lippes, 10 Jan 1843; Elijah Dyer, bm.

Holmond, Thomas & Amelia Goforth, 24 Sept 1849; m by Saml Walsh, J. P.

Holsclar, James & Malinda Land, 4 March 1839; James Land, bm.

Holt, Ambrose & Nancey Murrah, 14 Oct 1794; Wm. Murrah, bm.

Holt, Benjamin & Sarah Little, 26 Jan 1797; Ambrose Holt, bm.

Holt, James & Mahaly Law, 14 Nov 1831; Alfred B. Laws, bm.

Holt, John & Elizabeth Pogue, 21 Sept ___; John Isbell, bm.

Honeycut, Tillmon & Emmaline Meyers, 6 Nov 1856; James Culres, bm; m 7 Nov 1856 by W. Day, J. P.

Hood, John & Mahala Hood, 19 Aug 1826; Charles Hood, bm.

Hood, Martin & Rody Brown, 20 Nov 1817; Robt. Hayes, bm.

Hood, Robert & Elizabeth Watts, 7 Dec 1845; Caleb Minton, bm.

Hood, Thomas & Sarah Morgain, 6 March 1781; Isaac Elledge, Robert Hamrick, bm.

Hooper, Abraham & Sarah Fitzpatrick, 7 Jan 1806; Samuel Bicknell, bm.

Hooper, Elijah & Marcy Williams, 15 Dec 1800; William Hooper, bm.

Hooper, William & Patiance Young, 17 March 1800; Elijah Hooper, bm.

Hootes, William & Mary Childers, 21 Oct 1858; m 22 Oct 1858 by M. A. Parks, J. P.

Hoots, Jacob & Fanny Combs, 2 Sept 1816; Isaac Stover, bm.

Hoots, Jacob & Nancy Hall, 30 Dec 1824; Wiley Combs, bm.

Hoots, Jacob & Mary Childers, 24 April 1856; Hiram Childers, bm; m 24 April 1856 by W. F. Adams, Baptist minister.

WILKES COUNTY MARRIAGES, 1778-1868

Hoots, Stephen & Delpha Spicer, 5 Jan 1859; Daniel Billings, bm; m 5 Jan 1859 by William J. Combs, D. D.

Hopkins, Lisles & Salley Alford, 22 Sept 1808; Thos Duerson(?), bm.

Hopper, John & Anna Wilson, 22 March 1785; Joseph Tanner, bm.

Hopkins, John & Pharibia Handy, 12 Nov 1864; Thomas Handy, bm; m 13 Nov 1864 by John Hall, J. P.

Horton, David & Sary Dula, 20 Nov 1817; Thos Dula, bm.

Horton, Jesse & Hannah Lewis, 27 Nov 1806; Benjamin Bicknell, bm.

Horton, Joshua & Rachel Howard, 2 Oct 1805; Philip Howard, bm.

Horton, Wm. & Patsy Pendlegrass, 24 Jan 1824; Saml Nicholson, bm.

Houpt, John W. & Margaret Cornell, 8 Sept 1834; John Correll(?), bm.

Howard, Benja. & Milley Rose, 9 Oct 1816; Sterling Rose, bm.

Howard, Christopher & Hanah Johnson, 5 Dec 1809; Wm Rousseau, bm.

Howard, Cornelius & Philadelphia Hagler, 7 April 1822; Mark Mullins, bm.

Howard, Findly & Mary Brown, 31 Jan 1850; Rufus W. Martin, bm; m 31 Jan 1850 by Thos. Roberts, J. P.

Howard, George & Betsey Jones, 23 Feb 1799; Hezekiah Crumpton, bm.

Howard, John & Anna Grant, 11 April 1806; John Chambers, bm.

Howard, John & Betsey Jarvis, 8 March 1831; Wesly Howard, bm.

Howard, Larkin & Sarah Warren, 13 Jan 1836; Alfred Warren, bm.

Howard, Phillip & Frankey Sails, 16 Jan 1801; John Cambers, bm.

Howard, Wiley & Harnet Saintcler, 13 Feb 1843; James Roberson, bm.

Howel, Leonard & Suzanna Wingler, 16 Aug 1856; Elijah Wingler, bm.

Howell, Geo. W. & Elizabeth A. Phillips, 11 Jan 1866; Jas. H. Ferguson, bm; m 18 Jan 1866 by C. C. Ferguson, J. P.

Howell, Sherrod & Elizabeth Ferguson, 27 March 1838; John Barnes, bm.

Howell, William & Sally Winglor, 23 Jan 1833; John Dancy, bm.

Hubbard, Benjamin & Rosanah Dyer, 26 Jan 1784; Josiah Dyer, bm.

Hubbard, Benjamin L. & Mary Elizabeth Jane McKenzie, 22 Nov 1831; Wm. S. Spencer, bm.

WILKES COUNTY MARRIAGES, 1778-1868

Hubbard, David & Nancy Stafford, 22 Sept 1808; Isham Hubbard, bm.

Hubbard, Green & Susannah Parkes, 12 Aug 1826; Nathan Brown, bm.

Hubbard, Henderson & Delphey Eastridge, 6 Dec 1827; Esquire Parker, bm.

Hubbard, Isom & Elizabeth Grayson, 30 July 1834; John B. Crysel, bm.

Hubbard, Isom & Matilda Moore, 16 March 1852; John F. Parlier, bm; m 20 March 1852 by A. Gilreath, J. P.

Hubbard, James D. & M. Tedders, 1 Aug 1843; W. G. Johnson, bm.

Hubbard, Joel & Sarah Gilreath, 18 Feb 1823; Benj. J. Parks, bm.

Hubbard, John & Hanah Earpe, 10 July 1817; J. Hubbard, bm.

Hubbard, John & Elizabeth Williams, 18 Nov 1856; Isham Hubbard, bm; m 20 Nov 1856 by W. W. Wright, J. P.

Hubbard, Nathl & Sinthy Davidson, 13 July 1805; Wm. Brown, bm.

Hubbard, Samuel F. & Permelia Spencer, 8 June 1853; Thomas J. Matherly, bm; m 8 June 1853 by Thomas Land, J. P.

Hubbard, Wm. H. & Jane E. Sayner, 12 Dec 1846; D. C. Stinson, bm.

Huckerson, Jacob & Alcy Reynolds, 12 Dec 1815; Ivy Reynolds, bm.

Hudson, William & Sarah Trivett, 16 Jan 1850; Thomas Hamby, bm; m by Saml Walsh, J. P.

Huffman, Andrew & Sarah Crain, 14 July 1828; David Huffman, bm.

Huffman, Benjamin & Martha L. Cardwell, 19 Dec 1865; J. M. Eller, bm; m 21 Dec 1865 by Rev. Jas. McNiel.

Huffman, David & Zibby Bullous, 4 July 1832; Eli Forester, bm.

Hughes, Jonathan & Abigale Jackson, 11 July 1786; William Jackson, bm.

Hughman, Jacob & Sary Crain, 24 Feb 1817; John Church, bm.

Hull, Daniel & Mary Busby, 8 Dec 1788; John Johnson, bm.

Hulme, Robert & Frances Cleton, 4 Nov 1793; Wm. Hulme, bm.

Hulme, William & Susanna Patterson, 23 March 1787; George Hulme, bm.

Humphrey, Dennis & Sarah Gittins, 29 ___ 1803; David Humphrey, bm.

Humphrey, John & Telitha Story, 7 Jan 1834; Thomas Story, bm.

Humphry, David & Sally Stansbury, 11 Jan 1806; John Humphry, bm.

WILKES COUNTY MARRIAGES, 1778-1868

Humphry, John & Winne Fields, 21 July 1802; Owen Humphrey, bm.

Humphry, Owens & Mary Lea, 24 Feb 1796; Thomas Fields, bm.

Humphry, Owen Jr. & Susanna Brown, 20 Oct 1796; Owen Humphrey, bm.

Humphry, William & Polly Fields, 12 Jan 1804; Owen Humphry, bm.

Humphry, Young & Eliza Anderson, 14 Feb 1839; James Wood, bm.

Humphrys, Spencer & Milley Gordon, 7 July 1778; George Gordon, bm; consent from Milley Gordon, wit by George McNiel, Mary Gordon.

Huneycut, Daniel & Edney Gray, 12 Feb 1856; Daniel W. Huneycutt, bm.

Hunt, Henry & Patsey Johnson, 22 May 1829; Wm. Sale, bm.

Hunt, James & Diana A. Martin, 16 Dec 1828.

Hunt, John A. & Eliza Parks, 21 June 1867; m 22 June 1867 by M. A. Parks, J. P.

Hunt, Nathan D. & Elizabeth S. Hackett, 5 Jan 1842; J. T. Bryan, bm.

Hunt, Thos. A. J. & Sarah Hickerson, 4 May 1865; D. C. Thurmond, bm; m 18 May 1865 by W. D. Van Eaton, Minister.

Hurt, James & Anne Marten, 14 Nov 1799; James Meredith, bm.

Hurt, Micajah P. & Saryan Fields, 20 Jan 1838; Ansel Parkes, bm.

Hutchison, B. C. & Jane Sparks, 10 April 1858; E. M. Hutcheson, bm.

Hutchison, Francis & Emeline E. Sebastian, 16 Dec 1854; Robert P. Brooks, bm; m 21 Dec 1854 by Eli Grimes, of M. E. C. S.

Hutchison, Hardin & Elizabeth E. Haul, 20 Feb 1843; Elza Reynolds, bm.

Hutchison, John E. & Sidney L. Brown, 3 Sept 1853; Francis Hutchison, bm.

Hutchison, William & Martha Hall, 15 June 1844; Hardin Hutchison, bm.

Hutson, Joseph A. & Mary Goforth, 30 Nov 1850; William Hutson, bm.

Hutson, Robert & Nicey Reade, 20 Sept 1838; Thomas Roberts, bm; m 21 Sept 1838 by Thomas Holms(?), J. P.

Hynes, William & Polley Poe, 19 March 1814; Saml Hynes, bm.

Incle, Daniel & Elisabeth McDaniel, 16 Sept 1860; William Incle, bm.

WILKES COUNTY MARRIAGES, 1778-1868

Ingle, Simpson & Martha C. Stroud, 14 Feb 1867; Charles E. Tilley, bm; m 14 Feb 1867 by Rev. Wm. J. Chapel.

Ingold, Fredric & Jane Felps, 20 Nov 1865; John Inscore, bm.

Ingole, John & Elisabeth Johnson, 11 Aug 1853.

Ingram, Zedeciah & Margret Grayham, daughter of James Graham, 13 Jan 1794; James Graham, bm.

Ingule, Nathaniel & Liddy Bauguess, 25 Sept 1853; Robert J. Bauguess, bm; m 25 Sept 1853 by John Gentry.

Inscore, Jerdin Snr & Rebeckey Oakley, 21 Aug 1853.

Inscore, John & Eliza Caroline West, 13 Sept 1847; James Byrd, bm.

Inscore, Joshua, son of Rubin & Rith Inscore, & Mary Shotts, daughter of Andy & Millie Shotts, 6 June 1867; m 7 June 1867 by Rev. Wm. J. Chapel.

Inscore, Joshua M. & Mary Glass, 3 Sept 1861; m by Eli Johnson, 4 Sept 1861.

Inscore, Wm & Rutha Byrd, 8 Feb 1844; John Johnson, bm.

Inscour, James & Nancy M. Shew, 3 Feb 1852; m 3 Feb 1852 by Eli Johnson, J. P.

Inscour, Fielding & Elizabeth Oakley, 9 Aug 1849; John Myes, bm.

Irvin, Andrew & Lucey Wyatt, 19 Aug 1828; Thornton Kilbey, bm.

Irvin, Francis & Ann Mullins, 10 July 1803; Thomas Erwin, bm.

Isaacs, Elijah Jr. & Anne Robins, 18 Jan 1780; Nathaniel Robins, bm.

Isbel, Benj. & Martha Parkes, 11 Feb 1818; George Parkes, bm.

Isbell, Pendleton & Sarah Henderson, 1 Jan 1781; Aaron Pinson, Thomas Shurley, bm.

Isbell, Thomas & Discretion Howard, 13 Dec 1781; Godfrey Isbel, bm.

Isbel, Thomas & Lucinda Petty, 20 Aug 1829; Joseph Hackett, bm.

Isenhour, Joseph & Letty Barnes, 12 Oct 1837; Henry Parin, bm.

Isenhour, Thomas & Mary Land, 11 May 1861; m 12 May 1861 by J. H. Brown.

Isreael, Isham & Judy Strange, 22 Dec 1801; Archelaus Strange, bm.

Israel, John & Sarah Edmiston, 12 May 1795; Robt. Edmisten, bm.

Israel, Michael & Sarah Coffey, 26 Feb 1800; Lewis Coffey, bm.

Israel, Solomon & Nancy Allaway, 28 Feb 1797; Robert Edmundson, bm.

WILKES COUNTY MARRIAGES, 1778-1868

Ivey, Robt & Lucey Johnson, 25 June 1830; Ruffin Ivey, bm.

Jacks, David & Rachel Johnson, 16 June 1821; John Johnson, bm.

Jacks, Richard & Mary Triplett, 24 Jan 1806; Allen Robenett, bm.

Jacks, Richd. & Priscillah Tucker, 8 April 1819; David Jacks, bm.

Jacks, William & Sarah Netherly, 12 May 1783; Wm. Sloan, bm.

Jackson, Danl & Prudence Stanbury, 11 Aug 1807; David Stanbury, bm.

Jackson, Isaiah & Susannah Reddin, 12 March 1820; William Jackson, bm.

Jackson, James & Abgil Fairchild, 3 Feb 1779; Samuel Castle, bm.

Jackson, James & Martha Chambers, 21 Dec 1799; Elisha Chambers, bm.

Jackson, John & Louisa Coffey, 15 Aug 1820; Larkin Coffey, bm.

Jackson, Levy & Elizabeth Sellars, 24 Aug 1780; John Sellers, bm.

Jackson, Micajah & Milley Brown, 27 Sept 1814; Aaron Cook, bm.

Jacoway, Archibald & Susanna Gilreath, 29 Dec 1804; Henry Gilreath, bm.

James, Cyrus & Elizabeth Fields, 15 Sept 1829; Thomas Fields, bm.

James, John L. & Charlotte M. Hendren, 26 Jan 1848; James W. Hendren, bm.

James, Joseph & Kily Saintclear, 18 Aug 1815; Joel Vannoy, bm.

James, Lee L. & Kissia Jones, 26 March 1833; Joseph James, bm.

James, Spencer & Nancy Fields, 14 March 1832; Joshua Pinnel, bm.

James, Thomas B. & Meriah C. Saintclair, 3 Oct 1855; M. H. Gwyn, bm; m 7 Oct 1855 by S. C. Wellborn, J. P.

Janr, John & Efferller Fletcher, 7 Dec 1790, George Hulmc, bm.

Jarvis, Charles & Elisabeth Ball, 17 Dec 1811; Asa Rash, bm.

Jarvis, Charles & Sarah Howard, 20 April 1825; Parmenas Johnson, bm.

Jarvis, Henry C. & Marthey Mabery, 23 Aug 1866; William Kemp, bm; m 28 Aug 1866 by J. F. Somers, J. P.

Jarvis, James & Presila Watts, 21 Jan 1862; John W. Tagsdol, bm; m 22 Jan 1862 by John M. Grimes, Minister of N. C. Conf.

Jarvis, James Junr. & Lidda McBride, 4 Oct 1809; John Jarvis, bm.

WILKES COUNTY MARRIAGES, 1778-1868

Jarvis, James M. & Julia Ann Garner, 21 June 1865; Linsey Jarvis, bm; m 22 June 1865 by Henry Chambers, J. P.; oath of allegiance to U. S. by James M. Jarvis, sworn to by Henry Chambers, J. P.

Jarvis, John & Salley Chambers, 19 March 1811; James Jarvis, bm.

Jarvis, John & Susan Garvis, 2 Sept 1851; Wayla Jarvis, bm; m 2 Sept 1851 by William Goforth, minister.

Jarvis, John N. & Dicey Lunsford, 2 Nov 1839; George Chambers, bm.

Jarvis, Levi & Nancy Roberts, 2 Jan 1861; m 5 Jan 1861 by G. B. Parks.

Jarvis, Linsey & Sary Brown, 24 Feb 1851; William W. Somers, bm.

Jarvis, Linsey, son of James & Lydia Jarvis, & Matilda Write, m 24 Sept 1868 by Israel Hollor, Baptist minister.

Jarvis, Noah & Liddy Jarvis, 10 Jan 1842; William Jarvis, bm.

Jarvis, Noah & Liddy Walker, 18 March 1849; William McKay, bm.

Jarvis, R. F. & Martha Pardew, 10 Aug 1864; A. A. Bicknell, bm; m 14 Aug 1864 by Eld. R. W. Wooton, Baptist minister.

Jarvis, Wayleigh & Elizabeth Brown, 28 Dec 1852; Howard Summers, bm; m 30 Dec 1852 by Wm. Chappel, Eld.

Jarvis, Welmuth & Susey Brown, 27 Feb 1843; James Rash, bm; m 3 March 1843 by Thomas Roberts, J. P.

Jarvis, Welmuth & Dicey Jarvis, 28 Sept 1855; Thurston Redding, bm; m 30 Sept 1855 by William Goforth, Baptist minister.

Jarvis, William & Elizabeth Crabb, 6 May 1826; Henry Mitchell, bm.

Jarvis, William & Sally Dillard, 1 June 1830; John Jarvis, bm.

Jarvis, William & Nancy Jarvis, 19 Oct 1864; John Nooe, bm; m 15 Dec 1864 by Rev. R. W. Wooton.

Jasop, Jacob & Sarah Lee, 28 Feb 1786; William Lee, bm.

Jenings, Allen & Anne Sprinkle, 7 April 1830; John Jinings, bm.

Jenings, Thomas & Elisabeth McBride, 22 Oct 1861; H. C. Summers, bm.

Jenings, Willey & Rebecca Felts, 17 March 1842; Charles Jenings, bm.

Jenkins, Jonah & Polly Smart, 12 Feb 1825; M. L. Hill, bm.

Jenkins, Lewis B. & Frances Vickers, 29 June 1853; m 29 June 1853 by A. Gilreath, J. P.

Jennings, Abraham & Sarah Adams, 22 Dec 1835; George Owens, bm.

Jennings, Ezekiel & Polley Mabery, 3 Oct 1810; John Felts, bm.

WILKES COUNTY MARRIAGES, 1778-1868

Jennings, John & Sally Wyatt, 3 Feb 1835; Isaiah McGrady, bm.

Jett, John & Ann Burns, 21 Oct 1778; Charles Burns, bm.

Jett, John & Naomy Webb, 5 April 1787; Benjamin Duggar, bm.

Jinings, John & Susannah Felts, 29 Jan 1827; George Wheatley, bm.

Jinkins, John & Lucy Brooks, 5 Sept 1835; Joseph Porter Jr., bm.

Jinkins, John & Rody Church, 14 Jan 1836; David Gray, bm.

Jinkins, Solomon & Laney Ellis, 5 Oct 1822; John Brooks, bm.

Jinnens, John & Nancy Irwin, 17 Feb 1819; Thomas Jarvis, bm.

Jinnings, D. S. & Amanda Malviny Brown, 5 Oct 1861; m 5 Oct 1861 by A. B. Dansy, J. P.

Jinnings, Elijah & Betsy Abshire, 25 July 1812; William Brown, bm.

Jinnings, Elijah & Melinda Jinnings, 23 Aug 1860; m 26 Aug 1860 by P. R. McGrady, J. P.

Jinnings, Henry & Susanah McGrady, 19 Sept 1851; Henry Adams, bm.

Jinnings, Isaac & Edney B. Bingham, 17 Nov 1845; A. Church, bm.

Jinnings, John & Polley Hearrald, 14 Jan 1853; m 20 Jan 1853 by John Owens, D. D.

Jinnings, John D. & Rebeca E. E. Ellis, 15 Sept 1853; m 15 Sept 1853 by L. Sebastian, J. P.

Jinnings, Levi & Martha Dancey, 8 Oct 1855; Alexander Chatham, bm.

Jinnings, William & Mary Ann Dancey, 17 Dec 1852; Alexander Dancey, bm.

Johnson, Abraham & Leuisey Yates, 2 March 1822; Rowland Judd, bm; consent from John Yates.

Johnson, Albert & Eliza Ann Ray, 26 May 1858; J. L. Tulburt, bm.

Johnson, Ambrose L. & Nancey Laws, 20 Dec 1833; Hasten E. Parkes, bm.

Johnson, Andrew & Patsey Caul, 19 July 1810; John Sullivan (Sillivan), bm.

Johnson, Anthony & Anne Maberry, 1 Nov 1822; William Sale, bm.

Johnson, Anthony & Elizabeth Denney, 3 April 1824; Wm Sale, bm.

Johnson, Ashly & Lucinda Warren, 30 Oct 1824; David Shatterly, bm.

Johnson, Benjamin & Lucy Gray, 8 Feb 1785; Charles Johnson, bm.

WILKES COUNTY MARRIAGES, 1778-1868

Johnson, Benjamin & Delicia Chandler, 11 Feb 1789; Lewis Johnson, bm.

Johnson, Benjamin P. & Leucy Crocy, 27 Dec 1848; John Byrd, bm.

Johnson, Charles & Susana Sparks, 2 March 1784; John Bolin, bm.

Johnson, Calvin L. & Rosana J. Dowell, 23 Feb 1861; m 26 Feb 1861 by Israel Hollar, Baptist minister.

Johnson, Daniel & Nancy Holeman, 18 Dec 1799; William Johnson, bm.

Johnson, Daniel & Fanny Pig, 24 March 1819; David Wilkins, bm.

Johnson, Duke & Deborah Johnson, 31 Jan 1827; Noel Johnson, bm.

Johnson, E. H. & Caroline Hendrix, 2 Nov 1865; John W. Martin, bm; m 3 Nov 1865 by Henry Chambers, J. P.

Johnson, Edward & Susannah Johnson, 27 Sept 1827; William Gamble, bm.

Johnson, Elee & Salley Wheatley, 1 March 1821; Henry York, bm.

Johnson, Eli F. & Milley Johnson, 13 Aug 1857; Enoch Staley, bm.

Johnson, Elza & Elisabeth Gimes, 28 Sept 1837; Solomon Grimes, bm.

Johnson, Enock & Martha Caudle, 5 June 1841; Jesse Caudill, bm.

Johnson, F. P. & Luisa Caudill, 17 Oct 1865; Wm. M. Harrald, bm; m 22 Oct 1865 by Wilson Walker, J. P.

Johnson, Franklen & Millea Byrd, 27 Aug 1860; m 27 Aug 1860 by John Brown, Esqr.

Johnson, Gabrel P. & Lucindia Johnson, 9 Sept 1867; m 12 Sept 1867 by H. A. T. Harris.

Johnson, George & Sarah Ann Johnson, 19 Nov 1800; Lewis Johnson, bm.

Johnson, George W., son of Patsey Johnson & Eliza Whittington, daughter of A. G. Whittington, m at the house of William Hall, 22 Dec 1867 by William Hall.

Johnson, H. B. & C. L. Kelly, 17 June 1846; T. L. Kelly, bm.

Johnson, James & Nancy Allexander, 12 Sept 1816; David Hickerson, bm.

Johnson, James & Winney Johnson, 29 Nov 1828; Joshua Johnson, bm.

Johnson, James M. W. & Amanda C. Stone, 24 March 1853; Andrew Porter, bm; m 27 March 1853 by A. Porter, J. P.

Johnson, James H. & Dicey Anner Anderson, 15 Aug 1866; George P. Johnson, bm; m 16 Aug 1866 by G. W. Hayes, J. P.

Johnson, Jeffry & Polly Reynolds, 11 June 1828; John Brewer, bm.

WILKES COUNTY MARRIAGES, 1778-1868

Johnson, Jese F. & Mary E. Grimes, 1 Jan 1860; m 1 Jan 1860 by ___.

Johnson, Jessee & Elizabeth Hamby, 31 May 1821; Charles Philips, bm.

Johnson, Jesse & Sarah Adams, 31 Aug 1836; Eli Reeves, bm.

Johnson, Joel & Nancy Parkes, 11 March 1811; Jas. Laws, bm.

Johnson, John & Peggey Sparkes, 17 Jan 1782; Aniram Allen, bm.

Johnson, John & Sarah Taylor, 16 Feb 1782; Isaac Garison, bm.

Johnson, John & Elizabeth Gillem, 15 Feb 1821; George Johnson, bm.

Johnson, John & Edney Gray, 9 May 1826; Elee Johnson, bm.

Johnson, John & Fanny Inscore, 5 Oct 1859.

Johnson, John, son of Ennee Johnson, & Feaba Lynes, daughter of Alan Lynes, 3 Sept 1867; m 22 Sept 1867 by J. B. Spicer, J. P.

Johnson, John & Lovina Crain, 28 May 1823; James Crain, bm.

Johnson, John G., son of John & Edney Johnson, & Susanah Shew, daughter of Henry and Sally Shew, 4 Sept 1867.

Johnson, John H. & Nancy Alexander, 15 March 1846; Robt Martin Jr., bm.

Johnson, John M. & Martha Stamper, 5 Dec 1866; B. F. Johnson, bm; m 6 Dec 1866 by W. Joines, J. P.

Johnson, Joseph & Mary Staley, 7 Feb 1816; Jacob Staley, bm.

Johnson, Joseph & Dicey Stanly, 11 April 1812; Christopher Howard, bm.

Johnson, Joseph & Dianer Byrd, 2 May 1863; m 2 May 1863 by Eli Grimes, L. D. of M. E. Church S.

Johnson, Keseier & Jincy Norman, 29 Aug 1848; Annis Horten, bm.

Johnson, Leander & Franky Johnson, 17 Dec 1811; Saml Johnson, bm.

Johnson, Lewis & Susanna Chandler, 20 Dec 1789; Timothy Chandler, bm.

Johnson, Lewis & Rissy Wood, 11 Aug 1807; Joseph Wood, bm.

Johnson, Lewis & Nancy Lamarah Martin, 22 Jan 1829; Benj. Martin, bm.

Johnson, Malan & Sarah McCrary, 13 Nov 1843; John McCrary, bm.

Johnson, Mason & Elisabeth Baugus, 12 Nov 1829; Elsa Johnson, bm.

Johnson, Moses Jr. & Susanah C. Glass, 8 Jan 1852; Henry Glass, Jr., bm; m 8 Jan 1852 by Eli Johnson, J. P.

WILKES COUNTY MARRIAGES, 1778-1868

Johnson, Noah & Rebecca Dishmore, 24 July 1852; Wm. Dishmore, bm; m 26 July 1852 by L. J. Bicknell, J. P.

Johnson, Noel & Mitiday Walker, 25 April 1852; John Chambers, bm; m 25 April 1852 by R. W. Wooten, J. P.

Johnson, Noel & Hannah Luis, 17 April 1856; John Chambers, bm; m 20 April 1856 by L. J. Bicknell, J. P.

Johnson, Nooh & Sarah Pilkington, 15 April 1861; m by H. Hayes, J. P., 21 April 1861.

Johnson, Permanes & Sally Felie, 14 May 1816; Thos Witherspoon, bm.

Johnson, Philip & Poly Gaines, 6 Aug 1788; Thomas Allin, bm.

Johnson, Presly & Nancy Dickinson, 15 Feb 1815; William S. Hays, bm.

Johnson, R. M. & M. A. Faw, 21 Sept 1858; Robert Yates, bm; m 21 Sept 1858 by J. Yates, J. P.

Johnson, Robert & Rebekah McBride, 27 March 1805; James McBride, bm.

Johnson, Rubin & Nancy Greenle, 30 Oct 1788; Wm Johnson, bm.

Johnson, Samuel & Barbara Johnson, 28 Nov 1805; George Jonson, bm.

Johnson, Saml & Susanah Billings, 27 March 1848; Willis Childers, James Childers, bm.

Johnson, Samuel B. & Susanna Alexander, 25 Nov 1816; Jesse Gambill, bm.

Johnson, Thos & Doshe Nunnery, 8 Jan 1805; Thos Johnson, bm.

Johnson, Thos & Lucey Edwin, 5 Dec 1780; Joseph Herndon, bm.

Johnson, Thomas & Delphia Carter, 18 July 1805; Wm Sabastin, bm.

Johnson, Thos T. & Elisabeth Cox, 15 Aug 1865; Alexander Lipford, bm; m 17 Aug 1865 by J. W. Church.

Johnson, Wayett & Marthey Hollan, 7 May 1852; George W. Chambers, bm; m 20 May 1852 by W. W. Wright, J. P.

Johnson, Wesly & Elisabeth Warren, 13 April 1824; Byrd Stone, bm.

Johnson, William & Anna Dier, 23 Feb 1789; Ambrose Parks, bm.

Johnson, Wm & Elizabeth Stubblefield, 26 May 1798; Wm Lenoir, bm.

Johnson, William & Letty Johnson, 24 Aug 1818; Leander Johnson, bm.

Johnson, William & Mahala Cook, 25 Oct 1832; Mark Cook, bm.

Johnson, Wm & Rebecca Caudell, 21 July 1836; Andrew Porter, bm.

WILKES COUNTY MARRIAGES, 1778-1868

Johnson, William & Nancy Curry, 12 Jan 1842; John Johnson, bm.

Johnson, William & Rebeca Nance, 25 Feb 1852; m 29 Feb 1852 by W. W. Wright, J. P.

Johnson, Wm. B. & Frances E. Foster, 29 Oct 1838; John S. Johnson, bm.

Johnson, William M. A. & Elizabeth Sheen, 10 Nov 1854; m 11 Nov 1854 by M. H. Wheatly, J. P.

Johnson, William Parkes & Elizabeth Anderson, 18 April 1818; James H. Fyffe, bm.

Johnson, Wm. L. & Jane Boman, 11 Jan 1866; John J. Foster, bm.

Johnson, William W. & Sarah Crouse, 4 July 1853; James McCann, bm; m 12 July 1853 by Ansel Parks.

Johnson, Williams & Elizabeth Johnson, 21 Jan 1822; William Parkes Johnson, bm.

Johnson, Zachariar & Rebeca Suites, 29 Nov 1864; Elias Johnson, bm.

Johnston, Aaron & Nancy Hais, 7 Dec 1802; Lewis Thronbarly, bm.

Johnston, David & Peggy M. M. Julietty Johnson, 23 Sept 1852; J. M. W. Johnson, bm; m 24 Sept 1852 by Eli Johnson, J. P.

Johnston, Francis & Hanna McGee, 22 Dec 1807; Danl Meddows, bm.

Johnston, James & Susana Holton, 27 Jan 1792; Alexr. Holton, bm.

Johnston, James & Elizabeth ___, 18 Jan 1806; John Johnson, bm.

Johnston, Jas. & Winna Johnson, 25 May 1851; Maredath Henderson, bm.

Johnston, Joshua & Elisbeth Burnett, 2 Nov 1852; Noel Johnston, bm; m 3 Nov 1852 by Con. Gray, J. P.

Johnston, Joshua & Sarah Glass, 29 Oct 1855; William J. Chappel, bm.

Johnston, Noel & Lettuce Marlow, 15 Dec 1829; Saml Johnson, bm.

Joines, Hamilton & Nancy J. Clanton, 4 Jan 1859; m 5 Jan 1859 by Wm. H. Hubbard, J. P.

Joines, Hugh & Susanah Barker, 23 Dec 1851; Hamilton Joines, bm.

Joines, Jesse F. & Sarah Tompson, 15 Jan 1859; m 16 Jan 1859 by J. D. Hubbard, J. P.

Joines, John W. & Elvira Broyhill, 11 Jan 1834; Riley Laws, bm.

Joines, John W. & Margarett L. Wilcoxon, 15 June 1854; m 18 June 1854 by Wm. H. Hubbard, J. P.

Joines, Magar & Sally Caudle, 24 April 1825; Moses Joines, bm.

Joines, Moses & Luanah Hopper, 20 March 1820; Jerimiah Cordle, bm.

WILKES COUNTY MARRIAGES, 1778-1868

Joines, S. F. & Nancy McGrady, 9 July 1864; Thos B. Caudill, bm; m 10 July 1864 by William Hall.

Joins, Pendextor & Lucey Rector, 26 Feb 1820; Allen Bruce, bm.

Joley, Wesley & Nancy Cockerham, 8 Oct 1850; Mardy Thorton, bm.

Jolley, James & Aney Handy, 18 March 1851; Mardath Thorton, bm.

Jolley, John & Elizabeth Spicer, 18 Feb 1845; Jesse Billings, bm.

Jolley, Silas & Louisey Fortner, 16 Aug 1835; Elisha Carley, bm.

Jolly, Thomas J. & Dorces L. Byrd, 15 Oct 1865; John A. Billings, bm; m 18 Nov 1865 by W. F. Adams, Baptist minister.

Jones, Andrew J. & Rebecca Foster, 1 April 1839; Alford M. Foster, bm.

Jones, Austin & Nancy Laws, 2 Sept 1828; William Kilby, bm.

Jones, Benj. & Sally Case, 30 Oct 1804; Thomas Jones, bm.

Jones, Catlett & Nancy Dula, 8 Sept 1801; Edmd. Jones, bm.

Jones, Edmund & Ann Lenoir, 25 Oct 1798; ___ Gordon, bm.

Jones, Elbert W. & Amelia E. Webber, 29 June 1850; Phineas Horton, bm.

Jones, Gabriel & Mary Robins, 18 Nov 1792; Thos Foster, bm.

Jones, George & Sarah Transom, 13 Feb 1837; Wm. B. Transom, bm.

Jones, Harden & Nelley Web, 14 July 1802; Elijah Lanus(?), bm.

Jones, Hugh A. & Margaret Conly, 14 Aug 1835; Jesse Foster, bm.

Jones, James & Isabella Wright, 21 Dec 1778; Thomas Jones, bm.

Jones, James & Anne Felts, 29 Jan 1825; Hardy Wells, bm.

Jones, John & Salley Williams, 21 March 1809; Joseph Jones, bm.

Jones, John & Mary Presly, 26 Aug 1816; Joseph Jones, bm.

Jones, John & Prissilla Ferguson, 24 Oct 1827; James Bowman, bm.

Jones, John & Diannah Bishop, 26 July 1828; James M. Norble(?), bm.

Jones, John & Fanny Watson, 3 Oct 1848; Ephraim Davis, bm.

Jones, John & Marthew Laws, 17 March 1820; John Laws, bm.

Jones, Joseph & Ellender Wallas, 9 Jan 1779; Charles Walker, Jesse Greer, bm.

Jones, Joseph & Polley Johnson, 13 Nov 1807; Benja. Jones, bm.

Jones, Joseph D. & Mary Foster, 5 Dec 1814; Killis Foster(?), bm.

WILKES COUNTY MARRIAGES, 1778-1868

Jones, Lewis & Salley Robins, 3 Oct 1796; John Dula, bm.

Jones, Morton & Alsea Cleveland, 18 June 1807; John Foster Jr., bm.

Jones, Robt & Lenny Davis, 27 Feb 1821; John Bishop, bm.

Jones, Roland & Anne N. Stokes, 31 Aug 1844; Joseph W. Hackett, bm.

Jones, Russel H. & Permelia Fletcher, 14 Sept 1826; Lewis D. Jones, bm.

Jones, Samuel & Nancy Walker, 13 April 1825; Hardy Wells, bm.

Jones, Thos & Francis Mentin, 27 July 1837; Thos Lane, bm.

Jones, Thos & Susanah Hoofman, 15 Sept 1851; Ephraim Day, bm; m 18 Sept 1851 by Saml Walsh, J. P.

Jones, Wm & Rachell Backor, 11 Aug 1783; Edward Harris, bm.

Jones, Wm & Nancey Mitchel, 27 Dec 1802; Moses Mitchel, bm.

Jones, William & Elizabeth Hood, 1 Feb 1827; James Hood, bm.

Jones, William & Elisabeth Madison, 31 March 1827; Hardy Wells, bm.

Jones, William & Permealy Milam, 10 Aug 1832; John Wellborn, bm.

Jones, William & Nancey Jackson, 13 Dec 1834; Isaac Parlier, bm.

Jones, William B. & Elvira Mattba, 22 Oct 1842; John McKay, bm.

Jonson, John & Nancy Deboard, 22 Feb 1826; Joseph Debord, bm.

Jordan, John & Sarah Keling, 30 Jan 1786; William Davis, Mason Wheatley, bm.

Joyner, Hugh & Nancy Ellis, 20 Dec 1828; Willis Ellis Jr., bm.

Joyner, John & Flower Mastin, 22 Dec 1823; John Marstin, bm.

Judd, Jeremiah & Francis Kilbey, 3 Jan 1830; Larkin Shepherd, bm.

Judd, Nathan & Christena Grime, 6 April 1805; Daniel Kessler, bm.

Judd, Perry & Elizabeth McQuerry, 10 June 1823; Joseph D. Baldwin, bm.

Judd, Rowland & Phanney Mullins, 24 Aug 1781; Danl White, bm.

Judd, Thomas & Elizabeth Darnal, 6 March 1821; Archabal Owens, bm.

Kallar, Nicholas Jr. & Eve Kallar, 3 Sept 1821; Nicholas Kallar Sr., bm.

Kapp, C. H. & Martha Spicer, 15 Nov 1862; H. J. Spicer, bm; m 16 Nov 1862 by Rev. C. Sparks.

WILKES COUNTY MARRIAGES, 1778-1868

Kearby, William & Rachel Parks, 3 Dec 1800; Francis Kerby, bm.

Kearley, Joel & Margaret Bentley, 6 May 1828; Joel Kearley, bm.

Keeling, James & Patsy Reading, 8 Oct 1811; Carlton Keeling, bm.

Keeling, William & Susanna Lay, 13 March 1794; Richard Lay, bm.

Kees, John & Sally Keller, 17 Feb 1829; Alfred Dula, bm.

Kees, Solomon & Elizabeth Walters, 4 Dec 1856; John W. Waters, bm.

Kilbey, Henry & Mary Harmon, 3 March 1807; John Fletcher, bm.

Kelin, Leonard & Ann Thomson, 14 April 1784; Carlton Keeling, bm.

Kell, William & Amelia Johnson, 6 Oct 1842; Jesse Caudell, bm.

Keller, John & Phoeba Alexander, 1 April 1830; Eli Borders, bm.

Keller, Quiller & Mary Bentley, 5 Oct 1835; Jonas Keller, bm.

Keller, Solomon & Oriller Andres, 13 Sept 1860; m 26 Dec 1860 by ___.

Keller, Wm & Barbarra Blackburn, 15 Dec 1858; m 16 Dec 1858 by Elder Jas. McNeil.

Kelley, Benjamin & Fanney Coots, 11 Feb 1819; Francis Pourter, bm.

Kelly, Saml D. & Amelia E. Martin, 26 Sept 1838; Wm. Martin, bm.

Kelly, Thomas D. & Phoe C. Bryan, 15 Feb 1824; Hugh Jones, bm.

Kemp, Hugh R. & Lucinda Wellborn, 25 Oct 1860; m 15 Nov 1860 by D. W. Parks, J. P.

Kemp, John & Ruth Coleman, 11 May 1825; Joshua Souther, bm.

Kemp, Matthew & Everline Felps, 24 March 1830; Hugh R. Williams, bm.

Kemp, Richmond & Elizabeth Souther, 7 Jan 1826; Joshua Souther Junr., bm.

Kemp, Robert & Jan Mason, 15 Oct 1848; Willborn Siddin, bm.

Kemp, Wilborn & Rebecca Hooper, 15 Oct 1830; Jerome B. Souther, bm.

Kemp, Wilborn & Eisabeth Nicholson, 21 Feb 1832; Jerome Souther, bm.

Kennedy, Norwood & Lucinda Johnson, 12 Feb 1862; James Gentry, bm; m 13 Feb 1862 by Rev. R. Sparks, D. D.

Kenneday, William & Rachel Parkes, 14 Aug 1801; Thos. Allen, bm.

Kennaday, Churchwell H. & Susan Creed, 6 Nov 1849; P. C. Cockerham, bm.

WILKES COUNTY MARRIAGES, 1778-1868

Kerbey, Francis Jr. & Nancy Sparks, 30 Aug 1813; Thomas E___, bm.

Kerby, John & Sinthey Smith, 23 Feb 1794; James Penlee, bm.

Kerby, John Jr. & Sally Elmore, 15 Feb 1806; John Kerby Senr., bm.

Kerr, Whitfield & Miss Maria Louisa Wilson, 29 Aug 1828; Th. Wilson, bm.

Ketchum, Ackling & Adaline A. Wingler, 8 April 1835; Taton Woodel, bm.

Keys, Hiram & Sarah Bareer, 27 Dec 1829; Thomas Dula, bm.

Keys, John & Caroline Phillips, 5 April 1853; John W. Waters, bm; m 8 April 1853 by Nathl. Church, J. P.

Keeze, Jacob & ___, 11 March 1783; Benja. Guest, bm.

Kilbay, Michael & Suker Brown, 10 Sept 1781; Jonathan Wall, bm.

Kilby, Abraham & Naomia Dancey, 27 Aug 1839; Thornton Kilby, bm.

Kilby, Benj. & Emily Kilby, 21 March 1827; M. L. Hill, bm.

Kilby, Linvel & Fanny Vannoy, 27 Oct 1821; Lovel Kilby, bm.

Kilby, Adam & Rebecca Bolling, 1 Aug 1820; Henry Trustey, bm.

Kilby, Adam & Mercy Nicholas, 26 Jan 1840; A. E. Nicholas, bm.

Kilby, Auterey, slave of Saml Kilby, & Phoeba Grinton, a mulatto, 15 April 1830.

Kilby, Abram, son of Abram & Elisabeth Kilby, & Susanah Jenkins, daughter of Coder & Lenne Jenkins, 14 March 1868; m 14 March 1868.

Kilby, Henry G. & Martha A. Willcoxson, 14 June 1863; James C. Kilby, bm; m 15 June 1863 by A. A. Whittenton, J. P.

Kilby, J. W. & Polly Gambill, 24 Oct 1836; David Gray, bm.

Kilby, James & Margaret Robins, 24 March 1792; Johnson Owins, bm.

Kilby, James & Jane Jinnings, 3 Feb 1841; Jas. E. Reynolds, bm.

Kilby, James, son of John W. Kilby, & Amanday M. Brown, daughter of Overby Brown, m in the ridg Road near Wesly Kilby, 11 Jan 1868 by Wm. A. McNeil, J. P.

Kilby, James Welborn & Rachel Collert, 6 Sept 1828; John Whittenton, bm.

Kilby, John W. & Martha Wilcoxson, 20 Nov 1839; R. W. Kilby, bm.

Kilby, John W. & Delila A. Bumgarner, 17 June 1863; Simeon Bumgarner, bm; m 17 June 1863 by A. A. Whittenton, J. P.

WILKES COUNTY MARRIAGES, 1778-1868

Kilby, Joseph E. & Elizabeth Cooper, 17 Oct 1835; Elijah Nicholds, bm.

Kilby, Lovel & Rachel Tinsley, 19 July 1819; Larkin Holding(?), bm.

Kilby, R. W. & Elizabeth Barlow, 10 July 1841; W. G. Johnson, bm.

Kilby, Samuel & Casander J. Shumate, 3 Feb 1855; m 4 Feb 1855 by S. J. Gambill.

Kilby, Thornton & Lucy Shepherd, 10 Oct 1822; Andrew Irwin, bm.

Kilby, Thornton & Betsey Colvert, 27 Nov 1829; William H. Kilby, bm.

Kilby, Thornton & Sarah Yeats, 19 Feb 1847; John Whittington, bm.

Kilby, W. P. & Clarrissa Dancy, 28 Oct 1865; C. F. Vannoy, bm.

Kilby, William & Elisebeth Hall, 12 April 1805; Abra. Kilby, bm.

Kilby, Wm. S. & Ann Hines, 2 Aug 1854.

Kilpaterick, Josiah & Virginia C. Brown, 9 Feb 1867; Wm. Harriss, bm; m 14 Feb 1867 by Wm. A. Foster, J. P.

Kimbro, Joseph & Clary Hays, 11 Dec 1824; Tillous W. Bussell, bm.

Kimbrough, Goldman & Mary Allen, 18 March 1792; Thos Allen, bm.

Kindal, James & Polley Dula, 13 Oct 1795; John Dula, bm.

Kindall, James & Selenia Dula, 12 July 1848; Joel Brookshire, bm.

Kindall, John & Elizabeth Triplet, 22 Oct 1811; William Kindle, bm.

Kindall, John W. & Mary Foster, 26 Nov 1847; Charles Harris, bm.

Kindall, Thos & Rebecka Holdmon, 25 Jan 1814; W. F. Campbell, bm.

Kindall, Thomas & Margerett Pasley, 3 Feb 1824; John Northern, bm.

Kindall, William & Elizabeth Hagler, 28 Oct 1793; Jno Maret, bm.

Kindall, William & Nancy Brown, 9 April 1827; Wm. Kindall, bm.

King, Alfred & Mary Adams, 17 Feb 1841; William Shoemate, bm.

King, Jacob & Betsy Bennet, 13 Jan 1783; Russel Jones, bm.

Kinne, Southy(?), & Elizabeth Bath(?), 1 March 1862.

Kirby, Simon & Aly Holt, 21 Dec 1806; John Kirby, bm.

Kirk, Calven J. & Adline Triplet, m 15 Sept 1858 by E. B. Philips, J. P.

110

WILKES COUNTY MARRIAGES, 1778-1868

Kirk, W. P. & L. E. Triplett, m 1 Nov 1858 by E. B. Philips, J. P.

Knight, Ambrose & Malinda Bradley, 10 Dec 1830; Thomas Land, bm.

Knight, Ambrose & Polly Levingston, 10 Aug 1839; Reuben Knight, bm.

Knight, Burton & Frankey Levingston, 5 Oct 1835; Pickens Carlton, bm.

Knight, James & Ruth Crouch, 30 Oct 1830; Thos Land, bm.

Knight, James & Lucinda Knight, 15 Sept 1855; Thos Knight, bm.

Knight, John & Elizabeth Humphrey, 19 Oct 1824; Thomas Coffey, Jr., bm.

Knight, John & Franky Land, 23 Oct 1833; Thos Moltbey, bm.

Knight, Reuben & Lette Farguson, 24 Dec 1798; Elijah Triplett, bm.

Knight, Reuben & Mahala Land, 7 Sept 1829; James J. Burch, bm.

Knight, Thomas & Lucy Stanton, 24 Dec 1799; Reuben Knight, bm.

Knutt, William & Mary Edleman, 30 July 1816; Chapman Adams, bm.

Krouse, Solomon J. & Elizabeth Johnson, 23 July 1859; Gary G. Spencer, bm.

Kyle, Alexr. & Anna Swanson, 9 Aug 1826; James McGinnis, bm.

Lad, Franlen & Vicy Ried, 14 March 1852; m by Wm. S. McNiel, J. P.

Ladd, Amos & Nancy Felts, 4 Dec 1829; Wm. Felts, bm.

Ladd, Amos & Sary Sparkes, 8 Sept 1859; Aaron Ladd, bm; m 8 Sept 1859 by John Brown, J. P.

Ladd, Joseph & Millay Shewmaker, 18 Nov 1851; Richmond Speks, bm; m 19 Nov 1851 by R. W. Wooton, J. P.

Ladd, Milton & Mary Reynolds, 24 Jan 1811; Elisha Reynolds, bm.

Lakey, Head & Elizabeth Brooker, 28 Oct 1839; Willis Hollaway, bm.

Land, James & Ede Livingston, 5 Jan 1807; John Livingston, bm.

Land, James Jr. & Jinney Murphy, 20 Dec 1839; Charles Carlton, bm.

Land, John & Nancy Earp, 20 March 1817; Isam Hubbard, bm.

Land, Jonathan & Elizabeth Isbell, 27 Dec 1779; Livingston Isbell, bm.

Land, Jonathan & Margarett Mooney, 23 Sept 1828; James Mooney, bm.

WILKES COUNTY MARRIAGES, 1778-1868

Land, Linvill & Roda Proffet, 3 Aug 1849; William Triplitt, bm.

Land, Thomas & Jane Calton, 6 Nov 1814; Wm. Brown, bm.

Land, Thomas Jr. & Matilda Carlton, 30 Aug 1831; Silas Carlton, bm.

Land, Wilson & Rebecca Miller, 22 Oct 1836; Alfred Foster, bm.

Landsdown, Nathaniel & Nancy Farchilds, 15 April 1799; Peter Campbell, bm.

Landsdown, John & Mary Holton, 16 Sept 1786; Joshua Carter, bm.

Landsdown, Reuben & Selah Morgan, 3 Aug 1803; John Hamrick, bm.

Landsdown, Simon & Sarah Stanly, 10 Feb 1838; J. E. Mastin, bm.

Landtrip, Amos & Marey McGill, 3 March 1802; Laurence Pearson, bm.

Lane, Benj. H. & Martha C. Williamson, 10 June 1852; m 10 June 1852 by Wm. H. Hubbard, J. P.

Lane, Braxton & Betsey Underwood, 3 Jan 1827; H. B. Satterwhite, bm.

Lane, Edward & Mary Hampton(?), 7 June 1830; Thomas Lane, bm.

Lane, Jacob & Eveline Taylor, 23 Aug 1863; P. R. McGrady, bm; m 23 Aug 1863 by P. R. McGrady, J. P.

Lane, James & Frances Parsons, 8 Feb 1841; Wm. Gilbert, bm.

Lane, James & Caroline C. Brown, 26 Oct 1865; (no bm); m 26 Oct 1865 by Thos P. Parleir, J. P.

Lane, James, son of James & Annie Lane & Mary Parsons, daughter of Richard & Nancy Roberts, m 17 Oct 1868 by Smith Ferguson.

Lane, Jerry & Mary Furkbull, 1 Oct 1835; Isaac Parleir, bm.

Lane, John & Susan Cockerham, 28 Nov 1839; Thos H. Saintclair, bm.

Lane, John & Sally Raigen, 23 Jan 1836; Jesse G. Lee, bm.

Lane, Joseph & Polly Ann Mitchell, 8 April 1847; M. A. Allen, bm.

Lane, Martin & Matilda Brookshir, 3 March 1866; John W. Joines, bm; m 4 March 1866 by H. Hayes, J. P.

Lane, Nathaniel G. & Harriet Transon, 6 May 1835; Nathan Ward, bm.

Lane, Peter & Elizabeth Hampton, 17 March 1825; Lamuel Doss, bm.

Lane, Thomas & Elizabeth Chrisley, 3 June 1813; Wm. P. Waugh, bm.

Lane, Thomas & ___, 18 Dec 1850; J. F. Shepherd, bm.

112

WILKES COUNTY MARRIAGES, 1778-1868

Lane, William & Arminda Walker, 2 July 1851; Samuel K. Hartin, bm.

Lang, John R. & Polley Abshire, 15 Oct 1840; Walter Abshire, bm.

Langford, Richard & Rebecca Miller, 26 July 1824; John J. Miller, bm.

Langle, Charles & Nancy Ginkings, 29 Nov 1824; Peter Warran, bm.

Lankford, Elisha & Hanner Person, 19 Aug 1818; Thomas Earp, bm.

Lassenter, James & Elizabeth McAnn, 8 Jan 1850; John Lassenter, bm.

Laurance, Malachi & Ibsy Grimsley, 30 Aug 1817; John Grimsley, bm.

Laurence, Henry & Lany Vinsant, 22 Feb 1813; George Laurence, bm.

Laurance, James & Mary Cate, 5 Jan 1790; John Cate, bm.

Laws, Alfred & Hanah Lovit, m 31 Oct 1854 by S. C. Wellborn, J. P.

Laws, Andrew J. & Elizabeth Minton, 27 Feb 1845; Joshua Fletcher, bm.

Laws, Ausbon & Elizabeth Price, 24 Feb 1855; m 11 March 1855 by E. B. Philips, J. P.

Laws, Braxton & Leuesey J. Saterwhite, 20 Aug 1861; m 21 Aug 1861 by Wm. H. Hubbard, J. P.

Laws, C., son of Joshua & Caroline Laws, & Amanda Roberson, daughter of John & Armenia(?) Roberson, m 5 Jan 1868 by Rev. Jas. McNeil.

Laws, Daniel P., son of John & Rebecca Laws, & Mary R. Bently, daughter of J. J. & Margaret Bently, m 5 Feb 1868 by Elder James Kirby.

Laws, David & Martha Mitchel, 22 Feb 1779; James Mitchel, Caleb Law, bm.

Laws, David & Jinny Vannoy, 3 June 1811; John Caws, bm.

Laws, David & Susan Clanton, 3 May 1825; John Laws, bm.

Laws, David & Matildy Lazenby, 10 March 1862; E. L. Laws, bm; m 13 March 1862 by J. D. Hubbard, J. P.

Laws, David & Elisabeth Miller, 30 April 1811; Jno Laws, bm.

Laws, E. L. & Mary Elusenbery, 10 Feb 1862; David Laws, bm; m 13 Feb 1862 by J. D. Hubbard, J. P.

Laws, Elijah & Pricilla Ann Davidson, 11 March 1833; Joshua Laws, bm.

Laws, James & Rosanna Laws, 2 Nov 1807; Shadrach Laws, bm.

Laws, James & Nancy Harden, 1 Nov 1820; John Laws, bm.

WILKES COUNTY MARRIAGES, 1778-1868

Laws, Jason R. & Elizabeth Kilby, 19 April 1827; Benj. J. Parks, bm.

Laws, Jesse & Ester Rose, 15 Aug 1815; John Laws, bm.

Laws, Jesse & Rebecca Blanton, 12 April 1832; James Ayers, bm.

Laws, Jesse J. & Elizabeth Saunders, 27 April 1846; Nathl. Duncan, bm.

Laws, Joel J. & Martha Grayson, 27 Sept 1836; Jason R. Laws, bm.

Laws, John & Sally Teague, 2 Nov 1802; David Laws, bm.

Laws, John & Amy Laws, 19 Dec 1814; Joseph Laws, bm.

Laws, John & Nancy Lane, 25 Nov 1822; Joel Vannoy, bm.

Laws, John & Mary Laws, 6 Feb 1851; Wm. R. Presnell, bm.

Laws, John Senr. & Jane Adams, 27 July 1791; David Hickerson, bm.

Laws, Joseph R. & Elizabeth Laws, 25 May 1811; Joel Vannoy, bm.

Laws, Joshua & Caddy Caroline Lane, 1 March 1819; Willson Rhoads, bm.

Laws, Levi & Margeratt Church, 14 May 1818; John Church, bm.

Laws, Masten & Maryann Brothern, 23 Dec 1855; m 1 Jan 1856 by Alexander Gilreath, minister.

Laws, Meshack & Elizabeth ____, 31 July 1815; John Laws, bm.

Laws, Meshack & Luisinda Ares, 25 Dec 1820; Thomas Person, bm.

Laws, Moses & Sarah Stanley, 26 Feb 1839; Thos. H. Saintclair, bm.

Laws, Riley & Alsey Stanly, 10 May 1834; Thos. H. Saintclair, bm.

Laws, Shadrach & Mary Trible, 14 Jan 1779; John Laws, John Greer Esqr., bm.

Laws, Thomas & Elizabeth Hamby, 2 June 1832; Jerden (Jorden) Hamby, bm.

Laws, Timothey L. & Margret Price, m 24 Dec 1854 by E. B. Philips, J. P.

Laws, Timothy & Amey Laws, 20 Dec 1821; Joseph R. Laws, Reubin Hamby, bm.

Laws, Welcome William & Milley Low, 25 Jan 1782; Joshua Greer, bm.

Laws, William & Susanna Laws, 25 May 1818; David Laws, bm.

Laws, Wm & Betsy Jines, 12 Jan 1826; Timothy Laws, bm.

Laws, William & Selah Lipps, 9 Oct 1849; Richard Tomlinson, bm.

WILKES COUNTY MARRIAGES, 1778-1868

Laws, William M. & Charlotte Cook, 29 Dec 1823; William Dotson Jr., bm.

Laws, William W. & Delana Segraves, 4 Aug 1830; Sherwood Segraves, bm.

Laxon, Thomas & Polley Carlton, 9 Aug 1811; Stephen Tilley, bm.

Laxton, Wilson & Eveline Calton, 23 Dec 1833; Greenville Hagler, bm.

Laxton, Wilson & Ruth Grier, 10 Aug 1848; Chas. Hickerson, bm.

Lay, David & Mary Lay, 26 March 1794; David Lay Senr., bm.

Layne, James & Elizabeth Montgomery, 12 Nov 1819; John Parleir, bm.

Laysonberry, Alexander & Rosana Laws, 22 Feb 1840; John Duncan, bm.

Leach, Richard & Elizabeth Hulin, 31 Jan 1784; Jonathan Heathman, bm.

Leach, William & Milley Hulin, 14 June 1781; William Hendren, bm.

Leadbetter, Alfred & Mary Ann E. Atkins, 17 Nov 1866; John Q. A. Bryan, bm.

Lee, Galonton W. & Winna Wiles, 18 April 1858; m 18 April 1858 by Eli Grimes, L. D. of M. E. C. S.

Lee, Obediah & Elisabeth Hines, 15 Oct 1822; Joseph Lee, bm.

Lenderman, Henry & Eve Shaw, 2 Nov 1805; Leonard Lenderman, bm.

Lenderman, Henry & Mary Mailsey Whittington, 5 May 1829; John W. Whittington, bm.

Lenderman, John W. & Dianah E. Forrester, 25 Oct 1858; John T. Forster, bm; m 31 Oct 1858 by A. A. Whittenton, J. P.

Lenderman, Samuel & Eliza Mikel, 13 May 1841; Robert Yates, bm.

Lenderman, Wm & Elizabeth Sturt, 22 Sept 1842; David Bumgarner, bm.

Lenoir, Thos & Peggey Robins, 17 Feb 1789; Andw Bryan, bm.

Lenoir, Thos & Milley Loving, 12 Sept 1796; Charles Gordon, bm.

Lett, Reuben & Catharine Parsons, 19 Feb 1831; William Watts, bm.

Lewis, Abraham & Nancy Emily Lewis, 6 March 1844; Charles Hayes, bm.

Lewis (Luis), Andrew & Sarah Estep, 7 April 1856; Noel Johnson, bm; m 9 April 1856 by L. J. Bicknell, J. P.

Lewis, Burton & Mary H. Harris, 18 Sept 1866; m by C. R. S. Simpson, J. P.

WILKES COUNTY MARRIAGES, 1778-1868

Lewis, Daniel & Salley Allen, 17 March 1813; Thomas Allen, bm.

Lewis, David & Mary Hendren, 6 Jan 1823; John Saintclair, bm.

Lewis, Jacob & Hannah Waters, 2 Nov 1819; Lewis Waters, bm.

Lewis, Jacob & Ellen Tharp, 28 Dec 1866; D. C. Eastep, bm; m 28 Dec 1866.

Lewis, James & Nancy Brown, 26 Oct 1819; Joshua Lewis, bm.

Lewis, James & Emley Perdue, 11 Sept 1859; Thomas Lewis, bm; m 11 Sept 1859 by John Brown, J. P.

Lewis, James & Martha Brown, 3 Nov 1861; George W. Chambers, bm; m 3 Nov 1861 by G. B. Parks.

Lewis, James M. & Lemia A. Carmichael, 4 Dec 1862; Benjamin F. Petty, bm; m 17 Dec 1862 by R. W. Barber.

Lewis, Joseph & ___, 7 Feb 1822; Hartwell Hays, bm.

Lewis, Joshua & Salley Johnson, 4 March 1809; Jn. Johnson, bm.

Lewis, Joshua & Caroline Chambers, 1 Nov 1841; Joseph Lewis, bm.

Lewis, Lemmuel & Sely Borgus, 23 May 1818; Manuel Borgus, bm.

Lewis, Lemmuel & Sely Borgus, 23 May 1818; Manuel Borgus, bm.

Lewis, Mordecai & Mary Bradly, 10 Oct 1801; James Bradly, bm.

Lewis, Nathaniel & Elizabeth Downs(?), 26 Oct 1807; Joshua Lewis, bm.

Lewis, Minrod & Miry Bishop, 24 March 1861; Stephen Canter, bm.

Lewis, William & ___, 13 Aug 1806; John Standley, bm.

Lewis, William & Mary Foster, 1 Jan 1828; John M. Foster, bm.

Lewis, William & Delphia Estep, 2 Dec 1840; William Inscore, bm.

Lewis, William B. & Mary Adelaide Chambers, 21 May 1822; M. Stokes, bm.

Lineback, Lewis & Matilda Holeman, 16 Dec 1827; Wm. P. Waugh, bm.

Liney, J. O., son of Matilda Linney, & Matilda York, colored, m 25 Oct 1868 by J. S. Call, J. P.

Lion, Calven & Nancy Waddel, 17 Jan 1865; Augustus Prewitt, bm.

Lion, Meredith & Melindia Sparks, 23 Aug 1838; Jacob Lyon, bm.

Lipford, Anthony & Anny Adkins, 23 Dec 1833; George Bradly, bm.

Lipps, James & Franses Noris, 14 April 1820; John Noris, bm.

Lipps, John & Martha Chuck (Church?), 29 Sept 1814; Benj. McNeil, bm.

WILKES COUNTY MARRIAGES, 1778-1868

Lipps, John F., son of John & Martha Lipps, & Mary V. Yates, daughter of Robert & Jerusha Yates, 28 Sept 1867; m by J. W. Church, J. P.

Lipps, Martin & Eda Holmon, 21 Feb 1837; Enoch McNiel, bm.

Lips, Thomas & Sarah Vines, 1 May 1780; Dawson Sewell, bm.

Little, Lewis & Catheren Odom, 2 April 1829; Wm Odom, bm; Peter Barnes, wit.

Little, Masias & Mary Darnold, 30 Aug 1858; m 30 Aug 1858 by H. Hutchison, J. P.

Littlejohn, Eli & Susanna Fourd, 1 Jan 1780; Jacob Kees, bm.

Livingston, Cornelious & Nancy Brown, 14 June 1828; Wyatt Carlton, bm.

Livingston, John & Rachel Freman, 29 Oct 1782; James Fletcher, bm.

Livingston, John & Charity Carrel, 17 Dec 1801; John Parker, bm.

Livingston, John & K Mela Carlton, 5 May 1832; Cornelius Livingston, bm.

Livingston, John Jr. & Nancy Ferguson, 21 Jan 1834; Joseph Barlow, bm.

Livingston, John Sr. & Mary Dyson, 23 April 1838; Lindsey Livingston, bm.

Livingston, Linsay & Cinith Crouch, 27 Dec 1838; Cornelius Livingston, bm.

Livingston, Orrell & Polly Dula, 29 June 1838; Martin Livingston, bm.

Lockard, John & Margaret Smith, (no date, during admn. of Gov. Alexander Martin); James Smith, bm.

Locke, William C. & Martha D. Martin, 10 March 1835; John S. Johnson, bm.

Lodging, James & Mary Speers, 9 June 1817; William Judd, bm.

Logan, James & Abigail Phillips, 31 May 1821; Jno Joyner, bm.

Loggins, Johnathan & Syntha Ellis, 5 March 1835; George Ketchum, bm.

Logins, Joseph & Rachel Cox, 29 May 1805; Cristefer Gullit, bm.

Lomack, Peter & America Waid, 26 Dec 1856; Milton H. Gwyn, bm.

London, Amos & Salley Redding, 29 Sept 1818; William Jackson Jr., bm.

Long, Calvin & Louisa Stamper, 13 Jan 1866; Owen Waggoner, bm; m 14 Jan 1866 by P. R. McGrady, J. P.

Long, Joel & Elizabeth McKinney, 7 Jan 1802; Isaac Storey, bm.

WILKES COUNTY MARRIAGES, 1778-1868

Long, John & Elizabeth Gambill, 3 Aug 1836; James Boman, bm.

Long, Levi & Martha Handy, 1 June 1858; m by Jas. M. Gambill, 1 June 1858.

Long, Solomon & Nancy E. Abshire, 28 Nov 1849; R. C. Martin, bm.

Long, Wm & Cathe. Sipe, 9 Nov 1846; Jno Rolan, bm.

Long, Welborn & Aggy Rhods, 23 July 1860.

Longbottom, Elisha & Hannah Jarvis, 23 Oct 1823; Jos. Longbottom, bm.

Longbottom, Franklin & Sintha Mahatha, 30 Jan 1855; m by John Brewer, Esqr.

Longbottom, James & Leah Lakey, 24 May 1825; Benj. F. Martin, bm.

Longbottom, Luckky & Ann Jarvis, 27 Feb 1822; Joseph Longbotom, bm.

Longbottom, Wm. & Polley Mize, 19 April 1821; Joseph Longbottom, bm.

Longworth, John & Matilda Ferguson, 25 Feb 1813; Burges Longworth, bm.

Love, Ingram & Hiley Parker, 16 May 1823; Reubin Standley, bm.

Love, James A., son of Rebecca Love & Rhoda C. Duncan, daughter of John & Rebecca Duncan, m 18 Aug 1867 by Elder J. Kerly, bm.

Love, John & Peggey King, 23 May 1789; James Allen, bm.

Love, John & Salley Fletcher, 24 Sept 1819; James Love, bm.

Love, Thos & Caroline Johnson, 17 July 1827; Joseph Ray, bm.

Love, John & Nancy Brown, 1 Aug 1860; Eli Franklin Johnson, bm.

Love, William & Sally Brian, 24 Feb 1816; John Sparks, bm.

Love, William & Susanah Combs, 17 Aug 1860.

Lovelace, Isaac & Elizabeth Longbottom, 15 May 1809; William Beall, bm.

Loveless, Jeremiah & Phebe Lips, 30 Jan 1816; James Minton, bm.

Lovett, A. H. & Elizabeth Billings, 31 July 1855; Wm. Canter, bm; m 31 July 1855 by S. C. Welborn, J. P.

Loving, Gabriel Junr & Rachel Lisk, 27 Aug 1781; Gabl. Lovin, bm.

Loving, John & Fanney Parks, 27 Dec 1800; Thos. Allen, bm.

Low, Isaac & Mary Preston, 7 May 1787; Lewis Demoss, bm.

Low, Isaiah & Nancy Person, 29 Jan 1834; Isaac Bebber, bm.

WILKES COUNTY MARRIAGES, 1778-1868

Low, Saml & Ann Cupp(?), 29 March 1788; Thos Low, bm.

Lowder, Job & Sarah Ratcliff, 5 March 1827; Dd. Roussau, bm.

Lowe, David & Elizabeth Vickas, 20 Oct 1807; Vincent B. Hale, bm.

Lowe, Isaac & Sarah Hardgraves, 8 Sept 1790; Francis Hardgraves, bm.

Lowe, Isaac Jr. & Sarah Adams, 23 Aug 1805; Philip Price, bm.

Lowe, Joshua & Polly Teague, 1 Oct 1805; John Laws, bm.

Lowe, Joshua & Lucinda Hubbard, 9 June 1818; James Roberson, bm.

Lowe, Martin & Clarinda Laws, 18 Nov 1860; m 19 Nov 1860 by J. D. Hubbard, J. P.

Lowe, William & Ann Owen, 5 Feb 1800; Isaac Lowe, bm.

Luffman, John, son of William & Elizabeth Luffman, & Eliza Carter, daughter of Benjamin and Mary Carter, m 15 Aug 1867 by B. T. Wall, J. P.

Luffon, John & Famy Hanes, 12 May 1856; Daniel Hanes, bm; m 12 May 1856 by A. Parks.

Lufmon, Eli & Sarah Hanes, 28 Dec 1852; Isom L. Dickerson, bm.

Lufmon, James R. & Elizabeth Thomas, 5 Jan 1859; Daniel Hanes, bm; m 6 Jan 1859 by B. T. Wall, J. P.

Lufmon, John & Lucinda Cimmons, 4 Nov 1857; J. R. Lufmon, bm; m 4 Nov 1857 by B. F. Johnson, J. P.

Lumsden, John & Susan S. Wellborn, 6 Aug 1843; W. G. Johnson, bm.

Lundy, David & Elizabeth Lowe, 19 Feb 1816; John Lowe, bm.

Lundy, John K. & Elizabeth A. Parker, 11 Nov 1863; J. J. Call, bm; m 12 Nov 1863 by R. F. Hackett, J. P.

Lunsford, Archd. & Elisabeth Deboard, 5 Feb 1816; Jonathan Lunsford, bm.

Lunsford, Augustin & Lydia Wats, 1 Oct 1788; Lewis Recter, bm.

Lunsford, Elijah & Nancy Nicholson, 27 July 1832; Emmanel Lunsford, bm.

Lunsford, Emmanuel & Sarah Deboard, 13 Jan 1832; Ira Deboard, bm.

Lunsford, James & Nancy Becknall, 5 Dec 1815; William Brown, bm.

Lunsford, Joel & Teny Brown, 20 March 1811; John Stanly, bm.

Lunsford, Nathan & Dinary Stout, 2 Nov 1816; Jesse Adams, bm.

Lunsford, Reuben & Elizabeth Fletcher, 27 Feb 1833; Robert Cecil, bm.

WILKES COUNTY MARRIAGES, 1778-1868

Lunsford, Stepherd & Dolly Becknold, 15 Aug 1834; Daniel Rash, bm.

Lunsford, Turner & Elizabeth Clark, 29 April 1830; George Fourboush, bm.

Luntsford, Charles & Elizabeth Handy, 31 Dec 1846; Alston Yeats, bm.

Lusk, Samuel & Mary Towson, 28 Dec 1821; James Townson, bm.

Luther, Jordon & Hannah Vincanon, 29 July 1856; Christopher Bingham, bm; m 30 July 1856 by James Purvis.

Lycan, Jacob Gooding & Dolley Cook, 16 Dec 1779; Joseph Porter, bm.

Lyan, Absolom & Prudy Crous, 23 Nov 1853; James Lyan, bm; m 24 Nov 1853 by Ansel Parks.

Lyan, Jacob & Jane Gentry, 23 Dec 1855; John S. Parks, bm; m 23 Dec 1855 by Ansel Parks.

Lyan, Miles G. & Jane Lyan, 23 Dec 1857; Timothy Sparks, bm; m 24 Dec 1857 by J. M. Gambill, J. P.

Lyon, Alexandria & Mary Blackburn, 27 Sept 1827; Joel Sparks, bm.

Lyon, Austen & Nancy Caudle, 4 Feb 1828; Solomon Lyon, bm.

Lyon, Jacob & Malindy Sparkes, 6 June 1846; James Durham, bm.

Lyon, James & Polley Gentry, 21 March 1821; Jonathan Gentry, bm.

Lyon, Jesse & Frankey Holbrook, 17 July 1815; William Holbrook, bm.

Lyon, John & Hulda Durham, 11 Sept 1857; Allen Lyon, bm.

Lyon, Jonathan & Jinsa T. Walls, 22 Oct 1848; John D. Purdue, bm.

Lyon, Thomas M. & Ruth Wood, 19 May 1865; M. R. Wood, bm.

Lyon, Volentine & Mary Gentry, 4 Oct 1816; Artha Gentry, bm.

Lyon, Voluntine & Rachel Wales, 16 Jan 1835; Jacob Lyon Jr., bm.

Lyon, William & Jane Woody, 24 Dec 1818; Risdon Cooper, bm.

Lyon, Wm Jr. & Sally Holbrook, 2 Aug 1819; John Holbrook, bm.

Lyon, Willy & Amelia Cordell, 18 Oct 1860; M. L. Darnall, bm.

Lyons, William & Mary C. Hughs, 25 Feb 1863.

McBee, John M. & Susan Grogan, 21 Dec 1866; Joseph Grogan, bm; m 23 Dec 1866 by Thos L. Parleir, J. P.

McBride, Daniel & Elisabeth Green, 10 Jan 1804; Richd. Cunningham, bm.

WILKES COUNTY MARRIAGES, 1778-1868

McBride, Martin G. & Martha Martin, 14 Aug 1844; W. G. Johnson, bm.

McBride, D. L. & Almeda Harris, 8 March 1866, m by Thomas Howell.

McBride, Danniel L. & Mary Sale(?), 11 Jan 1837; John McBride, bm.

McBride, James & Elizabeth Walker, 25 Nov 1823; Robt Johnson, bm.

McBride, John J. & Elisabeth Gray, 3 Dec 1831; Thos. Witherspoon, bm.

McBride, Martin & Elisabeth Gray, 19 Feb 1810; George Gray, bm.

McBride, Martin G. & Sarah J. Harris, 10 Feb 1866; W. D. W. Swaim, bm; m 10 Feb 1866 by Thomas Howell.

McBride, William & Elizabeth Heathman, 5 Nov 1799; James McBride, bm.

McCann, A. L. & E. L. Douglass, 11 Feb 1862; T. H. McCann, bm; m 11 Feb 1862 by Rev. Wm. J. Combs.

McCann, D. J. & M. T. Parks, 12 Feb 1867; T. M. Parks, bm; m 14 Feb 1867 by Rev. R. Sparks, LL. D.

McCann, James & Nancy Smith, 10 Jan 1817; Reuben Suttle, bm.

McCann, John M., son of Marion & Rachel McCann, & Mary Hanks, daughter of James & Lucinda Hanks, m 24 Nov 1867 near Nancy Hanks, by John Hughes, Baptist minister.

McCann, Marion & Rachel Smith, 20 Oct 1849; Simon Smith, bm.

McCann, Wuton & Thursa Phillips, 9 May 1865; J. E. Perkins, bm.

McCann, Pary & Elizebeth Harris, 21 Feb 1856; Hugh Hanks, bm; m 21 Feb 1856 by A. Parks.

McCann, Richard & Charity Smith, 26 Oct 1829; Ira Deboard, bm.

McCann, T. H. & Hariet Poe, 20 Dec 1858; Marion McCann, bm; m 20 Dec 1858 by William J. Combs, D. D.

McClelland, John N. & Martha J. Parkes, 16 May 1834; Wm. Martin, bm.

McClewer, William & Malindy Seegraves, 25 Oct 1831; Britain Seegraves, bm.

McCloud, Isham & Mary Fair, 17 April 1833; Lewis D. Merriman, bm.

McCloud, Tennison & Holley Wells, 24 Dec 1825; William Wells, bm.

McCord, John & Marey Runnolds, 12 March 1804; Nelson Robinett, bm.

McCoy, Charles & Delilah Gilreath, 4 Oct 1815; M. Scroggs, bm.

WILKES COUNTY MARRIAGES, 1778-1868

McCoy, George M. & Jane Redding, 3 Aug 1861; John Robins, bm; m by Alfred Warren, J. P.

McCoy, Patrick & Mary Pitman, 24 Sept 1784; Wm. Newberry, bm.

McCrary, Thomas & Nancey Murrah, 16 Dec 1796; Samuel Smith, bm.

McCrary, Wm & Jane Caudle, 12 Jan 1845; Wm. Wiles, bm.

McDaniel, Elisha & Milley Wheatley, 10 Oct 1820; Henry McDaniel, bm.

McDaniel, Elisha & Polly Wheatley, 2 Aug 1832; Joel Wadkins, bm.

McDaniel, George B. & Martha L. Redding, 6 Feb 1854; m 15 Feb 1854 by Z. B. Adams, D. D.

McDaniel, Henry & Charloty Herbin, 12 Jan 1805; James Sheppard, bm.

McDaniel, Henry & Harriet McNeil, 26 Sept 1856; James C. McNiel, bm; m 12 Oct 1856 by A. A. Whittington, J. P.

McDaniel, Henry Jr. & Elizabeth Adams, 24 Dec 1833; Wm. F. Adams, bm.

McDaniel, Henry & Melia M. Gaultney, 20 May 1866; J. P. Adams, bm.

McDaniel, Marshal & Elizabeth Love, 4 March 1811; F. W. Irion, bm.

McDaniel, son of Joseph McDaniel & Eliza E. Wellcoxson, daughter of Wm. C. Willcoxson, m 2 March 1868 by Wm. A. McNiel, J. P.

McDaniel, Thomas & Lewizey Kerry, 11 Oct 1854; W. R. Whittington, bm; m 12 Oct 1854 by A. A. Whittenton, J. P.

McDaniel, William Jr. & Milly Herbin, 19 Feb 1805; Wm. McDaniel, bm.

McDaniel, William Jr. & Amelia Martin, 15 Aug 1834; Richd. Parker, bm.

McEntire, Lewis & Nelly Sullivan, 8 Jan 1830; John Grasty, bm.

McEwen, Archd. & Polley Sharp, 12 June 1807; Thomas Mitchell, bm.

McEwen, Archabal & Letty Brown, 20 Sept 1813; James McEwen, bm.

McGee, Holland & Nancy Wright, 3 May 1831; William Triplet, bm.

McGee, James & Polley Crouch, 27 March 1800; John McGee, bm.

McGee, John & Nancy Dotson, 11 Aug 1800; Isaac Hagler, bm.

McGee, John & Betsy Smith, 2 Sept 1818; Samuel Millender, bm.

McGee, William & Sarah Lowe, 16 Oct 1794; John Johnson, bm.

McGinney, John & Flora Witherspoon, 29 Aug 1790; John Witherspoon, bm.

WILKES COUNTY MARRIAGES, 1778-1868

McGinnis, Ephraim & Susannah Swanson, 21 Nov 1859; m 21 Nov 1859 by Pickens Carlton, J. P.

McGinnis, Hugh & Frances L. Holte, 13 Feb 1850; Jas. H. Ferguson, bm.

McGinnis, John & Priscilla Walker, 14 Dec 1835; Robert Williams, bm.

McGlamry, George & Salley Yates, 31 Oct 1820; John Yates, bm.

McGlamry, David & Suanah Eller, 30 Oct 1823; consent from Peter Eller, and William Eller, stating that Suanah is over 15 years of age.

McGlemory, Jesse & Melissa Lenderman, 1 Jan 1849; Robt. H. Yates, bm.

McGlemory, E. M. & Selpha M. Eller, 4 Feb 1858; Harrison Church, bm.

McGlemory, George F. & Amanda J. Beshep, 17 Jan 1862; Leander Eller, bm; m by Wm. S. McNeil, J. P.

McGlemory, John, son of David & Susanah McGlemory & America Jane Byers, daughter of Polly Byers, m 25 Dec 1867 by Wm. A. McNiel, J. P.

McGrady, Andrew & Pheeby Jinnings, 9 Feb 182__; Lewis Shepherd, bm.

McGrady, Edmond & Sarah Porter, 5 Oct 1841; Walter Absher, bm.

McGrady, John & Polly Long, 24 Jan 1855; J. H. Adams, bm; m 25 Jan 1855 by L. Sebastian, J. P.

McGrady, Linville & Elender Hall, 29 Jan 1862; W. M. Caudill, bm.

McGrady, Patrick R. & Susanah Owens, 16 March 1849. (no bm).

McGrady, Peter & Polley Sparkmon, 7 April 1814; Wm. McGrady, bm.

McGuire, Anderson & Mary Eliza Stinnet, 20 Dec 1857; m 20 Dec 1857 by Byme P. Walsh, J. P.

McGuire, John & Amelia Vanoy, 27 ___ 1836.

McKay, John H. & Elizabeth Cass, 9 Nov 1850; John M. Lane, bm.

McKay, Samuel & Mary Martin, 25 Sept 1808; Robert Gordon, bm.

McKee, John & Nancy M. Church, 14 Oct 1841; Wm. H. McNiel Jr., bm.

McKinnie, Thomas & Tabitha Wood, 12 Oct 1807; John Adams, bm.

McKinsey, Alexr. & Ann Coffey, 28 Oct 1793; Cleavland Coffey, bm.

McKinzie, Kenneth & Betsey Witherspoon, 20 March 1794; Nebuzarah Coffey, bm.

WILKES COUNTY MARRIAGES, 1778-1868

McLain, Isaac D. & Hariet E. Perkins, 19 Feb 1867; D. C. Woodruff, bm.

McClain, David & Jane Wilcoxson, 28 Jan 1846; Samuel C. Wellborn, bm.

McLean, Duncan & Louiasy Holder, 25 Feb 1851; S. C. Wellborn, bm.

McLean, Rorn & W. J. Holder, 17 April 1852; S. C. Welborn, bm; m 18 April 1852 by S. C. Wellborn, J. P.

McMullin, John & Jean Dula, 28 Jan 1797; William Demoss, bm.

McNeil, G. B. & M. A. Vannoy, 4 April 1866; A. M. Vannoy, bm; m 12 April 1866 by Rev. Jas. McNeil.

McNeil, James & Mary Dancy, 2 Nov 1852; William Eller, bm; m 23 Nov 1852 by A. A. Whittenton, J. P.

McNeil, John C. & Rebecca Ferguson, m 21 Nov 1866 J. H. Brown, M. G.

McNeil, Joseph & Elisabeth Viars, 11 Nov 1824; John Montgomery, bm.

McNeil, Wm. S. & Polly Willcoxon, 23 Dec 1833; Daniel Willcoxon, bm.

McNile, Alfred & Francis M. Vannoy, 4 Nov 1844; John Eller, bm.

McNiel, Alfred & Sarah Ann Bullis, 24 Oct 1866; J. H. McNiel, bm; m 25 Oct 1866 by Wm. S. McNiel, J. P.

McNiel, Benj. & Elisebeth Lips, 28 Aug 1805; Abr. Kilbey, bm.

McNiel, Eli & Fanny Eller, 8 Feb 1839; George McNiel, bm.

McNiel, George & Susan Vannoy, 21 Nov 1822; Larkin McNiel, bm.

McNiel, George W. & Louisa Triplett, 29 Jan 1849; Martin McGlemry, bm.

McNiel, J. O. & S. A. Stunt, 5 Sept 1866; Geo. H. Brown, bm; m 6 Sept 1866 by Rev. Jas. McNeil.

McNiel, James & Fanny Dula, 17 Jan 1849; Martin Parsons, bm; m 18 Jan 1849 by Wm. Church.

McNiel, James H. & Susana McNiel, 4 Feb 1845; W. H. McNiel, bm.

McNiel, Jesse A. & Susannah A. Taylor, 4 March 1860; J. R. Dancy, bm; m 6 March 1860 by W. S. McNeil.

McNiel, Joel & Nancy Ball, 6 Jan 1836; Enoch McNiel; bm.

McNiel, John G. & Polly Nichols, 1 Feb 1860; J. P. W. Nicholls, bm; m 1 Feb 1860 by Wm. S. McNiel, J. P.

McNiel, Larkin & Nelley Ferguson, 2 Oct 1837; Daniel Bumgarner Jr., bm.

McNiel, Martin & Agness Norris, 19 March 1834; Joel McNiel, bm.

WILKES COUNTY MARRIAGES, 1778-1868

McNiel, Oliver & Delila Ellor, 4 Aug 1828; George McNeil, bm.

McNeil, Wm. & Martha E. Roberson, 30 Nov 1843; Alfred McNiel, bm.

McNiel, Wm. H. & Sally Kilby, 10 March 1843; Wm. Eller, bm.

McNiell, John & Rachel Eller, 19 Aug 1820; John Eller, bm.

McQuay, Morgan & Polly Case, 18 June 1816; Larkin Sheppard, bm.

McQuerry, John & Lucinda Kilbey, 21 Sept 1825; William Hart, bm.

McQuerry, James & Rachel Jinnings, 13 March 1826; Perry Judd, bm.

McSkelton, Major & Nancy Brown, 15 June 1827; John Brown, bm.

Mabary, Henry & Susanna Morgan, 5 March 1856.

Mabery, Alven & Nancy Ann Mahaffey, 16 June 1866; John W. Sturdivant, bm; m 16 June 1866 by J. F. Somers, J. P.

Mabery, Frederick & Rachel Barns, 27 Jan 1821; Randal Wilborn, bm.

Mabery, James & Marth Reddin, 6 Dec 1806; William Ridden, bm.

Mabery, James & Ann Marlow, 10 Feb 1838; Joseph Millsaps, bm.

Mabery, John & Nancy Hollas, 23 March 1854; John Jarvis, bm; m 26 March 1854 by Alfred Warren, J. P.

Mabery, Randol & Nancy Mitchel, 5 Oct 1839; Robert Mitchel, bm; m 8 Oct 1839 by Thomas Roberts, J. P.

Mabery, William & Mary Sale, 3 Oct 1839; Aaron Felts, bm.

Mabry, Howell & Malissa Marlow, 1 Jan 1842; John E. Gortney, bm.

Mabry, Randall & Gemima Cook, 27 Jan 1779; Abra. Cook, bm.

Maburey, James & Mahaley Hollis, 7 Feb 1843; Nathan Reding, bm.

MacCrary, Christopher & Polly Wiles, 4 Feb 1823; Iven(?) Abshire, bm.

MacCrary, Joseph & Sarah E. Cheek, 11 April 1802; William C. Byrd, bm.

Maderson, Lewis F. & Marcy Buckin, 14 Feb 1843; John L. Felts, bm.

Madison, Wiley B. & Matilda M. Sale, 23 Sept 1856; m 24 Sept 1856 by L. D. Swaim, Baptist minister.

Magee, A. W. & Anna Land, 13 Jan 1856; Thomas C. Carlton, bm; m 17 Jan 1856 by W. S. McGee, J. P.

Magee, David & Mary Cook, 23 March 1793; William Magee, bm.

Magee, Ralph & Christener Hagler, 5 March 1796; Isaac Hagler, bm.

WILKES COUNTY MARRIAGES, 1778-1868

Magee, Ralph & Ruth Davidson, 30 March 1802; James McGee, bm.

Magee, Ralph & Lucinda Livingston, 16 Sept 1822; Benjamin Howard, bm.

Mahafey, William & Lidey Myers, 36 Aug 1851; Isaac Money, bm; m 30 Aug 1851 by John Brown, J. P.

Mahaffey, John & Polly Johnson, 10 March 1836; David Gray, bm.

Mahaffy, John F., son of Thomas & Mary Mahaffy, & Sarah E. Stone, daughter of William & Rebecca Stone, m March 1868 by J. N. Haynes.

Mahaffey, Thos & Patsey Mahaffey, 13 Nov 1830; Samuel P. Smith, bm.

Mahaffey, William F. & Marthey Hendricks, 15 Oct 1856; Joseph Myers, Jr., bm; Richard Walker, wit; m 15 Oct 1856 by W. Day, J. P.

Mahaffey, William F. & Nancy Gregory, 31 Dec 1857; Cader Pruitt, bm.

Mahaffey, William M. & Emeline Childers, 21 Nov 1858; James Mahaffey, bm.

Mahaffey, Wm. R. & Candis Crouse, 17 Nov 1841; A. Porter, bm.

Main, Henry & Nancy Watters, 25 Oct 1831; Eaton Ball, bm.

Majors, John & Nancy Wright, 31 Oct 1782; John Wilson, bm.

Maltba, Thomas & Cinthy Land, 5 Sept 1838; Linsay Livingston, bm.

Maltba, Thomas E. & Elizabeth Ferguson, 27 April 1840; Charles Carlton, bm.

Maltbay, Peter & Elizabeth Livingston, 28 Feb 1822; Orril Livingston, bm.

Maltbey, William & Nancy Land, 30 May 1809; James Land, bm.

Mangum, Daniel & Elizabeth Harbin, 4 Nov 1815; John Sillivan, bm.

Manord, Larkin & Phebey Phillips, 18 Dec 1811; Henry Laurence, bm.

Manuel, George E. & Mary Hamby, m 29 Aug 1861 by Amos Church, J. P.

Maret, John & Betsey Kendol, 13 Nov 1792; Robert Shearer, bm.

Marten, Thomas & Marey Cunningham, 16 Jan 1804; Langston Cunningham, bm.

Marley, Benjn. W. & Frances Lowes (Lawes?), 26 March 1849; Masten Laws, bm.

Marley, John & Hannah Barns, 25 Nov 1805; Michael Swaim, bm.

WILKES COUNTY MARRIAGES, 1778-1868

Marley, John B. & Prudence Holder, 12 April 1837; Robt. L. Steele, bm.

Marley, John F. & Milley C. Oliver, 15 Nov 1855; Joseph Price, bm; m 15 Nov 1855 by Wm. H. Hubbard, J. P.

Marlour, Mark & Lowra Carter, 15 April 1784; Wm. Roberts, Wm. Jolley, bm.

Marlow, Albert & Casse A. Mullis, 22 Oct 1857; m 29 Oct 1857 by L. D. Swaim, Baptist minister.

Marlow, Benjamin & Rachel Swiem, 24 July 1812; Michael Swaim, bm.

Marlow, Beveda & Sarah Moore, 7 Feb 1844; James Marlow, bm.

Marlow, Elbert & Sely Cook, 3 Feb 1866; H. H. Hayes, bm; m 8 Feb 1866 by H. Hayes, J. P.

Marlow, Elom & Viney V. Williams, 7 Feb 1837; Jos. M. Mabery, bm.

Marlow, Hilley & Sinah Marlow, 15 Feb 1842; Phineas Marlow, bm.

Marlow, James & Peggy Davis, 2 April 1811; Mark Marlow, bm.

Marlow, James & Mary Marlow, 9 Feb 1815; Richard Cook, bm.

Marlow, James & Polly Gilreath, 30 July 1834; Jeremiah Gilreath, bm.

Marlow, James H. & Rebecca Law, 16 Nov 1852; Phineas Marlow, bm; m 19 Nov 1852 by A. Gilreath, J. P.

Marlow, James M. & Dolly E. Anderson, 17 Dec 1866; Wilbur J. Ball, bm; m 20 Dec 1866 by H. Hayes, J. P.

Marlow, Joel & Sarah Davis, 18 ___ 1822; Ephraim Cook, bm.

Marlow, John & Charlotte Vickus, 5 Sept 1832; Wm. W. Harden, bm.

Marlow, John & Polly Dishman, 5 Oct 1835; Jefferson Dishman, bm.

Marlow, Joseph & Martha Gilreath, 14 July 1829; Joel Marlow, bm.

Marlow, Melven & Rebecca Hays, 20 Jan 1862; Henry H. Hayse, bm; m 21 Jan 1862 by Wm. Tedder, Baptist minister.

Marlow, Thomas & Charity Mickleroey, 18 March 1822; Jeremiah Gilreath, bm.

Marlow, Thos & Ruth Becknall, 1 Feb 1825; Shadrach Stanley, bm.

Marlow, Wesley G. & Suphire Moore, 26 Sept 1866; W. M. Marlow, bm; m 29 Sept 1866 by H. Hayes, J. P.

Marsh, John & Nancy Baugus, 5 Aug 1828; Jesse Caudle, bm.

Marshall, Charles & Rachael Hawkins, 4 July 1838; David Gray, bm.

WILKES COUNTY MARRIAGES, 1778-1868

Marshall, William & Mary Martin, 6 Jan 1817; James Martin, bm.

Marstin, John & Elizabeth Head, 7 Jan 1822; Stephen Gentle, bm.

Marstin, Thomas & Oliff Rose, 27 July 1803; Uriah Parks, bm.

Martin, Alexander J. & Elizabeth Curry, 19 Nov 1838; John E. Martin, bm.

Martin, Ambrose & Rebecah Redding, 6 Nov 1809; William Redding, bm.

Martin, Augustus H. & S. V. Corpening, 8 May 1858; M. A. Parks, bm; m 11 May 1858 by Wm. Parks, J. P.

Martin, B. R. & Mary C. Johnson, 7 July 1866; E. M. Felts, bm; m 10 July 1866 by John Sale, J. P.

Martin, Benjamin & Fanney Martin, 13 Jan 1797; James Martin, bm.

Martin, Benjamin F. & Salley Rousseau, 27 June 1825; Robert Martin, bm.

Martin, Benjamin & Jane Lindsey, 25 May 1867; m 26 May 1867 by M. A. Parks, J. P.

Martin, Charles & Catharine Hoard, freed people, 23 March 1867; Daniel McGrady, bm.

Martin, Henery & Mary Sales, 21 Jan 1782; Wm. Reddin, bm.

Martin, Isaiah & Lucinda Bumgarner, 7 Dec 1833; N. Garland Lane, bm.

Martin, J. B. & S. E. Partette, 14 Jan 1867; S. T. Sale, bm; m 16 Jan 1867 by W. F. Adams, Baptist minister.

Martin, James & Elvira Bryan, 27 Aug 1806; Robert Martin, bm.

Martin, James & Amelia Anderson, 7 Oct 1817; Thos. A. Gordon, bm.

Martin, John E. & Martha J. Mastin, 27 Feb 1866; m 28 Feb 1866 by Rev. Wm. P. Chapel.

Martin, John & Susana Bunge, 2 Feb 1797; Thos Martin, bm.

Martin, John & Elizabeth Martin, 20 Oct 1800; Benjn. Martin, bm.

Martin, John & Amelia Jones, 10 Dec 1805; Robert Martin, bm.

Martin, John & Diana Martin, 17 July 1806; James Martin, bm.

Martin, John & Patsey Parkes, 14 Jan 1828; Thos Witherspoon, bm.

Martin, John Jr. & Sarah Sales, 19 Nov 1835; William Sale, bm.

Martin, John H. & Mary Jane Edwards, 3 Nov 1847.

Martin, Robart G. & Lucy Gilreath, 16 Dec 1815; Azel Sharpe, bm.

Martin, Robert Jr. & Fanney Alexander, 29 Jan 1834; John Martin, bm.

WILKES COUNTY MARRIAGES, 1778-1868

Martin, Rufus W. & June Hickerson, 16 April 1851; C. L. Cook, bm; m 30 April 1851 by W. R. Frier, Minister of St. Paul's Church, Wilkesboro.

Martin, Thos & Elisabeth Sale, 4 Sept 1810; Elias Sale, bm.

Martin, Thomas & Martha Perdue, 25 Sept 1838; William Redding, bm.

Martin, Turner & Jemmimah Hays, 18 Dec 1810; Hicks Combs, bm.

Martin, William Alberto & Martha Clalinda Nelson, 21 Oct 1830; James Stuart, bm.

Martin, William C. & Sarah Martin, 12 April 1824; Thos. Witherspoon, bm.

Martin, Zachariah & Rebecca Hubbard, 12 Nov 1783; Stephen Tribble, bm.

Marymore, Briant & Martha Ferguson, 18 Sept 1818; Smith Ferguson, bm.

Mason, Wm. & Cina Lunsford, 10 Jan 1831; James Chambers, bm.

Mason, Winsor & Rosanah Shoemaker, 7 May 1859; Albert Harden, bm; m 8 May 1859 by G. B. Parks.

Massey, James & Jrushe Day, 9 April 1855; William Massy, bm.

Massey, Permanus & Disey Dishman, 23 Sept 1842; Archabald Dishman, bm.

Massy, Isriel & Nancy Day, 9 April 1856; James Massey, bm.

Massy, Pinkney & Ludisi Ann Collens, 21 April 1863; Noah Tucker, bm; m 2 April 1863 by J. M. Gambill, J. P.

Massy, William & Mary A. Tolbert, 8 Feb 1851; James Massy, bm.

Mastin, Alexander & Martha Currey, 17 Sept 1849; James Perdue, bm.

Mastin, Benjamin & Malinda W. Danold, 19 Nov 1829; William Mastin.

Mastin, James & Harriett Joyner, 15 July 1840; Nathan Ward, bm.

Mastin, James F., son of Benj. & Malinda Mastin, & Virginia Martin, 13 Nov 1867, m 14 Nov 1867 by W. F. Adams, Baptist minister.

Mastin, Joseph H. & Martha Joyner, 13 Nov 1844; Obadiah Sprinkle, bm.

Mastin, Thomas T. & Caroline Jarvis, 2 Jan 1862; Joseph Coringder, bm; m 2 Jan 1862 by W. F. Adams, minister.

Mastin, W. J. & Nancy C. Edwards, 22 Nov 1865; W. F. Parkes, bm; m 23 Nov 1865 by J. M. Gambill, J. P.

Mastin, William E. & Manda M. Becknell, 15 March 1856.

WILKES COUNTY MARRIAGES, 1778-1868

Maston, Thomas A. & Sarah C. Maston, 25 Aug 1863; John Corthing, bm.

Matherly, Jefferson & Nancy Lipford, 25 Jan 1867; m 25 Jan 1867 by J. W. Church, J. P.

Matherly, William & Sally Stephens, 16 March 1805; Wilson Stephens, bm.

Mathis, Alexander & Filas Redding, 5 Feb 1854.

Mathis, James J. & Nancy Felts, 14 March 1848; Enoch S. Mathis, bm.

Mathis, Wiley & Nancy Brooks, 2 Jan 1815; McK. McCoy, J. Johnson, bm.

Mathis, Goodwin & Mary Walker, 14 June 1817; Jessee Walker, bm.

Matney, John & Cinthy Urp, 22 Sept 1846; Sanford Dula, bm.

Matthews, Ambrose & Mary Call, 16 Sept 1813; James Andrews, bm.

Matthews, James & Polly Chambers, 7 May 1807.

Matthews, James & Salley Clark, 29 Jan 1822; Ansel Matthews, bm.

Matthis, Aberham & Mary Curry, 5 March 1854; John Chambers, bm.

Matthis, John & Elisabeth Steward, 21 Oct 1824; Ansel Matthis, bm.

Maxwell, Tunis H. & Martha Wilcoxen, 26 Nov 1866; W. H. Norman, bm.

Mayberry, John & Susanah Sprinkle, 3 Sept 1830; Howell Barker, bm.

Maynard, James & Chaney Smith, 10 March 1808; William Maynard, bm.

Meadows, Harvey & ___, 4 Aug 1840; Daniel Meadows, bm.

Meadows, W. C. & Mary E. Price, 1 April 1867; Wm. L. Price, bm; m 3 April 1867 by James Kerley.

Mebry, Randolph & Senith Marlow, 9 Dec 1834; Thos Millsaps, bm.

Medder, John & Mary Combes, 26 Dec 1849; Welmouth Jarvis, bm.

Meguire, John & Elizabeth Field, 25 July 1818; William Field, bm.

Mehaffey, Moses & Susannah Kerley, 4 March 1820; Jas Mehaffey, bm.

Meriman, William D. & Lorana Page, 10 Dec 1818; Isaac Peasley, bm.

Merrow, John W. & Rody Stanbury, 14 April 1818; Wesley Reynolds, bm.

Meriman, Owen & Jane Colvard, 4 Nov 1834; David Gray, bm.

WILKES COUNTY MARRIAGES, 1778-1868

Messick, Elza & Lucy Gilliam, 5 Dec 1815; Leonard Messick, bm.

Messick, James J. & Mary A. Triplett, 20 Jan 1857; Thos. J. Gilreath, bm.

Messick, John Nelson & Salley Nicholson, 11 March 1814; Henry Brown, bm.

Messick, Wily & Malinda Bround, 29 July 1825; Eliza Messick, bm.

Meys, Milton & Marthey Michell, 2 Oct 1858; Richard Prescott, bm.

Michael, Rily & Mary Watson, 5 March 1841; m 5 March 1841 by Wm. Church.

Micheal, Jacob & Salvy Yeats, 10 July 1816; John Yeats, bm.

Michel, Henry & Mary Smith, 18 Aug 1856; Wesly Smith, bm; m 18 Aug 1856 by A. A. Whittenton, J. P.

Michel, James M. & Nancy A. Talor, 2 Sept 1860; by A. A. Whittenton, J. P.

Michel, Joseph W. & Susanna King, m 26 June 1864 by Wm. Parks, J. P.

Mikel, David Jr. & Minerva Swiney, 13 Jan 1831; Shadrach Minton, bm.

Mikel, John & Louisa Bethany Minton, 19 Dec 1825; John J. Miller, bm.

Milam, Adam & Matilda Foster, 20 March 1848; Wm. Eller, bm.

Milam, Benjamin & Milly Parsons, 14 Feb 1831; Abner Trible, bm.

Milam, John W. & Larraw A. Church, 3 May 1865.

Milam, Thomas C. & Eveline Minton, 16 Jan 1856; Samuel Curtice, bm; m 17 Jan 1856 by Amos Church, J. P.

Milam, William C. & Tabitha Bunton, 10 April 1855; John S. Dockrey, bm; m 11 April 1855 by A. M. Foster, J. P.

Milam, William J. & Martha Minton, 21 April 1856; m 24 April 1856 by G. Sumerlin, J. P.

Miles, John & Polly Adams, 12 Nov 183; Elze Johnson, bm.

Miles, Smith & Elizabeth Simmons, 14 Aug 1865; Alfred Elledge, bm.

Miles, William H. & Martha Blackburn, 25 Oct 1866; J. A. Miles, bm.

Milliner, Samuel & Patsy Nolen, 28 Sept 1806; Wm. Nolen, bm.

Miller, A. B. & Mary McNiel, 27 Jan 1859; m 27 Jan 1859 by Elder Jas. McNiel.

Miller, Alexander & Sarah E. Call, 7 June 1855; Joshua Johnston, bm; m 7 June 1855 by S. P. Smith, minister.

WILKES COUNTY MARRIAGES, 1778-1868

Miller, Christian & Phebea Brown, 13 Dec 1844; Abslum Bare, bm.

Miller, David & Mary Eller, 12 March 1842; Eli McNiel, bm.

Miller, David S. & Mary C. Forester, 20 Dec 1854; A. C. Allen, bm.

Miller, Francis & Delilah Hampton, 31 Oct 1827; Jsaiah Hampton, Jno. B. Crysel, bm.

Miller, H. C. & Mary Jane Bennet, 24 Dec 1857; m by Jas. McNiel, M. G.

Miller, H. Nelson & Elizabeth C. Vannoy, 18 March 1835; J. H. Perkins, bm.

Miller, Thomas & Holloy McNiel, 12 Nov 1803; Jas. McNiel, bm.

Miller, Henry Jr. & Mary A. Nicholds, 9 Nov 1835; Jeremiah Lane, bm.

Miller, Henry H. & Martha Lewis, 24 July 1866; L. J. Hendrix, bm; m 25 July 1866 by J. K. Hendrix, J. P.

Miller, Henry Harrison & Nicey Land, 10 Oct 1837; John Hagler, bm; m 10 Oct 1837 by Wm. Church.

Miller, Jerry & Jemima Bone, 7 Dec 1836; Danel Bone, bm.

Miller, Jesse & Elizabeth Proffet, 18 Nov 1830; John Boman, bm.

Miller, John & Polly Triplett, 8 Oct 1833; Enoch McNiel, bm.

Miller, John & Elizy Tugman, 24 March 1866; m 24 March 1866 by Larkin Pipes, M. G.

Miller, John J. & Margaret Hunt, 25 Jan 1824; Ambrose Foster, bm.

Miller, Joseph & Nancy Bingham, 6 July 1807; Henry Miller, bm.

Miller, Leonard & Elizabeth Church, 30 Dec 1828; Danl. Bumgarner, bm.

Miller, Thos. C. & Lizzie Land, m 9 Sept 1866 by J. K. Hendrix, J. P.

Miller, William & Judith Edwards, 4 Aug 1807; James Allison, bm.

Mills, Burton J. & Louisa Young, 13 Nov 1858; H. C. Mills, bm; m 19 Dec 1858 by B. F. Johnson, J. P.

Mills, Hardy & Frances Carpenter, 3 Dec 1785; Dickson Nailer, bm.

Mills, Hur & Margaret Tucker, 19 May 1835; David Tucker, bm.

Mills, John & Alley Coffey, 19 March 1804; James Whitesides, bm.

Mills, William & Salley Strutton, 30 June 1802; Hezekiah Strutton, bm.

Millsaps, J. C. & Jane Hendren, 21 Jan 1864; John W. Smith, bm.

WILKES COUNTY MARRIAGES, 1778-1868

Millsaps, Litten & Margaret Quen, 4 Feb 1834; Thomas Millsaps, bm.

Millsaps, Thomas & Mary Harrison(?), 24 Jan 1785; Joseph Harrison, bm.

Milton, James & Anny Foster, 22 June 1859; Wm. T. Farguson(?), bm.

Milton, Zachariah & Elizabeth Bruce, 2 Dec 1807; David A. Bruce, bm.

Milum, Jonathan & Martha Crane, 7 May 1864; Henry C. Eller, bm; m 15 May 1864 by J. W. Church.

Milum, William & Polley Cruise, 28 Dec 1803; Mordaca Cruise, 28 Dec 1803; Mordaca Cruse, bm.

Minish, Lewis & Mary Dun, 11 April 1847; George Felts, bm.

Minish, Wm. W. & Julyann Bagly, 24 Dec 1856; Moses Walls, bm.

Minks, Hiram T. & Nancy Adams, 23 Dec 1828; Thomas J. Stokes, bm.

Minten, Joel & Rachal Church, 5 May 1865.

Minting, Hugh & Elizabeth Joines, 26 Jan 1849; Joseph A. Brown, bm; m by Saml Walsh, J. P.

Minting, Hugh & Malaan Byers, 6 Aug 1858; William Sanders, bm; m 26 Nov 1858 by G. Sumerlin, J. P.

Minting, John & Emaline Keeton, 16 July 1849; William Minting, bm; m by Saml Walsh, J. P.

Minting, William & Ruthy Ruton, 9 Oct 1849; Thomas B. Jones, bm.

Minton, Abram & Phebe C. Philips, 27 June 1859; James Dudley, bm; m 30 June 1859 by Wm. A. Phillips.

Minton, Alfred & Bethena Eller, 26 Oct 1848; Thomas H. Foster, bm.

Minton, Caleb & Elizabeth Green, 10 Jan 1839; Jesse Minton, bm.

Minton, George & Rebeckea Curch, 24 Nov 1814; Jno. Hickerson, bm.

Minton, Hugh & Elizabeth Martin, 10 July 1834; James Minton Jr., bm.

Minton, Hugh & Mary Blackburn, 24 Feb 1858; m 25 Feb 1858 by Jas. McNeill, mg.

Minton, James & Ireney Brog, 4 March 1833; Wm. Minton, bm.

Minton, Jesse & Violett Adams, 13 Sept 1806; John Minton, bm.

Minton, Jesse & Mary Minton, 22 Oct 1838; Joseph W. Calloway, bm.

Minton, Jesse L. & Mira Curtis, 13 Nov 1846; Madison Minton, bm.

WILKES COUNTY MARRIAGES, 1778-1868

Minton, Jesse W. & Alley A. Church, 13 March 1856; Calvin Church, bm.

Minton, Lovlace & Susan Sumerlin, 14 Nov 1835; Abner Trible, bm.

Minton, Madison & Milly Minton, 26 Dec 1848; Thomas Green, bm.

Minton, Purvis & America Bishop, 26 Sept 1865; Leander Eller, bm; m 28 Sept 1865 by Rev. Jas McNeil.

Minton, Thos C. & Sarah Ann Nichells, 10 April 1866; J. W. Nicholls, bm; m 10 April 1866 by Rev. Jas. McNeil.

Minton, William & Hannah Summerlin, 10 Oct 1820; Abner Trible, bm.

Minton, W. T. & M. A. Johnson, 31 Dec 1865; J. L. Faw, bm; m 31 Dec 1865 by Rev. Jas. McNeil.

Minton, Winborn & Lemira Church, 23 Feb 1843; Caleb Minton, bm; m by Saml Walsh, J. P.

Mirick, Thomas & Frances Church, 28 Aug 1822; Moses Swaim, bm.

Mires, Joseph & Lidda Wallace, 29 Oct 1810; Stephen Matthews, bm.

Misner, John & Molly Webster, 23 Feb 1782; John Cleveland, bm; Nathan Coffee, wit.

Mitchel, David & Cary Webb, 31 July 1851; Nimrod Lewis, bm; m 31 July 1851 by Saml. Walsh, J. P.

Mitchel, Gabriel & Marthey Mabary, 28 Feb 1855; John Mabery, bm; m 6 March 1855 by L. J. Bicknell, J. P.

Mitchel, James & Catherine Sidney Deer, 9 Jan 1823; William Deer, bm.

Mitchel, Moses F. & Fanney S. Jarvis, 20 Jan 1867; E. F. Roberts, bm; m 24 Jan 1867 by J. F. Somers, J. P.

Mitchel, William & Tabitha Dyer, 6 Nov 1801; Elijah Dyer, bm.

Mitchel, William & Elizabeth Stonepheer, 9 March 1818; Lewis Triplett, bm.

Mitchell, Anderson & Lottey Brown, 2 April 1831; Jesse Ferguson, bm.

Mitchell, Asa & Nancy Hall, 4 April 1811; Henry Kilby, bm.

Mitchell, Edmund J. & Sally Mabery, 8 March 1842; Robert Mitchell, bm.

Mitchell, Elijah & Marther Eller, 8 Sept 1823; Gipson Adams, bm.

Mitchell, Henry & Martha Bentley, 5 Aug 1828; James Bentley, bm.

Mitchell, James & Elizabeth Hatton, 20 Dec 1827; Jayson R. Laws, bm.

Mitchell, Joseph W. & Susanna King, 25 July 1864; W. W. White, bm.

WILKES COUNTY MARRIAGES, 1778-1868

Mitchell, James M. & Nancy A. Talor, 2 Sept 1860; Enoch Staly, bm.

Mitchell, Jonathan & Gille Watson, 3 May 1803; Reuben Hamby, bm.

Mitchell, Joshua & Elizabeth Hambrick, 26 Aug 1778; Spencer Humphries, Thomas Hambrick, bm.

Mitchell, Joshua & Rebeca Motherly, 8 Aug 1805; John Motherly, bm.

Mitchell, Matison & Elizabeth Gold, 10 Feb 1848; Wriley Green, bm.

Mitchell, Merry & Sally Allman, (no date, during admn. of Gov. William R. Davie); Joshua Mitchell, bm.

Mitchell, Moses & Dilley Geer, 30 Dec 1800; William Mitchell, bm.

Mitchell, Moses & Elizabeth Grant, 3 Aug 1801; James Jarvis, bm.

Mitchell, Thos Jr. & Charity Tucker, 23 Oct 1827; Thomas W. Mitchell, bm.

Mitchell, Thomas W. & Lenora Gwyn, 5 June 1817; M. Thurmond, bm.

Mitchell, William Junr. & Sarah Hayes, 30 Oct 1798; Willm. Mitchell, bm.

Mize, John & Sary Keton, 28 April 1808; John Keton, bm.

Mize, William & Nancy Longbottom, 24 June 1817; William Davis, bm.

Mock, James A. & Jane A. Allen, 3 Oct 1860; m 3 Oct 1860 by S. J. Jinnings, J. P.

Montgomery, Hugh & Lina Johnson, 11 Sept 1826; George Horn, bm.

Montgomery, John & Nancey Curtiss, 24 Feb 1825; Jesse Guilbert (Gilbert), bm.

Montgomery, Samuel & Franky Swanson, 2 March 1811; William Swanson, bm.

Mony, Isaac & Lucind Myars, 6 March 1842; Thomas Myers, bm.

Mony, Martin & Mary Colemon, 15 Feb 1852, John Chambers, bm; m 15 Feb 1852 by L. J. Bicknell, J. P.

Mony, Moses & Nancy Ball, 22 Jan 1851; John Chambers, bm.

Moody, Benjamin & Elizabeth Lansdown, 9 Jan 1803; Reuben Landsdown, bm.

Mooney, Harvin & Millee Land, 19 Jan 1830; Silas Cox, bm.

Mooney, Wm & Susana Hunt, 9 Dec 1795; John Walker, bm.

Mooney, Wm & Abigail Medlock, 7 Oct 1855; Thomas Andrews, bm; m 5 Oct 1855 by Pickens Carlton, J. P.

WILKES COUNTY MARRIAGES, 1778-1868

Moore, Alexander & Darinda Ball, 27 Feb 1861; m 28 Feb 1861 by William Tedder, Baptist minister.

Moore, Anderson & Susanah Dishmon, 28 May 1857; m 31 May 1857 by Israel Hollar, Baptist minister.

Moore, James & Susanna Epperson, 12 Sept 1788; David Elston, bm.

Moore, James & Kisah Hayse, 19 Feb 1847; Wilson Moore, bm.

Moore, Jesse & ___, 16 July 1807; Thos Clark, bm.

Moore, Jesse & Judy Price, 1 Dec 1824; Jacob Estep, bm.

Moore, Wm & Rachel Ferguson, 6 Feb 1815; Isom Felts, bm.

Moore, Wm. F. & Mary Baugess, 2 Sept 1841; Vinsent Baugess, bm.

More, James & ___, 25 July 1792; John Goodrich(?), bm.

More, James & Mary Stanley, 29 May 1817; Jacob Estep, bm.

More, Robin & Sophy Anderson, 10 Aug 1822; Starling More, bm.

More, Wilson & Mary Hayse, 19 March 1844; Jacob Estep, bm.

Moreland, William & Rosanah Curtis, ___ July 1832; Owen Moremon(?), bm.

Morgan, Charles & Charee Morgain, 21 Jan 1780; Isaac Morgan, bm.

Morgan, Ezekiel & Kisiah Norman, 1 May 1817; Asa Rash, bm.

Morgan, James & Martha Martin, 22 March 1815; Joshua Morgan, bm.

Morgan, John & Polley Brock, 5 Feb 1818; Isham Hubbard, bm.

Morgan, Jos. & Sarah Rash, 21 Feb 1793; William Rash, bm.

Morgan, Joseph & Ruth Cass, 10 May 1819; Ezekiel Cass, bm.

Morgan, Joshua & Mary Adams, 4 Oct 1810; John Adams, bm.

Morgan, Lenard & Mary Low, 11 July 1822; John Morgan, bm.

Morgan, Lewis & Patsey Adams, 16 Oct 1817; Joshua Morgan, bm.

Morgan, Mark & Jincy Adams, 29 May 1830; Isaac Adams, bm.

Morgan, Theophilus & Polly Fitchpatrick, 20 Jan 1834; Aquilla Williams, bm.

Morgan, William & Rebecka Wellborn, 20 July 1814; J. W. Gordon, bm.

Morgan, Wm. W. & Elizabeth Moore, 3 Nov 1818; Moses Cass, bm.

Morgin, Allen & Jane Waits, 31 July 1820; Thomas Morgin, bm.

Morris, George & Sarah Coleson, 17 Jan 1782; Adoniram Allen, bm.

Morris, James & Amanda Adams, 24 Sept 1847; Thos. Morris, bm.

Morris, John & Mary Hicks, 17 Feb 1816; Ansil Matthews, bm.

WILKES COUNTY MARRIAGES, 1778-1868

Morris, Joseph & Rachel Waller, 20 Dec 1819; John Martin(?), bm.

Morris, Wm. M. & Matilda Triplett, 23 Oct 1865; John Nooe, bm; m 26 Oct 1865 by T. L. Triplett, minister.

Morrison, Archabald & Darcus Kerby, 16 July 1831; Riley Curbey, bm.

Morrow, John & Polley Hank, 22 May 1827; Leonard Bumgarner, bm.

Mott, Jas. J. & Caroline T. Hendrix, 8 July 1856; C. M. Suddeth, bm.

Moxley, Alfred & Polly Caudle, 28 July 1832; Ralph Holbrook, bm.

Mulles, Hillery & Mary Mitsteade, 8 Jan 1835; Solomon Chapman, bm.

Mulles, John & Darlett Stanley, 22 Feb 1811; Wm. Hendron, bm.

Mullies, William & Rebeck Nickelson, 20 Aug 1850; Abel Reed, bm.

Mullins, Demarkes & Sary Heret, 16 Dec 1815; William Hagler, bm.

Mullis, Andrew & Patsey Combs, 12 July 1832; Nelson Anderson, bm.

Mullis, Geo. P. & Sary M. Cass, 16 Dec 1854; Samuel J. Cass, bm.

Mullis, James & Nancy Chambers, 30 Jan 1817; John Mullis, bm.

Mundy, Wm & Polley Baker, 8 Jan 1823; Benjamin Mundy, bm.

Murah, Fedrick & ___ Day, 27 Aug 1794; Nicholas Day, bm.

Murphey, Timothy & Kessiah Baugus, 16 June 1825; Thomas Grimsley, bm.

Murphy, Eli & Mary Mitchel, 29 May 1818; Thomas Barns, bm.

Murrell, Robert M. & Rachel Loving, 22 Nov 1827; George Taylor, bm.

Murrah, Wm & Elizabeth Crider, 17 Nov 1794; Ambrose Holt, bm.

Myers, Andrew Jackson & Barbery A. D. Jarvis, 7 Dec 1845; John Myers, bm.

Myers, John & Clarey Howard, 24 Sept 1839; Thomas Myers, bm; m 26 Sept 1839 by Thomas Roberts, J. P.

Myers, John W., son of A. E. & Eliz. Myers, & Sarah A. Staley, daughter of Jacob & Sernettie Staley, m 15 Sept 1867 by N. F. Myers, J. P.

Myers, Joseph & Sarah Low, 12 Jan 1783; Wm Carr, bm.

Myers, Thomas & Marget Cury, 27 Sept 1842; John Myers, bm.

Nailer, Dickson & Mary Carpenter, 28 June 1785; Stephen Carpenter, bm.

WILKES COUNTY MARRIAGES, 1778-1868

Nance, B. A. & Dicey Anderson, 23 Dec 1865; Wm. R. Queen, bm; m 28 Dec 1865 by H. Hayes, J. P.

Nance, Elis & Martha Smithy, m 15 Feb 1854 by W. W. Wright, J. P.

Nance, J. Y. & Mary Ball, 9 Nov 1865; Wm. R. Queen, bm; m 16 Nov 1865 by H. Hayes, J. P.

Nance, John & Gincy Combs, 24 Sept 1822; Joseph James, bm.

Nance, Vincent & Roxana Dilingham, m 2 Dec 1858 by H. Hayes, J. P.

Nance, William & Sally Parker, 15 Dec 1823; William Combs, bm.

Napper, Hughs & Gemima Roberts, 7 Jan 1803; Richard Roberts, bm.

Nawl, John & Sarah Gambil, 21 March 1785; Jas. Gambill, bm.

Neal, Q. F. & S. A. Rousseau, 21 March 1848; L. B. Carmichael, H. T. Dyer, bm.

Nelson, Hugh & Sally Day, (no date, during admn. of Gov. James Turner); Hugh Day, bm.

Nelson, Wm. A. & Sarah Simmons, 11 May 1861; H. M. Bumgarner, bm; m by Wm. S. McNeil, J. P.

Nelson, Robert & Matilda Campbell, 23 Dec 1831; William Wells, bm.

Nelson, Thos & Jane Robins, 19 Aug 1827; Edward Day, bm.

Nelson, William & Missouri Simmons, 10 Jan 1856; Jesse Pipes, bm; m 11 Jan 1856 by G. W. Hendrix, J. P.

Newbery, Wm & Nanney Bond, 10 Feb 1783; John Smith, bm.

Nichols, Abraham & Catharine Eller, 13 Jan 1835; Elijah Nicholds, bm.

Nicholas, John & Elizabeth Bishop, 27 Sept 1828; Jesse Laws, bm.

Nicholds, William & Elizabeth Holdaway, 19 Dec 1807; Jerema Chrisel, bm.

Nicholls, Abram & Nancey E. Bishop, 11 April 1866; Adam Staley, bm; 12 April 1866 by Rev. Jas. McNiel.

Nicholls, Elija & Margarett Bullison, 21 Jan 1820; John Nicholls, bm.

Nicholls, Elijah & Sarah Ann Nicholds, 29 Dec 1846; Wm W. Roberson, bm.

Nicholls, Henry H. & Matilda Minton, 31 Jan 1866; Wm. Edmisten, bm.

Nicholls, James B. & Mary A. McKee, 26 Jan 1860; James Nicholls, bm; m by Wm. S. McNeil.

Nicholls, Jno. & Elizabeth Nicholls, 19 April 1849; Absalom Bullis, bm.

WILKES COUNTY MARRIAGES, 1778-1868

Nicholls, John & Clarissa Harlow Bishop, m 7 Dec 1855 by William Church.

Nicholls, Jos. W. & Amelia Dancy, 9 June 1861; J. R. Dancy, bm.

Nicholls, Peter H. & Martha C. Church, 5 Feb 1867; W. W. Roberson, bm; m 7 Feb 1867 by Rev. Jas. McNiel.

Nichols, John & Rebecca Millum, 9 April 1839; Joseph Nicholls, bm.

Nichols, Joseph & Nancy Bullis, 17 Aug 1824; John Bullis, bm.

Nichols, Wm. B. & Cintha E. Roberson, 8 Dec 1858; m 8 Dec 1858 by Elder Jas. McNiel.

Nicholson, James & Susannah Sale, 20 June 1816; Beverly Coleman, bm.

Nicholson, Lazarus & Phoebe Coleman, 11 March 1809; Beverly Coleman, bm.

Nicholson, Wm. & Jinsey Sale, 26 Feb 1820; Jas. Cass, bm.

Nicholson, Wm. & Patsey Sale, 25 Jan 1823; Wiley Pilkinton, bm.

Nickols, John & Mary Yates, 12 July 1813; Wm. Lambert, Jno Finley, bm.

Nickelson, Joseph & Rebeckah Young, 20 Jan 1801; Samuel Nickelson, bm.

Nickelson, Martin & Elisebeth Nickelson, 25 Dec 1841; William Nickelson, bm.

Nickelson, William & Delphey Speakes, 25 May 1838; William Nickelson, bm.

Nickolds, Joseph E., son of Abram & Catherine Nickolds, & Maria Sumlin, daughter of Golris(?) Church, m 5 Feb 1868 by Wm. A. McNiel, J. P.

Noble, James & Tobatah Pardue, 29 Aug 1808; Beavel Pardue, bm.

Nooe, John & S. M. Vannoy, m 4 July 1857 by S. P. Smith.

Noland, William R. & Judy Allen, 27 July 1805; James Patton, bm.

Noling, Philip & Milley Hall, 21 Oct 1806; John Ferguson, bm.

Norman, Amos & Elisebeth Mabery, 19 Oct 1859; G. B. Parks, bm; m 20 Oct 1859 by G. B. Parks.

Norman, Clemans & Nancy Norman, 6 Aug 1854; James McCann, bm; m 6 Aug 1854 by Ansel Parks.

Norman, Early J. & Lucindy Wilborn, 28 Jan 1855; Lee Davis Welborn, bm.

Norman, Eli & Clarissa Lee, 23 Dec 1849; William Harris, bm.

Norman, Elijah & Rachale Bra___, 24 Oct 1850; Elisha Coleman, bm.

WILKES COUNTY MARRIAGES, 1778-1868

Norman, George & Rachel McBride, 7 March 1818; Jesse Baker, bm.

Norman, Isaac & Nancy Morgan, 16 Sept 1809; James Morgan, bm.

Norman, James L. & Mary Colemon, 15 Feb 1849; Jessee Ceeter, bm.

Norman, Levi & Mary E. Philips, 17 Aug 1854; John B. Philips, bm.

Norman, Thomas & Rhoda Grier, 10 Jan 1786; Isaac Norman, bm.

Norman, Thomas & Ruth Morgan, 2 Nov 1821; John Coleman, bm.

Norman, Wm. M. & Mary Carter, 11 Dec 1866; N. J. Walls, bm.

Norman, Wilson & Roxy Carter, 21 Aug 1837; Wilson Luffman, bm.

Norris, David & Matilda Proffet, 23 Sept 1843; Linvil Land, bm.

Norris, Elihu & Nancy Secres, 20 Feb 1827; W. Calphin Welsh, bm.

Norris, Ephraim & Mary Murphy, 7 April 1792; Thomas Cottrel, bm.

Norris, Jesse F. & Selena Triplett, m 23 Feb 1856; by Saml Walsh, J. P.

Norris, Jessee & Charlotte Holeman, 30 Aug 1830; Wm. Brown, bm.

Norris, John & Patsy Parsons, 8 ___ 1813; A. C. Adie, bm.

Norris, Joseph & Milly Elledge, 24 Feb 1825; John Norris, bm.

Norris, William & Hanah Case, 8 June 1802; William Allison, bm.

Northern, William & Polley Holeman, 29 Dec 1802; John Hodge, bm.

Northern, John & Salley Kindol, 19 Dec 1821; Phillip Walsh, bm.

Northern, Thomas & Lucinda Foster, 2 June 1825; Joseph D. Jones, bm.

Nothern, Edmd. & Ellender Roberts, 18 Aug 1793; John Roberts, bm.

Nothern, Solomon & Polley Church, 24 Dec 1793; Joseph Farguson, bm.

Nuberry, Thomas & Rebeckah Jones, 1 Jan 1780; James Jones, bm.

Oakley, James & Mary Inscore, 14 Nov 1852; m 14 Nov 1852 by Con. Gray, J. P.

Oglesby, Micajah & Mary Wilborn, 21 May 1840; S. Chaply Wellborn, bm.

Oliver, George & Caroline Sales, 13 Dec 1851; Alexander Church, bm; m 14 Dec 1851 by Const. Gray, J. P.

Oliver, Jesse & Amanda Spencer, 7 May 1825; Allen Parks, bm.

Oliver, Wm & Jane E. Devenport, 24 Jan 1844; James Marsh, bm.

Olliver, William & Jane Spencer, 6 May 1830; Elisha Petty, bm.

WILKES COUNTY MARRIAGES, 1778-1868

Olvey, Henrey & Nancey Parkes, 21 Jan 1845; Jacob Delinger, bm.

Olvey, John & Lucy Sale, 28 Feb 1807; Fielder Olvey, bm.

ONeil, Timothy & ___, 27 Sept 1793; Ambrous Powell, bm.

O Rielly, James C. & Polly Gordon, 22 March 1805; Nathl. Gordon, bm.

Orr, John & Mary Laws, 25 Aug 1824; Larkin Jones, bm.

Osbern, Ephraim & Sucky Abshire, 8 Feb 1832; David Osbern, bm.

Osbern, Joseph & Sally Talor, 25 April 1822; Jesse Harwood, bm.

Osborn--see also Ausbon

Osburn, David & Cintha Mosely, 6 Sept 1827; Job Lowder, bm.

Owen, Archbel & Nancy Judd, 22 Dec 1810; Johnson Owen, bm.

Owen, Barnet & Elizabeth Wooten, 6 June 1834; Abner Wooten, bm.

Owen, David & Winifred Mullens, 16 Dec 1780; John Robins, bm.

Owen, David & Nancy Lowe, 4 Aug 1800; Isaac Lowe, bm.

Owen, George F. & ___, 6 March 1854; John Jinnings, bm.

Owen, Solaman & Margret Adams, m 9 Dec 1860 by H. H. Dent, J. P.

Owen, William & Rachael Padget, 20 Oct 1793; Thomas Cox, bm.

Owens, George & Polly Ginnings, 29 Oct 1832; Martin Owens, bm.

Owens, George W. & July Ann Cheeks, 25 June 1853; John G. Owens, bm; m 26 June 1853 by P. R. McGrady, J. P.

Owens, James S. & Leaner L. Wyatt, 2 April 1867; R. P. McGrady, bm.

Owens, John & Rebekah Linch, 5 Oct 1797; James Mullins, bm.

Owens, John & Mary Vanoy, 2 Nov 1815; Enock Vanoy, bm.

Owens, John Jr. & Pheba Jinnings, 10 March 1835; Martin Owens, bm.

Owens, John C. & Susanna Winkler, m 16 Aug 1860 by H. Hutchison, J. P.

Owens, Levi & Saline Grimsley, 28 Oct 1866; J. M. Grimsley, bm; m 29 Oct 1866 by H. C. Sebastian, J. P.

Owens, Martin & Susannah Ginnings, 29 Oct 1832; George Owens, bm.

Owens, Richd. & Rachel Montgomery, 13 Dec 1795; Jno. Dobson, bm.

Owens, Solomon & Suana Bowlin, 6 April 1818; Arch. Owen, bm.

Owens, Solomon & Suana Adams, 18 Sept 1823; Henry Hays, bm.

WILKES COUNTY MARRIAGES, 1778-1868

Owens, William & Sally Dunkin, 5 April 1811; James Bently, bm.

Owens, Wm. A. & Matilda Walker, 21 Feb 1860; m 22 Feb 1860 by Wm. Hall, minister.

Owens, Wm. H. H. & Jenny Church, m 15 Jan 1860 by P. R. McGrady, J. P.

Owens, Zacariah T. & Nancy M. Shepard, 25 Dec 1865; Larkin Owens, bm; m by Nachaniel Church, minister.

Padgett, Wm. R. & Nancy Liviston, 8 Dec 1812; Jno. H. Petty, bm.

Paine, Henry & Elizabeth Barnes, 15 Oct 1833; John Barnes, bm.

Palmer, W. & Elizabeth Greer, 14 March 1853; Isaac S. Call, bm; m 13 April 1853 by Wm. H. Hubbard, J. P.

Palmerly, John & Rebecca Cross, 1 Dec 1785; Wm. Spicer, bm.

Pardew, A. J. & Martha E. Lewis, 1 Jan 1866; J. F. Salmons, bm.

Pardew, Branly M. & P. E. Pagit, 19 Dec 1843; Joel Wadkins, bm.

Pardew, E. M. & Dovey Baker, 23 Dec 1865; m 26 Dec 1865 by J. N. Haynes, J. P.

Pardew, J. L. & Martha L. Byrd, 10 Nov 1865; W. Childers, bm; m 15 Nov 1865 by W. F. Adams, Baptist minister.

Pardew, John A. & Evline Darnel, 28 Sept 1853; James Darnal, bm; m 29 Sept 1853 by Wm. Burcham, J. P.

Pardew, Leander & Jain McBride, 24 May 1856; Joel M. Pardew, bm.

Pardew, Thomas & Matilda Martin, 23 Oct 1853; Chatman Lewis, bm.

Pardiew, William & Luzena Osborne, 30 July 1831; Wm. M. Hicks, bm.

Pardue, Bevelly & Jinsey Day, 4 Dec 1839; Chapman Lewis, bm.

Pardue, J. F. & Lizbeth Poter, 23 Jan 1867; J. F. Pardue and Elizebeth Porter, m 24 Jan 1867 by J. N. Haynes.

Pardue, James & Malinda Stout, 4 Jan 1831.

Pardue, James & Martha Pardue, 22 Aug 1867; James Sale, bm; m 22 Aug 1867 by John Sale, J. P.

Pardue, John A. & Amma Darnall, 1 Nov 1847.

Pardue, Thos & Nancy Marsten, 2 Feb 1826; James Pardue, bm.

Pardue, John & Mary Tucker, 4 Nov 182_; Wm Pardue, bm.

Pardue, William & Adaline Hemrick, 17 Aug 1859; Benjamin Walker, bm.

Parker, Alexander & Sarah Hayes, 27 Sept 1855; Ambrose Johnson, bm; m 28 Sept 1855 by W. W. Wright, J. P.

Parker, Bezel & Sarah Tedder, 2 Oct 1828; Reuben Stanley, bm.

WILKES COUNTY MARRIAGES, 1778-1868

Parker, David & Charity Combs, 10 June 1805; Francis Barnard, Esqr., bm.

Parker, G. L. & Mary A. Barnett, 22 Dec 1866; Lafayette Hampton, bm; m 24 Dec 1866 by G. W. Hayes, J. P.

Parker, George & Rebeca Wilson, 13 Dec 1854; Micager Lewis, bm.

Parker, James & Jammey Roberts, 26 Aug 1847; Howard Walker, bm.

Parker, John & Franky Parker, (no date, during admn. of Gov. Benj. Williams); Jess Greenstreet(?), bm.

Parker, John & Elizabeth Carrel, 9 Jan 1793; Isaac Walker, James Carrel, bm.

Parker, Martin & Jane Hatten, 22 March 1836; Joseph Standly, bm.

Parker, R. H. & Mary S. Hendren, 24 Nov 1865; J. W. Moore, bm; m 26 Nov 1865 by Rev. Wm. J. Chapel.

Parker, R. L. & Sarah Roberson, 21 Nov 1866; G. H. Brown, bm.

Parker, Richard & Anny Stanely, 15 Oct 1805; Samuel Anderson, bm.

Parker, Richard & Susannah Smoot, 17 March 1807; Shadrach Stanley, bm.

Parker, Samuel S. & Elizabeth Call, 10 Dec 1859; m 10 Dec 1859 by S. P. Smith.

Parker, Shadrach & Francis Combs, 27 Sept 1800; George Combs, bm.

Parker, Squire & Polley Estridge, 22 March 1819; Benj. Pendlegrass, bm.

Parker, William & Candis Austin, 27 Oct 1810; William Austin, John Parker, bm.

Parker, William F. & Sarey A. Coock, 22 Oct 1844; H. F. Freeman, bm.

Parker, William H. & Nancy E. Thornburg, 7 Feb 1863; John M. Bouchelle, bm.

Parker, William R., son of John & Vise Parker, & Amelia Fletcher, daughter of Spencer & Barthenia Fletcher, m 16 Aug 1867 by Jno. Parleir, J. P.

Parkes, Alfred & Loisa Pinkard, 3 Dec 1827; James D. Parkes, bm.

Parkes, Allen W. & Fanny Miller(?), 11 Jan 1823; Benjamin H. Brown, bm.

Parkes, Benj. J. & Catharine Wellborn, 19 Nov 1825; Bernard Franklin, bm.

Parkes, Felix B. & Frances L. Hampton, 29 Sept 1849.

Parkes, Hasten E. & Ruth Laws, 4 June 1831; Benjamin L. Hubbard, bm.

WILKES COUNTY MARRIAGES, 1778-1868

Parkes, James D. & Sarah Phillips, 18 May 1824; Wm. Grayson Jr., bm.

Parkes, Maredith & Nancy Denney, 16 Oct 1821; William Walsh, bm.

Parkes, Thos & Salley London, 30 Nov 1811; Reuben Parks, bm.

Parks, Aaron & Omy Stubble, 2 Nov 1784; Thomas Parks, bm.

Parks, Ambrose & Franfes L. Isbell, 2 Dec 1790; James Gray, bm.

Parks, Ansel & Mary Crumpler, 13 Jan 1838; Thos Crumpler, bm.

Parks, Benjamin & Elizabeth Branch, 3 Nov 1779; John Parks, bm.

Parks, D. C. & Mary M. Roberts, 22 Feb 1864; John P. Parks, bm.

Parks, Edmond & Lemira Ellis, 29 Dec 1835; Danl. McBride, bm.

Parks, Henry & Pattie Justice, 9 Dec 1782; Benj. Herndon, bm.

Parks, Jas. M. & Mary Bryan, 14 Dec 1816; Jas. Martin, bm.

Parks, John & Betsy Parks, 10 Dec 1795; Benjamin Parks, bm.

Parks, John & Martha Felts, 22 April 1809; Silas Reynolds, bm.

Parks, John J. & Martha J. Johnson, 18 Feb 1862; Thomas M. Parks, bm; m 19 Feb 1862 by J. M. Gambill, J. P.

Parks, Jonathan & Elizabeth Cannaday, 27 Jan 1800; Reuben Parks, bm.

Parks, Joshua & Ruth Franklin, 14 Sept 1811; Thomas Parks, bm.

Parks, Sendolph D. & Lucinda C. Petty, 28 Aug 1850; A. L. Rousseau, bm.

Parks, M. A. & Mary L. Hickerson, 12 Jan 1866; A. L. Roussau, bm; m 22 Jan 1866 by R. W. Barber.

Parks, Moses & Nancy Davice, 27 July 1801; Thos Allen, bm.

Parks, Reuben & Hanah Reynolds, 11 Nov 1788; Benjamin Parks, bm.

Parks, Rufus, son of Richmond & Milly Parks, & Alice Hackett, daughter of Orrange & Matilda Hackett, 8 Oct 1867.

Parks, Samuel & Sally Kearby, 23 Dec 1802; William Curby, bm.

Parks, Theophilus C. & Olley Williams, 4 Nov 1850; J. P. Parks, bm; m 6 Nov 1856 by Thos Roberts, J. P.

Parks, Thos Junr & Rachel Hoot, 6 March 1805; Joseph Walls, bm.

Parks, Uriah & Sally Green, 22 May 1805; James Patton, bm.

Parks, Uriah & Rachel Johnson, 28 Aug 1809; Allen Robinett, bm.

Parks, Wiley M. & Mary E. Kemp, 19 Nov 1864; Linsey Jarvis, bm; m 29 March 1864 by Rev. R. W. Wooton.

Parks, William & Rhoda Vanwinkle, 1 Oct 1788; Ambr. Parks, bm.

WILKES COUNTY MARRIAGES, 1778-1868

Parks, William & Matilda Bryan, 7 Feb 1814; Richard Parks, bm.

Parleir, George W. & Mary Cook, 15 Jan 1856; Hicks Hendren, bm.

Parlier, Isaac & Mary Soot, 2 Aug 1799; Jeremiah Crisel, bm.

Parleir, Jacob & Fanny Dougthit, 27 Aug 1829; J. W. Wellborn, bm.

Parleir, Jacob & Elizabeth Watts, 29 Dec 1838; Bazell Burlison, bm.

Parleir, John & Betsey Bullis, 27 June 1800; Benjamin Bruce, bm.

Parleir, John & Arreney Triplett, 7 Nov 1832; James Parleir, bm.

Parleir, John F. & Mary E. Gilreath, 23 March 1854; m by Wm. J. Chaple, Eld.

Parleir, James & Lucreacy Phillips, 19 Dec 1827; Isaac Parlier, Jr., bm.

Parlier, Jonathan & Beckey Shin, 12 Feb 1811; Hugh Campbell, bm.

Parlier, Jonothan & Rhoda L. Gilreath, 15 Nov 1852; Chas. Hickerson, bm; m 15 Nov 1852 by Wm. J. Chappel, Eld.

Parlier, Noah B. & Mary Elizth. Parlier, 10 Feb 1849; William Parlier, bm.

Parlier, William R. & Sarah C. Ellis, 21 May 1844; Evin Ellis, bm.

Parliette, John & Susannah E. Sale, 22 Aug 1859; James P. Sale, bm; m 31 Aug 1859 by W. F. Adams, Baptist minister.

Parmely, Ephraim & Mary Hinds, 11 Jan 1779; William Spicer, James Bunyard, bm.

Parr, Benjamin & Patsey McKenney, 25 July 1790; Henry Jones, bm.

Parson, James & Mary Sever, 7 Aug 1846; Jesse Yates, bm.

Parson, Thos & Alsa Roberts, 1 Aug 1846; Luther Swanson, bm.

Parsons, Alfred C. & Martha J. Roberts, 25 May 1866; C. M. Pryor, bm; m 24 May 1866 by J. W. Church.

Parsons, E. H. & S. E. Parsons, 23 Dec 1865; W. M. Parsons, bm; m 24 Dec 1865 by J. W. Church, J. P.

Parsons, George & Belinda Farchild, 18 March 1835; John Parsons, bm.

Parsons, George H. & Marey Robeds, 5 Jan 1853; m 5 Jan 1853 by E. B. Philips, J. P. (bride given as Marey Roberts on certificate).

Parsons, James & Massey Church, 3 Feb 1817; Hugh Hays, bm.

Parsons, J. C. & Rebecca Powel, 25 Jan 1862; W. M. Parsons, bm; m 26 Jan 1862 by J. W. Church.

WILKES COUNTY MARRIAGES, 1778-1868

Parsons, Jesse & Betsey Lay, 26 March 1794; David Lay Sr., bm.

Parsons, Jesse F. & Elisabeth A. Hethham, 23 June 1867; Calvan W. Whittenton, bm.

Parsons, John & Polly McNiel, 24 Jan 1837; David Gray, bm.

Parsons, John & Alpha E. Curtis, 21 Sept 1865; R. M. Foster, bm; m 24 Sept 1865 by D. Wellborn, minister.

Parsons, Jonathan & Mary Church, ___ 182_; John Church, bm.

Parsons, Johnathan F. & Elisabeth Griffing, 24 Aug 1861; W. N. Pearce, bm; m 26 Aug 1861 by A. A. Whittenton, J. P.

Parsons, Martin & Elizabeth M. McNeill, 3 Jan 1845; George W. McNiel, bm; m 5 Jan 1845 by Wm. Church.

Parsons, Paton & Angenette Pilkington, 2 June 1860; William Pilkington, bm.

Parsons, Rufus Gordon, son of John Parson, & Nancy Phillips, daughter of John Phillips; m 31 Aug 1867 by William Church, J. P.

Parsons, Thomas & Elizabeth Dyer, 8 May 1837; James McNiel, bm.

Parsons, Thomas & Senah C. Shewmaker, m 8 April 1867 by C. E. S. Simpson, J. P.

Parsons, William F. & Rebeca C. Parson, m 8 Nov 1865 by James McNeil.

Parsons, William R. & Darcus Pusser, 19 July 1845; James Watts, bm.

Parsons, Wm. R. & Caroline Person, m 16 April 1865 by Smith Ferguson, M. T.

Passons, James & Piety Joines, 1 Feb 1792; John Neil, bm.

Patterson, Oliver H. & Callie A. Blacknell, 18 Nov 1864; James W. Hackett, bm; m 8 Jan 1865 by Rev. R. W. Wooton.

Patterson, Saml F. & Phoebe C. Jones, 6 May 1824; Walter R. Lenoir, bm.

Patton, Neily & Elizabeth Vannoy, 26 April 1806; Joseph Patton, bm.

Payn, Jonas & Rodey Smirthes, 18 Feb 1804; Joseph Sanders, bm.

Payn, William W. & Rebecca Tugman, 23 Jan 1833; John Mitchell, bm.

Payne, Alfred B. & Marthey Vanoy, 27 March 1836; m 27 March 1836 by Wm. Church.

Payne, George & Ann Fugett, 3 Sept 1779; Wm. McCain, bm.

Payne, Wm. F. & Martha Carmiller Church, 30 June 1863; Henry H. Church, bm; m 30 June 1863 by J. W. Church.

Payne, Zebalum & Charity Lipps, m 23 July 1835 by Wm. Church.

WILKES COUNTY MARRIAGES, 1778-1868

Peanix, William & Miss Mary M. Wilburn, m 27 July 1865 by Henry Chambers, J. P.

Pearce, Francis M. & Elizabeth B. Haviner, 15 Nov 1847; John Eller, bm.

Pearce, John & Sarah Shepherd, m 1 Jan 1852 by A. A. Whittenton, J. P.

Pearce, Nelson & Milley Keller, 20 Jan 1834; John Keller, bm.

Pearce, Wm & Nancy C. Bane(?), m 12 Feb 1860 by J. W. Church, J. P.

Pearson, Alexander & Amanda Kilby, 19 Nov 1847; Wm. S. Kilby, bm.

Pearson, Charles & Betsey Custephen, 18 May 1812; Charles Custephen, Charles Adams, bm.

Pearson, Enoch & Patsy Walker, 12 March 1833; Thos Pearson, bm.

Pearson, James & Sarah Mitchell, 5 Aug 1803; David Dickoson, bm.

Pearson, James B. & Dianah Wright, 6 Oct 1852; Thomas S. Earp, bm; m 7 Oct 1852 by Wm. H. Hubbard, J. P.

Pearson, Joel & Luisy Watts, 8 Jan 1850; George Watts, bm.

Pearson, John A. & Nancy Calton, 9 Jan 1819; Lewis Carlton, bm.

Pearson, Jonathan & Anne Palmer, 11 Feb 1813; David Cockerham, bm.

Pearson, William A. & Sarah Hampton, 5 Aug 1852; Jas. H. Broyhill, bm; m 5 Aug 1852 by Wm. H. Hubbard.

Pearson, Wm. W. & Dianah Wallice, 28 April 1842; W. G. Johnson, bm.

Peden, Sandy, son of Ferebee Peden, & Sally Williams, daughter of Sarah Williams, all colored, m 6 July 1867 by C. R. S. Simpson.

Pedle, Mark & Mary Maudlin, 3 May 1814; Peter Davis(?), bm.

Pendergrass, Baley & Ruth Rash, 22 April 1833; Raleigh Pendergrass, bm.

Pendergrass, Benjamin & Martha Hall, 18 Dec 1861; Rolley Pendergrass, bm.

Pendergrass, Durry & Jane Mise, 26 May 1846; Raleigh Pendergrass, bm.

Pendergrass, Raleigh & Mary Malinda Brooks, 7 Jan 1859; m by Wm. Parks, J. P.

Pendergrass, William & Matildy Brewer, 7 Feb 1862; Findley Howard, bm; m 9 Feb 1862 by Wm. Parks.

Pendley, Adolphus W. & Ireny Triplett, 21 Dec 1841; Eli Coffey, bm.

WILKES COUNTY MARRIAGES, 1778-1868

Pendley, Jonathan & Elizabeth Fields, 28 Dec 1795; James Pendley, bm.

Pendley, Thomas & Nancy Coffee, 1 Sept 1818; Jesse Compton, bm.

Penix, Pernis & Elizabeth Hays, 1 April 1867; Wm. J. Chapel, bm; m 2 April 1867 by Rev. Wm. J. Chapel.

Pennel, C. Mandly & Camely Buch, 19 Jan 1867; Jesse Gilbert, bm; m 20 Jan 1867 by J. K. Hendrix, J. P.

Pennel, Joseph & Mary Bouthe, 16 July 1833; William Pennel, bm.

Pennel, Samuel & Susannah Gilbert, 27 Nov 1821; Edmund Jones, bm.

Pennel, Wm & Minerva A. Carlton, 5 Jan 1850; Sylvester McCalup, bm.

Pennel, Young & Sarah Pennel, 22 March 1836; Paul A. Reace, bm.

Penney, James & Sally Ferguson, 9 April 1821; James Smith, bm.

Perdew, William A. & Elisebeth Lewis, 7 Jan 1854; m 12 Jan 1854 by S. D. Swaim.

Perdew, E. M. & Dovey Baker, 23 Dec 1865; Franklin Pardew, bm.

Perdew, William & Lindey Alvey, 6 Nov 1809; Jas. Brown, bm.

Perdue, J. F. & Elizabeth Poter, 23 Jan 1867; C. N. Bruce, bm; m by Rev. J. K. Baldwin.

Perdue, John & Fannay Wootten, 4 Sept 1856; Thirston W. Redding, bm; m 21 Sept 1856 by S. D. Swaim, Baptist minister.

Perdue, Robert & Lear(?) Ausbeon, 27 April 1837; Chapman Davis, bm.

Perdue, Sale & Peggey Riston, 26 June 1817; Robert Perdue, bm.

Perdue, Silas & Malinda Sparkes, 23 Feb 1838; James Sale, bm.

Perdue, Thomas & Salley Hummey, m 30 Oct 1851 by John Brown, J. P.

Perkins, Peter & Elizabeth Brown, 18 May 1800; William Perkins, bm.

Perkins, R. J. M. & Matilda E. Martin, 30 June 1856; m 1 July 1856 by James Purvis.

Person, Charles & Mary Gullett, 6 June 1816; Jesse Gullett, bm.

Person, Samuel & Elisabeth Pernater, 31 March 1814; Moses Thornton, bm.

Person, Samuel & Polly Lunsford, 2 Aug 1821; Moses Cockerham, bm.

Person, Thomas & Agness Lane, 13 Feb 1822; Benjamin Grayson, bm.

Persons, Jas. & Drewsilla Hamon, 5 July 1805; John McQueary, bm.

WILKES COUNTY MARRIAGES, 1778-1868

Persons, William & Elisabeth Chandler, 28 Dec 1809; Reuben Parks Jr., bm.

Persons, William & Milley Darnald, 18 July 1817; John Thornton, bm.

Perteet, William P. & Nancey Felts, 31 Oct 1865; E. M. Woodruff, bm; m 31 Oct 1865 by Henry Chambers, J. P.

Peters, Elisha & Ann Jones, 2 Sept 1823; Allen Jones, bm.

Pettey, Eli & Dianna Harrison Martin, 3 March 1810; William W. Martin, bm.

Petty, Abram & Este Gordon, colored, m 16 Jan 1867 by C. R. S. Simpson, J. P.

Petty, John of Surry County, & Mary Sanders, 15 Jan 1791; John Sanders, bm.

Phair, Joseph & Polley Morgin, 29 Jan 1803; Ambr. Park, bm.

Phelps, Charles & Elizabeth D. Adams, 31 July 1821; Wm. Todd, bm.

Phelps, Richmond P. & Mary J. McCoy, 3 Jan 1843; J. G. Barnett, bm.

Phelps, Samuel & ____, 16 Sept 1806; Thomas Normand, bm.

Philips, Richard & Ann Doss, 25 Oct 1827; George Shepherd, bm.

Philips, George & Nancy Powel, 16 Dec 1858; m 16 Dec 1858 by Wm. H. Philips.

Philips, James & Maryan Keys, 24 Dec 1851; John Keys, bm; m by Nathl. Church, J. P.

Philips, James H. & Sarah Lewis, 11 March 1852; William L. Franklin, bm; m 11 March 1852 by Ansel Parks.

Philips, Joel & Jurana Barnes, 2 Oct 1814; John N. Greer, bm.

Philips, John B. & Jane C. Marshal, 21 Sept 1854; John J. Parks, bm; m 21 Sept 1854 by Ansel Parks.

Philips, Johnathan & Margaret Keys, 26 June 1849; D. W. Adkins, bm.

Philips, Michajar & Nancy Parks, 19 Oct 1846; Martin Parks, bm.

Philips, Nathan, son of Eli & Matilda Philips, & Martha Malissa Woody, daughter of Jonathan P. & Martha Woody, 26 Oct 1867.

Philips, William & Jemima Yates, 29 March 1828; Tillman Yeats, bm.

Philips, Wm. D. & Francis Pearson, 24 Feb 1845; Elisha B. Philips, bm.

Philips, William D. & Sarah E. Triplett, 28 Feb 1850; John W. Parleir, bm.

WILKES COUNTY MARRIAGES, 1778-1868

Philips, Wm. H. & Caroline Lindermon, 6 Aug 1844; James H. Whitington, bm; m by Saml Walsh, J. P.

Philips, Wm. M. & Carline Gibbs, 3 Jan 1850; A. W. Kennedy, bm.

Phillips, E. B. & Nancy E. Greenwood, 31 July 1865; J. J. Parlier, bm; m 1 Aug 1865 by J. K. Rose.

Phillips, Eli & Matilda Vyers, 24 March 1834; Wm. Tomlinson, bm.

Phillips, Elijah & Michel Bumgarner, 24 Aug 1836; Solomon Chapman, bm.

Phillips, Elisha B. & Mary Ferguson, 15 July 1848; James Parler, bm.

Phillips, Ephraim & Rebecca Phillips, 14 Aug 1784; Elias Phillips, bm.

Phillips, Hugh & Fanny Caroline Farechild, 17 Oct 1857; John W. Waters, bm; m 20 Oct 1857 by Wm. H. Phillips.

Phillips, Isaac & Elizabeth Orron, 4 Jan 1837; Archer Brown, bm.

Phillips, Jacob & Elizabeth Cope, 12 Feb 1820; Archer Brown, bm.

Phillips, Meredith & Judith Snow, 18 May 1825; Larkin Manord, bm.

Phillips, Micajah & Elizabeth Willey, 17 Sept 1824; Joseph Davis, bm.

Phillips, Peter & Lucinda Forterner, 23 Dec 1834; Richard Chapman, bm.

Phillips, Robert F. & Rebeca Parsons, m by Nathaniel Church, pastor of the Christian Church, 26 Sept 1865.

Phillips, William P. & Mary Powel, 19 Dec 1865; J. M. Powel, bm.

Philyam, Archibald & Elizabeth Yarber, 6 Oct 1849; James Cottral, bm.

Pierce, John E. & Elisabeth C. Nicholls, 27 Oct 1864; Leander E. Whittington, bm; m 27 Oct 1864 by A. A. Whittenton, J. P.

Pierce, John H. C. & Margaret Jenkins, 3 Jan 1866; Leander E. Whittington, bm.

Piles, John & Eloirah Wellborn, 15 Oct 1840; Hugh Montgomery Wellborn, bm.

Pilkinton, Murphey & Elizabeth Yates, 6 April 1853.

Pilkinton, William & Hila Westloch, 19 Dec 1822; Isom Felts, bm.

Pilkinton, Carney & Sarah Hamby(?), 14 April 1846; Thos Lane, bm.

Pilkinton, John & Lidda Busey, 21 Oct 1826; Wm Pilkinton, bm.

WILKES COUNTY MARRIAGES, 1778-1868

Pilkinton, Wesley & Louisa Yates, 5 March 1853; m 5 March 1853 by Wm. S. McNiel, J. P.

Pinion, Moses & Anner Barnes, 4 April 1825; George Swaim, bm.

Pinnel, Thomas & Elizabeth Berry, 17 April 1824; Joshua Curtis, bm.

Pipes, Hiram & Elizabeth Morris, 5 Nov 1816; Eli Pettey, bm.

Pipes, Jesse & Julia Triplette, 21 Sept 1856; F. F. Hendrix, bm; m 9 Oct 1856 by G. W. Hendrix, J. P.

Pipes, Thomas & Julia Barlow, 15 March 1845; Linville Land, bm.

Plott, Amos & Fanney Gomble, 22 Dec 1828; Nathan Gamble, bm.

Poe, Mathias & Salley Grimsley, 25 May 1807; James Grimsley, bm.

Poe, Mathias & Lucinda Wingler, m 22 Nov 1862 by John Hall, J.P.

Pollard, Wm & Rachael Holdaway, 14 June 1826; Thos W. Mitchell, bm.

Pope, John & Susanah Barnes, 6 Sept 1860; m 7 Sept 1860 by Pickens Carlton, J. P.

Poplin, John & Polly Brown, ___ 18__; Abel Gotly, bm.

Porter, A. R., son of Joseph & Rachel Porter, & Jayn Walker, daughter of Wilson & Mira Walker, m 12 Sept 1867 by A. E. Myers.

Porter, Andrew W. & Mary Coffee, 24 Dec 1831; John Jacobs, bm.

Porter, Constant & Lucinda Higgins, 6 Jan 1848; Josiah Brewer, bm.

Porter, Elisha & Malinda Brewer, 18 Jan 1844; Thos. L. Kelly, bm.

Porter, Franklin & Polley Hagins, 17 Jan 1856; Constant Porter, bm.

Porter, James T. & Joannah Petty, 17 April 1854; Geo. Wythe Gleaves, bm.

Porter, John & Salley Shew, 1 Feb 1825; John Shattely, bm.

Porter, Joseph & Rachael Johnson, 1 Jan 1836; John K. Baldwin, bm.

Porter, Oller & Viney Stone(?), 1 Jan 1865; m 15 Jan 1865 by J. N. Haynes, J. P.

Porter, William & E. Poter, 6 Sept 1866; William Blackburn, bm.

Porter, Wm. F. & Elizabeth Johnson, 27 Jan 1864; Harison Soots, bm.

Porter, Frances & Millindey Johnston, 27 Nov 1802; Thomas Johnston, bm.

WILKES COUNTY MARRIAGES, 1778-1868

Poter, George Leland, son of Elisha & Malinda Poter, & Semira Johnson, daughter of Louis & May Johnson, 17 Aug 1870; m 21 Aug 1870 by A. Wiley, J. P.

Poter, Welborn C. & Elizabeth Johnson, 6 Feb 1851; m 6 Feb 1851 by Eli Grimes, L. D. of M. E. Church South.

Potter, John & Polley Darnall, 18 Nov 1826; John Darnall, Junr., bm.

Poulions, Paul & Hezeiah Lantrip (sic), 4 July 1801; (no bm listed).

Pourter, James Junr. & Millenda Burnet, 26 April 1825; Joel Cargile, Youn N. Brooks, bm.

Powel, William & Rachel Smith, 7 Jan 1800; William Cash, bm.

Powell, James & Nancy Linderman, 16 Jan 1834; George Holder, bm.

Powell, Mason & Clary Brown, 11 Aug 1820; Warren Powell, bm.

Powell, Thomas & Agnis Roper, 17 June 1782; John Yates, Larkin Cleveland, bm.

Pratt, George & Celer Davis, 18 Dec 1847; Thos K. Davis, bm.

Pratt, John F. & Martha J. Ragesdel, m 16 Sept 1860 by Wm. H. Hubbard, J. P.

Presnel. William L. & Mary Laws, 6 Feb 1851; m 9 Feb 1851 by Charles Carlton, J. P.

Presnell, Elias & Nancy Steed, 16 Sept 1821; John Pinley, bm.

Presnell, Elijah & Nancey Barnes, 14 Jan 1823; Israel Presnell, bm.

Presnell, Enoch & Elizabeth Presnell, 26 Feb 1832; Elijah Presnell, bm.

Presnell, Isaac & Elizabeth Chapman, 8 Feb 1819; Gabel Melone, bm.

Presnell, Israel & Melinda West, 12 Dec 1819; John Hooper, bm.

Presnell, James & Anna Presnell, 24 May 1849; Larken Laws, bm.

Presnell, Wm. & Susana Presnall, 22 Aug 1846; C. C. Ferguson, bm.

Prevett, Iredille & Mary Ball, 28 July 1827; Levi Ball, bm.

Previtt, Richard & Marey Mabery, 9 Oct 1858; Wesley Prewit, bm.

Previtt, Abram & Lucy Ball, 29 Jan 1854; Cader Prewitt, bm; m 4 Feb 1854 by Alfred Warren, J. P.

Previtt, James & Clarasay Millsaps, 9 Nov 1814; Fr. Barnard(?), bm.

Previtt, James & Patsey Brooks, 20 Jan 1817; Noah Prewitt, bm.

WILKES COUNTY MARRIAGES, 1778-1868

Previtt, Noah & Omey Deboard, 9 Nov 1820; Jacob Prewitt, bm.

Previtt, Wesley & Sarah an Rash, 9 Oct 1858; Richard Prewitt, bm.

Prevett, Wiliford Sr. & Lucy Garris, 21 March 1859; m 18 April 1859 by Jas. M. Gambill, J. P.

Prewit, Isaac & Chrlet (sic) Richardson, 21 May 1835; William Baugess, bm.

Prewit, Joel & Elisabeth Durham, 9 Nov 1835; Ralph Pruit, bm.

Prewitt, H. P. & Mary Wagoner, 31 May 1862; Owen Absher, bm; m 1 June 1862, by John Hall.

Price, James W. & Rosannah Kilbey, 27 Sept 1832; Jason R. Laws, bm.

Price, John & Mary Combs, 22 Oct 1800; William Mills, bm.

Price, John & Ginsey Hubbard, 14 March 1825; Joshua Laws, James Hayes, bm.

Price, John, son of Walter & Nancy Price, & Mary Watson, daughter of John & Mary Watson, 12 Jan 1868; m by J. W. Church, J. P.

Price, Joseph A. & Evaline Pearson, 11 Dec 1866; T. J. Vannoy, bm; m 12 Dec 1866 by D. Wellborn.

Price, Philip & Sarah Hayse, 7 June 1846; Henry Holder, bm.

Price, William & Nancy Hubbard, 30 March 1819; Phillip Price, bm.

Price, William L. & Martha Roberson, 18 Dec 1855; Rufus Laws, bm; m 19 Dec 1855 by Wm. H. Hubbard, J. P.

Prince, Alford & Nancy Smith, 28 Feb 1851; James Smith, bm.

Privat, Jackson & Nancy Tindle, 4 Oct 1856; Albert Madison, bm.

Privett, Ansel & Mary Baldwin, 25 Dec 1862; John Baldwin, bm; m 25 Dec 1862 by John K. Baldwin, minister.

Privet, Willias & Scintha Jaris, 12 Feb 1848; Noah Jervis, bm.

Privett, Abel F. & Sary C. Jarvis, 5 April 1867; T. P. Cobs, bm; m 7 April 1867 by J.F. Somers, J. P.

Privett, Cyrus & Elizabeth Wood, m 23 Jan 1853 by John Brewer, J. P.

Privett, Hiat & ___, 8 Oct 1835; Lindsey Wood, bm.

Privett, Hiram & Caroline Yeats, 18 Aug 1843; no bm.

Privett, J. M. & Matilda Bird, 20 Jan 1865; D. R. Holeway, bm; m 30 Jan 1865 by Eli Grimes, L. D. of M. E. C. S.

Privett, Lewis & Gincy Templeton, 21 Feb 1862; m 22 Feb 1862 by G. B. Parks.

WILKES COUNTY MARRIAGES, 1778-1868

Privet, Williford & Susannah Dorson, 13 July 1807; Thomas Durham, bm.

Privett, Williford Jr. & Huldah Sparkes, 22 Nov 1848; Thos. L. Kelly, bm.

Privette, John F. & Lyda J. Jarvis, 24 Dec 1866; m 28 Dec 1866 by J. F. Somers, J. P.

Priviett, Joshua, son of Wileford & Hulda Priviett, & Martha Caudill, daughter of Thomas & Metilda Caudill, m 13 Dec 1867 by J. E. Reynolds, J. P.

Privit, Micajah & Jenny Brown, 24 Nov 1840; Levi Rash, bm.

Privitt, Alexander & Martha Mahaffey, 15 June 1866; m 24 June 1866 by Wilson Walker, J. P.

Profit, Thomas & Sally Bingam, 7 June 1809; James S. Gullet, bm.

Profitt, Sam. & Lucy Shumate, 31 Aug 1805; Hiram Roussau, bm.

Profitt, Silvester & Nancy Tomkins, 26 Aug 1782; John Profit, bm.

Prophet, John & Elizabeth Holman, 1 April 1823; James Holman, bm.

Prophet, Thornton & Elizabeth Brown, 1 Nov 1838; Wilson Fairchild, bm.

Prophet, James & Jane Allison, 9 Nov 1850; John A. Eller, bm; m 9 Nov 1850 by Wm. Church.

Prophet, William & Polley Welch, 4 Feb 1829; McAlpin Welch, bm.

Pruit, Andrew, son of Joseph & Nancy Pruit, & Almeda Lee, daughter of Wm. & Jane Lee, 19 May 1868, m by J. I. Parks, J. P.

Pruett, Thomas & Margaret Montgomery, 24 April 1829; Jacob Oerand, bm.

Pruit, Augustus & Matilda Jentry, 8 Nov 1860; Stanly Gentry, bm; m 8 Nov 1866 by A. E. Myers.

Pruit, Benja. & Peggy Tyre, 11 July 1808; Carlton Keeling, bm.

Pumphrey, John & Elizabeth Shepherd, 26 June 1807; Andrew Shepherd, bm.

Pumphry, Elijah & Lucy Marstin, 20 Oct 1812; Andrew Sheppard, bm.

Purkins, R. & J. W. Hackett, 30 June 1856; J. M. Hackett, bm.

Purkins, Wm & Mary Tramson, 1 Jan 1840; W. B. Transor(?), bm.

Purson, Robert & Vary Wallas, 7 Feb 1849; Finly Howard, bm.

WILKES COUNTY MARRIAGES, 1778-1868

Queen, Alfred & Susan Brotherton, 25 July 1837; Francis Queen, bm.

Queen, F. A. & P. A. Lin, 10 Jan 1867, m by H. Hayes, J. P.

Queen, Francis & Lucey Anderson, 19 Sept 1837; Elis Queen, bm.

Queen, Hartwell & Mary Adline Laws, 15 Oct 1854.

Queen, Hughs & Martha L. Gilreath, 24 May 1848; Wm. Gilreath, bm.

Queen, James & Jemima Mabery, 19 Dec 1840; J. W. Sprinkle, bm.

Queen, Jesse & Nancy Millsaps, 29 Aug 1837; William Millsaps, bm.

Queen, R. B. & N. C. Parleir, 6 Dec 1865; Wm. Deal, bm; m 7 Dec 1865 by H. Hayes, J. P.

Queen, Sirus & Martha Cook, 18 April 1843; Evin Ellis, bm.

Queen, Wm. R. & Adline Nance, 23 Dec 1865; G. F. Nance, bm; m 4 Jan 1866 by H. Hayes, J. P.

Rabey, Frederick & Issabella Kerby, 28 Dec 1829; James Kerby, bm.

Ragsdel, Wm. H. & Luisa Ann Russel, 12 Oct 1866; G. H. Brown, bm; m 12 Oct 1866 by C. R. S. Simpson, J. P.

Rains, Jesse O. & Dorcas Baty, 4 Jan 1838; John J. Turnbill, bm.

Rains, John & Elizabeth Laine, 19 Jan 1814; Jeremiah Crisel, bm.

Rains, John & Nancy Edwards, 10 Aug 1827; Joshua Mitchell, bm.

Rankin, John & Taner Hendrix, 14 Feb 1831; Abram Hendrix, bm.

Rash, Amos & Rebeccah Colemon, 28 Sept 1851; Beverly Coleman, bm; m by Alfred Warren, J. P.

Rash, Asa & Nasey Colmon, 12 Nov 1800; Levey Rash, bm.

Rash, Charles & Ledia Cass, 18 Nov 1820; Lazarus Nickelson, bm.

Rash, Daniel & Sally Rash, 9 March 1824; Daniel Brown, bm.

Rash, Daniel & Margarett Brown, 25 July 1834; Daniel Rash, bm.

Rash, Daniel A. & Farity Speakes, 5 Nov 1847; William Nickleson, bm.

Rash, David & Nancy Livingston, 29 Jan 1835; Thos Barlow, bm.

Rash, Henry & Elizabeth Parker, 12 Aug 1856; John Browan, bm.

Rash, James B., son of William H. & Martha Rash, & Winney Caudill, daughter of Jackson & Polly Caudill, m at the house of Jackson Caudill, 30 Sept 1868 by Henry Jinnings, J. P.

Rash, James C. & Rebeca Brown, m 30 Jan 1859 by A. A. Whittenton, J. P.

WILKES COUNTY MARRIAGES, 1778-1868

Rash, John & Virlesie Bulloson, 20 Nov 1837; John B. Kilby, bm.

Rash, Joseph H. & Mary Church, 21 Feb 1828; John Vian(?), bm.

Rash, Levy & Jinney Jarvice, 17 April 1841; m 18 Apr 1841 by Thomas Roberts, J. P.

Rash, Lealdin, son of Merida & Sarah Rash, & Lucinda Miers, daughter of Elizabeth Miers, her father not known, 19 Aug 1867.

Rash, Luke & Nancy Rash, 13 Dec 1837; Thomas Roberts, bm.

Rash, Pery & Nancey Cash, 12 Aug 1804; Abr. Kilby, bm.

Rash, Wm W & Margaret Kilby, 13 Nov 1839; John B. Kilby, bm.

Ratliff, James & Sary An Holdbrooks, 13 Jan 1865; Anderson Russel, bm; m 15 Jan 1865 by Nathaniel Church, minister.

Ratliff, Jonathan & Sarah Palmer, 11 Feb 1813; David Cockerham, bm.

Ratliff, Nathan & Lidda Palmer, 2 April 1813; Jonathan Ratliff, bm.

Ray, Ambris & Susana Lycan, 16 Oct 1782; James Reynolds, bm.

Ray, Jesse & Honar Baker, 8 Jan 1782; Justice Bowling, bm.

Ray, Joseph & Mary Walker, 3 Aug 1854; m 27 Aug 1854 by Wm. J. Chappel.

Ray, Thomas J. & Miner Beach, 24 Dec 1839; Thomas Dulas Hall, bm.

Ray, William & Peggey Walsh, 14 June 1822; John Kindall, bm.

Read, Samuel & Elizabeth Marlow, 21 Nov 1833; Elisha Marley, bm.

Reading, John & Polley Brown, 21 Feb 1803; Henry Martin, bm.

Reading, Martin & Salley Martin, 15 Dec 1824; Wm. Reddin, bm.

Reaves, Hiram & Rachal Handy, 30 Jan 1845; John Adams, bm.

Reaves, Joshua & Providence Baker, 1 Nov 1796; Zebediah Baker, bm.

Reavis, A. H., son of Joseph & Elizabeth Reavis, & Elizabeth Lowe, daughter of Colic & Lidda Lowe, m 6 Oct 1868 by John W. Hall, Baptist minister.

Reavis, J. M. & Delila C. Ray, 6 Feb 1867; A. H. Reavis, bm; m 6 Feb 1867 by Alexander Gilreath, Mg.

Rector, Benjamin & Martha Baker, 12 April 1780; Theophilus Morgain, bm.

Rector, Lewis & Franky Lindford, 1 ___ 1788; James Wheatley, bm.

Rector, W. A. & Elizabeth Owen, 18 Oct 1858; N. P. Canter, bm; m 5 Nov 1858 by A. A. Whittenton, J. P.

WILKES COUNTY MARRIAGES, 1778-1868

Rector, Willis A. & Mary Ann Crouse (Crane?) (no date, probably 1840's); J. M. Owens, bm.

Rector, Willis A. & Nancy M. Nicholls, 1 Aug 1844; A. E. Nicholls, bm.

Redden, Jas. & Peggy Woodward, 30 May 1820; Grepts Maberry, bm.

Reddin, James & Nancy Denny, 1 Feb 1828; Wm. Reddin, bm.

Reddin, William & Delphy Brown, 6 Feb 1807; James Sale, bm.

Reddin, Williams & Martha Martin, 11 Dec 1832; Martin Redding, bm.

Redding, Hiram & Nancy Gilliam, 10 Nov 1844; William Redding, bm.

Redding, James & Lewenday Felts, 14 March 1846; Anderson Redding, bm.

Redding, J. O. & Martha Gillam, 6 March 1866; m 8 March 1866 by W. F. Adams, Baptist minister.

Redding, John & Salley Redding, 6 Oct 1848; Williams Redding, bm.

Redding, Nathan & Grace Jackson, 27 April 1813; John Redding, bm.

Redding, Nathaniel & Lucey Pinx, 23 Oct 1845; Samuel Wolis, bm.

Redding, Thurstain W. & Clary Walker, 15 Jan 1850; John Redding, bm.

Redding, Thomas S. & Martha Peryjohn, 5 March 1865; John M. Laws, bm; m 7 March 1865 by Jas. F. Somers, J. P.

Reddings, William & Salley Nickelson, 19 Dec 1842; John Redding, bm.

Reding, Anderson & Elizabeth Felts, 19 Dec 1840; John Felts, bm; m 24 Dec 1840 by Thomas Roberts, J. P.

Redmond, Daniel & Lidda Parkes, 2 Feb 1866; Lewis Welborn, bm.

Reece, Newton & Elizabeth Owens, 30 Oct 1865; John F. Reeves, bm; m 31 Oct 1865 by A. D. Dancy, J. P.

Reed, Henry & Elizabeth Crouch, 25 April 1823; Jacob Crouch, bm.

Reeding, William Jr. & Elizabeth Sale, 27 Sept 1828; Abel R. Wellborn, bm.

Reeves, Peter & Salley Redden, 29 April 1801; John Readin, bm.

Reeves, Howel & Nancy Wyatt, 11 March 1852; Joseph H. Adams, bm.

Reeves, John F. & Julia A. Hutchison, 16 Dec 1865; Henry Sebastian, bm; m 24 Dec 1865 by Wm. Hall.

WILKES COUNTY MARRIAGES, 1778-1868

Reeves, Richd. & Mary Bishop, 3 Jan 1850; Alfred M. Bishop, bm.

Reid, Irvin & Elizabeth Riddle, 2 March 1835; John Moore, bm.

Reily, Joseph B. & Levina Laws, 27 Sept 1790; Littleberry Laws, Joseph Laws, bm.

Revis, Samuel S., son of Joseph & Elizabeth Revis, & Lousinda Dowell, daughter of Joshua & Disy Dowell, m 24 Sept 1868 by John W. Hall, Baptist minister.

Revis, Saml & Merch McGlemry, 24 April 1863; John Adams, bm.

Reynolds, Elisha & Judith Eddins, 5 Aug 1786; William Reynolds, bm.

Reynolds, Elisha & Elizabeth Greer, 8 Feb 1800; James Patton, bm.

Reynolds, Eliza & Susana Jennings, __ April 1843; Elisha Porter, bm.

Reynolds, Harbert & Nancy Felts, 27 Jan 1842; H. C. Felts, bm.

Reynolds, James & Jane Miller, 20 Feb 1806; David Hickerson, bm.

Reynolds, Jinken & Marey Vanoy, 22 May 1802; William Elliott, bm.

Reynolds, Jinkin & Peggy Greer, 5 Nov 1804; John Greer, bm.

Reynolds, John & Elizabeth Brooks, 15 Oct 1846; no bm.

Reynolds, William & Polly Cook, 4 April 1781; Absalom Cleveland, bm.

Reynolds, Wm. E. & Susanah Adams, 6 Jan 1849; no bm.

Rhimer, Eli & Christeny Hodges, 9 Dec 1848; Joseph T. Bingham, bm.

Rhinehart, Augustus P. & Susan M. Smith, m 14 April 1865 by Z. B. Adams.

Rhoades, John A. & Bethany Brewer, 15 Jan 1866; m 15 Jan 1866 by Wilson Walker, J. P.

Rhoades, Wm. D. & Eliza J. Edwards, 29 Aug 1865; James E. Reynolds, bm; m 30 Aug 1865 by A. E. Myers.

Rhoads, Benjamin F. & Mary Elledge, 2 Feb 1849; Reubin Hall, bm.

Rhoads, W. M. & J. E. Havener, 15 Aug 1864; Joel Wadkins, bm.

Rhoads, Wesley & Peggy Adam, 30 April 1840; James Tindsley, bm.

Rhodes, John & Sarah Adams, 28 Aug 1833; John Holderway, bm.

Rhodes, Elijah & Susan Hall, 18 Dec 1830; Jessee Hays, bm.

Rice, Philip & Mary Lowe, 29 July 1799; Caleb Lowe, bm.

WILKES COUNTY MARRIAGES, 1778-1868

Rice, Wilson & Rodah Laws, 28 April 1861; m 28 April 1861 by J. D. Hubbard, J. P.

Richard, James & Rebeckea Chapman, 17 April 1821; David G. Laws, bm.

Richardson, Burrell & Elizabeth Adams, 27 June 1844; John M. Adams, bm.

Richardson, Claborn & Ann Hayse, 9 Aug 1844; W. G. Johnson, bm.

Richardson, Jeremiah & Elizabeth H. Smith, 8 June 1844; Jas. H. Smith, bm.

Richardson, John & Eveline Beaugess, 28 Dec 1865; Wm. Hall, bm. m 28 Dec 1865 by Wm. Hall.

Richardson, Noel & Delphia Adams, 11 Nov 1833; William Shoemate, bm.

Richardson, William & Fanney Wilcox, 27 March 1858; Isaiah McGrady, bm; m 28 March 1858 by William Hall, M. G.

Riddle, James & Jincy Combs, 25 Feb 1833; John Moore, bm.

Riddle, Jesse & Alcy Previtt, 14 Sept 1856; Findly Howard, bm.

Riddle, Wm & Mary Lewis, 24 July 1849; John Moore, bm.

Right, James & Milinder Carter, 23 June 1802; Wm. Sebastin, bm.

Rigs, Lott & Martha Porter, 24 Nov 1858; m 25 Nov 1858 by Wm. Parks, J. P.

Rigsby, Jonathan & Polley Sanders, 24 April 1824; Richd Sanders, Lewis Rigsby, bm.

Riley, Hugh & Catharine Westlock, 21 Jan 1811; Jesse Felts, bm.

Rise, John & Martha Ferguson, 4 Sept 1784; Jeremiah Forguson, bm.

Road, Herven & Sarah Perdue, 20 Oct 1838; Thos Perdue, bm.

Roads, Solomon & Fanny Adams, 11 Sept 1838; Hiram Roads, bm.

Robarts, Aaron & Anna Stover, 18 Feb 1800; Richard Parker(?), bm.

Robins, James L. & Elizabeth Camel, 7 Feb 1851; John M. Hawkins, bm; m 10 Feb 1851 by L. Sebastian, J. P.

Robbins, John P. & Mary Wyatt, 4 Sept 1843; James Cottrell, bm.

Robbnett, Joel & Surrena Brown, 17 Feb 1835; John Brown, bm.

Robearts, Zechariah & Nancy Absher, 8 Feb 1844; Isaac Adams, bm.

Roberds, John & Betsey Jones, 22 Jan 1816; John Rhodes, bm.

Roberds, John & Mary Mise, 28 Sept 1816; James McBride, bm.

WILKES COUNTY MARRIAGES, 1778-1868

Roberds, Richard & Nancy Person, 30 Oct 1817; Thomas Roberts, bm.

Roberds, Saml & Letha Brock, 21 Sept 1816; David Roberds, bm.

Roberds, Thomas & Mimey Chambers, 15 Aug 1805; Francis Barnard, bm.

Roberson, James & Leviny Hubard, 1 July 1815; Gipson Adams, bm.

Roberson, James & Sarah Holder, 17 March 1854; Peter McNiel, bm; m 17 March 1854 by Saml Walsh, J. P.

Roberson, John & Elenor Smithy, 9 Sept 1858; m 9 Sept 1858 by James Cal___, J. P.

Roberson, William & Elizabeth Davis, 2 March 1832; Saml. Wellborn, bm.

Roberts, Alfred & Edna Curey, 4 June 1849; Finly Howard, bm.

Roberts, Bennet & Sally Martin, 23 March 1816; Hartwell Hayes, bm.

Roberts, E. F. & Elizabeth Mitchell, 19 July 1865; m 20 July 1865 by Henry Chambers, J. P.

Roberts, Edwd. & Salley Wallace, 14 Aug 1824; Moses Joins, bm.

Roberts, Edward & Fanny Blankenship, 18 Jan 1828; David Mikel, bm.

Roberts, Eli P. & Luiser Henderson, 2 Nov 1865; J. M. Coleman, bm; m 2 Nov 1865 by J. F. Somers, J. P.

Roberts, Francis & Pattie Mise, 22 April 1783; Nathaniel Chambers, bm.

Roberts, George & Mary Parker, 26 June 1863; m 28 June 1863 by G. B. Parks.

Roberts, James & Nancy Wilson, 31 Dec 1827; Wm. Wilcoxson, bm.

Roberts, James & Sarah Gray, 30 Oct 1847; George Roberts, bm.

Roberts, Joel & Martha Holder, 14 Nov 1831; Saml Pennell, bm.

Roberts, John & Mary Osburn, 12 Feb 1782; Wm Roberts, bm.

Roberts, John & Anna Morgan, 8 July 1849; Henry Chambers, bm.

Roberts, John P. & Lucinda Poe, 9 April 1852; Joshua F. Dalton, bm; m 9 April 1852 by Ansel Parks.

Roberts, Joseph & Mary Robins, 7 Feb 1791; Colbey Rucker, bm.

Roberts, Mathew & Sary Brookshire, 16 Dec 1817; William Brookshire, bm.

Roberts, Thomas & Susan Gamble, 24 Dec 1811; Turner Hampton, bm.

Roberts, Thomas & Margarett Ginings, 23 Feb 1814; Thomas Ginnings, bm.

WILKES COUNTY MARRIAGES, 1778-1868

Roberts, Thomas & Jane Haines, 31 Dec 1821; Isaac Adams, bm.

Roberts, William & Dolley Duncan, 9 May 1780; Bennet Roberts, bm.

Roberts, William & Elizabeth Osborn(?), 22 June 1783; John Roberts, bm.

Roberts, Wm & Ann Vandergriff, 27 Jan 1784; Jacob Roberts, bm.

Robertson, David & Temperance Peasley, 22 Dec 1818; Isaac Peasley, bm.

Robeson, Wm & Nancy McGlemory, 13 Feb 1849; Peter Eller Jr., bm.

Robinett, Elisha & Mary Brown, 28 Nov 1825; James Robinett, bm.

Robinett, Isaac & Elizabeth Reynolds, 5 July 1799; Andrew Bryan, bm.

Robinett, Jesse & Charity Gordon, 29 May 1816; Thos Fletcher, bm.

Robinett, Jesse & Fanny Jones, 7 Feb 1807; Allen Robinett, bm.

Robins, John & Margaret James, 3 Jan 1827; William Robins, bm.

Robins, Reuben & Jane Turner, 29 April 1782; Edward Turner, bm.

Robins, Thomas & Mary Murphey, 4 Dec 1807; James C. Reilly, bm.

Robins, William & Nancy James, 15 April 1823; Thomas Robins, bm.

Robnett, Daniel & Mary Murphy, 25 March 1819; Elir Murphy, bm.

Robnett, Lazarus D. & Letty Chapman, 30 Dec 1833; Eli Forester, bm.

Rods, William & Sarah Mahathy, 17 Oct 1833; Calvin Adkerson, bm.

Rogers, Henry & Elizabeth Mitchell, 4 Feb 1845; Samuel Hamby, bm.

Rogers, Robert Wm. & Nancy Macinny, 15 Jan 1847; Jesse Billings, bm.

Rolen, John & Ann Riley, 9 Oct 1846; Wm. Long, bm.

Rone, John & Edy Curtiss, 27 June 1831; Nelson A. Strange, bm.

Roop, Christian & Polly McGrady, 24 Jan 1854; Calvin McGrady, bm; m 2 Feb 1854 by L. Sebastian, J. P.

Rose, Benjamin & Margaret M. Crickmore, 30 July 1823; Sterling Rose, bm.

Rose, Edward & Francis Dunkin, 6 Oct 1841; Ralph Holbrook, bm.

Rose, Harbert & Frances Gregory, 21 Dec 1834.

Rose, Isaiah & Mary Baugus, 17 March 1826; Andrew Pruett, bm.

Rose, John & Mary Hancock, 30 Oct 1779; Edward Harris, bm.

WILKES COUNTY MARRIAGES, 1778-1868

Rose, Thomas & Mary Fulks, 3 March 1826; Ralph Pruit, bm.

Rose, William & Agness Burchett, 10 Oct 1811; Robert Burchett, bm.

Rose, Wm & Cynthia Carter, 4 Sept 1830; Thomas Brinegar, bm.

Rose, William & Mary Jane Holaway, 16 Jan 1867; m 17 Jan 1867 by W. Joines, J. P.

Rose, Wyatt & Frances Triplette, 26 Aug 1846; James Tugman, bm.

Roughton, E. C., son of Elisha Roughton, of Yadkin County, & Martha V. Sale, daughter of William Sale, of Wilkes Co., m 19 July 1867 by E. Martin.

Roussau, Hillair & Bettey Hercondon, 13 April 1802; James Fletcher, bm.

Rousseau, Adison L. & Cynthia Parkes, 20 April 1847; Alexd. L. Hackett, bm.

Rousseau, Calvin & Matilda Fuller, 8 Dec 1865; no bm.

Rousseau, Hiram & Sarah M. Martin, 21 Nov 1809; John Martin, bm.

Rousseau, John & Sally Gordon, 9 Oct 1811; Nathl. Gordon, bm.

Rousseau, Reuben & Sally Baugus, 6 Aug 1825; Benj. F. Martin, bm.

Rousseau, Wm & Sarah Witherspoon, 23 May 1814; David Rousseau, bm.

Royal, John & Lucinda Wingler, 5 Sept 1865; James Wagoner, bm.

Royall, T. J. & Melvina Wyatt, 12 April 1867; John Royal, bm.

Royall, Thos & Elizabeth Hicks, 27 Feb 1819; Micajah Hicks, bm.

Roysdon, Nathan & Nancy Brown, (no date, during admn. of Gov. William R. Davie); Jacob Mast, bm.

Rupird, Elknah & Sarah Dichmon, 7 May 1856; Caleb Rupard, bm.

Rusel, John & Rachel Davis, 2 June 1821; John Person, bm.

Russel, Isaiah & Nancy E. Sothers, 29 March 1854; G. S. Powell, bm.

Russel, J. J. & Dosia M. Pearson, 17 Feb 1866; N. A. Russel, bm; m 20 Feb 1866 by D. Wellborn, Minister.

Russel, James & Elizabeth Gouger, 14 May 1811; Henry Gouger, bm.

Russel, James J. & Clarinda Saintclar, m 19 Jan 1858 by E. B. Philips, J. P.

Russel, Lewis W. & Caroline Earp, m 24 Nov 1853 by E. B. Philips, J. P.

WILKES COUNTY MARRIAGES, 1778-1868

Russel, N. A. & Nancey S. Ferguson, m 21 Jan 1862; by E. B. Philips, J. P.

Russel, Wm & Manervy Sharp, m 18 Feb 1858 by E. B. Philips, J. P.

Russell, Isaac & Elizabeth Davidson, 22 July 1843; James D. Hubbard, bm.

Russell, Wilson & Nancy Brookes, 13 Feb 1845; John Jenkins, bm.

Russill, J. P., son of Wilson & Nancy E. Russell, & M. J. Jourdin, daughter of Salley Jourdin, m 11 Sept 1867 by L. K. Baldwin, Minister.

Rutledge, William & Cloe Johnson, 3 April 1782; Jeffery Johnson, bm.

Ryon, Henry & Elizabeth Jones, 12 Feb 1780; John Adams, Jephs Moss, bm.

Ryon, Hiram & Susannah Phillips, 16 June 1818; Larkin Manord, bm.

Sabastian, Benj. & Elizabeth Adams, 8 March 1833; Eli Brown, bm.

Sabastan, Charles J. & Louisa E. Harrld, m 24 Nov 1864 by Wm. Hall.

Sabastin, Elijah & Phoe Brown, 23 Feb 1801; Jonathan Stamper, bm.

Saintclair, Hiram & Ann Stanley, 16 March 1820; Wilford Smith, bm.

Saintclaer, James A. & Annis Miller, 27 Oct 1824; Wm. Tucker, bm.

Saintclair, John & Nancy Johnston, 18 Oct 1806; John Chambers, bm.

Saintclair, John E. & Charlotte Triplet, 27 Feb 1830; A. N. Smith, bm.

St. Clair, Thos & Betsey Laws, 1 March 1826; no bm.

Saintclair, Thos. H. & Matilda Smythy, 17 Sept 1842; John Lane, bm.

Sale, Alfred & Cynisca Macbride, 11 Feb 1861; Benja. Walker, bm.

Sale, Cornelius & Nancy Martin, 5 May 1803; Richd. Allen, bm.

Sale, Elias & Sarah Sale, 21 Feb 1811; Henry Martin, bm.

Sale, Enoch & Salley Demmit, 18 April 1821; William Sale, bm.

Sale, George W. & Mary E. Camender, 26 Oct 1865; G. M. Woodruff, bm; m 28 Oct 1865 by W. F. Adams, Baptist minister.

WILKES COUNTY MARRIAGES, 1778-1868

Sale, Hiram & Margaret Mitchell, 12 July 1823; James Sale, bm.

Sale, Hiram, son of Silas & Elizabeth Sale, & Alice A. Stimson, daughter of Delucson & Omy Stimson, m 18 Dec 1867.

Sale, James & Milly Gray, 14 Jan 1822; Wm. Gray, bm.

Sale, James & Marth Lith Hendry, m 14 Jan 1867 by Seth Chambers, J. P.

Sale, James P. & Nancy Lewis, m 29 Dec 1859 by John Brown, J.P.

Sale, John & Susaner Maberay, 14 June 1802; John Felts, bm.

Sale, John & Prisilla Baker, 17 Oct 1809; James Sale, bm.

Sale, John & Patsey Martin, 26 Aug 1810; Thos Martin, bm.

Sale, John T., son of John & Lamira Sale & Nancy C. Mcbride, daughter of Daniel & Clary Mcbride, 27 Sept 1867; m 29 Sept 1867 by Seth Chambers, J. P.

Sale, Robert & Lucinda Brown, 23 July 1846; James Byrd, bm.

Sale, Saml & Nancy Reynolds, 1 March 1813; Thos Martin, bm.

Sale, Silas & Elizabeth Wilcoxson, 18 March 1831; Isaac Wilcoxson, bm.

Sale, William Jr. & Martha Walker, 16 Feb 1836; Wm Walker, bm.

Sales, John Jr. & Lemirah Gray, 19 Feb 1835; Ruffin Ivy, bm.

Salmons, Enoch & Vicey Fitzpatrick, 23 Sept 1829; Benjamin Brown, bm.

Salts, Jesse & Sally Briant, 15 Feb 1825; John Pierson, bm.

Samuel, Henery & Voilet Hendren, 3 May 1825; Micajah L. Samuel, bm.

Samuel, Mordecai & Ann Bange, 9 Aug 1780; Thos Bange, bm.

Sanders, Aaron & Avy Foster, 17 May 1847; Wm. L. Horton, bm.

Sanders, Abednego & Amey Cook, 11 Aug 1807; Richard Cook, bm.

Sanders, Charles & Louizy Holder, 2 Aug 1855; Thos D. Hall, bm; m 5 Aug 1855 by W. S. McGee, J. P.

Sanders, Cornelius & Sally Baker, 6 May 1807; Isaac Teague, bm.

Sanders, Isaac & Elizabeth Laws, 26 Dec 1843; J. F. Mitchell, bm.

Sanders, James & Nancy Patterson, 9 June 1787; Samuel Wilson, bm.

Sanders, James & Jinsey Biers, 5 March 1839; Francis Reynolds, bm.

Sanders, James & Mary Byers, 23 Feb 1848; John Eller, bm; m by Saml Walsh, J. P.

WILKES COUNTY MARRIAGES, 1778-1868

Sanders, James Gunnel & Charlotte Lane, 21 May 1817; James Layne, bm.

Sanders, John & Nancy Triplet, 22 Dec 1797; Robert Foster, bm.

Sanders, Joseph & Rebecca Watson, 2 Sept 1846; Nimrod Triplett, bm.

Sanders, Moses & Betsy Harris, 12 June 1789; Stephen Harris, bm.

Sanders, Moses & Elizabeth Davis, 10 Aug 1837.

Sanders, William & Lucinda Byeres, 16 Dec 1841; John B. Tomlinson, bm.

Sanderskey, Jacob & Mary McBenory(?), 6 Dec 1795; James McDowel, James Stewart, bm.

Sartain, Kelly & Nancy Beshears, 30 Oct 1816; John Viars, bm.

Sartin, James & Jane Benham, 7 Nov 1822; Thomas Rash, bm.

Sauer, Joseph & Catherine McPeters, 17 Jan 1822; George Johnson, bm.

Saunders, Richard & Gizzey Eller, 30 Oct 1829; Richard Wheeler, bm.

Saunders, William & Emiley A. Hendren, 20 Feb 1867; Oliver Hendren, bm; m 21 Feb 1867 by Rev. Wm. J. Chapel.

Sawyers, Wm. B. & Susannah Caul, 10 Jan 1820; Joseph Ray, bm.

Scarborough, James & Sarah Bradley, 18 Dec 1799; Saml McKenney, bm.

Scarborough, Jesse & Ann Shell, 22 May 1828; Wm. Bradley, bm.

Scarborough, John & Elizabeth Coffey, 15 Feb 1830; David E. Horton, bm.

Scare, Jerdin & Sry Miller, 13 June 1858.

Scarlott, Wm. F. & Louisa M. Gentle, 21 Feb 1860; m 22 Feb 1860 by Wm. H. Hubbard, J. P.

Scott, James & Dila Underwood, 2 Feb 1841; Joshua Pennel, bm.

Scott, John & Catherine McCloud, 3 Jan 1827; Samuel Wells, bm.

Scott, King & Charity Gilbert, 20 Sept 1828; Jordan Hamby, bm.

Scott, Larkin & Phebe Brown, 17 Sept 1866; Richard Sidden, bm; m 17 Sept 1866 by Wesley Joines, J. P.

Scott, Nathaniel & Sarah Herreford, 7 Dec 1780; Isaac Elledge, bm.

Scott, Samuel & Hannah Philips, 30 Oct 1798; Archd. Mitchell, bm.

Scroggs, A. A. & M. Matilda Parks, 12 May 1852; R. F. Hackett, bm; m 12 May 1852 by S. P. Smith, J. P.

WILKES COUNTY MARRIAGES, 1778-1868

Scroggs, Moses & Nancy McKoy, 30 Oct 1810; Silas Reynolds, bm.

Seawell, Jackson & Carline Miller, 28 Jan 1854; James Person, bm.

Sebastian, Lewis & Rachael Adams, 29 Nov 1831; Benjm. Sabastian, bm.

Sebastian, Wm. & Eliza Grimes, 31 Aug 1846; Wm. E. Reynolds, bm.

Sebastian, Lewis & Nancey Elledge, 22 Dec 1866; Wm. G. Sebastian, bm; m 25 Dec 1865 by H. C. Sebastian, J. P.

Sebastian, Wm. G. & Frankey A. Shumate, 22 Dec 1866; Lewis W. Sebastian, bm; m 23 Jan 1866 by A. W. Myers.

Segraves, William & Luvaney Elisebeth Crickmore, 8 April 1847; Johnathan Osbeon, bm.

Segraves, Sherard & Patsey Laws, 6 Oct 1830; Wm. Holdway, bm.

Setliff, John & Nancy Parkes, 16 Dec 1807; A. Tomlinson, bm.

Setser, Jacob & Sally Sherwood, 8 Oct 1833; John Setser, bm.

Settle, John, son of Reuben & Anie Settle, & Mary Lyon, daughter of Volentine & Rachel Lyon, m 10 Dec 1867 by L. D. Burcham, J. P.

Settle, Marion F. & Martha Greenwell, 19 Oct 1852; Lewis York, bm; m 20 Oct 1852 by Wm. F. Adams, Baptist minister.

Sewell, Dawson & Mary Lips, 2 June 1780; Henricus Stonesyfer, bm.

Sewell, Joseph & Mary Tompkins, 10 Dec 1779; Benjamin Hambrick, George Sheffield, bm.

Shackleford, William G. & Sarah Forguson, 27 Jan 1816; Fras. Barnard, bm.

Shadburn, Joel & Eliza Hamby, 8 Nov 1831; Jesse Gilbert, bm.

Sharp, Samuel D., son of James & Mary A. Sharp, & Isabel Sharp, daughter of John & Minerva Sharp, m 26 Dec 1867 by E. B. Phillips, J. P.

Shatley, John & Sarah Glass, 3 Sept 1845; Wm. W. Crysel, bm.

Shatley, Solomon & ____, __ Dec __; (bond torn).

Shatley, Wm. & Adeline Porter, 7 Nov 1848; John Johnson, bm.

Shatly, Absulem & Betsey Love, 19 Dec 1850; John Johnson, bm.

Shatly, John & Mary Shooe, 24 Nov 1813; James Cargile, bm.

Shatterly, David & Beckey Suits, 5 March 1811; John Shatterly, bm.

Shaver, James & Charity Luneford, 12 April 1820; John Brown, bm.

WILKES COUNTY MARRIAGES, 1778-1868

Shaver, Wm & Millinda Lunsford, 23 July 1829; James Shaver, bm.

Shaver, John & Elizabeth Smith, 12 Aug 1812; John Shavers Sr., bm.

Shearers, Robert & Sarah Kindal, 10 Nov 1789; Bartow Jones, bm.

Sheets, Adam & Susana Bare, 14 Nov 1844; Andy Sheets, bm.

Sheets, Andrew & Catherine Bare, 2 Oct 1834; Daniel Bare, bm.

Sheets, Henry & Emeline Wyatt, 29 Dec 1865; Nelson Wyatt, bm.

Sheets, Jesse & Sarah Wyatt, 23 Feb 1841; Andrew Sheets, bm.

Sheets, John & Polley Wyatt, 13 Oct 1828; Aaron Wyatt, bm.

Sheffield, Nicholas & Marey Martin, 24 April 1817; Andrew Cross, bm.

Shell, David & Elender Walsh, 10 Sept 1842; Bennet B. Walsh, bm.

Shelley, Benjamin & Nancy Jackson, 19 March 1783; Abijah Fairchild, bm.

Shelnut, John G. & Elisabeth White, 25 Dec 1819; John McGee, bm.

Sheperd, Presley & Ruth Woody, 28 Feb 1818; Jonathan Woody, bm.

Shepherd, Allen & Rosa Johnson, 10 Feb 1826; Andrew McGrady, bm.

Shepherd, James & Susana Dancy, 21 July 1842; Alexander Whittington, bm.

Shepherd, John & Sally Erwin, 24 Aug 1824; Larkin Shepherd, bm.

Shepherd, Martin & Mary Church, 8 Nov 1865; S. C. Walker, bm; m by Eli Grimes, L. D. M. E.

Shepherd, Abram & Elizabeth A. Kilby, 21 May 1865; C. F. Vanoy, bm.

Shepherd, Daniel & Mary Howell, 21 Jan 1826; H. B. Satterwhite, Daniel Lane, bm.

Shepherd, D. F. & America E. Whittington, 13 Feb 1867; J. S. Phouts, bm; m 13 Feb 1867 by A. A. Whittenton, J. P.

Shepherd, James & Fanny Vian, 3 Aug 1832; James W. Nicholls, bm.

Shepherd, James & Jelina Patric, 5 Sept 1865; James Wagner, bm.

Shepherd, John & Mary Kilbe, 13 Oct 1802; Reubin Kilby, bm.

Shepherd, John & Salley Vires, 3 Jan 1828; Henry Miller, bm.

Shepherd, John F. & Francis A. Willcox, 20 Feb 1840; Dennis Jennings, bm.

Shepherd, John W. & Sarah L. Curry, 24 Dec 1853; m by Wm. H. Hubbard, 25 Dec 1853.

WILKES COUNTY MARRIAGES, 1778-1868

Shepherd, Levi & Nancy Berry, 24 Aug 1864; Enoch Perry, bm.

Shepherd, Lewis & Rebeca Jennings, 20 Feb 1828; George Shepherd, bm.

Shepherd, Presley & Martha C. Ashley, 8 Nov 1861; W. R. Whittington, bm.

Shepherd, Samuel N. & Sufrona M. Barnes, 25 Dec 1857; m 25 Dec 1867 by E. B. Philips, J. P.

Shepherd, Wm & ____, (no date, probably 1840's); Henry Glass, bm.

Shepherd, William & Elizabeth Aimes, 4 Oct 1848; James M. Gregory, bm.

Shepherd, Wm. A. & Susan Austin, 17 Aug 1831; Jas. H. Norwood, bm.

Sheppard, Andrew & Nancy Cunningham, 9 Jan 1810; Benjamin Cunningham, bm.

Sheppard, James & Mary Sartain, 1 Sept 1779; Josiah Sartain, bm.

Sheppard, Larkin & Ally Irvin, 8 Nov 1817; John McNiel, bm.

Shepperd, Oustin & Rachel Cunningham, 29 Dec 1807; Thomas Mastin, bm.

Shepwash, John M. & Liddy Sprinkle, 8 July 1858.

Shew, Boston & Elisabeth Brewer, 18 Sept 1816; Simon Shew, bm.

Shew, Henry & Sarah Johnson, 27 Jan 1832; Nelson Johnson, bm.

Shew, Joel & Anne Stone, 1 Jan 1824; Lewis Keller, bm.

Shew, Phillip & Salley York, 4 Jan 1814; Henry Lenderman, bm.

Shew, Simon & Mary Sutes, 13 March 1817; Henry Lenderman, bm.

Shew, Wesley & Deby Love, 6 Sept 1852; m 6 Sept 1852 by W. W. Wright, J. P.

Shew, Wesley & Lulia Stone, 14 May 1853; Andrew Porter, bm; m 22 May 1853 by A. Porter, J. P.

Shewmate, James Elbirt & Mirecey Jolley, 30 Aug 1856; John Utzman, bm.

Shewmate, Daniel & Susanna C. Vannoy, 3 Feb 1859.

Shewmate, Henry & Nancy Crabe, 21 Feb 1856; James Crabe, bm; m 24 Feb 1856 by Israel Hollor, Baptist minister.

Shewmate, Thomas J. & Mare Ownes, 24 March 1852; m 24 March 1852 by L. Sebastian, J. P.

Shoe, Wm. P. & Martha Shoe, 9 Dec 1865; E. F. Johnson, bm; m 18 Dec 1865 by A. Porter, J. P.

Shoemake, Wm. B. & Susanah Felts, 13 Oct 1845; Anderson Myers, bm.

WILKES COUNTY MARRIAGES, 1778-1868

Shoemake, Andrew & Rebecca Lane, 19 May 1837; Wm. Laws, bm.

Shoemaker, Burril & Kezia Dichmon, 24 Aug 1852; m 26 Aug 1852 by R. W. Wooton, J. P.

Shoemaker, Evan & Sarah Anderson, 30 Nov 1850; Andrew Shoemaker, bm.

Shoemaker, John & Susanna McCain, 24 March 1813; W. F. Campbell, bm.

Shoemaker, Joseph & Ann Crabb, 28 April 1849; Moses Treadway, bm.

Shoemate, John & Nancy Handy, 22 Oct 1835; Noel Richardson, bm.

Shoemate, William & Polly Shoemate, 24 Jan 1834; John Shoemate, bm.

Shoemate, William Jr. & Polly Hall, 27 Jan 1858; Rueben Hayes, bm; m 31 Jan 1858 by L. Sebastian, J. P.

Shomate, Isaac & Amelia M. Wheatley, 6 Nov 1838; George Wheatley Jr., bm.

Shooe, Daniel & Dolly York, 16 June 1813; John Chambers, bm.

Shooe, John J. & Marthy M. Benton, 17 Feb 1858; m 17 Feb 1858 by Eli John, J. P.

Shoors, W. M. & Mary Myers, 23 May 1865; m 28 May 1865 by Israel Hollar, Baptist minister.

Shore, Philip & Martha J. Mahaffey, 27 Aug 1865; J. W. Felts, bm.

Shore, A Biram & Elizabeth Roussau, 24 May 1803; Wm. Roussau, bm.

Shores, David & Lucy Roussau, 18 Sept 1791; William Reynolds, bm.

Shores, Levi & Sarah Roussau, 30 March 1801; A Biram Shores, bm.

Shores, Ransom & Cyntha Tomlin, 4 Dec 1824; James Tharington, bm.

Shuford, C. & Emeline Martin, 10 July 1837; John J. Bryan, bm.

Shuford, Elkanah & Emilin Martin, 10 July 1837.

Shuford, Quincy Adams & Julia Ann Petty, 23 May 1849; Andw. A. Scroggs, bm.

Shumate, Enoch & Jane Brooks, 25 March 1866; m 26 March 1866 by H. C. Sebastian, J. P.

Shumate, Esley & Nancy Kilby, 5 Jan 1866; Wesley Shumate, bm; m 5 Jan 1866 by Jno. M. Brown, J. P.

Shumate, Jasper & Nancey Vannoy, 21 March 1853; m 26 March 1853 by John Owens, D. D.

WILKES COUNTY MARRIAGES, 1778-1868

Shumate, Mark & Susanah Stamper, 29 Nov 1830; Jacob Stamper, bm.

Shumate, Mark F. & Jane Hous, m 23 March 1856; by S. J. Gambill, J. P.

Shumate, Toliver & Lucinda Dancey, 15 Aug 1843; John Shumate, bm.

Shumate, Samuel & Caroline Shumate, 14 Aug 1866; Henry Sebastian, bm; m 14 Aug 1865 by Jno M. Brown, J. P.

Shumate, S. C. & Nancy Bullis, 21 April 1866; M. H. Sebastian, bm; m 22 April 1866 by H. C. Sebastian, J. P.

Sidden, Richard & Catharine Cacy, 25 Nov 1852; James Cacy, bm; m 25 Nov 1852 by Ansel Parks.

Sidden, William & Mary Caudill, 27 Feb 1867; m 28 Feb 1867 by W. Joines, J. P.

Silckson, J. Hew & Marthy J. Tilmon, 7 March 1847; James Tilmon, bm.

Silcocks, Ambrose & Rebecah Meadows, 25 Feb 1830; Jerome B. Souther, bm.

Silcocks, Andrew & Delvy Souther, 1 June 1825; Tillons M. Bussell, bm.

Sillivan, John & Hester Haruen(?), 5 March 1810; Turner Sillivan, bm.

Simmons, Stephen & Susanah Smith, 28 March 1865; no bm.

Simmons, Thomas & Elizabeth Holder, 11 Dec 1819; Edward M. Day, bm.

Simmons, William & Matilda Nelson, 29 Sept 1831; Russell Triplett, bm.

Simmons, William & Dicy Swanson, 1 Dec 1847; William Hodges, bm.

Simmons, William G. & Lidia A. Brown, 6 Jan 1856; J. F. Roberts, bm; m 8 Jan 1856 by James Roberts.

Simons, Alfred & Elizabeth Lewis, 6 May 1845; Jas. M. Hendrix, bm.

Simons, Theophilus & Sarah Sale, 22 Feb 1793; William Sale, bm.

Sims, Britton & Sucky Strutton, 1 June 1801; William Sims, bm.

Sisemore, David & Sally Jones, 6 Aug 1802; Thos Jones, bm.

Sisk, Gabriel & Mary Simpson, (no date, during admn. of Gov. William R. Davie); James Hogen, bm.

Sisk, Hareson & Dicey Norman, 12 April 1840; Paten Dimmett, bm.

Sisk, James & Salley London, 9 Sept 1809; Wm. Jeffry, bm.

Sisk, Jerel & Sary Norman, 4 June 1849; Elijah Norman, bm.

WILKES COUNTY MARRIAGES, 1778-1868

Sisk, John & Oney Strutton, 14 April 1798; Hezekiah Strutton, bm.

Sizemore, John & Jane Arms, 4 Dec 1831; John Ozborn, bm.

Slaton, Benjamin & Nancy Preston, 5 April 1788; Isaac Preston, bm.

Sloan, David & Susanna Majors, 19 Jan 1784; John Cleveland, bm.

Sloan, Robert & Rebekah Adams, 3 Dec 1812; James Davenport, bm.

Sloan, Thomas & Letitia Russell, 6 April 1811; Wm. Laws, bm.

Slone, William & Nancy Hood, 17 Jan 1820; Charles Hood, bm.

Smether, Reubin & Patty Chanler, 21 Dec 1778; Robt. Chandler, bm.

Smether, William & Mary Anderson, 8 May 1828; Evin Anderson, bm.

Smith, Alex. & ___, ___ 1784; Davd. Smith, bm.

Smith, Edward & Jane Linvill, 10 March 1780; Golson Stapp, Moses Guest, bm.

Smith, George & Elizabeth Robins, 3 Dec 1779; Nathaniel Robins, bm.

Smith, Jacob & Winna H. Hanks, 7 March 1861; m 7 March 1861 by B. T. Wall, J. P.

Smith, Jacob E. & Rebecca E. Millsaps, 1 May 1854; m 5 May 1854 by Wm. J. Chappel.

Smith, James A. & Martha Settle, 25 Sept 1862; Alfred P. McCann, bm; m 22 Sept 1862 by Rev. Wm. J. Combs.

Smith, John & Pheoby Maxfield, 22 Jan 1782; William Newbery, bm.

Smith, John & Elisabeth Barber, 21 Nov 1808; Michael Swaim, bm.

Smith, John & Elisabeth Hall, 12 Aug 1824; Owen Hall, bm.

Smith, John & Caty Brown, 10 Oct 1825; Daniel Brown, bm.

Smith, John & Matilda Ellis, 23 Dec 1847; Hugh Smith, bm.

Smith, John A. & Elsey Vine Treadway, 7 Sept 1862; Eli A. Treadaway, bm; m 7 Sept 1862 by J. D. Hubbard, J. P.

Smith, John B. & Panthie Hix, 26 July 1866; W. Dennis Mason, bm.

Smith, Joshua & Nancy Whitley, 10 Oct 1807; Jno Hickerson, bm.

Smith, Marion & Matilda Magee, 2 Feb 1859; m 2 Feb 1859 by Pickens Carlton, J. P.

Smith, Robert W. & Charity Edwards, 21 Oct 1852; E. W. Jones, bm; m 26 Oct 1852 by Z. B. Adams.

WILKES COUNTY MARRIAGES, 1778-1868

Smith, R. M. & Mary J. Lyndon, 30 Oct 1861; H. M. Bryan, bm; m 31 Oct 1861 by James Calloway, J. P.

Smith, R. P. & S. A. Baugus, 18 Dec 1865; E. M. Perdew, bm; m 26 Dec 1865 by J. N. Hayes, J. P.

Smith, Samuel & Amelia Matilda Martin, 4 Jan 1825; Benj. F. Martin, bm.

Smith, Thomas & Polley(?) Simmons, 26 Nov 1817; Malachi Robins, bm.

Smith, Thomas & Winney Pendergrass, 14 Oct 1819; Wyat Fletcher, bm.

Smith, Wilford & Zillar Fitzpatrick, 13 May 1820; Francis Barnard, bm.

Smith, Wm & Susanah B. Wallace, 17 Oct 1857; m 18 Oct 1857 by H. Hayes, J. P.

Smithey, J. W. & Selenia Church, 5 Feb 1856; Pendex Joines, bm; m 12 Feb 1856 by Wm. H. Hubbard, J. P.

Smithy, Harvey & Martha Lane, 21 June 1845; John Robinson, bm.

Smithy, Jesse & Millen Landsdown, 5 Oct 1816; John Usry, bm.

Smoot, Gideon S. & Elizabeth R. Gambile, 1 Oct 1844; Wm. M. Caudill, bm.

Smott, Hiram & Ginsey Ball, 13 Nov 1816; John Smoot, bm.

Smoot, John & Elviry Ball, 24 Sept 1819; Richard Parks, bm.

Smoote, James & Phawney Vickar, 28 Oct 1784; James Fletcher, bm.

Snider, Moses & Martha Hooper, 6 May 1806; Joshua Souther, bm.

Snow, James & Anna Norman, 7 April 1850; L. J. Norman, bm.

Sootes, James & Nancy E. Johnson, 18 Jan 1853; m by Eli Grimes, L. D. of M. E. Church South.

Soots, Elisha E. & Rebecky Felel (sic), 27 Aug 1857; John C. Felts, bm.

Soots, Harrison & Joanah Johnson, 20 Aug 1864; John A. Johnson, bm; m 28 Aug 1864 by J. K. Baldwin, Minister.

Sother, Henry & Hannah Lewis, 14 Dec 1852; Jno Lewis, bm; m 16 Dec 1852 by L. J. Bicknell, J. P.

Sothers, John & Susanna Watson, 17 March 1851; E. F. Foster, bm; m by A. Lipford, Baptist minister.

South, David, son of Samuel South, & Neates Taylor, daughter of Allen Stidem, m 21 Sept 1867 by A. A. Whittenton, J. P.

Souther, A. J. & Jincey Lewis, 6 Feb 1838; Francis Souther, bm.

Souther, Jerome & Sarah Souther, 15 July 1832; Samuel P. Smith, bm.

WILKES COUNTY MARRIAGES, 1778-1868

Souther, Jesey & Jain Combs, 1 April 1800; Joshua Souther, bm.

Souther, Joel & Patsey Brown, 3 July 1815; Hartwell Hayes, bm.

Souther, John & Polley Combs, 7 Dec 1824; Jesse Anderson, bm.

Souther, John & Sarah Christy, m 21 Jan 1854 by Israel Hollar, Baptist minister.

Souther, Joseph & Anna Dishmon, m 19 Jan 1868 by Israel Hollar, Baptist minister.

Souther, Joshua & Lidey Profett, 17 Sept 1801; John Profitt, bm.

Souther, Joshua & Mary E. Mullis, m 18 Jan 1860 by Rev. R. W. Wooton.

Souther, Joshua Jr. & Sarah Law, 2 April 1829; John Hays, bm.

Souther, Nelson & Matilda Bell, 8 March 1838; Joshua Bicknell, bm.

Souther, Wesly, son of A. J. & Jane Souther, & Ruth Jarvis, daughter of William & Sarah Jarvis, 25 Dec 1867.

Southers, Jerome B. & Sarah Southers, 7 July 1832; Ambrose Cook, bm.

Southerland, Daniel & Agness Rysdon, 24 Oct 1787; Robert Hall, bm.

Sparkes, Alexander & Mary M. Bryan, 12 June 1849; Francis Wood, bm.

Sparkes, Daniel & Mary L. Walker, 16 Feb 1843; Wm. Vannoy, bm.

Sparkes, Elijah, son of Selam Sparks, & Luisy Combs, daughter of Feling Combs, m 15 Sept 1867 by L. D. Burcham, J. P.

Sparkes, James & Carlotte Dickerson, 14 Jan 1850; Isiah Field, bm.

Sparkes, Joel & Charloty Durham, 21 June 1846; James Durham, bm.

Sparkes, Joseph & Marey Gray, 20 Sept 1842; George Chambers, bm.

Sparkes, Joshua, son of Timothy & Jane Sparkes, & Marianda Jolly, daughter of William & Malinda Jolly, m at William Jollys 10 Feb 1868 by J. Hughes, minister.

Sparkes, Noah & Rachiel M. McBride, 4 Dec 1851; m by S. D. Swaim.

Sparkes, Reuben & Belinda Gray, 5 Jan 1846; Joseph Sparkes, bm.

Sparkes, Samiel & Salley Ellis, 26 Oct 1852; William Redding, bm.

Sparkes, Solomon & Marey Day, 30 Jan 1838; Chapman Lewis, bm.

Sparkes, Wm. R. & ____, 12 April 1839; Samuel Sparkes, bm.

WILKES COUNTY MARRIAGES, 1778-1868

Sparks, Calbia & Sarah Pruet, 28 Dec 1822; Claborn Wadle, bm; consent from John Pruit, 25 Nov 1852.

Sparks, Georg W. & Elizebeth E. Johnson, 17 Oct 1855; Leander Johnson, bm.

Sparks, George & Elisabeth Armstrong, 24 Oct 1814; Westley Armstrong, bm.

Sparks, Hardy & Susanah Brown, 9 Jan 1815; James Sparks, bm.

Sparks, Joel & Nancy Blackborn, 27 July 1814; Claborn Waddil, bm.

Sparks, Joel & Miry Lane, 5 Sept 1844; Saml K. Hardin, bm.

Sparks, Joel & Mary Shalley, 23 Nov 1846; John Shalley, bm.

Sparks, John & Mary Parmely, 14 Aug 1781; James Bunyard, bm.

Sparks, Jonas & Mary Brown, 27 Sept 1817; John Brown, bm.

Sparks, Joseph & Sabry Demmit, 4 Feb 1822; Joseph Brown, bm.

Sparks, Lewis & Martha J. Spicer, 11 June 1866; R. B. Bryan, bm; m 12 June 1866 by Lander Johnson, J. P.

Sparks, Reuben & Phoeby Blackburn, 10 Oct 1828; Eli Blackburn, bm.

Sparks, Robert & ___, ___ 1845; Joel Sparks, bm.

Sparks, Ruben & Elizabeth J. Billings, 12 April 1862; Daniel Billings, bm.

Sparks, Samuel & Mary Alvey, 22 Oct 1814; Wiseman Alvey, bm.

Sparks, Solomon & Malinda Caudil, 1 April 1835; Hampton Holldaway, bm.

Sparks, Wm & Salley Jinings, 13 Sept 1828; William R. Sparks, bm.

Sparks, William R. & Salley Wilcockson, 13 March 1821; Reuben Sparks, bm.

Speaks, Elihu, son of Mussinetine & Ale D. Speakes, & Adlaide Kemp, daughter of Mathew & Evey Kemp, 23 Feb 1868; m 27 Feb 1868 by Israel Hollar, Baptist minister.

Speakes, Melton & Sarah Vickers, 17 May 1863; m 20 May 1863 by G. B. Parks.

Speaks, Hiram & Nancy Privett, 14 April 1863; m 19 April 1863 by G. B. Parks.

Spears, James & Mily Parsons, 21 Oct 1864; Paten Parsons, bm; m 21 Oct 1864 by A. A. Whittenton, J. P.

Speeks, James & Elizabeth Rash, 9 Nov 1847; Joel Lumford, bm.

Speer, Samuel & Jeane Turner, 27 May 1809; Henry Baugus, bm.

WILKES COUNTY MARRIAGES, 1778-1868

Spencer, Goodmon & Nancy Lee, 5 March 1865; T. M. Parks, bm; m 5 March 1865 by Rev. G. Ayers, Baptist minister.

Spencer, James, son of John & Martha Spencer, & Jane Walls, daughter of Jacob & Susan Walls, m 24 Oct 1867 by J. I. Parks, J. P.

Spencer, John & Aily Waters, 18 Oct 1827; Jesse Olliver, bm.

Spencer, Robert & Elizabeth C. Pratt, 11 Jan 1866; James Spensor, bm; m 11 Jan 1866 by J. M. Gambill, J. P.

Spencer, Wm. M. & Elizbeth Jones, 26 Dec 1850; Banestor Laws, bm.

Spencer, William & Martha C. Jones, 12 Oct 1833; B. Washington Newland, bm.

Sperry, Jesse & Elizabeth Profit, 8 July 1795; Jas. Fletcher, bm.

Spicer, Benjamin & Nancy Baugess, __ March 1816; William Holbrook, bm.

Spicer, Gideon & Mary A. Byrd, 8 Sept 1853; m 8 Sept 1853 by John Gentry.

Spicer, H. J. & Eda L. Ferguson, 11 Oct 1865; E. M. Wellborn, bm; m 12 Oct 1865 by Jacob Crouch, minister.

Spicer, Harden & Marth Johnson, 20 Jan 1829; Thomas Bryan, bm.

Spicer, Harvy & Nancy Phillips, 21 July 1864; James Hanks, bm; m 21 July 1864 by Rev. Wm. J. Combs.

Spicer, James & Jamsey Johnson, 19 Feb 1842; William Holbrook, bm.

Spicer, Joshua & M. J. Holbrook, 17 Nov 1866; J. S. Holbrook, bm.

Spicer, Joshua & Martha J. Holbrook, m 18 Nov 1866 by Rev. William J. Combs.

Spicer, William & Parmely Hoots, 19 May 1853; m by John Brewer, Esq.

Spicer, Wm & Jenny Baugus, 22 Feb 1817; Wm Spicer Senr., bm.

Spradlen, John & Betsey Chapman, 15 May 1802; James Robnett, bm.

Spradling, David & Elitha Tompson, 13 Sept 1792; Aaron Smith, bm.

Spradley, Joshua & Marget Irvin, 18 Jan 1780; John Chapman, bm.

Sprinkel, Samuel & Adline Gray, 26 Jan 1853; m 26 Jan 1853 by Wm. F. Adams, Baptist minister.

Sprinkle, Edward & Nancy Chapel, 10 Jan 1855; O. Sprinkle, bm; m 10 Jan 1855 by W. F. Adams, Baptist minister.

Sprinkle, Noah & Nancy E. Byrd, 10 March 1861; m 11 March 1861 by M. A. Parks, J. P.

WILKES COUNTY MARRIAGES, 1778-1868

Sprinkle, Obadiah & Elvirah Martin, 3 April 1866; Aaron Ladd, bm; m 4 April 1866 by W. F. Adams, Baptist minister.

Stacy, John W. & M. L. Allen, 21 July 1852; m 26 Aug 1852 by Wm. F. Adams, Baptist minister.

Stacy, Simon & Elizabeth Hulme, 9 Oct 1792; Thos Farguson, bm.

Staley, Adam & Peggy Cargill, 7 Nov 1808; James Parler(?), bm.

Staley, Adam & Nancy Kilby, 17 April 1843; Henry H. Ray, bm.

Staley, Andrew J. & Sarah E. Miller, 11 Feb 1858; m 11 Feb 1858 by Eli Johnson, J. P.

Staley, Jacob & Nelley Childers, __ Sept 1815; John Johnson, bm.

Staly, Alfred & Dianah E. Cleaveland, 2 Dec 1846; A. L. Rousseau, bm.

Staly, Enoch & Sarah Whittington, 2 Jan 1861; Wm. H. McNiel, bm; m 3 Jan 1861 by Rev. Jas. McNeill.

Staly, Esley & Martha A. Cleaveland, 15 Aug 1843; W. W. Finley, bm.

Staly, Jacob & Sernetta P. Buttery, 26 Jan 1847; A. Staly, bm.

Staly, Thornton, son of Adam Staly, & Susan E. Dancy, daughter of A. J. Dancy, m 24 Dec 1867 by A. A. Whittenton, J. P.

Stancey, James P. & Catherine R. Calloway, 8 Oct 1855; Matthew Locke, bm; m 11 Oct 1855 by Jos Puett(?), L. D.

Stamper, Jacob & Clary Laurence, 18 Nov 1826; Benj. J. Parks, bm.

Stamper, Joel & Nancy Cannaday, 29 July 1780; Moses Toliver, bm.

Stamper, Jonathan & Mary Sabasten, 23 Feb 1801; Elijah Sabasten, bm.

Stamper, Nathaniel & Sarah Gambel, 23 Aug 1800; Jonathan Parks, bm.

Stamper, Powell & Sarah Bowen, 9 Jan 1817; John Rousseau, bm.

Stamper, William & Nancy Willson, 7 Feb 1820; John Handy, bm.

Stanbery, Aaron & Patty Humphry, 15 Jan 1806; Wm. Dunsmore, bm.

Stansberry, John & Ann Earnest, 28 Nov 1811; David Stanbery, bm.

Standley, Jacob & Elizabeth Hunt, 26 Dec 1780; Bennet Roberts, David Harris, bm.

Standley, Jonathan & Margret McCane, 3 Aug 1780; Joel Copeling, Nicholas Angel, bm.

Standley, Noel & Ann Barnet, 29 Jan 1839; Sumon Lansdown, bm.

WILKES COUNTY MARRIAGES, 1778-1868

Standley, Shadrick & Hanner Becknell, 7 __ 1800; Samuel Anderson, bm.

Standly, Reubin & Margarett Hendon, 21 Aug 1816; James Standley, bm.

Stanley, Joel & Sucky McKinney, 11 Nov 1806; Joel Long, bm.

Stanley, John & Lucy Stanley, 9 April 1819; Joseph Stanley, bm.

Stanley, Joseph & Mary Johnson, 9 Oct 1811; Samuel Anderson, bm.

Stanley, Larken & Oma Laws, 11 July 1839; Riley Laws, bm.

Stanley, Nathan & Hannah Levy, 21 Feb 1807; James Fletcher, bm.

Stanley, Thos Jr. & Ellender Hooper, 21 Jan 1823; Ruben Standley, bm.

Stanley, William & Elizabeth Hays, 21 Jan 1819; Wm. Lawrence, bm.

Stanly, Howell & Elizabeth Hooper, 13 Jan 1826; Thos Stanly, bm.

Stanly, Harris & Sally Brown, 13 April 1811; John Stanley, bm.

Stanly, Nathan & Elizabeth Kemp, 28 Jan 1830; Ambrose Silcock, bm.

Stanly, Noel & Martha Love, 22 Aug 1829; Reuben Standley, bm.

Stansbury, Nathan & Polley Allen, 20 April 1817; John Stanbery, bm.

Stanton, James & Polly Johnson, 24 Aug 1801; Reuben Knight, bm.

Stapp, Akilis & Elizabeth Hagler, 24 March 1817; Thomas Stapp, bm.

Stapp, Joseph & Rachel Walter, 21 Feb 1818; Thomas Stapp, bm.

Starkey, Joseph & Sarah Hamton, 3 Feb 1780; Jesse Greer, Joseph South, bm.

Starnes, Samuel S. & Nancy M. Wellborn, 3 July 1816; M. Stokes, bm.

Stead, Thomas & Pheby Tucker, 15 Dec 1779; Abraham Demoss, Jesse Greer, bm.

Steed, James & Pheby Campbell, 13 Oct 1801; Thos Ellison, bm.

Steele, Henry & Rhoda Shores, 15 Sept 1823; Daniel Shores, bm.

Steele, Peter & Margaret Laxton, 13 Dec 1819; Richard Brown, bm.

Steele, Robert L. & Annis Waatts, 21 Sept 1817; Ambrose L. Parks, bm.

Steelman, Elihugh & Lidda Rose, 25 April 1859

Steelman, Elihugh & Nancy Chambers, 23 Jan 1865; m 25 Jan 1865 by J. F. Somers, J. P.

WILKES COUNTY MARRIAGES, 1778-1868

Steelman, James L. & Sarah Jane Duncan, 1 Nov 1866; Harper Adams, bm; m 2 Nov 1866 by H. Hayes, J. P.

Stephens, Andrew & Nancy Keys, 4 Dec 1847; Martin Keys, bm.

Stephens, Elisha & Sarah Tribble, 12 July 1784; Menoah Dyer, bm.

Stepp, Golson & Aliles Peniton, 23 July 1782; Abraham Demoss, bm.

Stepp, Thomas & Martha Robertson, 15 June 1823; Robert Stepp, bm.

Stewart, James & Elizabeth Brown, 9 Nov 1793; Nathl. Gordon, bm.

Stikeleather, Cain & Rebecca Lipps, 15 Dec 1866; no bm.

Stimson, D. C. & J. M. Clery, 17 Jan 1844; A. A. Scroggs, bm.

Stinson, John & Jane McDaniel, 16 March 1803; Hugh McDaniel, bm.

Stoker, John & Jane Keeling, 20 Oct 1804; Thomas Keeling, bm.

Stokes, M. S. & Sallie E. Triplett, 10 May 1858; E. Staley, bm; m 11 May 1858 by J. N. Barker, minister.

Stokes, Montfort & Rachel Montgomery, 6 Jan 1796; Lewis Demoss, bm.

Stone, Bird & Lucy Johnson, 20 Jan 182__; Simon Shore, bm.

Stone, John & Dililey Maynard, 8 April 1808; Jesse Caudill, bm.

Stone, John & Elizabeth Mahafy, 29 Oct 1836; John Brewer, bm.

Stone, John Senr & Malinda Jordin, m 18 Feb 1866 by Rev. J. K. Baldwin.

Stone, W. Franklin & Martha Joyner, 10 Dec 1866; m by W. F. Adams, Baptist minister.

Stone, William & Salley Baugus, 11 March 1828; John Johnson, bm.

Stoneseffer, Johann Heinrich & Eloner Burck, 27 Aug 1781; Isaac Garrison, bm.

Storie, Eli & Mary Carlton, 1 Oct 1828; David Hooton, bm.

Storie, Harven & Nancy Coffey, 13 Oct 1826; Eli Story, bm.

Storie, Isaac & Abigal Long, 18 Oct 1800; Joel Long, bm.

Storie, John & Susanna Green, 8 Feb 1821; William Green, bm.

Storie, Joshua & Dise Green, 2 Feb 1818; William Bradley, bm.

Storie, Joshua & Catharine Lewis, 31 July 1795; Joshua Storie, bm.

WILKES COUNTY MARRIAGES, 1778-1868

Storie, Robert & Rutha Lewis, 11 Sept 1802; Joshua Storie, Senr., bm.

Storie, Thomas & Clary Bradley, 6 Jan 1797; John Bradly, bm.

Storie, Thomas & Phebe Cox, 10 March 1824; Smith Ferguson, bm.

Storie, Benjamin & Nancy Hagler, 5 March 1806; Tho Lenoir, bm.

Story, Berrymon & Vienna Holmon, 22 Sept 1835; Wm. Foster, bm.

Stout, Hisekur & Dicy Holbome, 27 June 1811; John Prew, bm.

Stout, Johnathan & Rachel Eller, 3 Dec 1844; James W. Vannoy, bm.

Stover, Isaac & Margarett Hoots, 7 Dec 1818; Solomon Sparks, bm.

Strange, Archelaus & Elizabeth Coffey, 23 Nov 1802; Lewis Coffy, bm.

Stroud, A. M. & R. M. Parsons, 7 May 1865; m 6 May 1865 by ___.

Strutton, Absalom & Dorcas Shearman, 25 Oct 1806; John Kerbo, bm.

Strutton, Richard & Lyda Taylor, 7 July 1830; John Setsor, bm.

Stuard, John & Nancy Matthews, 30 July 1816; Ansel Matthews, bm.

Stuard, Samuel & Sally Coffey, 2 March 1824; Lewis Coffey, bm.

Studavant, John W. & Mima Mabry(?), 20 Sept 1857; John Mabery, bm.

Sudderth, Abraham & Elizabeth Gilreath, 20 April 1843; Abel H. Shuford, bm.

Suits, Joel & Nancy Pourter, 24 Nov 1825; Joel Cargill, bm.

Sullivan, Saml. & Charlotte Gilreath, 8 June 1825; D. C. Barrett, bm.

Summerling, Griffin & Patsey Cleveland, 4 Dec 1813; E. Watkins, bm.

Summerlin, Alfred & Mariah Speck, 21 Oct 1844; Allen Summerlin, bm; m by Saml Walsh, J. P.

Summerlin, Allen & Elizabeth Miller, 28 March 1846; Thomas Walsh, bm.

Summerlin, Martin & Mahala Keller, 1 Jan 1839; Joel Roberts, bm.

Summerlin, Presley & Mariah Pernell, 22 Dec 1846; John A. Eller, bm.

Summerlin, Thos & Ann Trible, 30 Oct 1843; Loveless Minton, bm.

Summerlin, Thos P. & Bathsheba Roberts, 1 Dec 1824; Abner Trible, bm.

WILKES COUNTY MARRIAGES, 1778-1868

Summerlin, James M. & Louisa Summerlin, 6 Oct 1866; E. A. Roberts, bm; m 7 Oct 1866 by J. W. Church, J. P.

Summerlin, Jesse C. & Mary Ann Hamby, 20 May 1848; James Hamby, bm.

Summerlin, Lazarus & Tempy Cross, 24 May 1815; Charles Pearson, bm.

Summers, James F. & S. M. Felts, 26 Dec 1859; m 6 March 1860 by L. D. Swaim, Baptist minister.

Summers, Thomas & Margarett Davis, 1 Dec 1815; James Allison, bm.

Summers, W. H. & Rebeka E. Brown, 17 Jan 1855; J. W. Felts, bm.

Summes, John & Seenay Meys, 18 March 1859; Seelius Pinden, bm.

Sumolin, Miles & Sarah Prophfet, 10 March 1814; Charles Person, bm.

Sutherland, Daniel & Grace Holdman, 7 March 1790; Wm. Lenoir, bm.

Suttle, Rueben & Polley McCann, 10 Jan 1817; James McCann, bm.

Suttle, William & Nancy Darnall, 8 April 1817; Solomon Alexander, bm.

Swaim, Charles & Rachel Russel, 17 Jan 1821; John Russel, bm.

Swaim, Michael & Elizabeth Barns, 7 Oct 1800; John Swaim, bm.

Swaim, Moses & Salley Stinson, 6 March 1821; Joshua Barnes, bm.

Swaim, V. D. & Dianah McBride, m 11 March 1866 by Thomas Howell.

Swan, Henry & Elizabeth Martin, 23 Oct 1832; Benjamin Martin, bm.

Swann, Richard & Elizabeth Robinett, 9 Oct 1812; James Robnet, bm.

Swanson, Anderson & Sarah Brown, 23 July 1839; John J. Walker, bm.

Swanson, James & Elizabeth Furgason, 12 March 1814; William Gray, bm.

Swanson, John & Sary Al Scotter, 5 April 1817; Wm Walker, bm.

Swanson, John & Polley Langford, 20 Feb 1819; Isaac Swanson, bm.

Swanson, R. E. & Elmyrah Triplett, m 22 Sept 1855 by E. B. Philips, J. P.

Swanson, Wm R & Margaret Adaline Tribble, 25 Feb 1848; Luther Swanson, bm.

Swinney, William A. & Leanor Cordill, 19 April 1838; Nathan Ward, bm.

WILKES COUNTY MARRIAGES, 1778-1868

Swinny, Edmund & Francis Duncan, 24 Oct 1831; Wm. C. Emmet, bm.

Tailor, Chas & Anne Cooke, 11 Dec 1783; James Tailor, bm.

Tailor, Joseph, of Rowan County, & Elizabeth Roberson, 6 Aug 1781; Isaac Mize, bm.

Tate, George B. & Sarah M. Davenport, 7 July 1831; Andrew Patterson, bm.

Taylor, Edward & Sarah Pourter, 31 Aug 1778; Joseph Hopkins Sr., bm.

Taylor, George & Jean Fletcher, 25 Jan 1826; Joseph Osbern, bm.

Taylor, Hance & ____, (no date); Lewis Demoss, bm.

Taylor, James & Sususana (sic) Cook, 21 April 1780; Benja. Bailis, bm.

Taylor, James & Easter, Osburn, 25 Oct 1830; Joseph Osburn, bm.

Taylor, James H. & Rebecca McNiell, 18 Jan 1854; m 18 Jan 1854 by Jas. McNiel, minister.

Taylor, John & Catharine Orsbern, 22 March 1822; Joseph Osbern, bm.

Taylor, William & Susan Fletcher, 23 Dec 1829; Isaac Fletcher, bm.

Taylor, William T. & Edith Craner, 15 Oct 1866; James W. Hackett, bm; m 16 Oct 1866 by J. D. Wilson.

Teague, Elisha & Elizabeth Michel, 29 May 1817; Joseph Teague, William Webster, bm.

Teague, Isaac & Nancey Mulles, 1 Oct 1836; Elijah Cearley, bm.

Teague, James & Loveviney Odom, 12 Feb 1835; Lewis Little, bm.

Teague, Magnes & Sarah Webster, 24 Jan 1809; Joseph Teague, bm.

Tedder, Elijah & Sarah Brock, 25 Sept 1828; William R. Mitchell, bm.

Tedder, Huston & Sarah Brooks, 13 Aug 1852; m by Eli Johnson, J. P.

Tedder, Joel & Amanda Sinclair, 5 Oct 1847; Wm Tedder, bm.

Tedder, Joel H. & Caroline Hix, 16 April 1859; A. Bell, bm; m 8 May 1859 by Thos. H. Saintclair, J. P.

Tedder, John & Nancy Parker, 13 Aug 1827; Wm Cox, bm.

Tedder, Wm & Rhody Eastept, 11 Feb 1846; Wellborn Nance, bm.

Tedder, Zachariah & Winney Eastridg, 7 Feb 1817; Jeramiah ____, bm.

Teder, Wm. H., son of Biddy Teder, & Mary Ridel, daughter of Debury Riddle, 19 Jan 1868; m 28 Jan 1868 by Rev. Wm. J. Chapel, Baptist minister.

WILKES COUNTY MARRIAGES, 1778-1868

Teder, Zaciere & Salley Brures, 29 Oct 1845; Willis Bereng, bm.

Templeton, James M., son of W. G. & Margret Templeton, & Caroline Eller, daughter of George & Mary Eller, 12 Oct 1867; m 13 Oct 1867 by J. W. Church, J. P.

Templeton, Solomon & Rebecca Wellborn, 6 Nov 1837; John E. Mastin, bm.

Templeton, John & Nancy Mitchell, 6 Feb 1862; A. Luckey Speakes, bm; m 6 Feb 1862 by G. B. Parks.

Tether, Benjamin & Mahalia Eastreg, 6 June 1826; Jeremiah Gilreath, bm.

Thomas, Henry M. & Mary Chapel, 27 March 1865; Ambrous J. Phillips, bm; m 27 March 1865 by J. I. Parks, J. P.

Thomas, Joel & Emily Hambrix, 4 Oct 1865; Henry M. Thomas, bm; m 5 Oct 1865 by J. K. Rose, Baptist minister.

Thomas, Wiley & Miry Horton, 28 March 1853; William S. Ferguson, bm; m 13 April 1853 by Smith Ferguson, minister.

Thomasson, William C. & Nancey E. Hampton, 14 March 1858; Cornelius J. Jones, bm; m 14 March 1858 by John Brown, Esqr.

Thomes, William & Mary Cockerham, 9 March 1859; H. L. Gambill, bm; m 10 March 1859 by J. M. Gambill, J. P.

Thompson, Closs & Rebeckah Wilson, 14 Sept 1787; Benjamin Coffey, bm.

Thompson, George W. & Elibeth (sic) Caudel, 1 Nov 1828; William Cordell, bm.

Thompson, Jas. G. & Sarah Pennel, 24 March 1828; Jesse Gilbert, bm.

Thompson, John A. & Ruth Dowell, 9 June 1859; m 12 June 1859 by Wm. H. Hubbard, J. P.

Thompson, Joseph & Martha Johnson, 5 Feb 1821; William Johnson Jr., bm.

Thompson, Roden & Clary Sale, 13 Sept 1806; Elias Sale, bm.

Thomson, Joseph & Mary Butrey, widow of Timothy Buttrey, 4 May 1806; Thos Allen, bm.

Thornberg - see Thronbergh.

Thornton, John & Susannah Cockerham, 11 Oct 1819; John Durham, bm.

Thornton, Meradeth & Mary R. York, 7 Feb 1860; Thos Byrd, bm.

Thronbergh & Elizabeth York, 18 June 1814; Henry Lenderman, bm.

Thronbergh, Jacob & Johanna Shoe, 27 Oct 1807; Leonard Lenderman, bm.

Thronburg, Lenard & Dolly Brewer, 18 Jan 1817; John Brewer, bm.

WILKES COUNTY MARRIAGES, 1778-1868

Thurmond, Meredith & Salley Gwyn, 3 Oct 1807; Wm. Martin, bm.

Thurmond, Willis & Elisebeth Jones, 14 Nov 1801; Benja. Jones, bm.

Thurston, Benjn. & Elizabeth Carrel, 24 Jan 1792; James Gwyn, bm.

Tiary, William & Mary Rash, 23 Feb 1818; Johnson Owen, bm.

Tidder, Wm & Elisabeth Ferguson, 8 March 1826; Jacob Estep, bm.

Tidline, Elxander & Elvira Holbrook, 1 Jan 1860.

Tidline, John A. & Marget Vollintine, 14 Jan 1855; Thomas Vollentine, bm; m 14 Jan 1855 by A. A. Whittenton, J. P.

Tilley, Benja. & Nancey Land, 29 March 1782; Coleson Stepp, bm.

Tilley, Edmund & Polly Holt, 31 Jan 1804; Henry Killion, bm.

Tilley, Edmund & Milla Goforth, 25 ___ 1847; Joel Brown, bm.

Tilley, George & Susanna Bryant, 29 Nov 1830; Edmon Tilley, bm.

Tilley, Henry & ___, 12 Oct 1792; Anns. Allen, bm.

Tilley, Lazarus & Sarah Davis, 9 Aug 1784; Philip Davis, bm.

Tillman, George & Hily Becknel, 16 Feb 1838; Andrew J. Souther, bm.

Tilly, Edmund & Sarah Furgison, 22 July 1796; Pearce Nowland, bm.

Tilmon, John & Cresey Fleatcher, 20 April 1844; Nelson Jarvis, bm.

Tindsley, James & Sarah Rhoads, 12 Dec 1840; James Kilby, bm.

Tinsley, David & Nancy Kilby, 28 Oct 1818; Charles Adams, bm.

Tinsley, Isaac & Elizabeth Perlin, 16 May 1811; Larkin Cash, bm.

Tinsley, Thos & Susanner Kilbey, 27 Jan 1800; James Hays, bm.

Tinsley, Thomas & Margerett Kilby, 26 Nov 1822; Daniel Bumgarner, bm.

Tipton, Joseph & Rebecca Cockerham, 30 Jan 1851; James C. Fulks, bm.

Tirey, Thomas & Sarah Taylor, 12 Sept 1799; George Koons, bm.

Tiser, Frederick & Elizabeth Stailey, 25 Dec 1811; Adam Stailey, bm.

Tolliver, Edmund & Patsey Higgins, 23 June 1827; Young H. Brooks, bm.

Tomlinson, Hiram & Malinda Lipps, 13 Sept 1860; J. H. Hines, bm; m 14 Sept 1860 by J. W. Church, J. P.

WILKES COUNTY MARRIAGES, 1778-1868

Tomlinson, William & Fanny Phillips, 15 March 1833; Eli Phillips, bm.

Tompkins, Benjamin & Elizabeth Hampton, 11 Jan 1799; Thomas Hampton, bm.

Tompkins, Daniel & Viney Johnson, 28 Aug 1826; John Hatley, bm.

Tompkins, James & Susannah Coffin, 27 April 1817; George Combs, bm.

Tompkins, James & Elizabeth Dier, 12 Nov 181__; W. Smith, Joel Vannoy, bm.

Tomson, George & Rebeca Young, 12 June 1801; Leonard Keeling, bm.

Townzen, John & Nancy Denney, 7 Sept 1780; Richd. Allen, bm.

Transon, James W. & Mary A. Rousseau, 16 Aug 1834; James H. Rousseau, bm.

Transon, Rufus & Jerusha Wright, 25 Feb 1860; m 26 Feb 1860 by S. P. Smith.

Transon, Rufus & Nena E. Hendon, 2 April 1867; Wm. Saunders, bm; m 4 April by Rev. Wm. J. Chapel.

Treadaway, Eli & Ruah Smith, 10 Feb 1861; m 10 Feb 1861 by Jno Parleir, J. P.

Treadway, Moses & Elizth. Massey, 28 April 1849; Joseph Shoemaker, bm.

Tribble, Elijah & Polley Brown, 17 ___ 1783; Charles Martin, bm.

Tribble, William & Lizy Speck, 21 Oct 1844; Andrew J. Blackburn, bm; m by Saml Walsh, J. P.

Trible, Abner & Suana Summerling, 17 June 1815; Thomas Compton, bm.

Trible, Abner & Rachel Walsh, 3 Sept 1844; McAlpin Walsh, bm; m by Saml Walsh, J. P.

Trible, Benja. & Feraby Johnson, 24 Jan 1781; Spillsbe Trible, bm.

Triplett, Enoch & Nancy Lipps, 25 Feb 1856; John B. Miller, bm; m 24 Feb 1856 by A. M. Foster, J. P.

Triplett, Joel & Milley Triplette, 25 Sept 1844; Miry W. Walsh, bm.

Triplett, John & ___, 26 Feb 1795; Robert Foster, bm.

Triplett, Russel & Elizth. Hendricks, 29 Nov 1831; Alfred Miller, bm.

Triplette, Elijah & Usley Knight, 24 Dec 1798; Reubin Knight, bm.

Triplett, Horton & Matilda Janus, 1 Feb 1836; Thomas Triplett Jr., bm.

WILKES COUNTY MARRIAGES, 1778-1868

Triplett, Horton & Sulena Pearson, 22 Jan 1851; William Hagler, bm.

Triplett, Jesse & Polley Triplett, 11 Jan 1828; Ransom Randal, bm.

Triplette, Jesse & Edy Dula, 22 Dec 1851; A. J. Walsh, bm; m 3 Feb 1852 by G. W. Hendrix, J. P.

Triplett, John & Sally Ferguson, 17 Jan 1826; Joel Waters, bm.

Triplette, John & Susannah Gilreath, 26 Feb 1827; Jesse Ferguson, bm.

Triplitt, Jesse & Susana Hodges, 26 April 1791; Richard Ferguson, bm.

Triplitt, Lindsey & Charlotte Lipps, 2 Nov 1861; J. W. Triplett, bm; m 4 Oct 1861 by J. W. Church.

Triplett, Martin & Nancey Brown, 27 March 1820; John Dula, bm.

Triplett, Martin & Polley W. Hall, 20 Feb 1822; Philip Walsh, bm.

Triplett, Mason & Mary Mullins, 28 March 1785; William Mullins, bm.

Triplett, Nimrod & Caroline Triplett, 17 March 1844; A. W. Pendley, bm.

Triplet, Sideney & Rebeckey Church, 18 July 1860; m 19 July 1860 by A. M. Foster, J. P.

Triplett, Thos & Susannah Triplett, 19 Feb 1849; Thos Ferguson, bm.

Triplett, Thos Jr. & Docia Dula, 1 Feb 1836; Horton Triplett, bm.

Triplett, Warren & Nancy Foster, 31 March 1832; William Wright, bm.

Triplett, Wm & Nancy Ferguson, 14 Feb 1785; John Webb, bm.

Triplett, William & Mary Bishop, 21 April 1827; Thomas Foster, bm.

Triplett, Wm & Martha Shepherd(?), 14 Aug 1847; Nathan Triplet, bm.

Triplette, Lewis & Prudence Roberts, 26 Dec 1818; John Triplitt, bm.

Triplit, Thomas & Elizabeth Triplett, 7 Jan 1822; Samuel Walsh, bm.

Triplitt, Ambrose & Harriet Secrese, 27 Feb 1854; William Triplitt, bm; m 27 Feb 1854 by P. Walsh, J. P.

Triplitt, Joel & Rebecca Gilreath, 5 Dec 1831; John Hagler, bm.

Triplitt, Lindsy & Fanny Foster, 2 Nov 1833; John Ferguson, bm.

WILKES COUNTY MARRIAGES, 1778-1868

Triplitt, Thomas & Jane Farguson, 25 Feb 1788; George Foster, bm.

Triplitt, William & Dianna Holmon, 6 Oct 1810; William Tugmon, bm.

Triplitt, Wm & Ann Waters, 21 March 1850; John B. Miller, bm.

Triplitt, Willington & Marthy Land, 6 May 1858; Thos Triplett, bm; m 6 May 1858 by J. F. Tugman, J. P.

Tritt, Elkana, son of Peter & Mary Tritt, & Elizabeth Davis, daughter of Benjamin & Emily Kilby, m 14 Nov 1867 by E. B. Phillips, J. P.

Trivitt, Elijah & Irreny Carlton, 4 April 1848; Linvil Land, bm.

Trivitt, Isaac & Nancy M. Curry, 22 March 1847; William Williams, bm.

Truman, John R. & Nancy Hamby, 4 Sept 1843; A. T. Ferguson, bm; m by Saml Walsh, J. P.

Trustey, Henry & Elizabeth A. Bruss, 26 July 1813; Thomas Law, bm.

Trusty, Allen & Sary Bruce, 5 Nov 1816; Solomon Debord, William Tucker, bm.

Tucker, Binion & Cinda Suttle, 27 Oct 1838; Washington Tucker, bm.

Tucker, James & Milley Carlton, 25 Aug 1826; Hiram Tucker, bm.

Tucker, James & Betey Royal, 26 July 1852; David Hames, bm; m 26 July 1852 by B. F. Johnson, J. P.

Tucker, John & Mary Hagler, 30 April 1825; David Earnest, bm.

Tucker, John & Belinda Reeves, 27 Jan 1855; Wm. H. Absher, bm; m 27 Jan 1855 by L. Sebastian, J. P.

Tucker, Noah, son of Wm. M. & Sarah Tucker, & Adline Anthony, daughter of Wm & Elizabeth Anthony, m 5 March 1868 by John K. Rose, Baptist minister.

Tucker, Silas & Betsey Robins, 9 Feb 1802; John Robins, bm.

Tucker, W. M. & Mary Darnall, 2 June 1853; James Darnall, bm; m 2 June 1853 by A. Parks.

Tucker, William & Susana Hampton, 20 Sept 1799; Jas. Williams, bm.

Tuder, James & Marthey Brookes, 19 April 1845; James Beng, bm.

Tugman, Edward & Sarah Sweeden, 16 March 1790; Saml. Besshop, bm; Charles Gordon, wit.

Tugman, James & Sarah Elmore, 28 Sept 1799; Francis Webb, bm.

Tugman, James & Malinda Brown, ___ 186_; B. F. Absher, bm.

WILKES COUNTY MARRIAGES, 1778-1868

Tugman, James F. & Lemada Hendrix, 11 Oct 1856; Samuel J. Ginnings, bm; m 28 Oct 1856 by G. W. Hendrix, J. P.

Tugman, James L. & Susanna McGrady, 25 Nov 1846; J. F. Tugman, bm.

Tugman, Wm & Mary Hawkins, 2 Nov 1824; Thomas W. Wilson, bm.

Tugman, Wm & Elizabeth Ferguson, 10 Feb 1838; John E. Mastin, bm.

Tulbert, Jesse & Jenny Brown, 2 April 1824; John Reddin, bm.

Turnbill, Benj. & Anne Yates, 23 Aug 1813; Robt Yates, bm.

Turnbill, James & Rhodie Good, 23 Aug 1798; Thomas Cole, bm.

Turnbill, John & Oliff Reed, 9 July 1782; Abraham Wiggins, bm.

Turnbill, John & Sally Holdaway, 26 Nov 1805; Jno Sinkler, bm.

Turner, A. L. & Pity Sidden, 11 Oct 1852; Richard Sidden, bm; m 12 Oct 1852 by Ansel Parks, J. P.

Turner, Edward & Lowersey Kelley, 27 Sept 1782; Thomas Turner, bm.

Turner, Edward & Sally Butry, 18 May 1805; David Mais, bm.

Turner, Henry & Marth J. Perdue, 16 April 1858; m 16 April 1858 by John Brown, J. P.

Turner, John E. & Mary M. Tildey Benge, 31 Jan 1861; Samuel Beng, bm.

Turner, Roger & Sarah Speed, 17 Nov 1779; Stephen Harris, bm.

Turnbull, John & Mary Russell, 23 Nov 1793; Joseph Herndon, bm.

Turnmire, P. W. & Cay Winkler, 26 Feb 1867; J. M. Nelson, bm.

Tyre, Joshua & Patsey Prewit, 11 March 1833; James Forrester, bm.

Tyre, Wm & Mary Ann Haynes, 8 March 1843; James Brewer, bm.

Underwood, Anderson & Mary Brookes, 1 Oct 1847; Montillmon Wade, bm.

Underwood, Claibern & Rebeckea Epps, 28 April 1821; William Ferguson, bm.

Underwood, Jos. & Elizabeth Lane, 13 April 1837; Jno B. Crysel, bm.

Underwood, Lewis Jr. & Polley Laurence, 16 March 1828; Henry Holder, bm.

Upchurch, G. B. & Maryann Welborn, 15 May 1866; Richard Shors, bm; m 16 May 1866 by W. H. Pardue.

Upchurch, Wm. B. & Emly Carline Cordall, 23 Nov 1851; Wm. R. Cordall, bm; m 23 Nov 1851 by Ansel Parks.

WILKES COUNTY MARRIAGES, 1778-1868

Usrey, John & Elisabeth Shaver, 30 Nov 1814; Jesse Smither, bm.

Utzman, John & Mary Adams, 24 Dec 1846; Jesse Howk, bm.

Utzman, John & Nancey Shumaker, 4 Oct 1865; Henry Souther, bm.

Vanderpool, Lewis & Polley Roach, 23 March 1831; Thomas Roberson, bm.

Vanhoy, John M. & Nancy Shomate, 29 March 1845; Wm. Hall, bm.

Vannoy, Abraham & Aley Eller, 22 April 1842; Wm. H. McNiel, bm.

Vannoy, Anderson & Martha Wheeler, 27 Oct 1852.

Vannoy, Andrew & Elizabeth Dogan, 29 Nov 1809; John Foster, bm.

Vannoy, Andrew & Nancy Powel, 12 April 1815; Abner Vannoy, bm.

Vannoy, Columbus F. & Mary V. Hall, 28 Dec 1866.

Vannoy, Daniel & Sarah Hickerson, 2 Oct 1779; Francis Reynolds, bm.

Vannoy, Enoch & Letea McGrady, 6 May 1823; Isaiah McGrady, bm.

Vannoy, Harvey S., son of Joel & Mira Vannoy, & Catherine Welborn, daughter of H. M. & Nancey D. Welborn, m 19 Sept 1867 by R. F. Hackett, J. P.

Vannoy, James & Sarah Sheppard, 5 Dec 1813; Larkin Sheppard, bm.

Vannoy, James H. & Mariah E. Whittenton, 20 Dec 1855; William R. Whittenton, bm; m 21 Dec 1855 by Wm. S. McNeil, J. P.

Vannoy, Jesse & Polley Sheperd, 11 Jan 1804; William Kilby, bm.

Vannoy, Jesse & Elizabeth Fairchild, 20 Sept 1837; John Eller, bm.

Vannoy, Jesse & Nancey Eller, 7 March 1846; Wade H. Colvard, bm.

Vannoy, Joel & Elisabeth Sinatclear, 18 March 1817; L. M. Hickerson, bm.

Vannoy, John & Rebecah McNiel, 8 Dec 1833; Wm. S. McNeil, bm.

Vannoy, John Jr. & Catharine Gambill, 28 March 1835; Wade H. Colvard, bm.

Vannoy, L. G. & Emeline Lenderman, 10 Oct 1868; James A. Vannoy, bm; m 11 Oct 1865 by J. W. Church.

Vannoy, Nathaniel & Peggey Tinsley, 5 Jan 1819; Amos Church, bm.

Vannoy, Neal C. & Emly C. Whittenton, 6 March 1859; W. R. Whittenton, bm; m 9 March 1859 by Rufus W. Colvard, J. P.

Vannoy, Noah & Charity Church, 23 Feb 1811; Francis Vannoy, bm.

Vannoy, Wm. K. & Matilda M. Wheeler, 23 Dec 1842; Wm. H. McNiel, bm.

WILKES COUNTY MARRIAGES, 1778-1868

Vannoy, William W., son of Joel & Mira Vannoy, & Susan E. Crowson, daughter of Adam S. & Nancey Crowson, m 7 July 1867 by Calvin Plyler.

Vannoye, Andrew & Susanna Sheppard, 18 Oct 1779; Joseph Tanner Whiteman, James Sheppard, bm.

Vannoye, Nathaniel & Fanny Owens, 7 Jan 1841; A. Tomlinson, bm.

Vanwinkle, Abraham & Carity Salley, 1 Feb 1787; Adoniram Allen, bm.

Vanzant, Isaac & Feby C. Cope, 24 March 1866; m 25 March 1866 by J. F. Somers, J. P.

Vest, Absalom & Hannah Raymond, 2 Aug 1808; John T. Mize, bm.

Viars, John B. & Anis Payne, 18 April 1837; David Gray, bm.

Viars, Robert & Elizabeth Powel, 9 Feb 1815; John Viars, bm.

Viars, Wm & Rebekah Kirby, 19 Feb 1808; Andrew Sheppard, bm.

Vicas, James & Sally Mullis, 22 Jan 1820; John Brooks, bm.

Vicas, John & Polley Mathis, 2 Dec 1828; Jeremiah Gilreath, bm.

Vicars, John S. & Nancy Ellis, 6 April 1833; Wm. Ellis, bm.

Vickas, Elias & Lucy Hopkins, 23 Oct 1778; Wm. Gilreath, Elijah Vickas, bm.

Vickas, Elijah & Sarah Childres, 29 Dec 1783; John Vickas, bm.

Vickers, Charles & Nancy Smoot, 28 June 1813; Samuel Anderson, bm.

Vickers, Wiley & Mariah Vickers, 4 July 1835; Ishom Hubbard, bm.

Vickers, Jesse H. & Martha Barnett, 5 Nov 1855; B. C. Gilreath, bm.

Vickes, John & Ann Johnson, 10 March 1817; Charles Vickes, Jeremiah Gilreath, bm.

Vickes, Sinsay & Sarey Sewmaker, 11 Nov 1858; James Walker, bm.

Vines, John D. & Nancy Lester, 28 May 1859; Alfred Warren, bm; m 29 May 1859 by John Gentry, J. P.

Volinetine, John H. & Marey Denney, 13 Sept 1848; Rufus Hampton, bm.

Waddell, Levi & Rachel Wiles, 1 April 182__; William Wiles, bm.

Wadle, Merdeth & Winna Lee, 9 April 1865; m 9 April by Jno M. Brown, J. P.

Wadill, J. T. & Maryann Brown, 26 Jan 1867 by Wilson Walker, J. P.

WILKES COUNTY MARRIAGES, 1778-1868

Waddell, John & Sarah Dunkin, 23 Jan 1834; Richard Baugus, bm.

Waddle, Abraham & Pheba Holbrook, 29 April 1858; m 29 April 1858 by Eli Grimes, L. D. of M. E. C. S.

Waddle, Clabourn & Sarah Previt, 5 May 1827; Atha Waddle, bm.

Waddle, James & Fanny Baugus, 19 March 1823; Calborn Waddle, bm.

Waddle, John & Margret Pennington, 6 June 1855; Live Waddle, bm; m 6 June 1858 by Eli Grimes, L. D. of M. E. C. S.

Waddle, Noey & Elizabeth C. Johnson, 10 Nov 1864; Daniel Brown, bm.

Waddle, Ruben & Amelia Billings, 27 Feb 1856; Daniel Billings, bm; m by John Brewer, Esq.

Wade, A. R. & Elisabeth Ratliff, 27 Aug 1859; Jas. R. Ratliff, bm; m 29 Aug 1859 by Elder Jas. McNeill.

Wade, Tillmon & ___, ___ 18__; John W. Baily, bm.

Wadell, Arthey & Levina Wiles, 3 Jan 1828; Robert Baugus, bm.

Wadker(?), Joel & ___ Perdue, 16 Dec 1830.

Wadkins, Andrew & Telitha Lunsford, 8 Jan 1823; Jesse Walker, bm.

Wadkins, John & Nancey Wainscott, 3 Aug 1819; Hughs Napper, bm.

Wadkins, John & Francis Chavis, 22 Jan 1846; Anderson Ferguson, bm.

Wadkins, John W. & Martha C. R___, 9 Nov 1854; Bevel M. Pardue, bm.

Wadkins, William & Frankey Adams, 21 Jan 1833; Wesley Adams, bm.

Wadkins, Wm & Elizabeth Shumate, ___ Oct 1858; m 3 Oct 1858 by Jas. M. Gambill, J. P.

Wadle, Burgess & Sarah An Boese, 29 Sept 1851; Ezra Debord, bm; m 30 Sept 1851 by B. F. Johnson, J. P.

Wagner, Matthias M. & Mary Fyffe, 9 March 1830; Zachariah Adams, bm.

Wagoner, W. D. & Mary Miller, 22 Feb 1867; m 22 Feb 1867 by J. W. Church.

Wakefield, Hamilton & Sary Goodwin, 1 Jan 1817; Ivy Reynolds, bm.

Wales, Samuel & Nancy E. Brown, 14 Aug 1845; Abel R. Wilborn, bm.

Walis, Martin & Anne Roberson, 18 Jan 1830; James Roberson, bm.

Walker, A. L. & Mary Jerden, 20 Jan 1866; H. C. Summers, bm; m 20 Jan 1866 by H. C. Somers, J. P.

WILKES COUNTY MARRIAGES, 1778-1868

Walker, Alfred & Susana Sale, 25 Dec 1841; Green McBride, bm.

Walker, Benjamin & Jane Sale, 30 Nov 1842; Alfred Walker, bm.

Walker, Charles & Susannah Gray, 13 June 1811; Wm Demmit, bm.

Walker, Charles & Mary Caroline Swanson, 2 March 1848; John Walker, bm.

Walker, Charles & Sarah Chambers, 20 Jan 1853; Noah Jarvis, bm; m 20 Jan 1853 by R. W. Wooton, J. P.

Walker, Daly & Hannah Smith, of Burke County, 27 Nov 1778; Charles Walker, Randler Walker, bm.

Walker, David & Fany Adams, 6 Feb 1795; Ambrose Walker, bm.

Walker, David & Frances Helen, 16 Nov 1816; W. W. Wright, bm.

Walker, David & Nelley Holderway, 30 Oct 1860; m 1 Nov 1860 by Wm. Tedder.

Walker, Eli & Suana Gamble, 13 Aug 1819; David Caudill, bm.

Walker, Eli & Sarah Roads, 7 Nov 1858; Simvel Walker(?), bm; m 8 Nov 1858 by L. Sebastian, J. P.

Walker, Francis M. & Phebe Cordill, 30 Dec 1866; W. L. Higgins, bm.

Walker, G. W. & Elisa J. Ferguson, 24 Feb 1859; m 24 Feb 1859 by E. B. Philips, J. P.

Walker, Hiram & Jane Kell, 31 May 1823; Benj. H. Brown, bm.

Walker, Howard & Martha Benton, 11 Sept 1792; Patrick McCay, bm.

Walker, Howard & Ailcy Parker, 27 June 1832; Nelson Anderson, bm.

Walker, Isaac & Rhoda Greer, 14 Jan 1786; George Elmore, bm.

Walker, Isaac & Sarah Roberds, 21 Jan 1834; Eli Bordens, bm.

Walker, J. W., son of L. R. D. & Cynthia C. Walker, & Sarah L. Ferguson, daughter of Chapman C. & Elizabeth Ferguson, m 24 Oct 1867 by Smith Ferguson.

Walker, James & Andrew Maxwill, 19 Jan 1700; Patrick McKay, bm.

Walker, James & Nancy Bradley, 11 Feb 1797; John Walker, bm.

Walker, James & Lucretia Hicks, 29 July 1819; Micajah Hicks, bm.

Walker, James & Fereby Wadkins, 24 May 1828; Leonard Walker, bm.

Walker, James H. & Nancy L. Wood, 8 Jan 1866; Elisha Smoot, bm; m 11 Jan 1866 by A. C. Myers.

Walker, Jerra P. & Martha Beshears, 3 March 1861; J. R. Hartin, bm; m 31 March 1861 by J. W. Church.

WILKES COUNTY MARRIAGES, 1778-1868

Walker, John & Sarah Cash, 5 Aug 1823; Isom Felts, bm.

Walker, John & Polley Barlow, 29 Sept 1825; Joseph Barlow, bm.

Walker, John & Hily Swanson, 17 Oct 1836; Enoch Pearson, bm.

Walker, John Junr. & Clary Sale, 6 Jan 1831; William Mabery, bm.

Walker, John F. & Nancy M. Abshire, 14 Aug 1852; W. P. Abshier, bm; m 19 Aug 1852 by L. Sebastian, J. P.

Walker, John O. & Sarah E. Davis, 24 Nov 1854 m by Eld. John G. Bryan.

Walker, Josiah & Lademia Butrey, 17 Feb 1867; Wm. J. Johnson, bm; m 17 Feb 1867 by Wilson Walker, J. P.

Walker, Leonard & Nancy Sale, 18 May 1822; Richard Walker, bm.

Walker, Renelder & Mary Wilcoxson, 27 Nov 1778; Charles Walker, Daly Walker, bm.

Walker, Richard & Sina Sale, 4 March 1820; Goodwin Mathis, bm.

Walker, Robert Jr. & Maryan Stamper, 13 Jan 1867; James F. Wood, bm; m 17 Dec 1867 by A. W. Myers.

Walker, Simial & Rebecca Wadkins, m 5 Jan 1862 by A. B. Dancy, J. P.

Walker, Sion & Nancy Hall, 31 Jan 1821; James Brown, bm.

Walker, Smith F. & Seenor Elmirah Reid, m 4 Sept 1855 by Pickens Carlton, J. P.

Walker, Turner & Elizabeth Heral, 4 April 1823; Goen Abshire, bm.

Walker, Thomas & Lucinda Lane, 12 Feb 1845; Charles Downs, bm.

Walker, Wesley & Alsy M. Barnett, 26 Feb 1866; John Ray, bm; m 26 Feb 1866 by Rev. Wm. J. Chapel.

Walker, Wilis M. & Rebecca Myres, 15 Dec 1858; m 16 Dec 1858 by L. Sebastian, J. P.

Walker, Wiles M. & Mary J. Ellis, 29 Dec 1865; R. B. Grimes, bm; m 29 Dec 1865 by Eli Grimes, L. D. M. E.

Walker, William & Betsey M. Danold, 10 Sept 1825; Adam Grimes, bm.

Walker, William & Sarah McBride, 26 Oct 1826; Wilie Pilkenton, bm.

Walker, W. M. & Sarah McDanel, 28 Aug 1863; James Wiles, bm; m 30 Aug 1863 by L. Sebastian, J. P.

Walker, Wm. C. & D. J. Handy, 15 Nov 1865; R. B. Grimes, bm; m 15 Nov 1865 by A. E. Myers.

Walker, Wm. H. & Maryan Johnson, 4 Jan 1859; Milton Walker, bm; m 6 Jan 1859 by L. Sebastian, J. P.

WILKES COUNTY MARRIAGES, 1778-1868

Walker, Wilson & Mirah Hall, 17 March 1851; John Walker, bm.

Walker, Zephaniah & Hannah S. Crouch, 26 Sept 1843; Isaac Walker, bm.

Wall, Burrell T. & Elizabeth Carter, 23 Dec 1842; David Haines, bm.

Wall, Joseph & Hope Cannaday, 19 Aug 1822; John Wall, bm.

Wallace, John G. & Elizabeth Clariton, 19 Dec 1854; W. E. Clanton, bm; m 24 Dec 1854 by Thos. S. Wellborn, J. P.

Wallace, Joseph G. & Caroline Roberson, 24 Jan 1859; m 27 Jan 1859 by A. Gilreath, minister.

Wallace (Wallis), Richard & Catharine Warren, m 20 Feb 1857 by S. P. Smith.

Walls, Eli P. & Eliza J. Newman, 31 Aug 1862; William Lyons, bm; m 31 Aug 1862 by James M. Gambill, J. P.

Walls, James & Polley Cannaday, 7 Nov 1821; Aron Cannaday, bm; consent from William Cannaday, father of Polley, 4 Nov 1821.

Walls, James J. & Mahuldah Jentry, 26 March 1856; N. J. Walls, bm; m 26 March 1856 by J. M. Gambill, J. P.

Walls, Moses P. & Eliza J. Begly, 2 March 1855; James J. Walls, bm; m 4 March 1855 by Wm. Burcham, J. P.

Walls, Nathan J. & Elizabeth Norman, 5 Sept 1865; J. M. Gambill, bm; m 7 Sept 1865 by J. M. Gambill, J. P.

Walls, Peter & Sarah Gentry, 31 March 1857; Nathan J. Walls, bm.

Walls, William B. & Martha E. Philips, 7 May 1856; John W. Fields, bm; m 7 May 1856 by A. Parks.

Walsh, Andrew & Franky Hall, 31 Dec 1814; Peter Ray, bm.

Walsh, B. H. & Sarah Ann Melton, 7 Feb 1866; m by Larkin Pipes, M. of G.

Walsh, Harry & Elizabeth Holdman, 10 Aug 1852; Calvin Walsh, bm; m 10 Aug 1852 by Thomas Land, J. P.

Walsh, John & Betsey Allen, 19 Jany 1805; Richd. Allen, bm.

Walsh, Larkin & Mary Philips, 1 Dec 1859; William Walsh, bm; m 3 Dec 1859 by A. M. Foster, J. P.

Walsh, McCalpin & Rebeca Profit, 30 May 1829; Andrew Hamby, bm.

Walsh, Phillip & Anna B. Huffman, 28 Aug 1865; J. M. Eller, bm; m 30 Aug 1865 by J. W. Church.

Walsh, Samuel & Mary Prophet, 6 Jan 1823; Thomas Northern, bm.

Walsh, T. F., son of Thomas & Elizabeth Walsh, & Malinda Cardwell, daughter of N. P. & Patsey Cardwell, m 2 Feb 1868 by J. W. Church, J. P.

WILKES COUNTY MARRIAGES, 1778-1868

Walsh, Thomas & Elizabeth Profit, 23 Sept 1824; William Profit, bm.

Walsh, Thomas & Susanna Walsh, 18 Feb 1852; Harry Walsh, bm; m 19 Feb 1852 by Saml Walsh, J. P.

Walsh, Turner Calvin & Francis L. Norris, 10 Sept 1855; Harvy Walsh, bm; m 10 Sept 1855 by A. M. Foster, J. P.

Walsh, William & Fanny Parkes, 29 Dec 1821; Marideth Parkes, bm.

Walsh, William H. & Greenetta Johnston, 1 Feb 1866; m 1 Feb 1866 by J. H. Brown.

Walsh, Wm. L. & Rebecca L. McGee, 11 Nov 1858; m 11 Nov 1858 by Elder Jas. McNiel.

Ward, Nathan & Mary Foster, 17 Aug 1837; David Gray, bm.

Warner, Samuel & Winneford Alexander, 8 Jan 1783; Stephen Cordial, bm.

Warren, Alfred & Marey Rush, 12 Sept 1850; George W. Chambers, bm.

Warren, Henry & Elcy Kez, 21 April 1830; David Gray, bm.

Warren, James P. & Sarah J. Word, 26 Dec 1866; J. M. Emerson, bm; m 28 Dec 1866 by J. N. Haynes.

Warren, Peter & Salley Owens, 2 March 1821; Robt Warren, bm.

Warren, Robert & Elizabeth Johnson, 20 Apr 1820; John Hatley, bm.

Waters, Isaac & Peggy Lard, 4 Feb 1806; Jeremiah Hampton, bm.

Waters, Joel & Rebecca Ferguson, 1 April 1826; Joel Vannoy, bm.

Waters, John W. & Mary Elizabeth Philips, 20 Dec 1854; Montgomery Cox, bm; m 21 Dec 1854 by A. M. Foster, J. P.

Waters, Joseph & Malinda Beshears, 22 Aug 1856; Thomas Kindall, bm; m 27 Aug 1856 by N. Church.

Waters, William & Elizabeth Bowman, 8 Dec 1778; Isaac Elledge, Moses Bowman, bm.

Watkins, Lewis & Margarett Holdman, 26 March 1819; John Hoopper, bm.

Watkins, Willis & Mary Perdue, 11 May 1832; William F. Adams, bm.

Wats, William & Peggy Parsons, 18 Dec 1830; Wright Earp, bm.

Watson, Allen & Malissa A. Payne, 5 June 1867; L. C. Hamby, bm.

Watson, Daniel & hlizabeth Biship, 6 Sept 1832; Thos Watson, bm.

Watson, David & Ali Davis, 8 Aug 1826; Ephraim Davis, bm.

Watson, David & Hily Hampton, 22 May 1841; Elihu Watson, bm.

WILKES COUNTY MARRIAGES, 1778-1868

Watson, Elbert & Mandy M. Davis, 11 Feb 1851; John M. Jones, bm; m by A. Lipford, Baptist minister.

Watson, James & Elizabeth Davis, 22 Feb 1822; Reubin Hamby, Ephraim Davis, bm.

Watson, James & Rachel Powel, 31 July 1851; Lindsey Triplett, bm; m 31 July 1851 by N. Church, J. P.

Watson, Jesse & Selah Adaline Watson, 23 March 1847; Thomas Watson, bm; m 23 March 1847 by ___.

Watson, John & Mary Bishop, 2 Oct 1822; Thomas Watson, bm.

Watson, John & Sarah Eller, 8 Feb 1823; Joseph Estep, bm.

Watson, Lemuel & Rhody Powel, 20 Jan 1855; G. S. Powel, bm.

Watson, Lewis & Clairey Ferguson, 28 Nov 1846; Samuel F. Hubbard, bm.

Watson, M. C. & F. B. Land, 7 May 1843; Willis Watson, bm.

Watson, Moses & Celia Laxton, 20 Feb 1827; Benj. J. Parks, bm.

Watson, Nelson & Nancy Pilkinton, 15 Nov 1844; Isaac Trivitt, bm.

Watson, Thomas & Garey Allen, 27 Dec 1814; L. M. Hickerson, bm.

Watson, Thomas & Nancy Banks, 16 Feb 1847; James Ates, bm.

Watson, Thomas & Elizabeth Triplett, 15 May 1847; Hiram Bishop, bm.

Watson, Warren & Catharine Watson, 6 Jan 1848; Jonathan Mitchell, bm.

Watson, William & Sussanna Bunting, 7 Aug 1853; Elijah Dyer, bm; m 7 Aug 1853 by Wm. Church, minister.

Watson, Willis & Elizth. Huffman, 23 Aug 1832; Thos Watson, bm.

Watters, John & Nancy Ellet, 18 Dec 1790; Francis Weeb, bm.

Watters, Joshan & Elizabeth Bowman, 18 Oct 1807; James Laws, bm.

Watts, George & Rebecca Parsons, 26 Feb 1840; Abednego Russel, bm.

Watts, James M. & Margerett E. Watts, 8 Sept 1866; J. H. Warren, bm; m 11 Sept 1866 by D. Wellborn, Minister.

Watts, James & Rebecka Jones, 15 Dec 1813; Benjamin Watts, bm.

Watts, James & Cloey Brown, 24 May 1831; William Russel, bm.

Watts, James & Francis L. Parks, 2 July 1831; Ambers L. Parks, bm.

Watts, John & Sarah Parsons, 31 Aug 1832; Thomas Earp, bm.

WILKES COUNTY MARRIAGES, 1778-1868

Watts, Nasia & Selina Davice, 19 Jan 1842; William P. Phillips, bm.

Watts, Nesiah & Nancy Ragesdle(?), m 24 June 1858 by E. B. Philips.

Watts, Reuben & Lurener Watts, 17 Feb 1833; Elisha Chapman, bm.

Watts, T. J. & Jamie Laine, 12 Oct 1865; T. B. Hester, bm; m 11 Oct 1865 by C. C. Ferguson, J. P.

Watts, William & Betsey Barns, 2 Feb 1808; Reuben Barns, bm.

Watts, William & Lydia Adeline Watts, 23 Sept 1846; James Watts, bm.

Watts, William, son of Jacob & Winey Watts, of Alexander County, & Jane Hackett, daughter of Luberto Hackett, all colored, 17 Sept 1868.

Watts, William, son of John & Sarah Watts, & Sarah H. Watts, daughter of George & Rebecca Watts, 5 Nov 1867; m 7 Nov 1867 by E. B. Phillips, J. P.

Waugh, James & Elizabeth Robinett, 24 July 1805; Robert Martin, bm.

Wayting, Joshua & Delily Markes, 4 April 1862; W. N. Pierce, bm.

Weaver, Solomon & Rachel Childers, 14 Feb 1820; Frederick Tiser, bm.

Weaver, Solomon & Martha Green, 5 March 1822; John Weaver, bm.

Webb, Darius & Salley Allen, 22 Aug 1811; Joseph Wall, bm.

Webb, Elijah & Martha Johnson, 2 Dec 1823; J. Mastin, bm.

Webb, Henry A. & Kissy Waddy, 6 Aug 1863; John B. Wooddy, bm; m 7 Aug 1863 by P. R. McGrady, J. P.

Webber, Abner P. & A. E. Smith, 20 Sept 1844; R. C. Martin, bm.

Webster, Elijah & Mary Fortner, 1 Sept 1827; Joel Vannoy, bm.

Webster, James & Elizabeth Fortner, 11 Feb 1834; George Swaim, bm.

Webster, Zachariah & Ruthy Baines, 31 Dec 1825; Joel Vannoy, bm.

Welborn, Daniel & Susanna Deal, 10 Feb 1836; Write Earpe, bm.

Welborn, F. D. & Mary M. Tulbert, 19 Aug 1866; G. H. Brown, bm; m 19 Aug 1866 by C. R. S. Simpson, J. P.

Welborn, Henry M. & Martha Jane Hampton, 20 Oct 1865, E. M. Felts, bm; m 8 Sept 1866 by H. C. Somers, J. P.

Welborn, James & Rebeccah Johnson, 18 Feb 1813; Lewis Johnson, bm.

WILKES COUNTY MARRIAGES, 1778-1868

Welborn, Randol & Rebecca Felts, 9 March 1865; m 16 March 1865 by J. F. Somers, J. P.

Welborn, John M. & Sintha An Naylor, 25 March 1862; Thos S. Welborn, bm.

Welborn, Mabery & Nancy Pritchett, 13 March 1862; Jessey Couch, bm; m 18 March 1862 by Elder R. W. Wooton.

Welborn, Miren(?), son of Sarah Welborn & Mima Williams, daughter of Anthony & Juda Williams, all colored), 21 Sept 1867; m by C. R. S. Simpson.

Welborn, Randal & Patsey Redden, 6 March 1824; John Brown, bm.

Welch, J. C. & Ann C. Triplett, 15 Sept 1866; J. J. Parlier, bm; m 16 Sept 1866 by Smith Ferguson, minister.

Welch, Phillip & Elizabeth Hall, 10 Dec 1810; John Stanley, bm.

Welch, William & Elisabeth Judd, 29 May 1823; David Eller, bm; consent from John Judd, father of Elisabeth, 29 May 1823.

Wellborn, Isaac & Elvira Tomlinson, 7 Feb 1828; S. Wellborn, bm.

Wellborn, Lewis J. & Susan Miranda Watson, 16 Dec 1848; Horton Triplett, bm.

Wells, Hardy & Patsey Felts, 19 April 1823; Miles Wells, bm; consent from Aason Felts, father of Patsey, 19 April 1823.

Wells, James & Rachel Brown, 6 Aug 1823; Miles Wells, bm.

Wells, James & Sarey Walker, 28 Dec 1841; Elisha Felts, bm.

Wells, John & Mary Fleat, 6 April 1780; William Overstreet, bm.

Wells, John & Lemira Walker, 14 Aug 1840; Alfred Walker, bm.

Wells, Miles & Elisabeth Martin, 21 Dec 1813; Daniel Wilcockson, bm; Amelia Martin, wit.

Wells, Moses & Winney Chandler, 21 Jan 1793; Wm. McGill, bm.

Wells, W. D. & Mary Billings, 6 May 1863; M. M. Billings, bm; m 7 May 1863 by John Hall, J. P.

Wells, William & Jane Day, 29 Oct 1819; Edward M. Day, bm.

West, Alexd. & Hanner Langley, 7 March 1781; Edmund Tilloy, bm.

West, Alexander B. & Nancy Land, 4 Feb 1851; William T. Ferguson, bm; m by A. Lipford, Baptist minister.

West, Ananias & Abigail Crouch, 7 Oct 1829; Wilson Laxton, bm.

West, Bales & Mary Swanson, 21 Aug 1818; John Hooper, bm.

West, Franklin & Cinthy Holder, 30 July 1844; Franklin T. Ferguson, bm.

West, John & Catherine West, 24 Aug 1859; m by A. M. Foster, J. P.

WILKES COUNTY MARRIAGES, 1778-1868

Wester, P. T. & Lossern(?) Wadkins, 25 March 1862; Henry ___, bm.

Whealor, Smith & Mary Cox, 12 May 1832; Geo. Ferguson, bm.

Wheately, Martin H. & Frances Shoate, 2 Nov 1858; m 2 Nov 1858.

Wheateley, Willis H. & Matilda Alexander, 12 Nov 1851; m 12 Nov 1851 by Eli Grimes, L. D. of M. E. Ch. South.

Wheatley, Agnus A. & M. J. Alexander, 15 Feb 1867; Joseph Spicer, bm.

Wheatley, D. M. & Mary Billing, 1 Feb 1865; m by Eli Grimes, L. D. of M. E. C. S.

Wheatley, Dr. F. & Sarah Jane Gambill, 17 April 1864; F. P. Johnson, bm; m 17 April 1864 by Eli Grimes, L. D. M. E. C. S.

Wheatley, George W. & Elizabeth M. Abshire, 22 Feb 1854; m 22 Feb 1854 by L. Sebastian, J. P.

Wheatley, John & Milly Robbins, 29 Sept 1827; Turner Hampton, bm.

Wheatley, Martin & Polley Johnson, 12 June 1821; Fedric Tiser, bm.

Wheatley, William & Elizabeth Kilby, 2 June 1815; Joshua Smith, bm.

Wheatley, Willis & Matilda Robbins, 6 Jan 1818; William Alexander, bm.

Wheatly, Thos & Elizabeth Sprinkle, 18 March 1836; Jerry Alexander, bm.

Wheatly, Thomas B. & Jane Alexander, 11 Oct 1859; Paten Dimmet, bm; m 11 Oct 1859 by John Brewer, Esqr.

Wheeler, Alfred & Mary Church, 14 Feb 1841; Absolom Wheeler, bm.

Wheeler, Daniel & Mandy Triplett, 14 Feb 1848; William Holder, bm.

Wheeler, Carson E. C. & Marthy Waters, 8 Aug 1848; John W. Waters, bm.

Wheeling, Edmund C. & Salley Winkler, 9 Jan 1833; William H. Dula, bm.

Wheelor, Absalom & Elizabeth Eller, 10 Jan 1832; Alex. Church, bm.

Wheeley, William W. & Mary L. Cleavland, 19 Dec 1829.

Whiggins, Abraham & Nancy Colvert, 15 Feb 1785; William Rutledge, bm.

White, Achilles & Sarah Fletcher Jr., 18 July 1831; Thomas Fletcher, bm.

WILKES COUNTY MARRIAGES, 1778-1868

White, Elisha & Mary Bunting, 27 Nov 1849; William T. Ferguson, bm.

White, John & Aly Yeats, 23 Feb 1838; Barnard Yates, bm.

White, Landy R. & Rebeca Fletcher, 3 June 1825; Whitfield Kerr, bm.

White, William & Marthy Keller, 30 Sept 1839; Hiram Keys, bm.

White, William W. & Delila F. McNiel, 23 July 1863; George W. Carter, bm; m 23 July 1863 by A. A. Whittenton, J. P.

Whiteachar, John & Martha Wilson, 25 Feb 1782; John Yeargain, bm.

Whitington, John & Francis Yeats, 5 Feb 1846; Abner Carmichael, bm.

Whitley, L. M. & Amelia Johnson, 7 March 1854; m 9 March 1854 by W. M. Parks, J. P.

Whitley, M. H. & Susan Shumate, 2 Nov 1852; m 2 Nov 1852 by S. J. Gambill, Esqr.

Whitlock, Jno & Elisabeth Preston, 4 April 1816; Samuel Person, bm.

Whitley, Samuel P. & Elisabeth Brown, m 7 June 1855 by Saml G. Gambill.

Whetstone, Henry & Polly Yates, 10 Nov 1805; James Patton, bm.

Whittington, A. M. & Elisabeth Linderman, 18 Dec 1826; Jno: Whittington, bm.

Whittenton, Allen A. & Polly Eller, 13 Dec 1838; Reubin W. Kilby, bm.

Whittenton, James W. & Polly Lenderman, 9 Feb 1827; James Whittenton, bm.

Whittington, Alexander G. & Susana Vannoy, 21 July 1842; James Shepherd, bm.

Whittington, Calvin W. & Martha Parsons, 5 Sept 1865; J. S. Huffman, bm; m 6 Sept 1865 by Rev. Jas. McNeil.

Whittington, Carter & Nancy Brown, 6 Feb 1801; Caleb Dyer, bm.

Whittington, Leander & Sallie E. Colverd, 15 March 1867; Benjamin F. Whittington, bm; m 17 March 1867 by B. C. Calloway, J. P.

Whittington, Leonard & Sarah Kilby,(no date, during admn. of Gov. William R. Davie); Wm. Demoss, bm.

Whittington, Thos C. B. & Elisabeth J. Law, 17 Nov 1855; James H. Vannoy, bm.

Whittington, Wm. K. & Amarica Eller, 6 March 1859; Neil C. Vannoy, bm; m 9 March 1859 by Rufus W. Colvard, J. P.

WILKES COUNTY MARRIAGES, 1778-1868

Whitton, Thomas & Mary Barnes, 3 March 1800; Robert Philips, Michael Swim, bm.

Wiet, Enoc & Rachel Sheets, 10 July 1819; Thomas Grifeth, bm.

Wiggins, Hardy & Dilala Laws, 6 Dec 1828; Thos Rutherford, bm.

Wilborn, Abel R. & Mary L. Cass, 12 Dec 1859; L. D. Welborn, bm; m 15 Dec 1859 by D. W. Parks, J. P.

Wilborn, Henry & Nancy Redding, 26 July 1821; Wm. Redding, bm.

Wilborn, Joel & Nansey Redding, 11 April 1849; Harrison Wilborn, bm.

Wilborn, John & Lucy Brown, 18 Sept 1830; John Brown, bm.

Wilborn, John & Mary A. Shors, 4 Jan 1860; A. R. Wilborn, bm.

Wilborn, Maberry & Elisabeth Green, 29 Dec 1815; James Mabery, bm.

Wilcockson, George & Nancy Yates, 10 Sept 1806; Hugh Yeats, bm.

Wilcockson, George & Nancy Demmit, 5 March 1830; William Wilcockson, bm.

Wilcockson, Isaac & Agness Love, 9 Nov 1817; William Love, bm.

Wilcockson, William & Mira Robins, 2 Jan 1833; Isaac N. Forney, bm.

Wilcoxen, D. J. & Celina Adkinson, 5 July 1854; m 6 July 1854 by Wm. H. Hubbard, J. P.

Wilcoxson, David & Nancy Love, 1 Nov 1828; Isaac Wilcoxson, bm.

Wilcoxson, Jesse & Fereby Denney, 16 Feb 1818; James Denney, bm.

Wiles, A. P. & Pheba H. Philips, 31 Jan 1865; Wilson Walker, bm; m 31 Jan 1865 by Eli Grimes, L. D. of M. E. C. S.

Wiles, D. F. & L. M. Holbrook, 18 Jan 1864; Wilson Walk, bm; m 18 Jan 1864 by Jno M. Brown, J. P.

Wiles, H. C. & S. L. Bilings, 17 Dec 1861; m 17 Dec 1861 by A. B. Dancey, J. P.

Wiles, Hiram & Sarah Ann Brewer, 27 April 1863; Wm. Garner, bm.

Wiles, Joseph & Dinah Comer, 3 March 1854; m by John Brewer, Esqr.

Wiles, Wm. H. & W. H. Wiles, 25 Oct 1866; J. A. Wiles(?), bm.

Willbanks, Bouman & Hannah Mathews, 6 Jan 1793; John Wiggins, bm.

Willcox, Jesse & Sally Denney, 18 July 1826; Wm. Reddin, bm.

Willcox, S. W. & Rebecca J. Vann, 21 Jan 1866; William McNeil, bm; m 17 March 1866 by Rev. Jas. McNeil.

WILKES COUNTY MARRIAGES, 1778-1868

Willcoxon, Meredith & Malinda Lenderman, 14 Dec 1833; Wm. S. McNiel, bm.

Willcoxson, Levi & Elizebeth Orsbern, 17 Dec 1822; Joseph Orsbern, bm.

Williames, Reace & Polley Felphs, 4 April 1800; Richard Dickanie, bm.

Williams, Acquiller & Elizabeth Hays, 18 April 1859; m 19 April 1859 by H. Hayes, J. P.

Williams, Aquila & Sarah Nicholson, 14 June 1828; Adley Smith, bm.

Williams, David & Catherine Milsaps, 4 Feb 1857; H. Hayes, bm.

Williams, E. H., son of Jos. W. Williams, & C. E. Nickolason, daughter of Wm. Nickolason, 26 May 1867; m by Rev. R. W. Wooton.

Williams, Hugh R. & Elizabeth Kemp, 25 Feb 1832; Larkin J. Bicknell, bm.

Williams, James & Sarah Barber, 25 Sept 1865; C. R. S. Simpson, bm.

Williams, Keylon & Delphia Duncan, 28 Nov 1840; Ellis Anderson, bm.

Williams, Martin & Maryann Barnet, 4 Oct 1844; Wm. Bennet, bm.

Williams, Martin & Sarah Caroline Hubbard, 3 April 1849; James Williams, bm.

Williams, Melville & Caroline Specks, 26 Jan 1857; Newman Mahaffy, bm.

Williams, Nelson M. & Joseaphin Booey, 5 Oct 1865; C. R. S. Simpson, bm; m 5 Oct 1865 by C. R. S. Simpson, J. P.

Williams, Philip & Elizabeth Bell, 26 Jan 1814; Julus Keeton, bm.

Williams, Robert & Sarah Metstead, 28 March 1828(?); Jno B. Crysel, bm.

Williams, Turner, son of Anea Williams, & Susannah Gray, daughter of Jackson Keedil, colored, m 21 Nov 1867.

Williams, William & Mary Curry, 17 Feb 1844; Evin Ellis, bm.

Willson, Levi & Sary Baker, 15 Feb 1817; James Chambers, bm.

Willson, Saml & Ann Paterson, 29 March 1782; James Patterson, bm.

Wils, Iven & Polly Privit, 6 Jan 1830; Abram Buttrey, bm.

Wilson, Corneilious & Betsey Roberts, 25 Jan 1819; Bennet Robberts, bm.

Wilson, Isaac & Mary Hagerman (no date, during admn. of Gov. Wm. R. Davie); John Reese, bm.

WILKES COUNTY MARRIAGES, 1778-1868

Wilson, Isaac & Patience Jones, 12 Nov 1811; John Wilson, bm.

Wilson, John & Bellee Reaves, 28 Oct 1784; James Reaves, bm.

Wilson, John & Nancy Burchett, 29 Oct 1811; Robert Burchitt, bm.

Wilson, William & Mary Wilson, 17 Aug 1787; Joseph Holeman, bm.

Windsor, John H. & Gemima C. Sale, 10 July 1865; m 10 July 1865 by Henry Chambers, J. P.

Wingler, Francis & Temperance Dancy, 23 Oct 1832; John Dancy, bm.

Wingler, Humphrey & Nancy Adams, 3 Nov 1866.

Wingler, Isom & Leucy Wyatt, 24 Dec 1859; m 29 Dec 1859 by Wm. Hall, minister.

Winkler, Joshua & Carolina Person, 19 Feb 1852; m 19 Feb 1852 by Wm. H. Hubbard, J. P.

Winscot, Christopher & Sarah Padget, 9 April 1796; John Roberts, bm.

Wisdom, Thomas & Catharine Stapp, 29 March 1779; Golston Stapp, bm.

Witherspoon, David & Elizabeth Gordon, 16 June 1791; John Witherspoon, bm.

Witherspoon, Jno & Betsey Dula, (no date, during admn. of Gov. Wm. R. Davie); Benja. Howard Junr., bm.

Witherspoon, Thos & Elizabeth Mastin, 29 Nov 1820; Ths. W. Wilson, bm.

Witherspoon, Wm. H. & Clara Pennal, 10 May 1866; J. S. Call, bm; m 3 June 1866 by Rev. Jas. McNeil.

Witherspoon, Wm. P. & Nancy Montgomery, 17 April 1845; Hezekiah Curtis, bm.

Wood, Hambleton, son of William & Elizabeth Wood, & Elizabeth Luffmon, daughter of Isaac & Mary Dickerson, m 3 Oct 1867 by Elicum Ayers, minister.

Wood, Henry & Prudey Burcham, 26 Feb 1842; John Walls, bm.

Wood, Hezekiah A. & Nancy H. Poplin, 19 July 1866; R. B. Bryan, bm; m by J. B. Spicer, J. P.

Wood, James & Nancy Couch, 3 Dec 1829; John Walls, bm.

Wood, James & Nancy Carter, 24 Jan 1833; Jeremiah Crysel, bm.

Wood, James & Mary Love, 11 Feb 1847; Absalom Bullis, bm.

Wood, James N. & Rebecca Reace, 1 Oct 1858; m by H. Hutchison, J. P.

Wood, Jesse & Margett Tate, 22 Feb 1780; Nathaniel Wood, Reuben Stringer, bm.

WILKES COUNTY MARRIAGES, 1778-1868

Wood, John Jr. & Nancy Burchett, 27 Jan 1830; Elisha Pratt, bm.

Wood, Joseph & Jenny Durham, 7 Dec 1805; Thos Durham, bm.

Wood, Joseph & Rosana Durham, 13 Feb 1818; W. F. Campble, bm.

Wood, Joseph & Susana Fletcher, 28 Feb 1845; Isaac Parlur, bm.

Wood, Lindsey & Caroline Johnson, 11 Oct 1841; Saml Steelmon, bm.

Wood, Melvin R. & Sarah Bolding, 9 April 1859; Miles G. Lyon, bm; m 10 April 1859 by Thomas Bryan, J. P.

Wood, Nathan & Susannah Wall, 17 Jan 1825; John Walls, bm.

Wood, Samuel & Elizabeth Nale, 20 Nov 1821; Gideon Debord, bm.

Wood, Thomas & Peggy Durham, 15 March 1808; Jos. Wood, bm.

Wood, Thomas & Apelona Longbotom, 1 Aug 1842; Joseph Wood, bm.

Wood, W. W. & Miss J. L. Harris, 1 Jan 1866; J. S. Claywell, bm; m by ___ 2 Jan 1866.

Wood, Wm. F. & Mary C. Foster, 19 Oct 1865; Saml P. Smith Jr., bm.

Wood, Wm H. & Lydia Baggins, 15 Sept 1866; W. G. Hix, bm.

Wood, Wm. M., son of Joseph & Mary Wood, & Meley Bell, daughter of Evin & Nancy Bell, m 8 Aug 1867 by William A. Foster.

Woodde, Jackson & Sarah Wyatt, 1 June 1855; Bryan Woodde, bm.

Woodde, James & Peggy Bryan, 31 Oct 1811; Jonathan Woodde, bm.

Woodde, Jonathan & Nancy Nicholls, 29 Sept 1810; Larkin Pumphrey, bm.

Woodde, Tatton & Caty Theiling, 11 Nov 1804; John Turnbill, bm.

Woodfin, Wm. H. & Rebeca D. Gilreath, 26 Nov 1863; m 26 Nov 1863 by Rev. Wm. J. Chapel.

Woodruff, Braxton & Margret L. McDaniel, 21 Feb 1862; Harrison Cook, bm; m 22 Feb 1862 by J. P. Adams, J. P.

Woodruff, Daniel D. & Nanccy Phillips, 3 Jan 1855, John F. Shepherd, bm; m 4 Jan 1856 by S. D. Swaim.

Woodruff, G. M. & Sarah C. Sales, 10 March 1854.

Woodruff, John J. & Amelia C. Martin, 12 Oct 1846; R. C. Martin, bm.

Woodruff, Moses & Mary Kennedy, 15 Oct 1850; Thompson Kennedy, bm.

Woodruff, Wm. & Sarah Gentry, 26 March 1855; Jefferson Gentry, bm.

WILKES COUNTY MARRIAGES, 1778-1868

Woods, Shadrach & Sarah Wyatt, 19 May 1866; A. Abshire, bm; m 20 May 1866 by A. B. Dancey, J. P.

Woody, Abram M. & Nancy Owens, 19 Sept 1860; m 20 Sept 1860 by H. Hutchison, J. P.

Woody, Bryant & Nancy Holbrook, 20 Dec 1864; J. B. Blackburn, bm; m 22 Dec 1864 by A. E. Myers.

Woody, Edmond & Saley Wilson, 27 Jan 1819; William Wilson, bm.

Woody, James & Dicey Nicholson, 4 Aug 1835; Aquilla Williams, bm.

Woody, William & Phebe Abshire, 23 Aug 1831; Lewis Shepherd, bm.

Wooten, William J., son of John & Sarah Wooten, & Matilda Warren, daughter of Hampton & Susanah Warren, m 21 Nov 1867 by J. N. Haynes, Baptist minister.

Workman, Christopher & Nancy Fletcher, 10 July 1822; Perry Judd, bm.

Wotson, Sanders & Hanah Codle, 15 Oct 1826; Benj. Codle, bm.

Wray, Joseph & Nancy Mathews, 19 Sept 1807; Thos Mathis, bm.

Wright, Elfonzo & Lucindey Cross(?), 1 July 1841; William Seegraves, bm.

Wright, Jno W. & Fanny A. Transon, m 18 July 1861 by S. P. Smith.

Wright, John & Rachell Forgas, 3 Sept 1781; Thomas Wright, bm.

Wright, John & Jane Lane, 17 June 1822; Daniel Lane, bm.

Wright, John W. & Matilda Brown, 18 Oct 18__; John Brown, bm.

Wright, Josiah & Nancy A. Reynolds, 26 Sept 1820; James Todd, bm.

Wright, Parker A. & Maryan P. Wright, 27 April 1821; Elisha D. Waldon, bm.

Wright, Wm. & Nancy Woody, 10 June 1807; John Gordon, bm.

Wright, Zadock & Phebe Bryan, 26 Nov 1851; Pleasant Cockerham, bm; m 26 Nov 1851 by Ansel Parks.

Wyatt, Aaron & Mary Vannoy, 7 April 1835; Larkin Church, bm.

Wyatt, Alfred & Mary D. Binghim, 14 Oct 1854; R. S. Bingham, bm.

Wyatt, David & Amelia Wingler, 22 April 1824; John Adams, bm.

Wyatt, George & Polly Jinings, 27 March 1826; John McQuerry, Jr., bm.

Wyatt, George W. & Sarah L. Brown, 3 Nov 1861; Wesly Adams, bm; m 3 Nov 1861 by John Hall, J. P.

WILKES COUNTY MARRIAGES, 1778-1868

Wyatt, J. A. & N. E. Dancy, 10 Feb 1866; Nathan Wyatt, bm.

Wyatt, John & Nancy Matildy Rash, 31 Oct 1854; James C. Rash, bm.

Wyatt, John & E. E. Rash, 14 April 1866; Jos. C. Rash, bm.

Wyatt, John C. & Mary M. Adams, 7 Aug 1864; P. R. McGrady, bm; m 7 Aug 1864 by Wm. Hall.

Wyatt, John G. & Mary Brown, 15 March 1859; Aaron Wyatt, bm.

Wyatt, Leonard & Susanah Owens, 25 Nov 1865; F. M. Adams, bm; m 26 Nov 1865 by A. B. Dancy, J. P.

Wyatt, Sidney & Caty A. Miller, m 18 Aug 1860 by A. A. Whittenton, J. P.

Wyatt, Vickry & Sarah Jinnings, 13 Dec 1840; George Wyat, bm.

Wyatt, Vickry & Sary Jane Wingler, 26 Sept 1866; John Royal, bm.

Wyatt, Wm. A. & Sarah P. Rash, 25 Feb 1865; Nathan Wyatt, bm; m 25 Jan 1865 by Wm. Hall.

Wysong, Jonathan & Luisa David, 18 Nov 1844; John L. White, bm.

Yaets, Thos & Abey Michell, 28 Oct 1817; Rueben Hamby, bm.

Yarnell, Stephen & Lidia Baird, 19 Sept 1795; Aron Yarnell, bm.

Yates, A. C., son of John & Elisabeth Yates, & M. B. Lipps, daughter of John & Martha Lipps, 13 Oct 1867; m 12 Oct 1867 by J. W. Church, J. P.

Yates, Barnard & Mary Vannoy, 26 Nov 1834; Peter Eller Jr., bm.

Yates, Barnat J. & Nancey Eller, 21 Sept 1847; Peter Eller, bm.

Yates, Henry & Elizabeth Holbrook, 28 Sept 1866; Hiram Privett, bm; m 7 Oct 1866 by J. Stout, J. P.

Yates, Jesse & Caroline Eller, 18 Jan 1848; Robert Yates, bm.

Yates, Jessee & Suanah Milem, 7 Oct 1823; Samuel Gold, bm.

Yates, John & Elizebeth Cleveland, 13 May 1803; Jesse Cleveland, bm.

Yates, John & Ailcy Wilcox, 7 April 1840; Barnet Yates, bm.

Yeargin, John & Elizabeth Nazary, 20 Jan 1782; Edwd Finch, bm.

Yeates, David & Nancy Hays, 22 Oct 1814; Reuben Hayes, bm.

Yeats, David & Elizabeth Church, 5 Jan 1847; David Gray, bm.

Yeats, David & Milly Lunsford, 26 April 1851; no bm; m 17 May 1851 by Wm. S. McNiel.

Yeats, John D. & Louzaney Pilkenton, 31 March 1861; M. Pilkenton, bm; m 21 April 1861 by J. W. Church.

WILKES COUNTY MARRIAGES, 1778-1868

Yeats, Tillman & Polly Bumgarner, 18 April 1831; Daniel Bumgarner, bm.

Yeats, Hugh Jr. & Sally Miller, 23 March 1840; Isaiah Martin, bm.

Yeats, Robert & Polley Forrester, 8 Jan 1803; Neel Butram, bm.

York, Elias & Fanney Reddin, 29 Feb 1808; John Chambers, bm.

York, Henry & Polly Ellis, 8 Aug 1816; Leonard Lenderman, bm.

York, Isaac & Caroline Finly, 13 Oct 1866; Emanuel Craner, bm; m 18 Oct 1866 by J. D. Wilson.

Yonna, Abraham & Elizabeth Lewis, 15 Oct 1842; Charles Hayes, bm.

Young, Joshua & Lucy Smith, 13 July 1843; William R. Fortner, bm.

Younger, Joseph & Elizabeth Gray, 6 Feb 1790; Richd. Allen, bm.

Zedes, Ezekiel & Hannah Vest, 7 April 1854; m by A. Gilreath, 9 April 1854.

INDEX

Abshear, Ezekiel 1
  Goin 1
  Phoebe 92
Absher, Abram 1
  Alfred B. 24, 24
  B. F. 186
  Ezekiel 1
  Fanney E. 79
  Jain 48
  John 1
  Nancy 159
  Owen 153
  Pollie 26
  Susan 83
  Walter 123
  Wm. H. 24, 186
Abshier, John 1, 92
  W. P. 192
Abshir, Goen 69
  Jane 1
  Sucky 25
  William 1
Abshire, A. 204
  Betsy 1, 101
  Elizabeth M. 198
  Goen 192
  Going 92
  Iven(?) 125
  Kisiah 25
  Leeta J. 24
  Nancy 35, 92
  Nancy E. 118
  Nancy M. 192
  Phebe 204
  Polley 113
  Sucky 141
  Walter 113
Adam, Peggy 158
Adams, Aby 3
  Amanda 136
  Amelia F. 44
  Bettey 27
  Calvin 3
  Caroline 39
  Chapman 111
  Charity 46
  Charles 147, 183
  Deborah 86
  Delphia 159
  Elisabeth 26
  Elisabeth L. 91
  Elizabeth 46, 122, 159, 163
  Elizabeth D. 149
  F. M. 205
  Fanney 82
  Fanny 39, 159
  Fany 191
  Frankey 190
  Franky 28
  Gipson 82, 134, 160
  Harper 70, 178
  Harrison 2
  Hellen 37
  Henry 3, 86, 101
  Hulda 35
  Isaac 136, 159, 161

Adams (cont.)
  J. H. 123
  J. P. 122
  James F. 84
  Jane 10, 16, 114
  Jesse 119
  Jincy 136
  Jno 2
  John 90, 123, 136, 156, 158, 163, 204
  John M. 159
  Joseph H. 1, 157
  Judy 1
  Margret 141
  Martha 28
  Mary 10, 91, 110, 136, 188
  Mary M. 205
  Mathew 77
  Moses 2, 69
  Nancy 12, 17, 19, 71, 78, 86, 133, 202
  Nelly 16
  Patsey 136
  Pegga 3
  Polly 3, 131
  Rachael 166
  Rebekah 171
  Sarah 100, 103, 119, 158
  Sarah C. 2
  Solomon 28
  Spencer 4, 4
  Suana 141
  Susan 2
  Susana 88
  Susanah 158
  Violett 133
  Welborn 3
  Wesley 190
  Wesly 204
  William 16, 87
  William, Snr. 3
  William F. 194
  Wm. 3, 19
  Wm. F. 122
  Wm. H. 72, 86
  Wm. R. 42
  Zachariah 190
Addames, Nancy 45
Addams, Jacob 46
  Jane 87
  Martha 71
Adie, A. C. 140
Adkerson, Calvin 161
Adkins, Alferd 4
  Anny 116
  D. W. 149
  Frankey 53
  John 17
  Lewis 67
  Marthe 67
  Nancy 45
  Sarah 67
  William 90
Adkinson, Celina 200
Afzmann, C. H. 25

Aidey, Elizabeth 65
Aimes, Elizabeth 168
Alby, Margret 59
Alexander, Cally 92
  Coleby 36
  Fanney 128
  Fanny C. 92
  J. H. 5, 42
  Jane 198
  Jerry 198
  Jery 15, 15
  John 8
  M. J. 198
  Mary 4
  Matilda 198
  Milia 38
  Nancy 103
  Phoeba 108
  Pritchet 11
  S. E. 85
  Solomon 4, 180
  Susanna 104
  William 4, 198
  Winneford 194
Alford, Ann 64
  Marcy 7
  Salley 95
Alison, James 78
Allaway, Nancy 98
Allen, A. C. 132
  Adoniram 136, 189
  Aniram 103
  Ann 77
  Anns. 183
  Benjamin 50
  Betsey 193
  David C. 38
  Elizabeth 93
  Garey 195
  J. 5
  James 118
  Jane A. 135
  Judy 139
  M. A. 112
  M. L. 176
  Marthy Emily 31
  Mary 38, 110
  Peggey 72
  Polley 177
  R. 34
  Richd 7, 71, 163, 184, 193, 206
  Salley 116, 196
  Sarah A. 7
  Thomas 116
  Thos. 108, 110, 118, 144, 182
  Wm 7, 74
Allerson, Elizabeth 78
  Mary 78
Allexander, Elisabeth 69
  Linsy 15
  Linza 5
  Nancy 102
  Sary 4
  Winney 15
Allin, Thomas 7, 104

Allison, James 73, 132, 180
  Jane 154
  Jesse 71
  Mary 67
  Polly 33
  Susannah 23
  Thomas 16
  William 140
  Wm 31
  Wm. D. 18
Allman, Sally 135
Alvey, Lidda 46
  Lindey 148
  Mary 174
  Suckey 23
  Wiseman 174
Amefield, R. F. 74
Anderson, A. M. 43
  Amelia 128
  Ausborn 13
  Charlot 44
  Dicey 138
  Dicey Anner 102
  Dolly E. 127
  Eanes 6
  Eliza 97
  Elizabeth 72, 105
  Ellis 201
  Enos 60
  Enzor 6
  Jesse 173
  John 61, 63, 63, 77, 84
  Keziah 6
  Lucey 155
  Malinday 13
  Mary 60
  Mary Ann 6
  Nancy 45
  Nelson 137, 191
  Richmond 74
  Robert 6
  Robinett 7
  Samuel 6, 143, 177, 177, 189
  Sarah 84, 169
  Sophy 136
  Wesley 6, 43
  William 6
Andres, Oriller 108
Andrew, James 76
  Jane 49
  Jas. 74
Andrews, James 130
  Thomas 7, 135
Angel, Nicholas 176
Anthoney, Elizabeth 31
Anthony, Adline 186
  Elizabeth 186
  Wm 186
Aprks, Reuben 4
Ares, Luisinda 114
Arms, Jane 171
Armstrong, Elisabeth 174
  J. C. 7
  Mary 94
  Westley 174
Arrington, John 43
  Sary 9
Asbher, John 69
Ashley, Martha C. 168
Ashly, Anderson 24
Ates, Elizabeth 80
  Hugh 80
  James 195
  Sarah 80
  Tempy 74

Ates (cont.)
  Wm. 74
Atkins, Jonathan G. 45
  Mary Ann E. 115
  Pheba D. 70
Auntney, Elizabeth 48
Ausbeon, Lear(?) 148
Ausbon, Elizabeth J. 49
Austill, Isaac 54
Austin, Candis 143
  Susan 168
  William 143
Ayers, James 114
  Robert 13
Ayleson, Susanna 5
Ayres, Moses 8
  Mourning 68
B_____, Russel 73
Backor, Rachell 107
Bagbey, Patsey 47
Baggins Lydia 203
Bagley, Juda Anne 38
Bagly, Julyann 133
Bailey, Alex 6
Bailis, Benja. 181
Baily, A. 83
  John W. 190
  Nathaniel 6
Baines, Ruthy 196
Baird, Ezekiel 47
  Lidia 205
  Susanna 47
Baits, Lucinda 74
Baker, Dovey 148, 148
  Enoch 8
  Honar 156
  Jesse 140
  John 8, 8
  Martha 156
  Mary 11
  Pattie 18
  Polley 137
  Prisilla 164
  Providence 156
  Sally 164
  Samuel 47
  Sary 201
  Zebediah 29, 156
Baldwin, Joseph D. 107
  John 153
  John K. 151
  Mary 153
Ball, Alcey 62
  Darinda 136
  Eaton 126
  Elisabeth 99
  Elviry 172
  Ginsey 172
  Hiley 66
  Imlah 9
  John 9
  Levi 9, 152
  Lucy 152
  Mary 88, 138, 152
  Milley 49
  Nancy 124, 135
  Sampson 66
  Silas 49
  Tobitha 76
  Wilborn J. 9
  Wilbur J. 127
Ballard, Devereux 58
Ballow, Elisabeth 9
  N. B. 9
Ballows, Martha 23
Ballrip, Ann 91
Bane, Nancy C.(?) 147
Bange, Ann 164

Bange (cont.)
  Thos 164
Banks, Henry 10, 10
  John 10, 16
  Nancy 195
Barber, Elisabeth 171
  James 10
  Rilla 10
  Sarah 201
Bare, Abslum 132
  Catherine 167
  Daniel 167
  Susana 167
Bareer, Sarah 109
Barker, Howell 130
  N. 60
  Nathl. 30, 40
  Peter Q. 11
  Sally 44
  Susanah 105
  William 10
  Wm. 82
Barlow, Eliphalet 10
  Elizabeth 33, 110
  Henry H. 11
  Jane 19
  Joseph 117, 192
  Julia 151
  Linvill 41
  Nancey 41
  Polley 192
  Thos 155
Barlton, Lucinda 28
Barnard, Fr.(?) 152
  Francis 160, 172
  Francis, Esqr. 143
  Fras. 166
  John 66
  Madelphia 40
Barnes, Anner 151
  Elizabeth 11, 142
  John 11, 95, 142
  Joshua 180
  Jurana 149
  Letty 98
  Lydia 84
  Marcy 8
  Mary 200
  Nancey 152
  Peter 11, 11, 117
  Ruth 37, 66
  Sarah 12
  Solomon 11
  Sufrona M. 168
  Susanah 151
  Thos 11
Barnet, Ann 176
  Delily 71
  Manley(?) 37
  Mary 37
  Maryann 201
  Polly 92
Barnett, Alsy M. 192
  J. G. 149
  Leathe W. 24
  Martha 189
  Mary A. 143
Barns, Betsey 196
  Elisabeth 66
  Elizabeth 180
  Hannah 126
  Mary 32
  Nancy 48
  Rachel 125
  Reuben 196
  Ruth 25
  Thomas 137
Barnett, D. C. 179

Barrit, J. A. 20
Bass, Elizabeth 73
　Jesse 77, 84
Bates, Barbary 46
Bath, Elizabeth(?) 110
Baty, Dorcas 155
Bauges, John 14
Baugess, John 15, 30
　Mary 136
　Nancy 14, 175
　Vinsent 136
　William 153
Baughuss, Nancy 27
Bauguess, A. J. 31
　Liddy 98
　Mary 83
　Robert J. 98
　Sealy 31
Baugus, C. H. 31
　Elisabeth 103
　Fanny 84, 190
　Henry 174
　Jane 92
　Jenny 175
　Kessiah 137
　Lidda 41
　Mary 161
　Nancy 127
　Richard 190
　Robert 190
　S. A. 172
　Salley 178
　Sally 162
　Sarah 20
　Vincen 17
　Vinson 17
Bauguss, David K. 12
　John 15
　Osburn 75
　Susan 15
Beach, Mary 47
　Miner 156
　Nesa 12
Beakins, Catey 90
Beall, William 42, 118
Bear, Aly 62
　William 62
Beaty, John W. 45
Beaugess, Eveline 159
Bebber, Isaac 118
Becknal, Sineth 24
　Elizabeth 14
　Nancy 119
　Ruth 127
Becknel, Hily 183
Becknell, Hanner 177
　Manda M. 129
Becknold, Dolly 120
Begly, Eliza J. 193
Bell, A. 191
　Alcy 43
　Archaful 43
　David 13
　Elizabeth 43, 201
　Evin 203
　Matilda 173
　Meley 203
　Nancy 203
　Nelly 52
　Suana 34
　Wm 14
Beng, James 186
　James M. 43
　Samuel 187
Benge, Mary M. Tildey 187
　Nancy 26
　Sarah 8, 14
　Willis 14

Benham, Jane 165
Bennet, Betsy 110
　Mary Jane 132
　Thomas L. 76
　Wm. 201
Bentley, Elisabeth 85
　Hannah 14
　James 134
　Margaret 108
　Martha 134
　Mary 108
　Squire 14, 85
Bently, Daniel 14
　J. J. 113
　James 142
　Margaret 113
　Mary R. 113
　Skewer 84
Benton, Francis 20
　Martha 191
　Marthy M. 169
Bereng, Willis 182
Berry, Elizabeth 151
　Nancy 168
Beshears, Aaron 14
　Aley 14, 14
　Malinda 194
　Martha 191
　Nancy 165
Beshep, Amanda J. 123
Bess, D. R. 35
Besshop, Saml. 186
Better, Elizabeth 80
Bevely, John 77
Bever, Elizabeth 49
　Isaac 50
Beverly, John 77
Bichill, Isom 52
Bicknell, A. A. 100
　Benjamin 95
　Joshua 173
　Larkin J. 201
　Mary 23
　Samuel 94
Biers, Jinsey 164
Bilings, S. L. 200
Billin, Ally 38
Billing, Jesse 161
　Mary 198
Billings, Amelia 190
　Daniel 95, 174, 190
　Elisabeth 4
　Elizabeth 118
　Elizabeth J. 174
　Hiram 15, 38
　J. T. 38
　Jesse 45, 106
　John 69
　John A. 106
　M. M. 197
　Mary 56, 197
　Nancy 15, 78
　Nelson 30
　Salley 39
　Sary Adaline 69
　Susanah 104
　Thomas 15
　William 38
　Wm 38
Bingam, Sally 154
Bingham, Christopher 120
　Edney B. 101
　Joseph T. 158
　Nancy 132
　R. S. 204
　Wm 38
Binghim, Mary D. 204
Bircham, Janelese 70

Bird, Benjamin 5
　Casandrew 5
　Lidia 77
　Matilda 153
Bishop, Abraham 16
　Alfred M. 158
　America 134
　Clarrisa Harlow 139
　Diannah 106
　Elisabeth 28, 28
　Elizabeth 138, 194
　Hiram 195
　John 28, 107
　Larkin 16
　Mary 158, 185, 195
　Miry 116
　Nancey E. 138
　Nancy 16, 46
　Rosanna 46
　Tabitha 28
Blackborn, Joel 92
　Nancy 174
Blackburn, Andrew J. 184
　Barbarra 108
　Candis 15
　Eli 174
　J. B. 204
　Jesse 17
　L. M. 17
　Locky 76
　Martha 131
　Mary 67, 120, 133
　Matilday 34
　Phoeby 174
　Polley 91
　Sarah 17
　W. B. 16
　William 151
　Wm. 91
　Wm. B. 17
Blackman, Elizabeth 87
Blacknell, Callie A. 146
Blankenship, Fanny 160
　Susan 81
Blanton, Rebecca 114
Blevens, Matilda 22
Blevins, Wm. 17
Boaze, Mary C. 51
Boese, Sarah An 190
Bogle, Joseph M. 50
Bolding, Sarah 203
Bolin, Hugh 59
　John 90, 102
　Mary 90
Bolings, Elizabeth 73
Bolling, Mary 79
　Rebecca 109
Boman, Almiah 93
　Elizabeth 18
　Feby 82
　James 118
　Jane 105
　John 132
　Mary 4
Bond, Charles 46
　Nanney 138
Bone, Ann 19
　Danel 132
　Jemima 132
Bones, James 19
Booey, Joseaphin 201
Booth, Rachel 70
Bordens, Eli 191
Borders, Eli 108
Borffet, William 66
Borgus, Manuel 116
　Sely 116
Boring, Sarah 91

209

Boswell, B. F. 26
Bouchelle, Clarinda J.
  E. 18
  John M. 143
  Thomas S. 18
Bouthe, Mary 148
Bowen, Sarah 176
Bowers, Frances 15
Bowges, Sarah 36
Bowlin, Suana 141
Bowling, Justice 156
Bowls, Elizabeth 40
Bowman, Elizabeth 194, 195
  James 81, 106
  Jesse 92
  Martha 68
  Moses 194
Boyd, Nancy 86
Bra___, Rachale 139
Bradburn, Thos 58
Bradbury, James 19
Bradley, Ann 7
  Calvin 71
  Clary 179
  Elizabeth 8
  Hannah 19
  Jackson W. 19
  James 19
  Laurance 7
  Malinda 111
  Nancy 10, 191
  Sarah 165
  William 178
  Wm. 165
Bradly, Caty 5
  George 116
  James 5, 116
  John 179
  Mary 116
Branch, Elizabeth 144
Branham, Joel 26, 63
Brassfield, Salley 61
  Thomas 61
Brewer, Bethany 158
  Dolly 182
  Elisabeth 168
  Henry L. 79
  James 187
  Jane E. 4
  John 19, 36, 102, 178, 182
  Josiah 19, 151
  Malinda 151
  Mary 20
  Matildy 147
  Nathaniel 79
  Sarah Ann 200
  Silas 9
  Siler 3
  Suckey 69
  Susanah 17
  Temperance 62
Brian, Sally 118
Briant, Sally 164
Brinegar, Thomas 162
Brock, Letha 160
  Nancy 41
  Polley 136
  S. Jane 94
  Sarah 181
Brog, Ireney 133
Brook, Permelia 3
Brooker, Elizabeth 111
Brookes, Marthey 186
  Mary 187
  Nancy 163
Brooks, Elizabeth 56, 158

Brooks, (cont.)
  Jane 169
  John 30, 47, 101, 189
  L. C. 24, 48
  Lucy 101
  Mary Malinda 147
  Mathew 3
  Nancy 38, 130
  Nancy E. 25
  Patsey 152
  Rebeccah 44
  Robert P. 97
  Sarah 30, 181
  Youn N. 152
  Young H. 183
Brookshair, Nancy 23
Brooksher, Polly 5
Brookshir, Matilda 112
Brookshire, Betsy 22
  Elisha 61
  Elizabeth 61
  Enoch 20
  Joel 21, 110
  Mary A. 58
  Nancy 21
  Prudence 33
  Sarah 61
  Sary 160
  Thos 61
  Thos. W. 74
  William 160
Broosher, Nancy V. 74
Bross, Mary 51
Brotherlin, Sarah M. 37
Brothern, Maryann 114
Brothertin, Isaac 21
Brotherton, Easter 89
  Hugh 73
  Milley 18
  Nancy L. 73
  Susan 155
Bround, Malinda 131
Browan, Janey 43
  John 155
Browder, Jincey 9
Brown, Adaline 54
  Alexr 1
  Amanda Malviny 101
  Amanday M. 109
  Archer 150, 150
  Benj. H. 191
  Benjamin 25, 164
  Benjamin H. 143
  Caroline C. 112
  Caty 171
  Charles 51
  Clary 152
  Cloey 195
  Daniel 24, 78, 93, 155, 171, 190
  Delphy 157
  Eli 24, 24, 79, 163
  Elijah 25
  Elisabeth 1, 199
  Elizabeth 24, 25, 69, 100, 148, 154, 178
  Ezekael 48
  Ezekel 69
  Ezekiel 26
  Francis 22, 23, 33
  G. H. 21, 52, 143, 155, 196
  George, 12, 12, 51, 66, 69, 69
  George F. 39
  Geo. H. 124
  H. 21
  H. A. 27

Brown (cont.)
  Henry 131
  Hugh 22
  James 22, 24, 76, 192
  James Harrison 63
  James M. 20
  Jas. 148
  Jenny 154, 187
  Jinny 1
  Jno. 25
  Joel 25, 183
  John 7, 12, 21, 21, 21, 22, 23, 36, 125, 159, 166, 174, 197, 200, 204
  John, Jr. 20
  Joseph 53, 174
  Joseph A. 133
  Judy 37
  Julia 22
  Larkin 24
  Leanah 3
  Letta 24
  Letty 122
  Letty J. 1
  Lidia A. 170
  Lottey 134
  Lucinda 164
  Lucy 6, 200
  M. C. 59
  Malinda 186
  Marey 82
  Margarett 155
  Marget 36
  Martha 116
  Martha C. 59
  Martin 90
  Mary 20, 39, 51, 69, 95, 161, 174, 205
  Mary S. 44
  Maryann 189
  Matilda 204
  Milley 99
  Minda 30
  Nancey 185
  Nancy 1, 1, 9, 12, 25, 93, 110, 116, 117, 118, 125, 162, 199
  Nancy C. 2
  Nancy E. 190
  Nancy L. 21
  Nathan 96
  Overby 109
  Patsey 9, 173
  Peter 83
  Phebe 165
  Phebea 132
  Pheby 84
  Phoe 163
  Polley 156, 184
  Polly 27, 63, 151
  Rachel 197
  Rebeca 69, 155
  Rebeca M.(?) 58
  Rebecca 42, 70, 84
  Rebecka 13
  Rebeka E. 180
  Rebekah 87
  Richard 177
  Rily 23
  Rody 94
  Sally 177
  Sarah 25, 26, 37, 86, 180
  Sarah Ann 47
  Sarah L. 204
  Sary 46, 100
  Sidney L. 97

Brown (cont.)
  Suker 109
  Surrena 159
  Susanah 21, 22, 48, 174
  Susanna 97
  Susannah 63
  Susey 100
  Temperounce(?) 44
  Tempy 24
  Teny 119
  Thomas 69
  Thos 25
  Virginia C. 110
  W. W. 39
  Walter 1
  Wesley 21, 24, 25, 26
  William 23, 101, 119
  Wm. 7, 24, 96, 112, 140
  Wm. F. 25
  Yancy 72
Broyhill, Elvira 105
  Francis 81
  James 24, 55
  Jas. 26
  Jas. H. 147
  Mary 24
  Rhoda 54
  Roda 26
  Sary 82
Bruce, Allen 106
  Benja. 92
  Benjamin 145
  C. N. 148
  David A. 133
  Elizabeth 133
  James(?) 27
  Sary 186
Brures, Salley 182
Bruse, Albert P. 89
Bruss, Elizabeth A. 186
Bryan, Andrew 26, 161
  Andw 115
  Cinderella 8
  Elisay J. 61
  Elvira 128
  Fanny 34
  H. M. 172
  J. J. 14, 22, 31, 77
  J. T. 97
  Jno. J. 61
  John J. 169
  John Q. A. 92, 115
  Mary 45, 144
  Mary M. 173
  Matilda 145
  N. D. 92
  Nanoy 18
  O. C. 30
  Peggy 203
  Phebe 204
  Phoe C. 108
  R. B. 56, 174, 202
  Robert B. 8
  Thomas 34, 175
Bryant, Ann 14
  Fanny 50
  Mary 11
  Thomas 19
Bu____, Elizh. 31
Buch, Camely 148
Buckin, Marcy 125
Buttery, Sernetta P. 176
Buhson, Samuel 27
Bullis, Absalom 39, 138, 202
  Benj. 27

Bullis (cont.)
  Betsey 145
  Bibba 39
  John 139
  Martha 27
  Mary M. 39
  Merah 39
  Nancy 39, 139, 170
  Sarah Ann 124
  Wesley 28
Bullison, Margarett 138
  Polly 46
Bulliss, Betsey 72
Bulloson, Virlesie 156
Bullous, Zibby 96
Bumgarner, Daniel 28, 124, 183, 206
  Danl. 132
  David 115
  Delila A. 109
  Elizabeth Jane 47
  Emeline 28
  Frances C. 45
  H. M. 138
  James C. 52
  John 28, 39, 91
  Joseph A. 28
  Leonard 137
  Lucinda 128
  Mary 28, 39
  Mary M. 52
  Michal 27
  Michel 150
  Nancey C. 27
  Phillip G. 44
  Polly 27, 206
  Rebecca 27, 28
  Simeon 28, 109
  Stephen 27, 28
  Susan 28
  Thomas 66
Bunge, Susana 128
Bunting, Hily 39
  Mary 199
  Sussanna 195
Bunton, Tabitha 131
Bunyard, James 145, 174
Burch, Benjamin 33
  Elisabeth 33
  James 28
  James J. 111
  Jane 11
  Kissia 33
  Ruth 33
Burcham, Mary E. 34
  Prudey 202
Burches, James 73
Burchet, Isaac 29
  Nancy 29
Burchett, Agness 162
  Lindy 79
  Nancy 202, 203
  Robert 162, 202
  Sarah 2
Burchfield, John 29, 49
  Salley 49
Burck, Eloner 178
Burd, Braxton 65
Burehot, Louiza Y. 3
Burgin, Rosie 78
Burgus, Nancy 68
Burguss, Ambrose 68
Burlison, Bazell 145
Burnes, Racheal 84
Burnet, Millenda 152
Burnett, Elisbeth 105
Burns, Ann 101
  Charles 101

Burns (cont.)
  Mary 96
Busey, Lidda 150
Buship, Clarisa 50
Bushup, Hiram 21
Bussell, John 40
  Salley 40
  Tillis 21
  Tillone M. 170
  Tillous (see Russell)
  Tillous W. 110
Bustle, Mary 13
Butram, Neel 206
Butrey, Lademia 192
  Mary 182
Butrum, John 29
  Nicodemus 29
Butry, Sally 187
Buttery, Abraham 2
  Emely E. 15
Buttrey, Abraham 30
  Abram 201
  John 30, 92
  Timothy 182
Buttry, Eveline 73
  Mary 24
Byant, Susanna 183
Byars, John 77
Byeres, Lucinda 165
Byers, America Jane 123
  Malaan 133
  Mary 164
  Mary Harriett 14
  Polly 123
Byrd, Braxton 30, 90
  Dianer 103
  Dorces L. 106
  Elender 30
  Elizebeth M. 77
  James 20, 98, 164
  John 29, 30, 74, 102
  Josiah 30
  Martha L. 142
  Mary A. 175
  Millea 102
  Nancy E. 175
  Peggy 2
  Rutha 98
  Thos 182
  William 30, 72
  William G. 125
  Wm. F. 48
Cacy, Catharine 170
  Henry 31
  James 170
Calaway, Marthy J. 85
Caldwell, Elam 53
  Joseph 83
Call, Daniol 3, 60
  Elizabeth 143
  Isaac 31, 82
  Isaac S. 65, 87, 142
  J. J. 119
  J. S. 73, 202
  Margaret 11
  Mary 60, 130
  Milly 19
  Nancy 31, 31
  Sarah 89
  Sarah E. 131
  William 31
Callaway, Shad. 81
Calloway, Caroline 52
  Catherine R. 176
  James 62, 66, 82, 85
  Joseph W. 133
Calton, Eveline 115
  Jane 112

211

Calton (cont.)
  Mary 5
  Nancy 147
Cambers, John 95
Camel, Elizabeth 159
Camender, Mary E. 163
Cammell, Sarah 44
Campbell, Hugh 56, 145
  Matilda 138
  Peter 112
  Pheby 177
  W. F. 110, 169
  W. T. 20
Campble, Mary 13
  W. F. 203
Campel, Alesebeth 1
Canaday, Aaron 31
  Alic 78
  Fanney 34
  Susannah 34
  William 78
Canadey, Fanney 75
Candill, Abner 1
Cane, Abel 32
  Malinda 32
Canler, Salley 90
Cann, Rhoda W. 40
Cannaday, Aron 193
  Elizabeth 144
  Hope 193
  Nancy 176
  Polley 193
  William 193
Cannon, Betsy 5
Canter, James M. 32
  N. P. 15, 156
  Stephen 116
Cantor, Wm. 118
Caogile, Salley 5
Cardwell, Betty 64
  Biddy 46
  Elizabeth 76
  Malinda 193
  Martha L. 96
  Mathew P. 76
  N. P. 193
  Patsey 193
  Peter 32
Carel, Elizabeth 31
Carender, Martha 84
Cargile, James 166
  Joel 152
  Peggy 65
Cargill, Joel 179
  Peggy 176
  William 63, 64
Carley, Elisha 106
  Elizabeth 33
  Sarah 26
Carlton, Ambrose 33
  Charles 33, 111, 126
  Irreny 186
  John 33, 33, 33, 33
  K Mela 117
  Lewis 33, 33, 147
  Martha E. 76
  Mary 178
  Maryan 59
  Matilda 112
  Milley 186
  Minerva A. 148
  Polley 115
  S. M. 70
  Silas 112
  Thomas C. 125
  Thos. 33, 33
  Wyatt 117
Carmichael, Abner 199

Carmichael (cont.)
  Carrie 84
  L. B. 7, 138
  L. E. 30
  Lemia A. 116
  M. L. 31
  W. W. 47
Carmichall, L. B. 64
Carothers, Edmond 72
Carpenter, Frances 132
  Mary 137
  Stephen 70, 137
Carr, Wm 137
Carrander, Joseph 34
  Tirza 34
Carrel, Benjamin 31
  Charity 117
  Elizabeth 143, 183
  James 143
  Luke 50
Cart, Moses 65
Carter, Benjamin 34, 119
  Caleb 34
  Cynthia 162
  Daniel 34
  Delphia 104
  Eliza 119
  Elizabeth 193
  George W. 199
  Henry 29
  Jno 34
  Joshua 34, 112
  L. H. 16
  Littleton 34
  Lowra 127
  Mahuldah J. 29
  Mary 34, 34, 119, 140
  Milinder 159
  Nancy 202
  Randy 35
  Rebecca 78
  Roxy 140
  Theney 65
  Wm. M. 34
Case, Frances 15
  Hanah 140
  Phebe 67
  Polly 125
  Sally 106
Cash, David 34
  Elizabeth 34
  Larkin 183
  Nancey 156
  Sarah 192
  William 152
Cass, Benj. W. 66
  Elizabeth 37, 43, 123
  Ezekiel 136
  F. W. 9
  Jas. 139
  Ledia 155
  Lotty 90
  Mary L. 200
  Moses 136
  Ruth 136
  Samuel J. 137
  Sary M. 137
Cast, Abegail 29
Castel, Elisabeth 40
Castevens, Mary 63
  Thomas 66
Castle, Samuel 99
  Tamer 62
Cate, John 113
  Mary 113
Caton, Susannah 69
Catton, Charlotte 10
  Livingston 10

Caudel, Elibeth 182
Caudell, Benjamin 35
  Elizabeth J. 58
  Jeremiah 17
  Jesse 50, 108
  Polley 16
  Rebecca 104
  Stephen 3
  Thomas 16
Caudil, Malinda 174
Caudile, Melinda 43
Caudill, Abner 3
  Adlaid 69
  Daniel 35
  David 191
  Frances 36
  Jackson 155
  Jackson J. 35
  Jesse 35, 102, 178
  Luisa 102
  Martha 154
  Mary 170
  Metilda 154
  Polly 35, 155
  Thomas 35, 154
  Thos B. 106
  W. M. 123
  Winney 155
  Winnie 35
  Wm. M. 23, 172
Caudle, Abner 26
  Elizabeth 36
  Jane 122
  Jesse(?) 12, 78, 127
  Johnson 36
  Martha 102
  Nancy 12, 120
  Polly 32, 137
  Sally 105
Caul, Jane 74
  Patsey 101
  Susannah 14, 165
Cauthin, William 51
Caws, John 113
Cawthin, William 51
Cearcley, Clement 8
Ceareley, Elizabeth 75
  Kizzah 8
Cearley, Elijah 181
Cecil, Robert 119
Cecill, Allen 36
Ceeter, Jessee 140
Cerby, Nancy 76
Cerley, Absolem 36
  Hiram 75
  Larkin 36
Cerly, Elisha 70
Cesell, Matilda 21
Chambers, Aaron 35
  Caroline 116
  Elisha 99
  Elizabeth 43, 51, 58
  George 100, 173
  George W. 104, 116, 194
  Henry 36, 51, 160
  James 129, 201
  John 9, 32, 32, 42, 43, 52, 61, 75, 95, 104, 104, 130, 135, 135, 135, 163, 169, 206
  Martha 99
  Mary Adelaide 116
  Max. 36
  Mimey 160
  Nancy 137, 177
  Nathaniel 160

Chambers (cont.)
  Polly 130
  Salley 100
  Sarah 191
  Seth 42
  Susannah 19
  Watson 60
  William 86
Champton, Liday 74
Chandler, Bailey 37
  Delicia 102
  Elisabeth 149
  Evin 171
  Sophina 79
  Susanna 103
  Timothy 103
  Winney 197
Chanler, Patty 171
Chapel, Betsy 61
  Eliza Ann 12
  Mary 37, 182
  Nancy 175
  Wm. J. 37, 37, 148
Chapell, Harrison 58
  Susanah 58
Chapman, Betsey 175
  Elisha 196
  Elizabeth 152
  Enoch 24, 37, 37
  John 37, 37, 175
  John, Junr. 37
  Letty 161
  Lewis 142
  Rebeckea 159
  Richard 37, 150
  Solomon 137, 150
Chappel, Levi 44
  William J. 105
Chapple, W. J. 47
Chatham, Alexander 101
Chavis, Clarissy 84
  Francis 190
Cheatham, Martin 80
Cheek, Eli M. 36
  Elmore 38
  Fanny 5
  Rebeccah 44
  Samuel 5
  Sarah E. 125
Cheeks, Eline 78
  Elizabeth 78
  July Ann 141
  William 78
Chesten, Saml. A. 39
Childers, Carolina 38
  Eliza 77
  Elizabeth 10
  Emeline 126
  Hamilton 38, 38
  Henry 43
  Hiram 94
  James 104
  Mary 94, 94
  Nancy 79
  Nelley 176
  Rachel 196
  Salley 15
  W. 142
  Willis 36, 38, 38, 104
Childres, Sarah 189
Childress, Michael 46
  Sally 38
Chout, Cabiat 52
Chrisel, Jerema 138
Chrisley, Elizabeth 112
Christy, Sarah 173
Chuck, Martha (Church) 116

Church, A. 101
  Aaron 38, 39
  Alex. 198
  Alexander 140
  Alley A. 134
  Alph C. 60
  Alpha E. 47
  Amelia 28
  Amos 126, 188
  Bethany 28, 50
  Betsey 28
  Calvin 47, 134
  Celah L. 38
  Charity 93, 188
  Elijah 28
  Elizabeth 132, 205
  Elizabeth A. 67
  Emeline 28
  Frances 134
  Francis 3
  Gabriel 81
  Golris(?) 139
  H. B. 67
  Hamilton B. 50
  Harrison 123
  Henry H. 146
  Hiram 40
  J. J. L. 9
  Jenny 142
  Joel 38, 39
  John 38, 96, 114, 146
  John, Jr. 14
  Larkin 204
  Larraw A. 131
  Lemira 134
  Louisa 60
  Lucinda 69
  Margaret 32
  Margeratt 114
  Martha 24, 70 (see also Chuck)
  Martha C. 139
  Martha Carmiller 146
  Martha J. 67
  Mary 46, 67, 146, 156, 167, 198
  Mary A. 17
  Massey 145
  Matilda 27, 56
  Nancy M. 123
  Nathaniel 40
  Polley 140
  Rachael A. 67
  Rachal 133
  Rachell 47
  Rebeckey 185
  Rhoda 38
  Robt. 28
  Rudy 101
  Sally 14
  Saraha 38
  Selenia 172
  Susanah 3
  William 14, 38
Cimmons, Lucinda 119
Clanton, Amelia 31
  Nancy J. 105
  Nellie 26
  Rutha E. 26
  Susan 113
  W. E. 193
  William 26
Clariton, Elizabeth 193
Clark, Barbary 44
  Elizabeth 120
  Jinsey 21
  Rebecah 23
  Salley 130

Clark (cont.)
  Thos 40, 136
Clary, Benjamin 20
Clawson, Charlotty 93
Claywell, J. S. 203
Cleaveland, Dianah E. 176
  Perliney E. 31
Cleavland, Mary L. 198
Clendennin, J. W. 14
Clery, J. M. 178
Cleton, Frances 96
Cleveland, A. M. 66
  Absalom 158
  Alsea 107
  Benja. 4, 14, 40
  Elizebeth 205
  Jesse 205
  John 134, 171
  Larkin 152
  Martha A. 176
  Patsey 179
  Robt 68
Cloud, Fanny 81
Cobb, Nancy 34
Cobs, T. P. 153
Cockerham, David 147, 156
  Elisabeth 51
  Franklin 40
  James 41
  James P. 10, 40
  Lettice D. 83
  Marth E. 88
  Martin 56
  Mary 182
  Milley 10
  Moses 148
  Nancy 106
  P. C. 108
  Pheba 48
  Pleasant 204
  Rebecca 183
  Roda 41
  Sarah 10
  Susan 112
  Susannah 182
Cockes, Reley 48
Cockrem, Eliza 30
Cocorum, William 53
Cocram, William 19
Codle, Benj. 204
  Hanah 204
Coffee, Mary 151
  Nancy 148
  Nathan 134
  Patsy 54
Coffey, Alley 132
  Ambrose 36, 41
  Ann 123
  Benet 41
  Benjamin 41, 42, 51, 87, 182
  Cassey 46
  Cleavland 123
  Eleanor 43
  Eli 41, 54, 147
  Elisa 86
  Eliza 5
  Elizabeth 60, 165, 179
  Filliam 41
  James 62
  Jane 41
  John 87
  Larkin 41, 55, 86, 99
  Lewis 41, 41, 98, 179
  Louisa 99
  Nancy 178
  Nebuzaradan 50
  Nebuzarah 123

Coffey (cont.)
  Newton 74
  Polley 42
  Reuben 54
  Sally 179
  Sarah 41, 98
  Tho 41
  Thomas 111
Coffin, Susannah 184
Coffy, Lewis 179
Colbert, Tempy 61
Cole, Job 51
  Thomas 60, 187
Coleman, Beverly 139, 139, 155
  Bevily 93
  Elisha 84, 139
  J. M. 160
  John 18, 140
  Phoebe 139
  Polley 40
  Ruth 108
  Saercy 93
  William S. 76
Colemon, Mary 135, 140
  Rebeccah 155
Coleson, Sarah 136
Collear, Aggia 93
  Jno 93
Collens, Ludisi Ann 129
  Sary 60
Collert, Rachel 109
Collier, Marel 42
Collins, Anne 68
Colmon, Nasey 155
Colvard, Jane 130
  Merey 14
  Payton 45
  Wade H. 188, 188
  Wm 14
Colverd, Sallie E. 199
Colvert, Betsey 110
  Nancy 198
Combes, Hicks 42
  Lucy 42
  Mary 130
Combs, Charity 143
  Clay 91
  Dicey 7
  Elizabeth 89
  Fanny 94
  Feling 173
  Francis 143
  Franky 15
  George 143, 184
  Gincy 138
  Hicks 129
  Hix 43
  Jain 173
  Jesse 87
  Jincy 159
  John 43
  John M. 43
  Luisy 173
  Martha 36, 91
  Mary 42, 153
  Nancy 89
  Patsey 137
  Pheba 15
  Polley 173
  Susanah 118
  Wiley 94
  William 138
Comer, Dinah 200
Comes, Clary 88
Compton, Jesse 5, 148
  Thomas 184
  Thos 43

Conly, J. M. 32
  Margaret 106
Coock, Elisa 94
  Sarey A. 143
Cook, Aaron 99
  Abra. 125
  Alsa 21
  Ambrose 173
  Amey 164
  Berton 46
  C. L. 63, 129
  Charlotte 115
  Delphia 55
  Dicy 60
  Dolley 120
  Emeline 87
  Ephraim 127
  Gemima 125
  George 5
  Harrison 203
  Henry 13
  Isaac 94
  Johnson 44, 44
  Mahala 104
  Mark 104
  Martha 155
  Mary 89, 125, 145
  Polly 158
  Richard 43, 127, 164
  Richard J. 31
  Sarah 44
  Sely 127
  Sususana 181
  William R. 44
Cooke, Anne 181
Coons, Maryann 4
Cooper, Anne Merier 77
  Elizabeth 110
  Mary 57
  Risdon 120
  Wm. L. 13
Coopper, Mary 77
Coots, Fanney 108
Cope, Elizabeth 150
  Feby C. 189
Copeling, Joel 176
Cordall, Emly Carline 187
  Wm. R. 187
Cordell, Amelia 120
  William 182
Cordial, Stephen 194
Cordill, Leanor 180
  Margaret 17
  Phebe 191
Cordle, Jerimiah 105
Coringder, Joseph 129
Corley, Ann 23
Cornell, Margaret 95
Corpening, S. V. 128
Correll, John(?) 95
Corthen, M. A. C. 60
Corthing, John 130
Corthon, Mahaley 54
Cost, Metilder 86
Cothern, Polly 51
Cotton, Betsey 52
Cottral, James 150
Cottreal, Miry L. 89
Cóttrel, Jane 25
  Thomas 140
Cottrell, James 159
  Miry E. 45
  Sarah 41
  Thomas 47, 60
Couch, Gemima J. 35
  Jessey 197
  Mary E. 29

Couch (cont.)
  Nancy 202
  Sarah 48
Coumbs, Sarah 6
Council, Jesse 61
Councill, Charlotte 61
Couthern, William W. 15
Cowles, America 54
  Calvin J. 18
Cox, Ambrose 45
  Andrew 3
  Elisabeth 104
  John 69
  Mary 198
  Matilda 90
  Montgomery 45, 194
  Phebe 179
  Rachel 117
  Reuben 63
  Sally 63
  Silas 135
  Sinthay 69
  Thomas 141
  Wm 181
Crabb, Ann 169
  Elizabeth 100
Crabe, James 168
  Nancy 168
Crabtree, Mary 86
Crain, Elizabeth 38
  James 27, 103
  Lovina 103
  Nancy 16
  Sarah 96
  Sary 96
Crane, James 93
  Martha 133
  Mary Ann (see Crouse)
Craner, Edith 181
  Emanuel 206
Creech, Jaremiah 62
Creed, Henry 12
  Mahala 29
  Nancy 12
  Susan 108
  Susanna 44
Crickmore, Anney 57
  Luvaney Elisebeth 166
  Margaret M. 161
  Salley 44
Crider, Elizabeth 137
Crisal, Jeremiah 27
Crisel, Jeremiah (Crysel) 37, 93, 145, 155
Crisp, Abel 46
  Jane 92
  Joel 92
Croach, George 33
Crocy, Leucy 102
Cross, Andrew 167
  Lucindey(?) 204
  Rebecca 142
  Rebekah 92
  Sary 80
  Tempy 180
Crouce, Sarah Emeline 81
  Abigail 197
  Cinith 117
  Elizabeth 157
  Hannah S. 193
  Jacob 46, 157
  Mary 64
  Nancy 33
  Polley 122
  Ruth 111
Crouder, S. A. 85
Crous, Prudy 120
Crouse, Candis 126

214

Crouse (cont.)
Henry 16
John 46
Mahaley 16
Mary Ann (Crane) 157
Nancy 46
Sarah 16, 16, 105
Crowel, Felicia 93
Crows, Martha 34
Mary 24
Rachel 32
Sarah 81
Crowse, Hiram 46
Crowson, Adam S. 189
Nancey 189
Susan E. 189
Cruise, Mordaca 133
Polley 133
Crumpler, Mary 144
Thos 144
Crumpton, Hezekiah 95
Winneford 41
Crysel, Elizabeth 26
James 41
James E. 26
Jeremiah 82, 202 (see also Crisel)
Jno. B. 132, 187, 201
John B. 96
Lorena Frances 26
Mary 91
Wm. W. 47, 166
Cryssel, Jerrymiah 26
Cuech, Suana 30
Culres, James 94
Cuningham, Elizabeth 58
Cunningham, Benjamin 168
Langston 126
Marey 126
Nancy 168
Rachel 168
Richd 8, 120
Cupp, Ann(?) 119
Curbey, Riley 137
Curby, William 144
Curch, Rebeckea 133
Curey, Edna 160
Currey, John 13
Martha 129
Mathey 13
Curry, Elisabeth 34, 74
Eliza C. 34
Elizabeth 66, 128
Emeline 51
George 34
Jno 36
John, Jr. 13
John S. 33
Linday 76
Martha 88, 89
Mary 130, 201
Nancy 85, 105
Nancy C. 87
Nancy M. 186
Prissilla 37
Rachel 74
Rachel M. 67
Rebecca 7
Sarah 32
Sarah L. 167
Curtice, Samuel 131
Curtis, A. J. 42
Alpha E. 146
Carrie L. 42
Edmund 45
Eliza 47
Hezekiah 65, 202
Jenny 14

Curtis (cont.)
Joshua 151
Mira 133
Rosanah 136
Susanah 38
Curtiss, Edy 161
Nancey 135
Cury, Marget 137
Custephen, Betsey 147
Charles 147
Dalton, Joshua F. 160
Dancey, Amanda C. 78
Edward 90
Lucinda 170
Martha 101
Naomia 109
Dancy, A. J. 176
Amelia 139
Clarrissa 110
J. E. 48
J. R. 124, 139
John 48, 95, 202
M. N. 2
Mary 124
N. E. 205
Noah 48
Susana 167
Susan E. 176
Temperance 202
Danold, Betsey M. 192
Malinda W. 129
Dansy, Elizabeth 48
Obediah 48
Darnal, Elizabeth 107
James 142
Darnald, Milley 149
Darnall, Amma 142
Caroline 40
James 5, 46, 186
John 64
John, Junr. 49, 152
M. L. 120
Mary 186
Nancy 38, 180
Phebe 38
Polley 152
Wade 38
Darnel, Evline 142
James 49
Darnell, Elizabeth 5, 49
Nancey 48
Wm. 49
Darnold, Mary 117
Davenport, James 171
Mary 41, 41
Sarah M. 181
W. 31
William 56
Daveson, Emmeline 80
Davice, Nancy 144
Selina 196
David, Ephraim 194
Luisa 205
Davidson, Edny E. 80
Elizabeth 81, 163
Pricilla Ann 113
Ruth 126
Sinthy 96
Davie, J. A. 67
Davis, Ali 194
Balinona 9
Bethania 15
Catherine 88
Celer 152
Chapman 148
Dicey 15
Elizabeth 60, 160, 165, 186, 195

Davis (cont.)
Ephraim 106, 195
James 85
Jane 50
Jesse F. 80
Jestus 49
John 15
John N. 50, 71
Joseph 150
Joshua 85
Lenny 107
M. C. 10
Mandy M. 195
Margarett 180
Mary 89
Mathew 77
Peggy 127
Peter(?) 147
Philip 183
Polly 26
Rachel 162
Rebeca 38
Rebecca 48
Sarah 127, 183
Sarah E. 192
Selenia 81
Thomas S. 50
Thos K. 152
William 50, 107, 135
Day, ___ 137
Carline 74
Edmond 20
Edward 138
Edward M. 170, 197
Elisabeth 31
Ephraim 107
Hugh 31, 45, 138
Jane 197
Jinsey 142
Jrushe 129
Laban 50
Lewis 24
Lucy 45
Marey 173
Nancy 129
Nicholas 137
Sally 138
Thos. 51
Deal, Susanna 196
Wm. 155
Deason, Wm. M. 2
Deaton, Sophia 48
Deboard, Elisabeth 118
Gedion 51
Ira 119, 121
Joseph 51
Nancy 107
Omey 153
Sarah 119
Wm. 26
Debord, Ezra 190
Gideon 203
Joseph 107
Solomon 186
William 51, 51
Decker, Mary 44
Deel, Saly 37
Deer, Catherine Sidney 134
William 134
Dehart, Jane 35
Delinger, Jacob 71, 141
Demit, William 71
Demmet, Willis 18
Demmett, Elizabeth 5
John B. 53
Demmit, Mary 71
Nancy 200

Demmit (cont.)
  Sabry 174
  Salley 163
  Wm 191
Demoss, Abraham 177, 178
  James 8
  Lewis 118, 178, 181
  William 124
  Wm. 199
Denne, Jas. 23
Denney, Eli 91
  Elizabeth 101
  Fereby 200
  Geo. 51
  George 21
  James 200
  Jane 25
  John 51
  Marey 189
  Mary 21
  Nancy 144, 157, 184
  Patsy 6, 43
  Polley 57, 81
  Sally 200
Denny, Geo. 25
  James 6
Devenport, Jane E. 140
Dichmon, Kezia 169
  Sarah 162
Dickanie, Richard 201
Dickens, Betsy 86
  James 52
  Louisa 57
Dickerson, Carlotte 173
  Charity 60
  Charty 64
  Esquire 30
  Isaac 202
  Isham L. 5
  Isom L. 119
  Kiziah 29
  Lotta 51
  Mary 202
  Nanney 78
Dickinson, Nancy 104
Dickoson, David 147
Dier, Anna 104
  Elizabeth 184
  James 52
Dilingham, Roxana 138
Dillard, Sally 100
Dimett, Jane 52
Dimmet, Paten 198
  Sary 5
Dimmett, Paten 170
Dimmit, Sally 8
Dimmitt, Willis 53
Dishman, Archabald 129
  Disey 129
  Jefferson 127
  Polly 127
Dishmon, Anna 173
  Irena 94
  John 93
  Susanah 136
Dishmore, Rebecca 104
  Wm. 104
Dobson, Jno. 141
Dockery, John S. 32, 53, 68, 80
  Martha 32
  Susan M. 68
  Suzanna 49
Dockrey, John S. 131
Dockry, John 16
Dogan, Elizabeth 188
Dogen, Sarah 65
Dorson, Susannah 154

Doss, Ann 149
  Lamuel 112
  Lemuel 20
Dostridg, Tempy 12
Dotson, Nancy 122
  William, Jr. 115
  Wm., Senr 13, 13
Douglass, E. L. 121
Dougthit, Fanny 145
Dowel, Amon 54
Dowell, Disy 158
  Joshua 158
  Levi 43
  Lousinda 158
  Peter 68
  Polly 36
  Rosana J. 102
  Ruth 182
  William 42
Downs, Charles 192
  Elizabeth(?) 116
Dudley, James 133
Duerson, Thos(?) 95
Duggar, Ann 29
  Benja. 29
  Benjamin 101
Duke, Elizabeth 6
Dula, Alfred 108
  Ally 54
  Anna A. 89
  Anna E. 90
  Bennet 12
  Betsey 202
  Docia 185
  Eada 7
  Edy 185
  Eliza 66
  Fanny 124
  Fanny E. 45
  Harry 55
  James 55
  Jean 124
  Jefferson 54, 54
  Jno 66
  John 11, 33, 55, 55, 89, 107, 110, 185
  Lois 93
  Marthy 89
  Milley 89
  Nancy 106
  Patsey 10
  Peggy 55
  Polley 110
  Polly 117
  Sally 53
  Sanford 54, 130
  Sarah C. 65
  Sary 66, 95
  Selenia 110
  Thomas 54, 109
  Thos 95
  William 8
  William H. 55, 198
  William L. 55, 71
  Wm 55
  Wm. C. 71
Duley, William 55
Dun, Lewesy 51
  Mary 133
Duncan, Ann 26
  Chapman 7, 12, 93
  Delphia 201
  Dolley 161
  Eliza Jane 70
  Eliza Louisa 72
  Francis 181
  John 18, 115, 118
  Manda 57

Duncan (cont.)
  Milley 7
  Nathl. 114
  Rebecca 71, 118
  Rhoda C. 118
  Sarah Jane 178
  William 55
  Wm. 52, 57
Dunken, Tempy 49
Dunker, William 55
Dunkin, Chapman 65
  Elizabeth 65
  Francis 161
  John 55
  Sally 142
  Sarah 190
Dunn, Martha Ann 37
Dunsmore, Wm. 176
Duram, Marthia 52
Durham, Charloty 173
  Elisabeth 153
  Elizabeth 85
  Hulda 120
  James 17, 56, 120, 173
  Jenny 203
  John 10, 10, 41, 52, 182
  Peggy 203
  Rosana 203
  Susanah 50
  Thomas 50, 154
  Thos 203
Dyer, Caleb 199
  Dicy 74
  Elijah 23, 94, 134, 195
  Elisha 61
  Elizabeth 146
  H. T. 138
  Josiah 95
  Menoah 178
  Milly 17
  Polly 80
  Rosanah 95
  Tabitha 134
  Wm. 4, 56, 80
Dyson, Mary 117
Earnest, Ann 176
  David 64, 186
Earp, Annie 26
  Benj. 57
  Caleb 57, 82
  Caroline 162
  Martha 50
  Nancy 111
  Thomas 113, 195
  Thomas S. 26, 147
  Thos 57
  Wright 194
Earpe, Hanah 96 /
  Write 196
Eastep, C. D. 116
  Elizabeth 88
Eastept, Rhody 181
Eastreg, Mahalia 182
Estridg, Winney 181
Eastridge, Delphey 96
Eddins, Judith 158
Edleman, Mary 111
Edminsten, Newnicy 38
Edmisten, Margarett 39
  Robt. 98
  Wm 41, 98, 138
Edmiston, Sarah 98
  William 68
Edmonson, Jas. 44
Edmundson, Dolley 41
  Robert 98

Edmuston, John 46
Edwards, Charity 171
  Eliza J. 158
  Judith 132
  Lucy 21
  Mary J. 16
  Mary Jane 128
  Nancy 20, 58, 155
  Nancy C. 129
  Sally 24
  William 58
  Wm. S. 49
Edwer, Elizabeth 45
Edwin, Lucey 104
Edwins, Sarah 37
Eles, Aggy 86
Elledge, Alfred 58
  Benjamin 5
  Isaac 52, 53, 82, 94,
    165, 194
  J. A. 131
  John 22, 45, 58, 87
  Joseph 91
  Mary 158
  Milly 88, 140
  Nancey 166
  Pegy 91
  Sarah 20
Ellen, David 57
Eller, Aley 188
  Alpha J. 65
  Amarica 199
  Anna(?) 59
  Bethena 133
  Caroline 182, 205
  Catharine 138
  David 197
  Elizabeth 198
  Elza 93
  Famy 22
  Fanny 124
  Franky 79
  George 182
  Gizzey 165
  Henry A. 60
  Henry C. 133
  J. M. 96, 193
  Jane 67
  John 124, 125, 147,
    164, 188
  John A. 60, 154, 179
  Lafayette 59
  Leander 134
  Leanor 123
  Lurany 67
  Marther 134
  Mary 39, 132, 182
  Nancey 188, 205
  Nancy 59
  Peter 59, 59, 60, 123,
    205
  Peter, Jr. 161, 205
  Rachel 125, 179
  Sarah 195
  Selpha M. 123
  Suanah 123
  William 123, 124
  Wm. 125, 131
Elles, Sary 15
Ellet, Nancy 195
Ellige, Sena 21
Ellis, Ascena 43
  Benjamin 6
  Ebey 47
  Elisabeth 53
  Evin 145, 155, 201
  Laney 101
  Leacia 74

Ellis (cont.)
  Lemira 144
  Mary 60
  Mary J. 192
  Matilda 171
  Nancy 107, 189
  Polly 206
  Priscilla 82
  Rebeca E. E. 101
  Salley 173
  Sary 6
  Syntha 117
  Willis, Jr. 107
  Wm. 189
Ellison, James 5
  Nancy 45
  William 52
  Wm 45
Ellor, Delila 125
Elmore, Charity 5
  George 191
  Sally 109
  Sarah 186
Elrod, C. D. 75
  Calloway 67
  Peter 61
  Susanna 58
Elston, David 31, 136
Elusenbery, Mary 113
Emerson, J. M. 194
Emmet, Wm. C. 181
Emmit, W. C. 4, 55
England, John 61
Epperson, Robert 61
  Robt 46
  Susanna 136
Epps, Rebeckea 187
Eskew, Merinda 1
Esque, Jane 92
Estep, Delphia 116
  Jacob 136, 136, 136,
    183
  Joseph 195
  Lucy 43
  Sarah 115
Estridge, Fanney 66
  Nathan 61
Evans, Mary 6
Eve, Elizabeth 33
  Mary 8
  Sarah 13
Erwin, Andrew 67
  Thomas 98
Fair, John A. 62
  Mary 121
Fairchild, Abgil 99
  Abijah 62, 167
  Bethany 59
  Elizabeth 188
  V. C. 59
  Wilson 154
  Wm. A. 32
Farchild, Belinda 145
  Mary 62
Farchilds, Frances 16
  Nancy 112
Farechild, Fanny Caroline 150
Fargason, John 62
Ferguson, Jane 186
  John 45
  Joseph 140
  Lette 111
  Liley 41
  Margret 45
  Mary 34
  Moses 41
  Thos 47, 176

Farguson (cont.)
  Wm. T.(?) 133
Faugerson, John 45
Faw, J. L. 134
  M. A. 104
Fedor, Elizabeth 14
Feeland, Nancy 14
Felel, Rebecky 172
Felie, Sally 104
Felphs, Polley 201
Felps, Everline 108
  Jane 98
  Rebecah 62
Felts, Aaron 125
  Aason 197
  Anne 106
  E. M. 128, 196
  Elisha 197
  Elizabeth 157
  Elizebeth 27
  George 133
  H. C. 158
  Isom 63, 136, 150, 192
  J. W. 180
  Jane 13
  Jesse 159
  Jinkins 63
  John 62, 100, 157, 164
  John C. 172
  John L. 63, 125
  Lewenday 157
  Lindsey 63
  Martha 144
  Nancey 149
  Nancy 111, 130, 158
  Patsey 197
  Rebecca 100, 197
  Ruthy 63
  S. M. 180
  Susanah 168
  Susannah 42, 101
  Wesley 23
  Wilie 63
  Wm. 111, 169
Fergerson, Nancy 23
Ferguson, A. T. 186
  Amanda 10
  Anderson 77, 190
  Asa T. 80
  C. C. 152
  Chapman 57, 191
  Clairey 195
  Eda L. 175
  Elisa J. 191
  Elisabeth 183
  Elizabeth 11, 57, 95,
    126, 187, 191
  Franklin F. 59
  Franklin T. 107
  Geo. 198
  George 11
  Ibby 77
  Jas. H. 95, 123
  Jesse 70, 134, 185
  John 24, 56, 63, 63,
    139, 185
  John H. 45
  L. C. 18
  Martha 129
  Mary 57, 150
  Mary A. 11
  Matilda 118
  Nancey C. 6
  Nancey S. 163
  Nancy 117, 185
  Nelley 124
  Prissilla 106
  Rachel 136

217

Ferguson (cont.)
  Rebecca 124, 194
  Richard 185
  Salley 93
  Sally 41, 148, 185
  Sarah E. 46
  Sarah L. 191
  Smith 33, 129, 179
  T. T. 81
  Thos 185
  William 187
  William S. 21, 67, 182
  William T. 24, 197, 199
  Wm. T. 71
Ferrington, Alexr. 64
Field, Elizabeth 130, 148
  Isiah 173
  James J. 34
  William 130
Fields, Elizabeth 99
  Francis 85
  J. W. 29
  John W. 193
  Martha 48
  Nancy 99
  Polly 97
  Reuben 41
  Salley 38
  Saryan 97
  Susan 70
  Thomas 64, 64, 64, 97, 99
  Wesley 85
  Winne 97
Finch, Edwd 205
Finley, J. F. 64
  Jno 139
  W. W. 176
Finly, C. J. E. 18
  Caroline 206
Finney, Sarah 34
Fitchpatrick, Polly 136
Fitts, Elizabeth 21
Fitzpatrick, Sarah 94
  Vicey 164
  Zillar 172
Fleat, Mary 197
Fleatcher, Cresey 183
Fletcher, A. E. 11
  Amelia 143
  Barthenia 65, 143
  Efferller 99
  Elizabeth 30, 119
  Elizebeth 73
  Hanny 65
  Hiram 65
  Isaac 181
  James 8, 117, 162, 172, 177
  James F. 3, 65
  Jas. 65, 175
  Jean 181
  John 26, 40, 65, 108
  Joshua 113
  Marray 21
  Mathew 65
  Nance 45
  Nancy 204
  Olly 29
  Permelia 107
  Rebeca 199
  Salley 118
  Sarah, Jr. 198
  Serah H. 13
  Spencer 65, 143
  Susan 181

Fletcher (cont.)
  Susana 203
  Susanner 68
  Thomas 198
  Thos 161
  Wesley 69
  William 82
  Wyat 172
  Bettey 36
Fogerson, Mary 55
Fondren, John W. 65
Foots, Auston 31
  Elizabeth 31
  Nancy Elizabeth 31
Forbush, Wm. 66
Forester, Alfred 75
  Eli 59, 96, 161
  Elizabeth 93
  John 18
  Mary C. 132
  S. J. 54
  Sarah 67
  William 66
  W. M. 10, 23
  Wm. M. 93
Forgas, Rachell 204
Forgason, Selah 12
Forguson, Elizabeth 50
  Jeremiah 159
  Joseph 13
  Martha 159
  Polly 68
  Sarah 166
  Thomas, Jr. 83
Forney, Isaac N. 200
Forrester, Delpha 76
  Dianah E. 115
  Eli 65, 66, 67
  Harret 82
  James 187
  Milley 66
  Nelley 18
  Polley 206
Forrister, Fielding 66, 70
Forster, John T. 115
Forterner, Lucinda 150
Fortner, Aaron 66
  Dread 32
  Elizabeth 196
  Felix 36
  Flud 66
  Louisey 106
  Mary 196
  Violet 24
  William R. 206
Fortunar, Darkes 36
Foster, A. E. 72
  Akilles 67
  Alford M. 106
  Alfred 112
  Allison 63
  Ambros 67
  Ambrose 53, 67, 132
  Annis 49
  Anny 133
  Anthony 67
  Avy 164
  E. F. 172
  E. W. 66
  Edia 63
  Elizabeth 36, 55, 67
  Fanny 185
  Frances E. 105
  George 74, 186
  James H. 40
  Jane E. 18
  Jesse 106

Foster (cont.)
  John 66, 67, 188
  John, Jr. 107
  John J. 16, 20, 56, 105
  John M. 116
  Killis 67, 106
  Lavina 67
  Lucinda 33, 140
  Mary 106, 110, 116, 194
  Mary Ann 56, 74
  Mary C. 203
  Mary E. 13
  Mary L. 59
  Matilda 131
  Nancy 81, 185
  Nancy E. 39
  Nelley 22
  Polley 56
  R. M. 146
  Rebecca 50, 106
  Robert 2, 56, 60, 165, 184
  Robert B. 27
  Sally 73
  Sarah Ann 67
  Thomas 185
  Thomas H. 133
  Thos 106
  Thos Harry 57
  Thos M. 67
  Wm. 179
Fougar, Mary 49
Fourboush, George 120
Fourd, Susanna 117
Fox, Bridget 68
  Francis 68
  James 68
  Sarah 20
Francis, Sarah 42
Franklin, Bernard 143
  James 29
  Lucy 29
  Phebe 61
  Ruth 144
  William L. 49, 149
Freeman, H. F. 143
Freman, Rachel 117
French, Wm. 55
Frost, Mary 53
Fry, Mary 79
Fuget, Elisabeth 14
  Susanah 60
Fugett, Ann 146
Fugit, John 14
  Melindy L. 86
Fulks, James C. 183
  Mary 162
Fuller, Matilda 162
Fur, Polly(?) 36
Furgason, Elizabeth 180
Furgison, Sarah 183
Furguson, Nancy 57
Furkbull, Mary 112
Fyffe, James H. 105
  John 29
  Mary 190
  William 29
Fyppe, Barborah 67
Gaines, Poly 104
Galey, Peggey 86
Gallaway, Robt. 26
Gamble, Sarah 176
Gambell, Francis 12
Gambil, Benjamin 69
  Sarah 138
Gambile, Elizabeth R. 172
Gambill, Catharine 188
  Elizabeth 118

Gambill (cont.)
  H. L. 182
  Henry 69
  Henry W. 69
  J. M. 193
  James M. 69
  Jas. 138
  Jesse 104
  Polly 109
  S. J. 170
  Sarah Jane 198
  Susannah 4, 4
  Thos 69
  Wm 69
Gamble, Nathan 151
  Suana 191
  Susan 160
  William 102
Garison, Isaac 103
Garland, Cloe 37
  Louisa 73
Garman, Wellborn 21
Garmon, Charles 50
Garner, Julia Ann 100
  Wm. 200
  Wm. D. 69
Garres, Viney 42
Garris, Lucy 153
  Wiley 69
Garrison, Isaac 40, 178
Garvis, Susan 100
Gaulteny, Martha 37
Gaultney, Melia M. 122
Gaultny, Cyrus 37
  Leviny 37
Geer, Dilley 135
Gentle, Adline 82
  Louisa M. 165
  Martha 2
  Sarah 74
  Stephen 128
  Thomas 74
Gentry, Artha 120
  Catharine 28
  Elisabeth 49
  Frances 69
  Gilbert 70
  James 108
  Jane 120
  Jefferson 203
  Jonathan 54, 120
  Mary 120
  Polley 120
  Poulena 58
  Sarah 193, 203
  Stanly 154
Getts, Sary 35
Gibbs, Carline 150
  Elitha 77
  J. 70
  Sarah Ann 75
Gibs, Nancy 44
Gibson, Jeremiah 14
  Sabrough 8
Gidong, Elizabeth 50
Giffy, Thomas 48
Gilbert, Charity 165
  Comfort 40
  Jeremiah 58
  Jesse 148, 166, 182
    (see also Guilbert)
  John 71
  Nancy 71
  Sarah 86
  Susannah 148
  Wm. 112
  Wm. M. 70
Gillam, Martha 157

Gillem, Elizabeth 103
Gilliam, J. W. 71
  Lucy 131
  Marey 22
  Nancy 157
  R. 85
  Richard 85
  Sarah 75
  Thomas 71
  Thos 57, 68
  Wm. 8, 71
Gilreath, Agness 20
  B. C. 189
  Charlotte 179
  Delilah 121
  Elizabeth 88, 179
  Elvira 87
  Gideon 72
  Henry 21, 60, 72, 99
  Jeremiah 71, 127, 127, 182, 189, 189
  Lucy 128
  Martha 127
  Martha L. 155
  Mary E. 145
  Polly 127
  Rebeca D. 203
  Rebecca 185
  Rhoda 44
  Rhoda L. 145
  Sarah 96
  Sarah E. 8
  Susanna 99
  Susannah 185
  T. J. 72
  Thos J. 27, 131
  W. 49
  William 72
  Wm. 65, 155, 189
Gimes, Elisabeth 102
Ginings, Margarett 160
Ginkings, Nancy 113
Ginness, Letes 25
Ginning, A. H. 17
Ginnings, Elijah 72
  Polly 141
  Samuel J. 187
  Susannah 141
  Thomas 160
Ginnon, Mary 50
Ginter, Chapman 65
  Elza 65
Gittins, Sarah 96
Glass, Henry 168
  Henry, Jr. 103
  Mary 98
  Phillip 43
  Sarah 105, 166
  Simon 72
  Susanah C. 103
Gleaves, Geo. Wythe 151
Goar, Nancy 21
Goforth, Amelia 94
  Delthe 17
  Lavina 66
  Lucy 67
  Mary 97
  Milla 183
  Samuel S. 72
  William 67
Goins, Bettey 27
Gold, Elizabeth 135
  Frances 33
  Samuel 205
  Sarah 80
Gomble, Fanney 151
Good, Rhodie 187
  Thomas 79

Goodon, W. 86
Goodrich, John(?) 136
  Sary 190
Gordan, Mary B. 23
  Rebecka 39
Gorden, Martha 23
  Sarah Chapman 90
  Sarah H. 22
Gordon, _____ 106
  Charity 161
  Charles 115, 186
  Charles, Junr. 61
  Elizabeth 202
  Este 149
  George 97
  Hugh 73
  Isabel 73
  J. B. 89
  J. W. 136
  John 204
  M. L. 64
  Mary 49, 97
  Milley 97
  Mira E. 22
  Nancy 73
  Nathl 9, 90, 141, 162, 178
  Polley B. 56
  Polly 141
  Robert 123
  Sallie 6
  Sally 162
  Sarah A. 64
  Thos. A. 128
  W. 73
Gortney, John E. 125
  Siras 73
  Vina 73
Gotly, Abel 151
Gouger, Elizabeth 162
  Henry 162
Gowforth, Eveline 53
Graham, James 98
  Moses 73
Grant, Anna 95
  Elizabeth 135
Grantum, Betsey 73
Grason, Benj. 51
  Betsy 51
Grass, Suanah 92
Grasty, John 53, 122
Gray, Adline 175
  Amey 67
  Ann 84
  Belinda 173
  Benjamin 57
  David 26, 38, 69, 101, 109, 126, 127, 130, 146, 189, 194, 194, 205
  Edney 97, 103
  Elisabeth 121, 121
  Elizabeth 47, 85, 206
  George 121
  James 40, 54, 73, 144
  John 57, 84
  July Ann 69
  Laura 75
  Lemirah 164
  Lucy 101
  Marey 173
  Mary 38, 65
  Milly 164
  Nancy 57
  Rebecca 74
  Salley 76
  Sarah 160
  Sary 7

219

Gray (cont.)
  Susannah 191, 201
  Tyrel 53
  William 67, 180
  Wm. 47, 74, 74, 164
Grayham, Lidy 55
  Margret 98
Grayson, Benj. 50, 74
  Benjamin 148
  Elizabeth 96
  Martha 114
  Susannah 82
  Wm., Jr. 144
Grear, Salley 66
Green, Bartlet 76
  Dise 178
  Elisabeth 120, 200
  Elizabeth(?) 74, 89, 133
  Irvis(?) 78
  John 75
  Larkin 74
  Lucey Ann 78
  Martha 196
  Martin 75
  S. H. 80
  Sally 144
  Susanna 178
  Thomas 134
  William 75, 178
  Wriley 135
Greenle, Nancy 104
Greenstreet, Delila 9
  Jess(?) 143
Greenwell, Martha 166
  Salley M. 84
  Sarah 56
Greenwilt, Fanny 40
Greenwood, Nancy E. 150
  Thomas C. 57
Greer, Ann 51, 90
  Aquila 75
  Edwin B. 75
  Elizabeth 142, 158
  Jesse 76, 106, 177, 177
  John 23, 32, 158
  John, Esqr. 114
  John N. 23, 76, 149
  Joshua 114
  Peggy 158
  Rhoda 191
  Sebrah 90
Gregory, Elizabeth 16
  Emily 83
  Frances 161
  Franklin 48
  James 12
  James M. 168
  Nancy 38, 126
  Sary 7
  Viney 79
  William 76
Grenter, Caroline 72
Grey, David 26
  Martha 88
  Nancy 32
Grier, Edwin B. 76
  John 22
  Rhoda 140
  Ruth 115
Grifeth, Thomas 200
Griffen, Elizabeth 44
  L. B. 44
Griffeth, Thomas 76
Griffey, Betsey 27
  William T. 59
Griffing, Elisabeth 146

Grigery, Sary Ann 82
Grigory, John N. 82
Grime, Christena 107
Grimes, Adam 15, 192
  Edn 59
  Eli 9
  Eliza 166
  Lucinda 63
  Mary E. 103
  R. B. 192, 192
  Sara L. 90
  Solomon 102
Grims, Virginia 83
Grimsley, Ibsy 113
  J. M. 141
  James 151
  John 23, 113
  Littleton 68
  Saline 141
  Salley 151
  Thomas 137
Grimsly, James 68
  Nancy 68
  Peggy 68
Grinton, Ann 82
  Mary 73
  Phebe 82
  Phoeba 109
Groce, Rachel 86
Grogan, Joseph 120
  Susan 120
Groon, Nathl. 23
Grunton, Rachal 85
Gryr, William(?) 65
Guest, Benja. 109
  Moses 51, 171
Guilbert, Jesse (Gilbert) 135
Gullet, James S. 154
  Vilet 61
Gullett, Jesse 68, 72, 148
  Mary 148
Gullit, Cristefer 117
Gunter, Jesse 81
  Mary 3
Guthey, Elizabeth 28
Guyn, A. S. 22
Gwyn, Caroline M. 73
  Enoch N. 77
  Hugh 52
  James 73, 183
  James, Jr. 1
  Lenora 135
  M. H. 99
  Milley 90
  Milton H. 117
  Salley 183
  Sarah 73
  Silva 78
  Tennessee 78
  Thos P. 22
  James, Junr. 43
Hackett, Alexd. L. 162
  Alice 144
  Elizabeth S. 97
  Hanner 78
  Heigh 78
  J. M. 154
  J. W. 154
  James W. 146, 181
  Jane 196
  Joseph 98
  Joseph W. 107
  Luberto 196
  Matilda 144
  Orrange 144
  R. F. 54

Hackett (cont.)
  Sarah A. 18
Hagens, Susy 78
Hagerman, Mary 201
Hagins, Nelson 12
  Polley 151
Hagler, Ann 24
  Benjamin 62, 78, 81
  Christener 125
  Elizabeth 110, 177
  Greenville 115
  Hans 78
  Isaac 24, 122, 125
  Jacob 78
  John 78, 78, 132, 185
  Mary 186
  Nancy 47, 179
  Philadelphia 95
  Skelton 78
  William 137, 185
  Wm. F. 75
Hagnor, Susanah 92
Haines, David 193
  Jane 161
Hains, Jain 1
Hairld, Calaway 90
Hais, Nancy 105
Hale, Vincent B. 119
Hall, Adam 49
  Aly 80
  Barsheba 79
  Bethany 7
  Caroline 36
  Delphia 60
  Elender 123
  Elisabeth 171
  Elisebeth 110
  Elizabeth 197
  Eppy 25
  Frances 91
  Franky 193
  Isam 73
  Jesse 79
  John 1, 3, 9, 12
  Larken 2
  Martha 97, 147
  Marthy 2
  Mary Ann 86
  Mary M. 79
  Mary V. 188
  Milley 139
  Mira 86
  Mirah 193
  Nancy 94, 134, 192
  Omea 3
  Oriller 41
  Owen 1, 79, 171
  Owen, Jr. 79
  Peggy 71
  Polley W. 185
  Polly 169
  R. R. 1
  Reuben, R. 15
  Reubin 158
  Robert 173
  Robin 1
  Robt, Jr. 25
  Sally 1
  Susan 158
  T. D. 9
  Thomas Dulas 156
  Thos D. 164
  Willis 60
  Wm. 159, 188
Hallaway, Matilda 35
Haly, Adaline 81
Hambey, Joel(?) 37
  Letty (?) 37

Hambrick, Benjamin 166
  Elizabeth 135
  Thomas 135
Hambrix, Emily 182
Hamby, Andrew 193
  Asa 81
  Bedy 71
  Eliza 166
  Elizabeth 103, 114
  Henry 81
  Hiley 68
  James 81, 180
  James S. 73
  Jerden (Jorden) 114
  Jno 81
  Joel 80
  Jordan 165
  L. C. 194
  Larkin 68
  Malinda 74
  Martin 71
  Mary 126
  Mary Ann 180
  Nancy 68, 80, 186
  Rachal 81
  Reuben 135
  Reubin 55, 80, 114, 195
  Riley 81
  Rueben 205
  Samuel 81, 161
  Sarah(?) 150
  Selah 73
  Susanah 22
  Thomas 80, 96
  Wesly 16
  William 18
  Wm. 23, 39, 46
  Zekel 80
Hames, David 186
Hammon, Jeremiah 81
  Mary 87
  Sally 81
Hammons, Marinda 14
Hamon, Drewsilla 148
Hampton, Abigal 46
  Ames 74
  David 51
  Delilah 132
  Delphia A. 22
  Elijah 82
  Eliza 166
  Elizabeth 80, 112, 184
  Frances L. 143
  Frankey 92
  Harris 82
  Hily 194
  Isaiah 2, 26, 31, 68
  Jeremiah 194
  John 82
  Josiah 81
  Jsaiah 132
  Judah 75
  Lafayette 143
  Margaret A. 5
  Martha Jane 196
  Mary 68, 112
  Mim 82
  Nancey E. 182
  Nancy 26, 55
  Rebecca 55
  Rody 26
  Rufus 51, 71, 89, 89, 189
  Sarah 147
  Suanna(?) 2
  Susana 186
  Thomas 184

Hampton (cont.)
  Turner 160, 198
  Welcome W. 82, 82
  Wm. 35
Hamrick, John 112
  Robert 94
Hamton, Sarah 177
Hamty, James(?) 33
Hancock, Mary 161
Handon, Sarah 53
Handy, Aney 106
  D. J. 192
  Elizabeth 120
  Hulda 15
  J. B. 83
  James 24, 82
  John 176
  Margrat 83
  Marion 83
  Martha 118
  Nancy 169
  Pharibia 95
  Rachal 3, 156
  Tabitha 79
  Thomas 95
  Thos 83
Hanes, Andrew 83
  Daniel 119, 119
  Famy 119
  Harrison 83
  James 85
  Julia 85
  Mary 83
  Mary E. 83
  Rebeca 83
  Sarah 119
  May Adlaid 65
Hank, Polley 137
Hanks, Catherine 17
  David 50
  Elizabeth 53
  Hugh 121
  James 12, 121, 175
  Jane 41
  Lucinda 121
  Mary 121
  Nancy 17, 41, 121
  Samuel 17, 64
  Suana 12
  Winna H. 171
  Wm. 41
Hanley, Rebeccah 13
Hanoy, Mahaly 83
  Samuel 83
Hansley, Polley 77
Hanson, Pattie 40
Harbin, Elizabeth 126
  Mary 85
  Thomas 26
Harden, Albert 129
  Nancy 113
  Wm. W. 127
Hardgrave, Francis 75
Hardgraves, Francis 119
  Sarah 119
Hardin, Jane 53
  Randay 37
  Saml K. 174
  Sarah 13
Haris, John 84
  Leusia 64
  William 64
Harlow, Clarisa 26
Harmon, Amos 60, 81
  Mary 108
  Rachel 26
Harnold, Elizabeth 24
Harp, Elizabeth L. 82

Harper, Catherine 68
  Thursey 45
Harrald, Charlotte 52
  Elizabeth 35
  John 52, 84, 84
  Martha 84
  Wm. M. 102
Harras, Martha 16
Harrington, Sion 24
Harris, Almeda 121
  Alsey 84
  Betsy 165
  C. H. 83
  Catharine 54
  Charles 110
  David 176
  Delina 61
  Edward 107, 161
  Elizabeth 32
  Elizebeth 121
  George W. 84
  Ibby 6
  J. F. 85
  J. L. 203
  James 75, 85
  John 54
  Lidia 21
  Maret 64
  Martha Jane 54
  Mary Ann 55
  Mary H. 115
  Nancy 85
  O. J. 85
  Polley 52
  Polly 7
  Prissilla 50
  Richard 48
  Sarah 29
  Sarah J. 121
  Sareyan 50
  Squire 64
  Stephen 8, 187
  Tempey 55
  William 52
  Wm. 78
Harrison, Benjamin 87
  Daniel 22
  Joseph 133
  Martha 87
  Mary(?) 133
Harriss, Wm. 110
Harrld, Louisa E. 163
Harrold, Wm. M. 25
Hart, John 32
  Rebecca 75
  William 125
Hartin, J. R. 191
  Samuel K. 113
Hartly, Sophier 80
Hartzog, E. C. 31
  Laben 44
Haruen, Hester 170
Harvin, Lusey 7
Harwood, Jesse 141
Hather, Sarah 52
Hatley, John 184, 194
  Jane 143
Hatten, Charles 89
Hatton, Elizabeth 134
Haul, Elizabeth E. 97
Havener, J. E. 158
Havenor, Nancy M. 87
Haviner, Elizabeth B. 147
Hawkins, Elexander 87
  Elizabeth 58, 84
  Emeline 29
  Ezekael 17

Hawkins (cont.)
  Ezekel 86
  Ezekiel 58
  John 71, 86, 86
  John M. 159
  Mahaley 86
  Mary 187
  Nancy 14, 76, 86
  Rachael 127
  Salley 3
  Sally 41
  Sarah 12
  Susanah 86
  W. F. 76
  Washington 58
Hayes, Charles 115, 206
  G. W. 65
  George 72, 87
  H. 201
  H. H. 127
  Harrald S. 88
  Harrel 57
  Hartwell 23, 29, 160, 173
  Henry 43
  Hugh 30
  Isaac 46
  James 153
  Jesse 79
  John 87
  Jonathan 43
  Reuben 169, 205
  Reubin, Jr. 3
  Robt. 94
  Sarah 135, 142
Haynes, Mary Ann 187
Hays, Anna 88
  Bettie 28
  Clary 110
  Elizabeth 148, 177, 201
  Ezecal 87
  George 41
  George W. 88
  Hartwell 116
  Henry 81, 87, 141
  Herrald 89
  Hugh 87, 87, 145
  James 183
  Jemmimah 129
  Jesse 79
  Jessee 158
  John 173
  Joseph 87
  Keziah 43
  Mary 87
  Nancy 205
  Rebecca 127
  Reuben, Jr. 1
  Reuben, Junr. 25
  Sally 53
  Sofie M. 28
  Suanah 81
  Susanah 17
  William S. 104
  Y. W. 88
Hayse, Ann 159
  Henry H. 127
  Jesse 88
  Kisah 136
  Mary 136
  Robert, Jr. 88
  Robt 58
  Sarah 153
  Sarah M. 58
Head, Catherine 20
  Elizabeth 128
Hearrald, Polley 101

Heathman, Elizabeth 121
  Jonathan 115
Heatley, Elizabeth 16
Helen, Frances 191
Hembee, Nancy E. 17
Hemby, James 19
Hemrick, Adaline 142
Henderson, J. E. 58
  Luiser 160
  Maredath 105
  Mary 42
  Sarah 98
Hendon, Margarett 177
  Nena E. 184
Hendren, Alsey 69
  Charlotte M. 99
  Cinda 32
  Emiley A. 165
  Hicks 145
  James W. 99
  Jane 132
  Jehu 32, 89
  Martha 32
  Mary 116
  Mary S. 143
  Oliver 89, 165
  Solomon 89
  Voilet 164
  William 89, 89, 115
  William W. 89
  Wm. 69, 89
Hendricks, Charlotte 17
  Elizth. 184
  Marthey 126
Hendrin, William 89
  Wyatt 31
Hendrix, Abram 155
  Anna 54
  Caroline 102
  Caroline T. 137
  China 89
  Darby 31
  Elijah(?) 22
  Emily 90
  F. F. 151
  Green 89
  Hansle 90
  Irina(?) 50
  Jas. M. 170
  L. J. 132
  Lemada 187
  Taner 155
Hendron, Joel J. 88
  Wm. 137
Hendry, Marth Lith 164
Heral, Elizabeth 192
  Tempy 24
Herald, Sarah(?) 26
Herben, Dorchas 30
Herbin, Charloty 122
  Milly 122
Hercondon, Bettey 162
Herendon, Philadelpha 73
Heret, Sary 137
Herndon, Benj. 144
  Benjamin 23
  Jos. 73
  Joseph 104, 187
  Polly 78
Herrald, Wm. 3
Herreford, Sarah 165
Herrold, Marthy 25
Hester, T. B. 196
Hethham, Elisabeth A. 146
Hickerson, Charles 32
  Chas. 58, 90, 115, 145
  David 102, 114, 158
  Eliza 77

Hickerson (cont.)
  Jno. 133, 171
  John 3
  June 129
  L. M. 188, 195
  Mary L. 144
  Nancy 54
  Patsie 77
  Sarah 97, 188
Hickes, Jas. 90
Hickeson, Joseph 76
Hickman, Sarah 54
Hicks, Christenas 16
  Elizabeth 162
  Lucretia 191
  Mary 136
  Micajah 90, 162, 191
  Thomas 90
  Wm. M. 142
Higgins, Dolly 2
  Geo. 29
  Hiley 91
  Hiram 91
  Jane 19
  Lucinda 151
  Mary Ann 25
  Nancy C. 60
  Patsey 183
  Polley 77
  S. D. A. 41
  Sally M. 15
  W. L. 191
  Willia 91
  Wilsson 91
  Wm. L. 41
Highfield, Elizabeth 66
Hill, Elizabeth 41
  M. C. 81
  M. L. 100, 109
Hincher, Sharlott 91
  William 91
Hinchey, Patterson 28
  Phebe An 28
  Wm. D. 91
Hindrix, N. W. 45
Hinds, Mary 145
Hines, Ann 85, 110
  Elisabeth 115
  J. H. 183
  Lewiza 28
  Mary Ann 85
Hinshaw, Mary Jane 62
  William 91
Hitchcock, William 33
Hix, Caroline 181
  Charles 16, 22, 45
  Charlotte 16
  John 54
  Margaret E. 16
  Panthie 171
  Pollie 91
  W. G. 74, 203
Hoard, Catharine 128
Hockkings, John 91
Hodge, John 140
  Polley 51
Hodges, Christeny 159
  John 92
  Susana 185
  William 170
Hogen, James 170
Holaway, Mary Jane 162
Holbome, Dicy 179
Holbrook, Caleb 35
  Elisabeth 69
  Elizabeth 205
  Elvira 183
  Emila 60

222

Holbrook (cont.)
  Frankey 120
  J. S. 175
  John 1, 120
  John, Jr. 84
  L. M. 200
  M. J. 175
  Martha J. 175
  Metilda 29
  Nancy 204
  Pheba 190
  Polly 17
  Ralph 5, 35, 137, 161
  Sally 120
  William 120, 175, 175
Holbrooks, C. B. 92
  Catharine 15
Holcomb, Thos 8
Holdaway, Elizabeth 138
  Rachael 151
  Sally 187
  Sary An 156
Holder, Carline 55
  Cinthy 197
  Elizabeth 170
  Ezekiah 51
  George 152
  Henry 72, 153, 187
  James 93
  Louiasy 124
  Louizy 164
  Martha 160
  Maryan 93
  Mirah 80
  Nancy 11
  Newman J. 11
  Prudence 127
  Sarah 160
  W. J. 124
  William 198
Holderfield, Elizabeth 61
Holderway, John 158
  Nelley 191
  Rebecca 91
Holding, Larkin(?) 110
Holdman, Elizabeth 193
  Grace 180
  Margarett 194
  Thomas 47
Holdmon, Rebecka 110
Holdway, Wm. 166
Holebrook, Susan 15
Holebrooks, Sukey 5
  Wm. 81
Holeman, Ann 59
  Charlotte 140
  Joseph 202
  Matilda 110
  Nancy 102
  Polley 140
  Polly 79
  Thomas 62
Holeway, D. R. 153
  Marth 30
Hollan, Marthey 104
Hollar, Israel 94
Hollas, Nancy 125
Hollawang, D. H. 35
Hollaway, Daniel 94
  John 46
  Mary 46
  Willis 111
Holldaway, Hampton 174
Holleman, Bennet 94
  John 7
Holler, Nancy 94
Hollis, Mahaley 125

Hollow, Theny 52
Holman, Elizabeth 154
  Enoch 16
  James 154
Holmon, Dianna 186
  Eda 117
  Vienna 179
Holt, Aly 110
  Ambrose 87, 94, 137
  Elizabeth 87
  Polly 183
Holte, Frances L. 123
Holton, Alexr. 105
  Mary 112
  Susana 105
Hood, Charles 94, 171
  Elizabeth 107
  James 107
  Lucus 27
  Mahala 94
  Nancy 171
Hoofman, Susanah 107
Hooper, Elijah 94
  Elizabeth 177
  Ellender 177
  John 152, 197
  Martha 87, 172
  Nathaniel 62
  Polley 56
  Rebecca 108
  William 94
Hoopper, John 194
Hoot, Rachel 144
Hooton, David 178
Hoots, Jacob 42
  Margarett 179
  Mary 69
  Parmely 175
Hoover, Ann 62
Hopkins, Joseph, Sr. 181
  Lucy 189
Hopper, Elizabeth 2
  Luanah 105
  Susanna 78
  Tempy 77
  Thos 78
Hoppis, Mary 24
Horn, Cyntha 19
  George 135
  Joseph 19
Horten, Annis 103
Horton, Betty 65
  David 92
  David E. 165
  Jane C. 45
  Leander 45
  Miry 182
  Phineas 45, 65, 106
  Wm. L. 164
Hous, Jane 170
Howard, Benja, Junr. 202
  Benjamin 126
  Christopher 103
  Clarey 137
  Cornelius 31
  Discretion 98
  Fily 94
  Findley 147
  Findly 159
  Finly 154, 160
  George 33
  Joseph 15, 86
  Mary 94
  Nancy 30, 31
  Nansy M. 94
  Philip 95
  Prudence 31
  Rachel 95

Howard (cont.)
  Sarah 47, 99
  Sary 86
  Wesly 95
  William 90
Howel, Elizabeth 70
  Nancy 66
  Sarah E. 19
Howell, Mary 167
  Nancy M. 63
Howk, Jesse 188
Howson, Charlot 72
Hubard, Leviny 160
Hubbard, Ben 25
  Benjamin L. 143
  Betsey 8
  Elisabeth 85
  Elizabeth 64
  Ginsey 153
  Hanner 82
  Isam 111
  Isham 96, 96, 136
  Ishom 189
  J. 64, 74, 96
  James D. 163
  Nancy 62, 153
  Polly 80
  Rebecca 129
  Samuel F. 195
  Sarah 21, 83
  Sarah Caroline 201
Huffman, Anna B. 193
  Benjamin 59
  David 96
  Elizth. 195
  J. S. 199
  Martha 59
  Rosanah 3
  Stephen 39
  Zibba 27
Hufman, Andrew 46
Hufmon, Martha 27
Hughs, Mary C. 120
Hulin, Elizabeth 115
  Milley 115
Hulme, Elizabeth 55, 176
  Geo. 5
  George 62, 96, 99
  Wm. 56, 96
Hummey, Salley 148
Humphrey, Catherine 64
  David 96
  Elizabeth 111
  Owen 64, 97, 97
  Rachel 64
  Susanna 64
Humphries, Spencer 135
Humphry, David 14
  John 96
  Owen 64, 97
  Patty 176
Huneycutt, Daniel W. 97
Hunneycut, Mary 89
Hunt, Cynisca 65
  Elizabeth 176
  Margaret 132
  Susana 135
Hutcheson, E. M. 97
Hutchison, Francis 97
  Hardin 97
  Julia A. 157
  Nancy 19
Hutson, Elisabeth A. 28
  Eliza 68
  Elizabeth 68, 80
  Joseph 68
  Mary 81
  Sarah C. 6

Hutson (cont.)
　William 97
Hynes, Saml 97
Incle, William 97
Ingmon, Jane 69
　Rachel 66
Inscore, Fanny 103
　John 98
　Mary 140
　Rith 98
　Rubin 98
　William 116
Irion, F. W. 122
Irvin, Ally 168
　Marget 175
Irwin, Andrew 110
　Nancy 101
Isaacs, Mary 77
Isbel, Elizabeth 63
　Godfrey 98
Isbell, Elizabeth 111
　Frances 62
　Franfes, L. 144
　John 94
　Livingston 111
　Nancey 25
　Prudence 33
　Susannah 11
　Thomas 10
　Thos 55, 56
　Wm. 32
Isbill, Polley 23
　Thomas 25
Iscore, Wm. 16
Israel, Catey 57
　Michael 6, 57
Ivey, Elisabeth 69
　Nancy 68
　Ruffin 69, 99
　Winey 68
Ivy, Ruffin 164
Jacks, David 99
　William 13
Jackson, Abigale 96
　Grace 157
　Micajah 44
　Nancey 107
　Nancy 167
　Sarah 63
　William 96, 99
　William, Jr. 117
Jacobs, John 59, 151
James, Elizabeth 64
　Joseph 13, 49, 52, 87, 99, 138
　Juda 79
　Margaret 161
　Nancy 161
Jams, Wilie(?) 85
Janus, Matilda 184
Jaris, Scintha 153
Jarman, Nancy 23
　Sarah 18
Jarves, Noah 37
Jarvice, Jinney 156
Jarvis, Alce 9
　Ann 118
　Barbery A. D. 137
　Betsey 95
　Caroline 129
　Dicey 100
　Elizabeth 9
　Fanney S. 134
　Hannah 118
　James 100, 100, 135
　John 99, 100, 125
　Liddy 100
　Linsey 100, 144

Jarvis (cont.)
　Lyda J. 154
　Lydia 100
　Nancy 100
　Nelson 183
　Noah 191
　Ruth 173
　Sarah 173
　Sary C. 153
　Thomas 101
　Wayla 100
　Welmouth 130
　William 100, 173
Jeffry, Wm. 170
Jenings, Charles 100
Jenkins, Coder 109
　Emily 52
　John 163
　Lenne 109
　Margaret 150
　Susanah 109
Jennings, Dennis 167
　Frances 24
　Rebeca 168
　Susana 158
Jentry, Mahuldah 193
　Matilda 154
Jerden, Edney 9
　Mary 190
Jervis, Noah 153
Jines, Betsy 114
　Irenah 13
Jinings, Daniel 15
　John 62, 100
　Myra 25
　Polly 204
　Salley 174
Jinnings, Charity 3
　Charles 63
　Jane 109
　John 141
　John D. 3, 60
　Levi 47
　Melinda 101
　Pheba 141
　Pheeby 123
　Polly 1
　Rachel 125
　Sarah 205
　Susana 20
　Susanah 47
Johnson, Adelphia 77
　Alsa J. 81
　Alsey 77
　Ambrose 18, 23, 54, 142
　Amelia 108, 199
　Andrew 88
　Ann 189
　B. F. 103
　Barbara 104
　Benjamin 38
　C_____ 87
　Candace 84
　Caroline 118, 203
　Celia A. 83
　Charles 101
　Cloe 163
　Deborah 102
　E. F. 168
　Edney 103
　Elee 103
　Eli 98
　Eli Franklin 118
　Elias 105
　Elisabeth 98
　Elizabeth 38, 43, 105, 111, 151, 152, 194
　Elizabeth C. 190

Johnson (cont.)
　Elizabeth M. 72
　Elizebeth 48
　Elizebeth E. 174
　Elsa 103
　Elza 77, 77
　Elze 131
　Emaline 54
　Ennee 103
　Eunice 3
　F. P. 198
　Fanney 13
　Feraby 184
　Frances 87
　Franky 103
　Franses A. 19
　George 103, 165
　George P. 102
　Hanah 95
　J. 130
　J. M. W. 105
　James 5
　Jamsey 175
　Jas. M. W. 72
　Jeffery 163
　Joanah 172
　John 96, 98, 99, 103, 105, 105, 122, 166, 166, 176, 178
　John A. 172
　John S. 26, 105, 117
　Joseph 77
　Joshua 22, 102
　Jn. 116
　L. 26
　Leander 104, 174
　Letty 104
　Levina 6
　Lewis 23, 88, 102, 102, 196
　Lina 135
　Louis 152
　Lucey 99
　Lucinda 108
　Lucindia 102
　Lucy 178
　Luisa 92
　M. A. 134
　Marth 175
　Martha 1, 182, 196
　Martha J. 144
　Mary 7, 18, 26, 177
　Mary C. 128
　Maryan 192
　Mason 12
　Matilda 6, 6
　May 152
　Mayland 85
　Milley 102
　N. E. 67
　Nancy 26
　Nancy C. 50
　Nancy E. 172
　Nelly 30
　Nelson 168
　Noel 6, 102, 115
　Parmenas 99
　Patsey 69, 91, 97, 102
　Patsy 23
　Peggy M. M. Julietty 105
　Polley 51, 106, 198
　Polly 85, 126, 177
　Rachael 151
　Rachel 88
　Rachel 2, 48, 83, 99, 144
　Rebeccah 196

224

Johnson (cont.)
  Robt 121
  Roda 3
  Rosa 167
  Salley 44, 116
  Saml 27, 103, 105
  Samuel 69
  Sarah 168
  Sarah A. 61
  Sarah Ann 102
  Semira 152
  Sethe 6
  Sidney 23
  Stephen 84
  Susannah 102
  Tasann 20
  Tasy 3
  Thos 104
  Viney 184
  W. G. 59, 68, 81, 96, 110, 119, 121, 147, 159
  William 26, 45, 69, 102
  William, Jr. 182
  William P. 6
  William Parkes 105
  Wm. J. 192
  Winna 74, 105
  Winne 69
  Winney 102
  Wm. 16, 77, 104
Johnston, David 6
Johnston, Greenetta 194
  John 51
  Joshua 87, 131
  Millindey 151
  Nancy 163
  Noel 105
  Thomas 151
Joiner, John 64
Joines, Ann 39
  Eli 65
  Elizabeth 133
  Elizabeth A. 55
  Hamilton 105
  John 7
  John W. 112
  Lucy 38
  Marryann 42
  Martha 36
  Mary A. (Jones) 67
  Mary Elizabeth 65
  Moses 105
  Pendex 172
  Piety 146
  Rachel 36
  S. F. 36
  Sarah 68
  Thos 36
Joinnel, Mary 80
Joins, Moses 160
Jolley, Mirecey 168
  Wm. 127
Jolly, Malinda 173
  Marianda 173
  William 173
Jones, A. J. 61
  Adam 19
  Allen 149
  Amanda C. 55
  Amelia 128
  Ann 23, 149
  Ann Eliza 90
  Bartow 167
  Benja. 106, 183
  Betsey 95, 159
  Catharine 84

Jones (cont.)
  Cordelia Ann 55
  Cornelius J. 182
  E. W. 171
  Edd. 17
  Edm. 49
  Edmd. 106
  Edmund 148
  Elisebeth 183
  Eliza L. 54
  Elizabeth 163
  Elizabeth Evelina 57
  Elizbeth 175
  Famett 8
  Fanny 67, 161
  G. 17, 73
  George W. 11
  H. L. 61
  Henry 145
  Hugh 66, 108
  James 75, 140
  John 49, 64, 81
  John M. 195
  John W. 50
  Joseph 106, 106
  Joseph D. 140
  Kissia 99
  Larkin 141
  Larkin G. 90
  Lewis D. 107
  Louisa 83
  Lucy 35
  Margaret 54
  Martha C. 175
  Mary A. (see Joines)
  Mary Louisa 47
  Matilda 30
  Morton 10
  Nancy 90
  Nelly 81
  Patience 202
  Patty 61
  Phebe 16
  Philedelpha 26
  Phoebe C. 146
  Polly 2
  Rasmus 61
  Rebecka 195
  Rebeckah 140
  Russel 13, 110
  Sally 170
  Sarah 75
  Susanah 9
  Thomas 106, 106
  Thomas B. 133
  Thos 84, 170
Jonson, George 104
  James 44
Jordin, Malinda 178
Jourdin, M. J. 163
  Salley 163
Joyner, Harriett 129
  Jno 117
  L. 45
  Martha 129, 178
  Susanah 18
Judd, Elisabeth 197
  Elisebeth 61
  Hanner 65
  John 59, 197
  Nancy 141
  Perry 125, 204
  Rowland 90, 101
  Talitha 59
  William 61, 84, 117
Juson, Jane 91
Justice, Pattie 144
Kallar, Eve 107

Kallar (cont.)
  Nicholas, Sr. 107
Kamp, Rebekah 23
Kannaday, Jane 85
Katon, Tabias 29
Kaylor, Sally 34
Kearby, Sally 144
Kearley, Joel 108
Keedil, Jackson 201
Keelan, Michael 48
Keeling, Carlton 108, 108, 154
  Jane 178
  Leonard 184
  Thomas 178
Keer, James 74
Kees, Jacob 117
  Sarah 40
Keeton, Emaline 133
  Julus 102
  Mary 55
  William(?) 5
Keland, Nancy 29
Keling, Sarah 107
Kell, Jane 191
Keller, John 147
  Jonas 108
  Lewis 79, 168
  Mahala 179
  Marthy 199
  Milley 147
  Sally 108
  Wm. A. 17
Kelley, Lowersey 187
Kelly, Ann 52
  C. L. 102
  T. L. 102
  Thomas D. 53
  Thos. L. 151, 154
Kemp, Adlaide 174
  Amanda A. 13
  Elizabeth 177, 201
  Evey 174
  Gabriel E. 35
  H. E. 29
  Mary E. 144
  Mathew 174
  Sarah 76
  William 99
Kendall, Elizy 21
Kendell, Elizabeth 72
Kendol, Betsey 126
Kendoll, Nancy 49
Kenedy, Sally 92
Kennaday, John 71
  Nancy 71
Kennedy, A. W. 150
  Amelia 37
  Mary 203
  Norwood 37
  Thompson 203
Kerba, Sidney 68
Kerbo, John 179
Kerby, Amelia 71
  Darcus 137
  Francis 108
  Isabella 45
  Issabella 155
  James 155
  John 19
  John, Senr. 109
  Rachel 84
  Sally 19
Kerler, Salley 24
Kerley, Nelly 22
  Susannah 130
Kerly, Elder J. 118
  Elizabeth 25

Kerr, Whitfield 199
Kerry, Lewizey 122
Kertee, William, Junr. 66
Kessler, Daniel 107
Ketchum, George 117
Keton, John 135
  Mary 55
  Sary 135
Keys, Elizabeth 9
  Hiram 199
  John 149
  Margaret 149
  Martin 178
  Maryan 149
  Nancy 178
Kez, Elcy 194
Kidwell, Rachael 29
Kilbe, Jean 51
  Mary 167
Kilbey, Abr. 124
  Francis 107
  J. W. 15
  Lucinda 125
  Matilday 10
  Reubin 3
  Rosannah 153
  Salley 27
  Sally 15
  Susanner 183
  Thornton 98
  William S. 57
Kilby, Abr. 156
  Abra. 110
  Abram 109
  Albey 48
  Amanda 147
  Benjamin 186
  Elisabeth 109
  Elizabeth 48, 65, 74, 85, 114, 198
  Elizabeth A. 167
  Emily 109, 186
  Faney 48
  Franky 75
  Henry 109, 134
  Humphrey 11
  James 183
  James C. 109
  John 65, 92
  John B. 91, 156, 156
  John W. 109
  Mansy B. 48
  Margaret 156
  Margerett 183
  Matilda 21
  Nancy 169, 176, 183
  Nancy M. 62
  Phebe 28
  R. W. 48, 109
  Rachael 25
  Reubin 167
  Reubin W. 10
  Sally 125
  Saml 109
  Sarah 199
  Sarrah 11
  Thornton 11, 42, 42, 47, 109
  Wesly 109
  William 106, 188
  William H. 110
  Wm. S. 48, 56, 70, 82, 147
Killion, Henry 183
Kindal, Sarah 167
Kindall, Caroline 45
  John 156

Kindall (cont.)
  John Dula 75
  Thomas 194
  Wm. 110
Kindell, James 45
Kindle, James(?) 41
  William 110
Kindol, Salley 140
King, Elizabeth 72
  Hanah 72
  Peggey 118
  Susanna 131, 134
Kirby, John 110
  Polly 45
  Rebekah 189
Kirk, Mary Ann 20
Knight, Edy 11
  Lucinda 111
  Reuben 111, 111, 177
  Reubin 184
  Thos 111
  Usley 184
Koons, George 183
Kurby, Elsy 13
Lacky, Elisabeth 12
Ladd, Aaron 111, 176
  Amos 62
Lain, Elender 40
Laine, Elizabeth 155
  Jamie 196
Lakey, Leah 118
Lam, Edward(?) 93
Lambert, Wm. 139
Lambill, Felix 70
Lan, John 47
Land, Ann 57
  Anna 125
  Cinthy 126
  Elizebeth 33
  F. B. 195
  Frankey 74
  Franky 53, 111
  James 94, 126
  Lettice 33
  Linvel 75
  Linvil 31, 140, 186
  Linvill 33
  Linville 151
  Lizzie 132
  Mahala 111
  Malinda 94
  Martha C. 89
  Marthy 186
  Mary 80, 98
  Millee 135
  Nancey 183
  Nancy 126, 197
  Nicey 132
  Nimrod 57
  Rebecca 33
  Susanny 74
  Thomas 111
  Thos 13, 111
Landsdown, Millen 172
  Reuben 135
  Sarah 31
Lane, Agness 148
  Amelia 22
  Annie 112
  Caddy Caroline 114
  Charlotte 165
  Daniel 167, 204
  Elizabeth 187
  Garland 2
  Henry W. 6
  James 112
  Jane 204
  Jeremiah 63, 132

Lane (cont.)
  John 163
  John M. 123
  Lucinda 192
  Martha 172
  Mary L. 25
  Miry 174
  N. G. 82
  N. Garland 128
  Nancy 114
  Nancy G. 47
  Polly 71
  Rebecca 169
  Thomas 47, 112
  Thos 81, 107, 150
Lanes, Nelley 11
Langford, Polley 180
Langley, Hanner 197
Lansdown, Elizabeth 135
  Sumon 176
  William 42
Lanthford, Sealica 81
Lanton, Sarah (see Laxton)
Lantrip, Hezeiah 152
Lanus, Elijah(?) 106
Lard, Peggy 194
Lassenter, John 113
Laurence, Clary 176
  George 113
  Henry 126
  Polley 187
Law, Caleb 113
  Elisabeth J. 199
  Mahaly 94
  Margaret 65
  Rebecca 127
  Sarah 173
  Thomas 186
Lawes, Charety 10
  Frances (see Lowes)
Lawrence, Wm. 177
Laws, Alfred B. 94
  Amey 114
  Amy 114
  Benestor 175
  Betsey 163
  Caroline 83, 113
  Catey 82
  Catharine 27
  Clarinda 119
  David 113, 114, 114
  David G. 159
  Dilala 200
  E. L. 113
  Eliza 58
  Elizabeth 14, 114, 164
  James 14, 195
  Jas. 103
  Jason R. 114, 153
  Jayson R. 134
  Jesse 138
  Jno 113
  John 106, 113, 113, 113, 114, 114, 114
  John M. 157
  Joseph 114, 158
  Joseph R. 68, 114
  Joshua 113, 113, 153
  Larken 152
  Levina 158
  Littleberry 158
  Martha 53
  Marthew 106
  Mary 32, 114, 141, 152
  Mary Adline 155
  Mary An 28
  Masten 126

Laws (cont.)
  Milley 8
  Nancey 101
  Nancy 106
  Nancy J. 76
  Oma 177
  Patsey 166
  Polley 14
  Rebecca 113
  Riley 105, 177
  Rodah 159
  Rosaña 115
  Rosanna 113
  Rufus 153
  Ruth 143
  Sela 82
  Shadrach 113
  Susanna 114
  Timothey 73
  Timothy 114
  Tinley (Louther) 21
  William 9, 14, 16, 74, 79
  Wm. 91, 169, 171
Laxton, Celia 195
  Jain E. 26
  Lewis 11
  Louisa 11
  Margaret 177
  Mary A. 59
  Nancey S. 27
  Sarah (Lanton) 25
  Wilcox 197
  Wilson 33
Lay, Betsey 146
  David, Senr. 115
  David, Sr. 146
  Hannah 8
  Jesse 13, 55
  Mary 115
  Nancey 13
  Richard 108
  Susanna 108
Layne, James 165
Lazenby, Matildy 113
Lea, Mary 97
Lee, Almeda 154
  Clarissa 139
  James M. 56
  Jane 154
  Jesse G. 112
  Joseph 115
  Nancy 175
  Sarah 100
  William 100
  Winna 189
  Wm. 154
Lenderman, Emeline 188
  Henry 108, 100, 102
  Leonard 40, 115, 182, 206
  Malinda 201
  Melissa 123
  Polly 199
  Sally 40
  Samuel 28
Lenoir, Ann 77, 106
  Betsy 5
  Jackson 78
  Lucy 47
  Mary 73
  Maryan 77
  Nancy 78
  Tho 179
  W. R. 54
  Walter R. 146
  Walter W. 43
  William B. 35

Lenoir (cont.)
  Wm 104, 108
  Wm. A. 47
Lepford, Anthony 19
Lester, Nancy 189
Levingston, Polly 111
Levy, Hannah 177
Lewis, Aly 87
  Ann 49
  Catharine 178
  Chapman 173
  Chatman 142
  Elisebeth 148
  Elizabeth 43, 170, 206
  Hannah 95, 172
  James 41
  Jincey 172
  Jno 172
  Joel 73
  Joseph 116
  Joshua 40, 116, 116
  Martha 132
  Martha E. 142
  Mary 80, 89, 159
  Micager 143
  Nancey 43
  Nancy 164
  Nancy Emily 115
  Nimrod 134
  Rebecca 13
  Rutha 179
  Sarah 13, 149
  Sary 80, 89
  Thomas 89, 116
Lin, P. A. 155
Linch, Rebekah 141
Linderman, Nancy 152
  Samuel 27
  Caroline 150
  Dolly 27
Lindford, Franky 156
Lindsey, Jane 128
Linear, Minerva Adaline 15
Linney, Matilda 116
Linvill, Jane 171
Lion, Allen 48
  James 70
  Pheny 29
Lions, Rachel 70
Lipford, Alexander 104
  Nancy 130
  Sarah Jane 56
  Wm. A. 4
Lippes, Caroline 94
Lipps, Cenith 40
  Charity 146
  Charlotte 185
  Elizaboth 45
  John 117, 205
  M. B. 205
  Malinda 183
  Martha 117, 205
  Nancy 184
  Rebecca 178
  Sarah 4
  Selah 114
Lips, Elisebeth 124
  Mary 166
  Nancy 70
  Phebe 118
Lisk, Rachel 118
Little, Lewis 37, 181
  Sarah 94
Livingston, Catharine 33
  Cornelius 117, 117
  Ede 111
  Elizabeth 126

Livingston (cont.)
  Jane 33
  John 34, 111
  Lindsey 117
  Linsay 126
  Lucinda 126
  Martha 93
  Martin 34, 117
  Nancy 34, 34, 155
  Orrel 5
  Orril 34, 126
  Sarah A. 7
Liviston, Nancy 142
Locke, Matthew 176
Loe, Isaac 19
Lomack, Nancy 49
London, John 40
  Salley 144, 170
Long, Abigal 178
  Alexr 36
  Joel 177, 178
  Polly 123
  Wm. 161
Longbotom, Joseph 118
Longbottom, Apelona 203
  Elizabeth 118
  Jos. 118
  Joseph 118
  Nancy 135
Longworth, Burges 118
Lorance, Lucy 84
Louther, Tinley (see Laws)
Love, Agness 200
  Betsey 166
  Deby 168
  Elizabeth 122
  James 118
  Martha 177
  Mary 202
  Nancy 200
  Peggy 64
  Rebecca 118
  Thomas G. 77
  Thoms 91
  William 200
Lovelace, Elizabeth 46
  Geo. 46
  Nancy 2
Loven, Milley 5
Lovin, Gabl. 118
Loving, Anne 50
  Elizabeth 68
  Gabriel 50
  Milley 115
  Rachel 137
  Wm. 68
Lovit, Hanah 113
Low, Anna 19
  Hannah 76
  Mary 136
  Milley 114
  Sarah 137
  Thos 119
Lowder, Job 141
Lowe, Caleb 158
  Charity(?) 42
  Colic 156
  Elizabeth 119, 156
  Isaac 119, 141
  Isaiah 12
  John 119
  Lidda 156
  Mary 158
  Nancy 141
  Sarah 122
Lowes, Frances (Lawes) 126

Luffman, Elizabeth 119
  William 51, 119
  Wilson 140
Luffmon, Elizabeth 202
  Rhoda A. 83
Lufmon, J. R. 119
  Wilson 35
Luis, Hannah 104
  Mitilday 42
Lumford, Joel 174
Lunceford, Fanny 53
  Joel 53, 65
Luneford, Charity 166
Lunsford, Cina 129
  Cynthia 79
  Dicey 100
  Emmanel 119
  Jonathan 119
  Marey 85
  Micajah 53
  Millinda 167
  Milly 205
  Polly 148
  Telitha 190
Lunsfords, Malsia 35
Lyan, James 120
  Jane 120
Lycan, Susana 156
Lyndon, Mary J. 172
Lynes, Alan 103
  Feaba 103
  M. G. 83
Lyon, Allen 120
  Elizebeth 70
  Jacob 83, 116
  Jacob, Jr. 120
  Jacob J. 68
  James 70, 70
  Jesse 92
  Mary 166
  Meredith 56, 83
  Miles G. 46, 203
  Nancy 83
  Rachel 166
  Solomon 120
  Volentine 166
Lyons, William 193
Mabary, Marthey 134
Maberay, Susaner 164
Maberry, Anne 101
  Grepts 157
  Sarah Ann 30
  Yrpts 23
Mabery, Elisebeth 139
  James 200
  Jemima 155
  John 134, 179
  Jos. M. 127
  Marey 152
  Marthey 99
  Minday 48
  Phoeba 77
  Polley 100
  Randol 77
  Randolph 37
  Sally 134
  Susannah 35
  William 192
Mabry, Mima(?) 179
  Randall 43
Mabury, Carlina 39
Macay, Spruce 8
Macbride, Cynisca 163
Macguire, Locky 89
Macinny, Nancy 161
Macrare, Margaret 68
Madison, Albert 153
  Elisabeth 107

Madison (cont.)
  L. F. 19
  Sarah Jane 19
Magee, Matilda 171
  William 125
Mahafe, Emma 89
Mahaffey, Caroline 23
  Celia 80
  Elizabeth 54
  James 126
  Martha 154
  Martha J. 169
  Patsey 126
  W. 23
  William 54
Mahaffy, John F. 54
  Mary 126
  Newman 201
  Thomas 126
Mahafy, Elizabeth 178
Mahatha, Sintha 118
Mahathes, Sintha 18
Mahathy, Sarah 161
Mahiffey, Thomas 80
Main, Charles 33
Mais, David 187
Majors, Susanna 171
Mallby, Lucinda 11
Malloy, Thos W. 57
Maner, Suana 23
Mangum, Bettie 66
Manor, Jas 76
Manord, Larkin 150, 163
Manton, Ann 77
Maret, Jno 110
Markes, Delily 196
Marlen, Cenia 9
Marley, Anna 11
  Elisha 156
  John (Marlow) 11
  Nancy C. 57
Marlow, Ann 125
  Elizabeth 43, 156
  Gennetta 87
  James 49, 127
  Jas. 44
  Joel 127
  John 53 (see also Marley)
  Joseph 71
  Lettuce 105
  Malissa 125
  Mark 127
  Mary 127
  Phineas 127, 127
  Senith 130
  Sinah 127
  Tempy 57
  Viney 44
  Vira 22
  W. M. 127
Marsh, Isaac 78
  James 140
Marshal, Jane C. 149
Marsten, Nancy 142
Marstin, John 107
  Lucy 154
Marten, Anne 97
Martin, Adelia 84
  Amelia 40, 42, 122, 197
  Amelia C. 203
  Amelia E. 108
  Amelia Matilda 172
  Anne 8
  B. O. H. P. 38
  Benj. 44, 103
  Benj. F. 118, 162, 172
  Benj. H. 8

Martin (cont.)
  Benjamin 180
  Benjn. 128
  Charles 184
  Diana 128
  Diana A. 97
  Dianna Harrison 149
  E. M. 88
  Elisabeth 197
  Elizabeth 53, 128, 133, 180
  Elvirah 176
  Emeline 169
  Emilin 169
  Fanney 128
  Giles 41
  Henry 156, 163
  Isaiah 206
  James 44, 72, 128, 128, 128
  Jas. 53, 144
  Jas. O. 32
  John 9, 26, 75, 128, 137, 162
  John E. 128
  John W. 102
  Marey 167
  Martha 75, 121, 136, 157
  Martha D. 117
  Mary 11, 29, 83, 87, 123, 128
  Mary A. 32
  Matilda 142
  Matilda E. 148
  Nancy 85, 163
  Nancy Lamarah 103
  Patsey 164
  Peggie 41
  Perry 84
  R. C. 118, 196, 203
  Robert 40, 128, 128, 128, 196
  Robt, Jr. 103
  Rufus W. 95
  Salley 63, 156
  Sally 160
  Sarah 129
  Sarah M. 162
  Sary 32
  Sophah 84
  Thomas 47, 47, 58
  Thos 128, 164, 164
  Tildey 36
  Virginia 129
  W. W. 17
  William 56
  William W. 149
  Wm. 47, 77, 108, 121, 183
Marting, Marry 1
Marymen, Briant 7
Mason, Jan 108
  Nancy 66
  W. Dennis 171
  Winsten 46
Massey, Elizth. 184
  James 129
  Polley 45
  Sally 69
Massy, James 129
  William 129
Mast, Jacob 162
Masten, Amelia 85
Masteon, Marey 38
  William 38
Mastin, Alexander 52
  Amelia 67

Mastin (cont.)
Benj. 129
Elizabeth 202
Elizabeth E. 18
Flower 107
J. 196
J. E. 26, 65, 83, 112
James 2, 58
Jno. E. 12
John E. 20, 23, 27,
 74, 182, 187
Laura J. 78
Leuisia 38
Malinda 129
Martha C. 31
Martha J. 128
Rebecca A. 18
Sarah W. 74
Thomas 70, 168
W. 79
William 18, 65, 129
Wm 24, 31
Mastion, Susan 52
Maston, Dolley 70
 Sarah C. 130
Matherly, Mary 37
 Thomas J. 96
Mathes, Frances 14
Mathews, Hannah 200
 Nancy 204
Mathis, Adline 93
 Enoch S. 130
 Goodwin 192
 Jas. 58
 Polley 189
 Thos 204
Mattba, Amelia 57
 Elvira 107
Matthews, Ansel 130, 179
 Ansil 136
 Nancy 179
 Stephen 134
Matthis, Amy 6
 Ansel 130
Maudlin, Mary 147
Maxfield, Pheoby 171
Maxwill, Andrew 191
May, Eli B.(?) 33
Mayfield, Malinday 25
Maynard, Dililey 178
 Larkin 85
 William 130
McAlroy, Sarah 55
McAnn, Elizabeth 113
McBenory, Mary(?) 165
McBride, Betsey 40
 Clary 63, 73, 164
 Daniel 63, 73, 164
 Danl. 144
 Dianah 180
 Elisabeth 100
 Green 191
 Isabella 54
 Jain 142
 James 104, 121, 159
 John 74, 121
 Lidda 99
 Martha 29
 Marthey 63
 Matilda 73
 Martin G. 84
 Mary 7
 Nancy C. 164
 Nansey 7
 Rachel 140
 Rachiel M. 173
 Rebekah 104
 Ruth 52

McBride (cont.)
 Sarah 192
 Saron 71
McCain, Susanna 169
 Wm. 146
McCalup, Sylvester 148
McCan, Nancy 83
 Sarah 17
McCane, Margret 176
McCann, Alfred P. 171
 James 88, 105, 139, 180
 Marion 121, 121
 Polley 180
 Rachel 121
 T. H. 121
McCartay, Mary 92
McCay, Patrick 191
McCloud, Catherine 165
McCollister, Crotia 65
McCoy, Mahaley 35
 Martha 12
 Mary J. 149
 McK. 130
McCrary, John 103
 Nancy 30
 Sarah 103
McCray, Christopher 4
 Elizabeth 4
McDanel, Ann 91
 Sarah 192
McDaniel, Elisabeth 97
 Elizabeth 3
 Francis A. 44
 Henry 122
 Hugh 178
 Jane 178
 Joseph 122
 Margret L. 203
 Thos. 3
 William 14
 Wm. 122
McDow_, Catharine 24
McDowel, James 165
 Martha E. 77
McEwen, Cyntha 22
 Elenor Sharpe 66
 James 122
 Milley 23
McEwin, Archd. 32
Mcfactridge, Ann 43
McGee, Bluiforrt 5
 Cinthy M. 32
 Hanna 105
 James 126
 John 122, 167
 Louisa 63
 Martha L. Mead 62
 Patsy 5
 Rebecca L. 194
 Susannah 78
McGill, Marey 112
 Nancy 58
 William 19
 Wm. 197
McGinnes, Nancy 70
McGinnis, James 111
 Willis 70
McGlemory, David 123
 Nancy 161
 Susanah 123
McGlemry, Caroline 44
 Martin 124
 Merch 158
McGlomery, Marthy 85
McGrady, Andrew 46, 167
 Calvin 161
 Catharine 3
 Daniel 128

McGrady (cont.)
 Dolly 21
 Frances 36
 Isaiah 101, 159, 188
 Letea 188
 Nancy 106
 P. R. 26, 112, 205
 Polly 161
 R. P. 141
 Susanah 101
 Susanna 187
 Wm. 20, 123
Mchaffey, Nancy Ann 125
McHay, Robert 8
McKay, John 107
 Patrick 191
 William 100
McKee, M. A. 40
 Mary A. 138
McKenney, Patsey 145
 Saml 165
McKensey, Mary 51
McKenzie, A. G. 62
 Mary Elizabeth Jane 95
McKinney, Elizabeth 117
 Rebeckah 55
 Sucky 177
McKinzy, Nancy 70
McKoy, Nancy 166
McLie, Archd. S. 66
McMillion, Mary 38
McMullen, Docia 55
McNeal, Elizabeth 27
McNeil, Benj. 116
 George 125
 Harriet 122
 James 17
 John 58
 Nancy 47
 William 200
 Wm. H. 39, 59
 Wm. S. 188
McNeill, Alvy J. 58
 Elizabeth M. 146
McNiel, Alfred 125
 Delila F. 199
 Eli 132
 Elizabeth 25
 Enoch 117, 124
 Fany 60
 George 97, 124
 George W. 146
 Holloy 132
 J. H. 124
 James 146
 James C. 59, 122
 Jas. 132
 Joel 124
 John 168
 Larkin 124
 Mary 59, 131
 Peter 160
 Polly 146
 Rebecah 188
 Sally 24
 Sarah 17
 Susana 124
 W. H. 124
 Wm. 70
 Wm. H. 176, 188, 188
 Wm. H., Jr. 123
 Wm. S. 201
Mcniel, Eliza 27
McNiell, Peter 39
 Rebecca 181
 W. A. 27
McNil, Elizabeth 23
McPeters, Catherine 165

McQuary, John 9
  Sally 9
McQueary, John 148
McQuerry, Elizabeth 107
  John 85
  John, Jr. 204
  Lucy 62
  Polly 35
  Wm 35
McQuin, Braxton 32
M'Dowel, Elizabeth 76
Meadows, Daniel 130
  Elizabeth 8, 22
  James 66
  Rebecah 170
Meddows, Danl 105
Medlock, Abigail 135
Medows, Martha 8
Mehaffey, Jas 130
Meirs, Nancy 2
Melon, D. A. 91
Melone, Gabel 152
Melton, Sarah Ann 193
Mentin, Francis 107
Meredith, James 97
Mereman, Owen 13
Merriman, Dovey 71
  Lewis D. 121
  Nancy 42
  William W. 47
Merrimon, Elizabeth 75
  Owen 75
Merrit, Elizabeth 10
Merryman, Jenney 33
  Lewis D. 24
Messick, Eliza 131
  Elsey A. B. 22
  Leonard 131
Metstead, Sarah 201
Meyers, Emmaline 94
Meys, Seenay 180
Michal, Hannah 82
Micheal, Frederick 64
Michel, Elizabeth 181
Michell, Abey 205
  Marthey 131
Mickleroey, Charity 127
Middleton, Nancy 51
Midleton, Ann 51
Meirs, Elizabeth 156
  Lucinda 156
Mikel, David 160
  Eliza 115
Mikell, Rebecca 25
Milam, Permealy 107
  Wm. J. 45
Milem, Suanah 205
Miles, J. A. 131
Millender, Samuel 122
Miller, Alfred 184
  Annis 163
  Carline 166
  Caroline 39
  Caty A. 205
  Cleary 28
  David 23
  Elisabeth 82, 113
  Elizabeth 53, 179
  Fanny(?) 143
  Hamson 9
  Henry 132, 167
  Jane 158
  Jesse 39
  John B. 184, 186
  John J. 113, 131
  Mary 67, 190
  Nancy 81
  Polley 23

Miller (cont.)
  Rebecca 112, 113
  Sally 206
  Sarah(?) 20, 27
  Sarah Adalaide 39
  Sarah E. 176
  Sry 165
  Susanah 31
  William 20
Millinde, Samuel 71
Milliner, Sarah 5
Mills, H. C. 132
  Judah 87
  Martha 70
  T. D. 62
  William 153
Millsaps, Clarasay 152
  Joseph 125
  Nancy 155
  Rebecca E. 171
  Thomas 133
  Thos 130
  William 155
Millum, Rebecca 139
Milsaps, Catherine 201
Milum, Marthaan 30
Minter, Malissa Parisice 32
  Thomas C. 14
Minting, William 133
Minton, Alfred 39
  Betsey 69
  Caleb 63, 94, 134
  Delila 59
  Elenor 57
  Eliza Ann 16
  Elizabeth 84, 113
  Eveline 131
  Fanny 66
  George 30, 59
  Hugh 84
  James 118
  James, Jr. 133
  Jesse 133
  John 68, 133
  Louisa Bethany 131
  Loveless 179
  Madison 133
  Martha 80, 131
  Mary 59, 133
  Matilda 57, 138
  Milly 134
  Nancy 73
  Rosannah 14
  Shadrach 131
  Vicey 38
  Wm. 133
Mise, Jane 147
  Mary 159
  Pattie 160
Mitchel, Elijah 88
  Gemima 86
  George 11
  James 113
  Martha 113
  Mary 22, 137
  Moses 107
  Nancey 107
  Nancy 11, 38, 88, 125
  Rachel 87
  Robert 125
  Thomas W. 34
Mitchell, Ann 35
  Archd. 165
  Asa 79
  Asey 79
  Elizabeth 160, 161
  Gilley 54

Mitchell (cont.)
  Henry 100
  J. F. 164
  James 8
  John 17, 82, 146
  Jonathan 195
  Joshua 58, 135, 155
  M. F. 30
  Margaret 164
  Nancy 182
  Polly Ann 112
  Robert 134
  Salley 11
  Sarah 16, 147
  Susanh 56
  Thomas 122
  Thomas W. 135
  Thos W. 151
  William 135
  William R. 181
  Willm. 135
Mitsteade, Mary 137
Mize, Isaac 181
  John T. 189
  Polley 118
  Sary 50
Molba, Thomas E. 93
Moltbey, Thos 111
Monday, Elizabeth 62
Money, Austion 76
  Howel 34
  Isaac 126
  Lucinda 34
  Thomas 51
Mongumry, Elizabeth 88
Montgomery, Elizabeth 115
  Jane 59
  John 124
  Margaret 154
  Margartt 21
  Nancy 202
  Rachel 141, 178
  Susannah 57
Mooney, James 111
  Margarett 111
  Sally 19
Moony, William 18
Moore, Alexander 9
  Anny 6
  Bidunt 41
  Cintha Elizabeth 43
  David E. 78
  Elizabeth 136
  J. W. 143
  James 6
  Jesse 36
  John 158, 159, 159
  Mary 9, 43, 88
  Matilda 96
  Nancey 13
  Rebekah 36
  Rily 43
  Robert 7
  Sarah 6, 127
  Suphire 127
  Wilson 88, 136
More, Starling 136
Moremon, Owen(?) 136
Morgain, Charee 136
  Sarah 94
  Theophilus 156
Morgan, Ailes 69
  Anna 160
  Catherine D. 4
  Charity 69
  Isaac 136
  James 140
  John 136

Morgan (cont.)
  Joshua 3, 136, 136
  Nancy 63, 140
  Ruth 140
  Selah 112
  Susanna 125
Morgin, Polley 149
  Thomas 136
Morris, Elizabeth 151
  George 8
  Henry 8
  James 1
  Mary 1
  Susanna 8
  Thos. 136
Morriss, Susannah 32
Mosely, Cintha 141
Moss, Jephs 163
Motherly, John 135
  Rebeca 135
Mulkie, James 79
Mullens, Winifred 141
Mulles, Nancey 181
Mullins, Ann 98
  Elizabeth 78
  James 141
  Mark 95
  Mary 92, 185
  Phanney 107
  William 185
Mullis, Casse A. 127
  John 137
  Mary E. 173
  Polley 18
  Sally 189
Mundy, Benjamin 137
  Mary 23
Mongumry, Caty 40
Murpha, Ann 11
Murphe, Archable 11
Murphey, Ama 60
  Mary 52, 161
Murphrey, Sary 11
Murphy, Elir 161
  Jinney 111
  Mary 140, 161
Murrah, Joshua 84
  Nancey 84, 94, 122,
  Wm. 94
Musgrove, Sarah 66
Myars, Lucind 135
Myers, A. E. 137
  Anderson 168
  Eliz. 137
  James 18
  John 88, 137, 137
  Joseph, Jr. 126
  Lidey 126
  Marinda 60
  Mary 169
  Thomas 30, 135, 137
Myes, John 98
Myres, Rebeca 18
  Rebecca 192
Nailer, Dickson 132
Nale, Elizabeth 203
Nance, Aly 72
  Biddy 43
  Belita 6
  Eliline 3
  Fatana 9
  G. F. 155
  Miles 9
  Milos 52
  Polly 53
  Rebeca 105
  Wellborn 181
  Wm. 13

Nancy, Adline 155
Napier, Zepha 34
Napper, Hughs 190
Naris, Sarah M. (Noris)
  64
Nathery, Easter 78
Naylor, Sintha An 197
Nazary, Elizabeth 205
Neil, John 146
Nelson, Hugh 51
  J. M. 187
  Martha Clalinda 129
  Matilda 170
Nesbitt, A. 4
Netherly, Sarah 99
Newberry, Thos. 86
  William 171
  Wm. 122
Newland, B. Washington
  175
Newman, Eliza J. 193
Nichells, Sarah Ann 134
Nichelson, Lazarus 42
Nicholas, A. E. 109
  Mary 79
  Mercy 109
Nicholds, Elijah 110, 138
  Frances Bethenia 50
  Mary A. 132
  Rebecca 28
  Sarah Ann 138
Nicholl, Susan 57
Nicholls, A. E. 157
  Elisabeth C. 150
  Elizabeth 138
  J. P. W. 124
  J. W. 134
  James 138
  James W. 27, 167
  John 138
  Jos. W. 57
  Joseph 139
  Lodemma 59
  Nancy 203
  Nancy M. 157
  Permealy 46
  Vilott 27
Nichols, Abraham C. 91
  Amandy 93
  James W. 28
  Joseph 28
  Matilda 49
  Moseph 27
  Polly 124
Nicholson, Dicey 204
  Eisabeth 108
  Jane Lucinda 91
  Nancy 119
  Saml 95
  Sarah 201
Nickelson, Elisebeth 139
  Lazarus 155
  Rebeck 137
  Rebekah 42
  Salley 157
  Samuel 139
  William 139, 139
Nickleson, James 35
  Samuel 27
  William 35, 155
Nickolason, C. E. 201
  Wm. 201
Nickolds, Abram 139
  Catherine 139
Nickolson, Salley 131
Niell, Wm. 36
Night, Elizabeth 42
Nisbett, A. 6

Noland, Delilah 50
  Nancy 87
  Peter 87
  Pierce 33
  Sarah 34
  Wm 61, 93
Nolen, Patsy 131
  Wm. 131
Nooe, John 100, 137
Norble, James M. (?) 106
Noris, Franses 116
  John 116
  Sarah M. (see Naris)
Norman, Anna 172
  B. F. 29
  Benjamin F. 34
  Catharine 88
  Dicey 170
  Eli 44
  Eligan 88
  Elijah 170
  Elizabeth 193
  Isaac 140
  James 86
  Jincy 103
  Kisiah 136
  L. J. 172
  Mary 46
  Nancey 42
  Nancy 139
  Rosanna 9
  Sary 170
  Thos 41
  W. H. 130
Normand, Thomas 149
Normon, Elizabeth 63
Norris, Agness 124
  Francis L. 194
  John 140
  Sally 81
Northern, John 110
  Thomas 193
Norwood, Jas. H. 168
Nott, Ephraim 43
  Mary 43
Nowland, Pearce 183
Nulby, Nancy N. 10
Nunnery, Doshe 104
Oakley, Elizabeth 98
  Rebeckey 98
Obarr, Robert 29
Odom, Catheren 117
  Loveviney 181
  Mary A. 37
  Matilda(?) 55
  Wm. 117
Oerand, Jacob 154
Oings, Rachel 50
Oldridge, Elizabeth 30
Oliver, Marthy 4
  Milley C. 127
Olliver, Jesse 175
  Wm. 80
Olvey, Fielder 141
Opkins, Rebecca 18
Orand, Sarah 66
Orr, John 55
Orren, Jacob 66
Orron, Elizabeth 150
Orsbern, Catharine 181
  Elizabeth 201
  Joseph 201
Osbeon, Johnathan 166
Osbern, David 141
  Joseph 28, 181, 181
Osborn, Elizabeth(?) 161
Osborne, Luzena 142
Osburn, Easter 181

Osburn (cont.)
  Jonathan 38
  Joseph 181
  Mary 160
  Susannah 28
Overstreet, Catharine 4
  William 197
  Wm. 4
Owen, Ann 119
  Arch. 141
  Caroline 7
  Elizabeth 156
  George 26
  Jesse F. 79
  Johnson 141, 183
Owens, Archabal 107
  Elizabeth 157
  Fanny 189
  George 100, 141
  Hanah 87
  Hila 79
  J. F. 1
  J. M. 157
  John G. 141
  John J. 25
  Larkin 142
  Martin 141, 141
  Nancy 204
  Salley 194
  Susanah 123, 205
Owins, Johnson 109
Ownes, Mare 168
Ozborn, John 171
Paden, Wm. W. 93
Padget, Nancy 91
  Rachael 141
  Sarah 202
  Wm. R. 50
Page, Lorana 130
Pagit, P. E. 142
Pague, Matha 56
Pain, Catherine 39
  Lucinda 19
  Martha J. 39
Pajet, Susy 45
Palmer, Anne 147
  Elisabeth 40
  Lidda 156
  Sarah 156
Pardew, Elizabeth 40
  Franklin 148
  Joel M. 142
  Lucinda C. 74
  Martha 100
  R. L. D. 77
Pardue, Beavel 139
  Bevel M. 190
  J. F. 142
  James 142
  Laura 90
  Martha 142
  Tobatah 139
  Wm 142
Parham, Martha 34
  Wm 34
Parin, Henry 98
Park, Ambr. 149
Parker, Ailcy 191
  Amanda 37
  David 43
  Diannah 4
  Elisabeth 15
  Elizabeth 155
  Elizabeth A. 119
  Elizabeth J. 30
  Esquire 96
  Franky 143
  G. B. 29

Parker (cont.)
  Hiley 118
  James 13, 45
  John 34, 34, 34, 43,
    72, 117, 143, 143
  Mary 160
  Nancy 181
  Richard 7, 159
  Richd. 122
  Sally 138
  Vise 143
  William F. 7
Parkes, Alfred 75
  Ansel 97
  Benj. J. 68
  Clavin 75
  Cynthia 162
  Cynthia Mackconer 11
  Elisabeth 5
  Fanny 194
  George 98
  Hasten E. 101
  James D. 143
  Jonathan 48
  Levenah 72
  Lidda 157
  Marideth 194
  Martha 98
  Martha J. 121
  Mary 11
  Nancey 141
  Nancy 103, 166
  Patsey 75, 128
  Peggay 74
  Rachel 75, 108
  Sally 34
  Susannah 96
  Uriah 5
  W. F. 129
Parks, A. 44
  Aaron 53
  Allen 140
  Allen W. 25
  Ambers L. 195
  Ambr. 144
  Ambrose 11, 74, 104
  Ambrose L. 177
  Ansel 17
  Benj. J. 18, 96, 114,
    176, 195
  Benjamin 144, 144
  Betsy 144
  Eliza 97
  Emily A. 43
  Fanney 118
  Francis L. 195
  G. B. 139
  J. P. 144
  John 144
  John J. 149
  John P. 144
  John S. 120
  Jonathan 176
  M. A. 128
  M. Matilda 165
  M. T. 121
  Mahala 53
  Martin 149
  Milly 144
  Nancy 48, 149
  Peggy 5
  Pissilla 72
  Rachel 108
  Reuben 144, 144
  Reuben, Jr. 149
  Reuben, Junr. 5
  Richard 34, 145, 172
  Richmond 144

Parks (cont.)
  S. A. 53
  T. M. 121, 175
  Thomas 144, 144
  Thomas M. 144
  Uriah 72, 128
Parleir, James 145
  John W. 149
  N. C. 155
Parler, James 150, 176
Parlier, Isaac 107, 112
  Isaac, Jr. 145
  J. J. 150, 197
  John 46, 77, 115
  John F. 89, 96
  Mary Elizth. 145
  Rachael 77
  Rebecca E. 89
  William 145
Parlur, Isaac 203
Parmely, Mary 174
Parr, Abner 7
  Hannah 7
Parson, John 146
  Marry 73
  Martha 63
  Rebeca C. 146
Parsons, Alfred 28
  Catharine 115
  Elviny 70
  Frances 112
  Geo. G. 49
  John 145
  Martha 199
  Martin 124
  Mary 58, 66, 112
  Meley 36
  Milly 131
  Mily 174
  Paten 174
  Patsy 140
  Peggy 194
  Polly 82
  R. M. 179
  Rebeca 150
  Rebecca 195
  Rody 72
  S. E. 145
  Samuel 41
  Sarah 195
  Sinthy 14
  W. M. 145, 145
  Wm. 51
  Wm H. 14
  Wm. N. 46
Parsuns, George 46
Partette, S. E. 128
Pasley, Margerett 110
Passmore, Rebecka 70
Passons, James 77
Paterson, Ann 201
Patric, Jelina 167
Patterson, Andrew 181
  Emela 51
  James 201
  Nancy 164
  Saml. F. 61
  Susanna 96
Patton, James 25, 139,
    144, 158, 199
  Jane 61
  Jas., Jr. 78
  Joseph 146
Pauley, Betsey 93
Paxsley, Isaac 12
Payn, Nersisey 14
Payne, Anis 189
  Malindy 39

Payne (cont.)
  Malissa A. 194
  Uriah 39
  Wm. W. 74
Pearce, Anna 8
  John (Pierce) 32
  W. N. 146
Pearson, Charles 180
  Dosia M. 162
  Elizabeth 82
  Enoch 192
  Evaline 153
  Francis 149
  Jn. W. 22
  John 21
  L. H. 57
  Laurence 112
  Sulena 185
  Thos 147
  Wm. 57
Peasley, Isaac 130, 161
  Temperance 161
Peden, Ferebee 147
  Mary S. 10
  Wm. W. 93
Pendergrass, Amey 20
  Raleigh 147, 147
  Roley 20
  Rolley 147
  Winney 172
Pendlegrass, Benj. 143
  Patsy 95
Pendley, A. W. 92, 185
  James 148
  William 64
Peniton, Aliles 178
Penix, Polly 6
Penlee, James 109
Penley, Leanah 64
Pennal, Clara 202
Pennel, Joshua 89, 165
  Sarah 148, 182
  Susanna 10
  William 148
Pennell, John 68
  Saml 160
Pennington, Margret 190
Perden, Lucinda 85
Perdew, E. M. 172
  Matilda 19
Perdue, _____ 190
  Elender 51
  Emley 116
  James 129
  Joel 50
  John D. 64
  Marth J. 187
  Martha 129
  Mary 194
  Robert 148
  Salley 20
  Sarah 159
  Serey 75
  Thos 159
  Wm. 23
Perkins, Hariet E. 124
  J. C. 37
  J. E. 121
  J. H. 132
  Simeon 5
  William 148
Perlair, Margaret 26
Perleir, Sarah 71
Perlin, Elizabeth 183
Pernater, Elisabeth 148
Pernell, Cathrine 60
  Mariah 179
Perry, Enoch 168

Person, Carolina 146
  Caroline 146
  Charles 180
  Ellenar 57
  Hanner 113
  James 166
  John 14, 162
  Nancy 118, 160
  Samuel 199
  Thomas 114
Persons, Milley 49
  Wm. 40
Pertoll, John 63
Peryjohn, Martha 157
Pettey, B. F. 18, 88
  Eli 2, 20, 91, 151
  Thornton 31
Pettijohn, Jane 84
Petty, Amely 31
  Benjamin F. 116
  Delia A. 53
  Elisha 140
  Jno. H. 142
  Joannah 151
  Julia Ann 169
  Lucinda 98
  Lucinda C. 144
  William 82
Pety, Leety 43
Pheranton, Alexander (see Ferrington)
Phesler, Christenah 85
Philips, Charles 103
  Dennis 69
  Eli 149
  Elisha B. 149
  Hannah 165
  John B. 140
  Johnston 40
  Martha E. 193
  Mary 193
  Mary E. 140
  Mary Elizabeth 194
  Matilda 149
  Nancy 61
  Pheba H. 200
  Phebe C. 133
  Robert 200
  Sarah M. 44
  Stephen 73
  Wm. D. 50
Phillips, Abigail 117
  Alcey 29
  Ambrous J. 182
  Caroline 109
  Eli 184
  Elias 150
  Elisath (sic) 43
  Elioha B. 13
  Elizabeth 11
  Elizabeth A. 95
  Fanny 184
  Hanah Louisa 72
  Jemima 22
  John 61, 146
  Judy 66
  Lucreacy 145
  Malinda J. 93
  Meredith 85
  Milley 61, 91
  Miriam 85
  Nancey 16, 203
  Nancy 21, 146, 175
  Phebey 126
  Rebecca 150
  Sarah 144
  Stephen 61
  Susannah 163

Phillips (cont.)
  Thursa 121
  William P. 196
Phipps, Jordan 50
Phouts, J. S. 167
Phrophet, Rachel L. 9
Pierce, John (see Pearce)
  W. N. 196
Pierson, John 164
Pig, Fanny 102
Pigg, Salley 51
Pilkenton, Louzaney 205
  M. 205
  Wilie 192
Pilkington, Angenette 146
  Sarah 104
  William 146
Pilkinton, Nancy 195
  Wiley 139
  Wm 150
Pinden, Seelius 180
Pinkard, Loise 143
Pinley, John 152
Pinnel, Joshua 99
Pinson, Aaron 98
Pinx, Lucey 157
Pipes, Jesse 138
  Rebecca 51
  Susanna 51
  Thomas 31, 80
Pitman, Mary 122
Poe, Hariet 121
  Lucinda 160
  Milley 73
  Polley 97
  Powel 49
  Sarah 91
Pogue, Elizabeth 94
  Hannah 19
  Joseph 19
Polard, Sally 87
Pool, Wm 8
Pollard, Americk 86
Poplin, Huldah J. 46
  Nancy H. 202
Porter, A. 72, 126
  Adeline 166
  Andrew 3, 88, 102, 104, 168
  Catherine 4
  Constant 151
  Elisha 158
  Elizabeth 142
  Jos. 43
  Joseph 120, 151
  Joseph, Jr. 101
  Lois 36
  Martha 159
  Martha L. 19
  Nancy 45
  Rachel 151
  Sarah 123
Poter, E. 151
  Elisha 152
  Elizabeth 148
  Lizbeth 142
  Malinda 152
  Mary 93
Poulson, Paul 52
Pourter, Francis 108
  Nancy 179
  Polly 9
  Sarah 181
Powel, Elizabeth 189
  G. S. 195
  J. M. 150
  Mary 150
  Nancy 149, 188

Powel (cont.)
  Rhody 195
Powell, Ambrous 141
  G. S. 162
  Jane 93
  Rebecca 72
  Rosannah 71
  Warren 74, 152
Powers, Kezia 61
Pratt, Elisha 203
  Elizabeth C. 175
  John 75
  Mary Ann 56
  Meriah 65
  Polley 52
  Sarah 24
Prescott, Richard 131
Presly, Mary 106
Presnall, Susana 152
Presnell, Anna 152
  Elijah 152
  Elizabeth 152
  Israel 152
  Josiah 71
  Wm. R. 114
Preston, Elisabeth 199
  Isaac 171
  Mary 118
  Nancy 171
Previt, Sarah 190
Previtt, Alcy 159
Prew, John 179
Prewit, Mary 54, 54
  Patsey 187
  Roady 17
  Wesley 152
  Williford 56
Prewitt, Augustus 116
  Cader 152
  Jacob 153
  Leoiny 49
  Noah 25, 152
  Richard 153
Price, Elizabeth 113
  Joseph 127
  Judy 136
  Margret 114
  Mary E. 130
  Nancy 153
  Philip 119
  Phillip 153
  Polley 43
  Walter 153
  Wm. L. 130
Pritchett, Nancy 197
Privett, Hiram 205
  Nancy 174
Priviett, Hulda 154
  Wileford 154
Privit, Polly 201
Profett, Lidey 173
  Nancy 65
Proffet, Elizabeth 132
  Matilda 140
  Roda 112
Profit, Elizabeth 175, 194
  John 154
  Miry 80
  Rebeca 193
  William 194
Profitt, John 173
  Sarah 8
Prophet, Mary 193
Prophett, Polly 66
Prophfet, Sarah 180
Prophit, John 15
  Nancy 15

Pruet, Cathrine 9
  Nancy 17
  Sarah 174
Pruett, Andrew 161
  Polley 93
  Williford 69
Pruit, John 174
  Joseph 154
  Nancy 154
  Ralph 153, 162
Pruitt, Cader 126
  J. P. 20
  Nina 13
  Ralph 92
  Williford 45
Pryer, Emily 4
Pryor, C. M. 145
  Ladosia 55
Pumphrey, Larkin 203
Pumphry, Henry 35
  Sally 35
Purdue, John D. 120
Pusser, Darcus 146
Queen, Alla M. 6
  Elis 21, 155
  Francis 155
  James 6
  Jane 21
  Wm. R. 138, 138
Quen, Margaret 133
Quinn, Alfred 21
Ragesdel, Martha J. 152
Ragesdle, Nancy(?) 196
Ragsdell, Elizabeth 20
  James J. 20
Raigen, Sally 112
Rains, John 55, 82
  Nancy 20
Randal, Ransom 185
Randell, Susanna 24
Rash, Ameus 42
  Asa 9, 42, 99, 136
  Betsey 42
  Charles 35, 42
  Cinthia 27
  Daniel 120, 155
  E. E. 205
  Elisabeth 58
  Elizabeth 9, 174
  Henry 21
  James 100
  James C. 205
  Jos. C. 205
  Levey 155
  Levi 52, 154
  Mancy 8
  Margret 35
  Martha 155
  Mary 76, 183
  Merida 156
  Nancy 156
  Nancy E. 35
  Nancy Matildy 205
  Ruth 25, 147
  Sally 136, 155
  Sarah 135, 156
  Sarah A. 62
  Sarah an 153
  Sarah P. 205
  Thomas 165
  Vancey 8
  William 35, 136
  William H. 155
Ratcliff, Sarah 119
Rathbone, Alce 62
Ratliff, Elisabeth 190
  Jas. R. 190
  Jonathan 156

Rauswell, Susannah 10
Ray, Delila C. 156
  Eliza Ann 101
  Elizabeth 50, 71
  Henry H. 176
  James 55
  Jesse (Wray) 18
  John 192
  Joseph 7, 14, 50, 118, 165
  Margaret E. 50
  Mary C. 70
  Peter 55, 193
  Thos 18
  William 54
Raymond, Hannah 189
Reace, Paul A. 148
Reade, Nicey 97
Readin, John 157
Reading, Patsy 108
Rease, Rebecca 202
Reaves, Bellee 202
  James 202
Reavis, A. H. 156
  Elizabeth 156
  Joseph 156
Recter, Lewis 119
Rector, Lucey 106
Redden, Patsey 197
  Salley 157
Reddin, Fanney 206
  John 187
  Marth 125
  Susannah 99
  Wm. 128, 156, 157, 200
Redding, Anderson 157
  Elisabeth 22
  Filas 130
  Hiram 71
  J. W. 88
  James 37
  Jane 122
  John 157, 157, 157
  Lewenday 12
  Martha L. 122
  Martin 157
  Nancy 200
  Nansey 200
  Rebecah 128
  Salley 117, 157
  Thirston W. 148
  Thurston 100
  William 82, 88, 128, 129, 157, 173
  Williams 157
  Wm 18, 22, 200
Reddings, Salley 76
Reding, Nathan 125
Reed, Abel 137
  Oliff 187
Reese, James 83
  John 201
  Margret M. 83
Reeves, Belinda 186
  Eli 103
  James 83
  John 60
  John F. 157
Regan, Peter 62
Reid, Seenor Elmirah 192
Reilly, James C. 161
Renols, Martha 5
Revis, Elizabeth 158
  Joseph 158
Reynolds, Alcy 96
  Clarasey 20
  Elisha 29, 111
  Elizabeth 62, 111

Reynolds (cont.)
  Elza 97
  Francis 164, 188
  Hanah 144
  Ivy 96, 190
  James 156
  James E. 158
  Jas. E. 109
  Mary 111
  Nancy 164
  Nancy A. 204
  Polly 102
  Sally 58
  Sarah 76
  Silas 144, 166
  Wesley 31, 62, 130
  William 40, 158, 169
  Wm. E. 1, 20, 67, 166
Rhoades, John A. 69
Rhoads, Nancy 60
  Sarah 183
  Willson 114
Rhodes, John 87, 159
  Sarah 87
  W. M. 2
Rhods, Aggy 118
  Bengaman 29
  Elizabeth 91
  J. U. 86
  Mary 29
  Merica 29
Richardson, Chrlet 153
  Eveline 12
  M. F. 83
  Margaret 79
  Noel 169
  Vicey 2
Richerson, Noel 82
  Peggey 82
Richeson, Matilda 3
Ridden, William 125
Riddle, Debury 181
  Elizabeth 158
  Polly 87
Ridel, Mary 181
Ried, Vicy 111
Riggins, Elizabeth 45
Right, Christeen 75
Rigsby, Lewis 159
Riley, Ann 161
  Lucinda 15
  Nancy 46
Risdin, Elizabeth 23
  Phana 19
Riston, Peggey 148
Rivett, Winney 17
Roach, Mary 29
  Polley 188
Roads, Hiram 159
  Polly 36
  Sarah 191
Robards, Richard 90
Robarts, William 77
Robberds, Izey 91
Robberson, James 80
Robberts, Bennet 201
  Marian 64
Robbins, Casander 63
  Matilda 198
  Milly 198
Robeds, Marey (Roberts) 145
Robenett, Allen 99
Roberds, David 160
  Delphy 53
  John 2
  Mary 91
  Rebecka 87

Roberds (cont.)
  Sarah 191
  Sary 35
  Sintha 2
Roberson, Amanda 113
  Anne 190
  Armenia(?) 113
  Caroline 193
  Cintha E. 139
  Elizabeth 181
  James 95, 119, 190
  John 113
  Keziah 89
  Lydia 60
  Martha 153
  Martha E. 125
  Mary C. 88
  Matilda 50
  Nancy 88
  Sarah 143
  Thomas 188
  W. W. 139
  Walter 88
  Wm. W. 62, 138
Roberts, Alsa 145
  Bathsheba 179
  Bennet 161, 176
  Betsey 201
  E. A. 180
  E. F. 134
  Elizabeth 77
  Ellender 140
  Fanny 12
  Ferebe 81
  Gemima 138
  George 22, 85, 160
  J. F. 170
  Jacob 161
  Jammey 143
  Joel 93, 179
  John 140, 161, 202
  Lu Annie T. 35
  Lusean M. 63
  Marey (see Robeds)
  Margerett 58
  Martha J. 145
  Mary M. 144
  Nancy 100, 112
  Phebe 60
  Prudence 185
  Rebecka 36
  Richard 112, 138
  Sally 22
  Sarah 83
  Thomas 83, 97, 156, 160
  Thos 37, 58
  Wm. 127, 160
  Zachariah 22
Robertson, John 12
  Martha 178
Robinett, A. 2
  Allen 144, 161
  Elizabeth 180, 196
  James 161
  Nancy 73
  Nelson 121
Robins, Ann 26
  Anne 98
  Betsey 41, 186
  Elizabeth 171
  Frances 50, 78
  Jane 18
  John 42, 47, 53, 81, 122, 141, 186
  Lucy 26
  Malachi 172
  Margaret 109

Robins (cont.)
  Margret 42
  Mary 106, 160
  Mira 200
  Nancy 36, 47
  Nathaniel 98, 171
  Peggey 115
  Salley 107
  Thomas 161
  Thos 49, 73
  William 161
Robinson, Elizabeth 18
  John 64, 172
Robison, E. C. 59
Robnet, James 180
Robnett, James 175
Rolan, Jno 118
Roland, Nancy 77
Roper, Agnis 152
Rose, Delpha A. 66
  Ester 114
  Lidda 177
  Milley 95
  Oliff 128
  Sally 47
  Sterling 47, 95, 161
Ross, Polley 25
Roughton, Elisha 162
Roussau, David 66
  Dd. 119
  Nancy 90
Rousseau, A. L. 144, 144, 176
  America C. 18
  David 8, 162
  Elizabeth 60, 169
  Hiram 154
  James H. 184
  John 176
  Lucy 169
  Mary A. 184
  S. A. 138
  Salley 128
  Sarah 169
  Wm 95, 169
Rowland, Charles 8
Roy, Mary 18
Royal, Betey 186
  John 162, 205
Royaland, Sarah 20
Royall, Thos 86
Roye, Elizabeth 46
Rucker, Colbey 160
  Sally 87
Runnolds, Marey 121
Runt, Polley 13
Rupard, Caleb 162
  Elknah(?) 53
Rupord, Calep 83
Rush, Marey 194
Russel, Abednego 195
  Anderson 156
  Isaac 31
  John 25, 180
  Luisa Ann 155
  N. A. 162
  Nancy 66
  Rachel 180
  William 66, 195
Russell, Letitia 171
  Lewis 49
  Mary 187
  Nancy E. 163
  Tillous (Bussell) 44
  Wilson 163
Rutherford, Thos 9, 200
Rutledge, William 198
Ruton, Ruthy 133

Ryans, Patsey 56
Ryon, Keziah 56
　Sarah 3
Rysdon, Agness 173
Sabasten, Elijah 176
　Mary 176
Sabastian, Benj. 9
　Benjm. 166
Sabastin, John 10
　Lewis 76
　Wm 104
Sabastion, William 21
Saberstin, Hezekih 10
Sail, Margaret 74
Sails, Frankey 95
　Susa 7
　Susannar 76
Saintclair, John 87, 116
　Meriah C. 99
　Rebecca Amanda 62
　Thos. H. 112, 114, 114
Saintclar, Clarinda 162
Saintclear, Kily 99
Saintcler, Harnet 95
Sale, Clary 182, 192
　Cornelius 65
　Elias 129, 182
　Elisabeth 129
　Elizabeth 9, 75, 157, 164
　Enoch 6
　Gemima C. 202
　Ginsey 74
　James 53, 142, 148, 157, 164, 164
　James P. 145
　Jamima 53
　Jane 191
　Jinsey 139
　John 74, 164
　Lamira 164
　Lucy 141
　Martha V. 162
　Mary(?) 121, 125
　Matilda M. 125
　Nancy 192
　Patsey 139
　Rebecah 8
　S. T. 128
　Sarah 163, 170
　Silas 164
　Sina 192
　Susana 191
　Susannah 139
　Susannah E. 145
　William 101, 128, 162, 163, 170
　Wm 69, 97, 101
Sales, Caroline 140
　Mary 128
　Nancy E. 63
　Sarah 128
　Sarah C. 203
　William 68
Salley, Carity 189
Salmons, J. F. 142
Samuel, Micajah L. 164
Sanders, John 149
　Joseph 146
　Linday 52
　Marey 4
　Mary 149
　Polley 159
　Richd 159
　Susaner 80
　William 133
Sartain, Josiah 168
　Mary 168

Saterwhite, Leuesey J. 113
Satterwhite, H. B. 112, 167
Saunders, Aaron 80
　Elizabeth 114
　Polley 64
　Sarah 48
　Wm. 184
Sawyers, Wm. B. 74
Saymer, Sarah 33
Sayner, Jane E. 96
Scisk, Jelico 54
Scoott, Henry 85
Scoott, Sarah 77
Scott, Elizabeth 55
　John 67
　Martha 67
Scotter, Sary Al 180
Scroggs, A. A. 178
　Andw. A. 169
　M. 121
Seamans, Stephen 73
Sebastian, C. F. 86
　Emeline E. 97
　Henry 157, 170
　Lewis 84
　Lewis W. 166
　M. H. 170
　William 2
　Wm. G. 166
Sebastin, Ailse 29
　Matilda 84
　Sarah Ann 58
　Wm. 159
Sebastine, Nancy 31
Sebastion, Sarah 26
Secres, Maran 59
　Nancy 140
Secrese, Harriet 185
See, Mourning 62
　Susy 64
Seeden, Easter 88
Seegraves, Britain 121
　Malindy 121
　William 204
Segraves, Delana 115
　Sherwood 115
Segroves, Sarah Ann 52
Sellars, Elizabeth 99
Sellers, John 99
Setser, John 166
Setsor, John 179
Settle, Anie 166
　Martha 171
　Reuben 166
Settles, Betty 64
Sever, Mary 145
Sewell, Dawson 117
　Joseph 77
Sewmaker, Sarey 189
Shackelford, W. 4
Shalley, John 174
　Mary 174
Sharp, Isabel 166
　James 166
　John 166
　Manervy 163
　Mary A. 166
　Minerva 166
　Polley 122
　Wm. B. 19
Sharpe, Azel 128
Shattely, John 151
Shatterby, Absolom 72
Shatterly, David 101
　John 166
Shaver, Elisabeth 188

Shaver (cont.)
　James 167
Shavers, John, Sr. 167
Shaw, Eve 115
Shay, David 61
Shearer, Robert 126
Shearman, Dorcas 179
Shearwood, Benjamin 20
Sheats, Daniel 49
Sheen, Elizabeth 105
Sheets, Adam 24
　Andrew 167
　Andy 167
　Rachel 200
Sheffield, George 166
　James 2
Shell, Ann 165
Shelley, Hanner 53
Shelly, Ellen 44
Shepard, Nancy M. 142
　Stephen 48
　Polley 188
Shephard, James 5
　Sarah 147
Shepherd, Alcey 48
　Andrew 154
　Elizabeth 154
　George 27, 39, 47, 149, 168
　J. F. 112
　James 199
　John F. 41, 203
　Larkin 107, 167
　Lewis 123, 204
　Lucy 110
　Martha(?) 185
　Mary 26
　Rebbecca 41
Sheppard, Andrew 154, 189
　George 3
　James 36, 122, 189
　Larkin 125, 188
　Rebeca 84
　Sarah 188
　Susanna 189
Shepwash, Sary 72
Sherwood, Sally 166
Shew, Henry 103
　Hessa 72
　Joel 72
　Nancy M. 98
　Salley 151
　Sally 103
　Simon 168
　Susanah 103
Shewmaker, Millay 111
　Sarah 56
　Senah C. 146
Shin, Beckey 145
　Sally 56
Shinn, T. S. 58
Shipp, Bartlett 73
Shoate, Frances 198
Shoe, Johanna 182
　Martha 168
　Sarah 72
Shoemaker, Andrew 169
　John 50
　Joseph 184
　Nancy 65
　Polly 83
　Rosanah 129
Shoemate, John 91, 169
　Mahaly 82
　Martha 91
　Nancy 91
　Polly 169
　William 82, 110, 159

236

Shomall, Amelia 1
Shomate, Elender 21
　Nancy 188
Shooe, Mary 166
Shore, Simon 178
Shores, A Biram 169
　Saniel 177
　Mary 8
　Rhoda 177
　Sarah 54
Shors, Mary A. 200
　Richard 187
Shorse, David 75
Shotts, Andy 98
　Mary 98
　Millie 98
Shoud, Sabia 52
Shue, J. O. 44
Shuford, Abel H. 179
Shumaker, Martha 89
　Nancey 188
Shumate, Calvin 24
　Caroline 79, 170
　Casander J. 110
　Eleanor S. 56
　Elizabeth 190
　Frankey A. 166
　John 170
　Lucy 154
　Martha 79
　Mary 21
　Polley 64
　Susan 199
　Toliver 24
　Wesley 169
Shurley, Thomas 98
Sidden, Pity 187
　Richard 30, 165, 187
Siddin, Willborn 108
Silcock, Ambrose 177
　Andrew 42
　Anna 42
Sillivan, John 126 (see also Sullivan)
　Turner 170
Simcock, Mary 19
Simmons, Elizabeth 131
　Jane 35
　Jinney 79
　Maryann 30
　Missouri 138
　Polley 93, 172
　Sarah 138
　Susanna 74
Simons, Sarah 47
Simpson, Ann 4
　C. R. S. 201, 201
　Mary 170
　Samuel 18
Sims, William 170
Sinatclear, Elisabeth 188
Sinclair, Amanda 181
Sinkler, Jno 187
Sipe, Cathe. 118
Sloan, Robert 14
　Saml 62
　Suca 79
　Wm. 99
Slone, Calvin 77
　Roberts 49
　William C. 12
Smart, Polly 100
Smirthes, Rodey 146
Smith, A. E. 196
　A. N. 163
　Aaron 175
　Adley 201

Smith (cont.)
　Adley 201
　Amelia M. 22
　Arrittey 34
　Betsy 122
　Cathrone 27
　Chaney 130
　Charity 121
　Davd. 171
　Delphia 4
　Dianah 86
　Diana L. H. 58
　Elisha 46
　Elizabeth 3, 16, 35, 46, 167
　Elizabeth H. 159
　Hannah 85, 191
　Hugh 171
　James 44, 49, 117, 148, 153
　Jas. H. 159
　John 60, 138
　John W. 132
　Joshua 22, 198
　Levici 44
　Lucy 206
　Margaret 117
　Mary 131
　Nancy 121, 153
　Olivia A. 22
　Patty 34
　R. M. 13, 54
　Rachel 121, 152
　Ruah 184
　Saml P., Jr. 203
　Samp P., Sr. 22
　Samuel 122
　Samuel P. 76, 126, 172
　Sarah 44, 54
　Simon 121
　Sinthey 109
　Sulila 46
　Susan M. 158
　Susanah 170
　W. 184
　Wesly 131
　Wilford 163
Smither, Jesse 188
Smithey, Emily 7
Smithy, Elenor 160
　Elvira 61
　Harvey 2
　Martha 138
　Rebecah 6
　Wm. 6
Smitsney, Elizabeth 7
　Jesse 7
　Mary 13
Smoot, Elisha 191
　Jno 9
　John 87, 172
　Nancy 189
　Susannah 143
Smyth, Susanna 33
Smythy, Matilda 163
Snow, Judith 150
Somers, William W. 100
　Winston 90
Soot, Mary 145
Soots, Harison 151
Sother, Marthyan 32
　Nancy E. 162
Sout, N. J. 58
South, Joseph 177
　Samuel 172
Souther, A. J. 173
　Andrew J. 52, 183
　Delvy 170

Souther (cont.)
　Elizabeth 71, 108
　Francis 172
　Henry 188
　Jane 173
　Jerome 53, 108
　Jerome B. 108, 170
　Joshua 23, 29, 108, 172, 173
　Joshua, Jr. 87
　Joshua, Junr. 108
　Rody 88
　Sarah 81, 172
Southers, Sarah 173
Sparkes, Cahles 56
　Elizabeth 47
　Huldah 154
　Jane 173
　Jincey 2
　Joseph 173
　Lusinda 83
　Malinda 148
　Malindy 120
　Mary 56, 93
　Peggey 103
　Reuben 2
　Samuel 173
　Sary 111
　Timothy 173
Sparkmon, Polley 123
Sparks, Amelia 12
　Arrena R. 15
　Bilenda 36
　Hannah 51
　James 174
　Jane 97
　Joel 17, 17, 120, 174
　John 91, 118
　Lizzey 50
　Margaret 70
　Martha 32
　Mary 72
　Matilda 70
　Melindia 116
　Mity 56
　Nancy 109
　Reuben 174
　Sally 56
　Sarah 78, 91
　Sary 5
　Selam 173
　Solomon 24, 179
　Susana 102
　Temperance 68
　Timothy 120
　William 91
　William R. 23, 70, 174
Speakes, A. Luckey 182
　Ale D. 174
　Archabel 9
　Delphey 139
　Farity 155
　Lewcreasey 82
　Mussinetine 174
Speaks, Aladelpha 13
Spear, Robert 62
Speck, Lizy 184
　Mariah 179
Specks, Caroline 201
Speed, Sarah 187
Speer, Francis 26
　Joseph 12
Speers, Mary 117
Speks, Richmond 111
Spence, Nancy E. 16
Spencer, Amanda 140
　Gary G. 111
　Elizabeth 18

Spencer (cont.)
  Jane 140
  John 175
  Martha 175
  Permelia 96
  Wm. S. 9, 95
Spensar, Robert 58
Spensor, James 175
Spice, Peggy 53
Spicer, Abigail 17
  Delpha 95
  Elizabeth 92, 106
  Gemima 70
  H. J. 92, 107
  Harden 70
  James 92
  Joseph 92, 198
  Joshua 92
  M. E. 4
  Martha 107
  Martha J. 174
  Nancy 92
  Salley 92
  William 145
  Wm 78, 142
  Wm, Senr. 175
Sprinkle, Anne 100
  Elizabeth 198
  J. W. 155
  Liddy 168
  Nancy 58
  O. 175
  Obadiah 129
  Rebecca 53
  Ruth 63
  Samuel 34
  Susanah 130
Stafford, Nancy 96
Stailey, Adam 183
  Elizabeth 183
Staley, A. E. 70
  Adam 62, 78, 138
  E. 178
  Ellender 54
  Enoch 102
  Jacob 103, 137
  Mary 103
  Sarah A. 137
  Sernettie 137
Stallings, Abraham 51
  Mary 51
  Samuel 61
Staly, A. 176
  Adam 176
  Enoch 135
  Esley 30
Stamper, Jacob 170
  Jesse 5
  Jonathan 83, 163
  Louisa 117
  Marinda 24
  Martha 103
  Mary 83
  Maryan 192
  Nancy 79
  Peggy 82
  Rachel 83
  Sta(?) 22
  Susanah 170
  William 79
Stanbery, David 176
  John 177
Stanbury, David 99
  Prudence 99
  Rody 130
Standley, Harris 25
  James 177
  John 116

Standley (cont.)
  Reuben 6, 13, 13, 177
  Reubin 118
  Ruben 177
Standly, Amy 9
  Joseph 143
  Reuben 45
Standsberry, Zevirah 56
Stanely, Anny 143
Stanfield, Kiziah 50
Stanley, Ann 163
  Darlett 137
  Jacob 13
  John 86, 177, 197
  Joseph 177
  Lucy 177
  Mary 136
  Nancy 6
  Reuben 36, 142
  Sarah 114
  Shadrach 127, 143
  Thomas 45
Stanly, Alsey 114
  Dicey 103
  John 119
  Joseph Y. 61
  Sarah 112
  Thos 177
Stansbury, Sally 96
Stanton, Lucy 111
Stapp, Catharine 202
  Golson 171
  Golston 202
  Thomas 93, 177, 177
Starnes, John 32
Steed, Nancy 152
Steele, Robt. L. 127
Steelman, H. D. 32
  James L. 55
  Saml. 58
Steelmon, Amelia 32
  Jane 50
  Saml 203
Stelman, Saml 15
Stephens, John 80
  Sally 130
  Wilson 130
Stephenson, Mira 25
Stepp, Coleson 183
  Robert 178
Stevens, Lewis 47
  Sarah 14
Stevingson, Mary 7
Steward, Elisabeth 130
Stewart, J.(?) 23
  James 42, 165
Stidem, Allen 172
Stilwell, Margarett 86
Stimson, Alice A. 164
  Delucson 164
  Omy 164
Stinnet, Mary Eliza 123
Stinson, D. C. 21, 96
  Elijah 34
  Polly 12
  Salley 180
Stoe, Anna 55
Stokes, Anne N. 107
  Hugh M. 36
  M. 116, 177
  Mary Adelaide 36
  Rebecca C. 61
  Sarah 78
  Thomas J. 133
Stone, Amanda C. 102
  Anne 168
  Byrd 104
  Eli (Story) 19

Stone (cont.)
  Lulia 168
  Mary J. 15
  Rebecca 126
  Sarah E. 126
  Thomas 10
  Viney(?) 151
  William 126
Stonepheer, Elizabeth 134
Stonesyfer, Henricus 166
Storey, Isaac 117
Storie, Joshua 178, 179
  Thomas(?) 45
Story, Eli 178 (see also Stone)
  Rachael 75
  Telitha 96
  Thomas 75, 96
Stout, Denary 119
  Malinda 142
Stover, Anna 159
  Isaac 94
Strane, Edney M.(?) 20
Strange, Archelaus 98
  Judy 98
  Nelson A. 90, 161
Strickland, Nancy 66
Stringer, Reuben 202
Stroud, Martha C. 98
Strutton, Hezekiah 132, 171
  Nancy 72
  Oney 171
  Salley 132
  Sucky 170
Stuart, James 129
  Jane 42
  Margaret 56
  Mary 42
  Samuel 42, 42
Stubble, Omy 144
Stubblefield, Elizabeth 104
Studavent, Elvira 71
Stunt, S. A. 124
Sturdivant, John W. 76, 125
Sturt, Elizabeth 115
Suddeth, C. M. 137
Suite, Susanah 73
Suites, Rebeca 105
Suits, Beckey 166
Sulivan, Eliza 12
Sullivan, John (Sillivan) 101
  Nelly 122
  Saml 54, 56
Sumerlin, Emelen 30
  Mary 23
  Susan 134
Sumlin, Maria 139
Summerlin, Allen 179
  Hannah 134
  Huldah 16
  Jesse C. 39
  Louisa 180
  Patsey 90
  Sarah 80
Summerling, Suana 184
Summers, Elizabeth 61
  H. C. 100, 190
  Howard 100
  Nancy 51
  Paul F. 80
Sumpter, Thomas W. A. 41
Sutes, Mary 168
Suttle, Cinda 186
  Hiram 52

Suttle (cont.)
　Maryann 10
　Milley 14
　Reuben 121
　Reuben, Junr. 40
Swaim, George 151, 196
　John 180
　Martha 11
　Michael 11, 126, 127, 171
　Moses 134
　W. D. W. 121
Swaling, Aan 63
Swam, Nancy 33
Swanson, Anna 111
　Betsy 40
　Dicy 170
　Elcy 74
　Hily 192
　Isaac 180
　Luther 145, 180
　Mary 197
　Mary Caroline 191
　Susannah 123
　Wesley 34
　William 135
Sweeden, Sarah 186
Sweeten, Keziah 28
Swiem, Rachel 127
Swim, Michael 200
　Polly 11
Swiney, Minerva 131
Swinney, Clarinda 7
Tagsdol, John W. 99
Tailor, James 181
Talor, Nancy A. 131, 135
　Sally 141
Tandley, Lucy 2
Tanner, Joseph 78, 95
　Joshua 91
Tate, George B. 37
　Margett 202
　Thos R. 8
Taylor, Eveline 112
　George 137
　Lyda 179
　Neates 172
　Sarah 103, 183
　Susannah A. 124
Teague, Elizabeth 32
　Isaac 48, 164
　Joseph 181, 181
　Polly 119
　Sally 114
Teashill, Limera 27
Tedder, Amandy M. 22
　Biddy 6
　Sarah 142
　Wm 181
Tedders, M. 96
Teder, Biddy 181
Temple, E. C. 50
Templeton, Gincy 153
　J. M. 88
　Margret 182
　W. G. 182
Terrel, Susanna 73
Tharington, James 169
Tharp, Ellen 116
Theiling, Caty 203
Thomas, Eliza J. 89
　Elizabeth 119
　Henry 17
　Henry M. 182
　Mary 17, 37
　Susan 17
　William F. 57
Thompson, Catherine 4

Thompson (cont.)
　Roxann 75
Thomson, Ann 108
　George W. 44
Thornburg, Nancy E. 143
Thornton, John 56, 149
　Merideth 30, 30
　Moses 148
　Susannah 54
Thorton, Maraday 16
　Mardath 106
　Mardy 106
Thronbarly, Lewis 105
Thurmond, D. C. 97
　Harrison 77
　Julia 52
　M. 135
　Salley 77
　Thos, J. 52
Tilley, Charles E. 98
　Edmon 183
　Edmond 34
　Edmund 197
　Elizabeth 20
　Mary 66
　Matilda 41
　Nancy 46
　Peggy B. 34
　Stephen 115
Tilmon, James 170
　Marthy J. 170
Tindle, Nancy 153
Tindsley, James 158
Tinsley, Nancy E. 2
　Peggey 188
　Rachel 110
Tire, Polly 79
Tiser, Fedric 198
　Frederick 54, 196
Todd, James 62, 204
　William 53
　Wm. 149
Tolbert, Mary A. 129
　Roxann 58
Tolbey, Nancy 29
Toliver, Moses 176
Tomkins, Nancy 154
Tomlin, Cyntha 169
Tomlinson, A. 85, 166, 189
　Archibald 55
　Elvira 197
　John R. 165
　Mary A. 20
　Nancy Jane 39
　Richard 114
　Wm. 150
Tompkins, Mary 166
　Phoby 8
　William 8
Tompson, Elitha 175
　Sarah 105
Tomson, Mary 68
Tomsson, Hannah(?) 43
Towell, Polly 23
Townson, James 120
Towson, Mary 120
Tramson, Mary 154
Transon, Sarah 106
　Wm. B. 106
　Fanny A. 204
　Harriet 112
Transor, W. B.(?) 154
Treadaway, Eli A. 171
Treadway, Elsey Vine 171
　Moses 169
Treble, Rebekah 57
　Shadrach 57

Tribble, Margaret Adaline 180
　Rebecca 87
　Sarah 178
　Stephen 129
Tribet, Lucindy 75
Trible, Abner 131, 134, 134, 179
　Ann 179
　Spillsbe 184
　Adline 110
　Charlotte 163
　Elizabeth 33, 62, 110
　Frances 62
　Marthey J. 70
　Nancy 165
　Nathan 185
　Noah 36
　Priscilla 62
　Sarah 56
　William 122
Triplett, A. L. 70
　Addleine 90
　Ann C. 197
　Anny 55
　Arreney 145
　Asa 55
　Balinda 55
　Caroline 185
　Edith 78
　Elijah 111
　Eliza 71
　Elizabeth 55, 185, 195
　Elmyrah 180
　Elsy 75
　Frances 90
　G. W. 7
　Horton 185, 197
　Ireny 147
　J. W. 185
　Jesse 80
　L. E. 111
　Lewis 134
　Lindsey 195
　Louisa 124
　Mandy 198
　Martha E. 91
　Mary 99
　Mary A. 131
　Matilda 137
　Milley 78
　Nancy 92
　Polley 185
　Russel 92
　Russell 170
　S. M. 33
　Sallie E. 178
　Sarah E. 149
　Selena 140
　Susannah 185
　Thomas 75
　Thomas, Jr. 184
　Thos 186
　William 90, 112
Triplette, Frances 162
　Julia 151
　Milley 184
　Nancy 20
　Nimrod 165
Triplitt, John 185
　Permina 92
　William 185
Tripplett, Talport 82
Tritt, Mary 186
　Peter 186
Trivett, Sarah 96
Trivitt, Isaac 195
Trustey, Henry 109

Tucker, Charity 135
  David 132
  Hiram 186
  Laura 49
  Levina 65
  Margaret 132
  Martha An 49
  Mary 142
  Noah 129
  Pheby 177
  Polley N. 31
  Priscillah 99
  Sallie 49
  Sally 75
  Sarah 186
  Washington 49, 186
  Willaim 186
  Wm. 163
  Wm. M. 186
Tuder, Emaline 12
Tugman, Ailsey 93
  Edmond 93
  Edward 28
  Elizy 132
  J. F. 187
  J. L. 71
  James 12, 89, 162
  Nancy 21, 35
  Rebecca 146
  William 93
Tugmon, William 186
Tulbert, Mary M. 196
Tulburt, Cintha 34
  J. L. 101
  Laurah 34
  Levi 34
Tumlin, J. C. 65
Turnbill, Delphia 34
  Elizabeth 37
  John 203
  John J. 155
Turner, Edward 161
  Jane 161
  Jeane 174
  Thomas 187
Tyra, Jane 54
Tyre, Peggy 154
Umphrey, Owen 82
Underwood, Betsey 112
  Dila 165
  James 20
  Lewis 9
  Rachel 77
Urp, Cinthy 130
Usry, John 172
Utzman, John 168
Vandergriff, Ann 161
Vann, Rebecca J. 200
Vannoy, _____ 8
  A. M. 124
  Abner 188
  Abram 59
  Aly 59
  Anderson 59
  Andrew 91
  C. E. 48
  C. Elizabeth 132
  C. F. 26, 48, 110
  Caroline 59
  Daniel 92
  Elizabeth 24, 59, 146
  Emeline C. 62
  Enoch 24
  Fanny 109
  Francis 29, 48, 188
  Francis M. 124
  James A. 188
  James H. 199

Vannoy (cont.)
  James W. 179
  Jinny 113
  Joel 61, 99, 114, 114,
    184, 188, 189, 194,
    196, 196
  John 39
  Katherine 61
  M. A. 124
  M. W. 78
  Martha 60
  Mary 1, 65, 204, 205
  Milley 48
  Mira 188, 189
  Nancey 169
  Nathanael 8
  Neil C. 199
  Phoebe 42
  Rebecka 90
  S. M. 139
  Sarah Carline 59
  Susan 124
  Susana 24, 199
  Susanna C. 168
  T. J. 6, 153
  W. W. 18, 32
  Wm. 173
Vanoy, Amelia 123
  C. F. 167
  Enock 141
  Marey 158
  Marthey 146
  Mary 141
Vanwinkle, Rhoda 144
Vest, Betsey 52
  Hannah 206
  Luisa 65
  Patsey 57
Vian, Fanny 167
  John(?) 156
Viars, Elisabeth 124
  John 165, 189
Vicar, Elizabeth 9
Vickar, Phawney 172
Vickas, Elijah 189
  Elizabeth 119
  John 189
Vickers, Frances 100
  Jesse H. 37
  Mariah 189
  Sarah 174
Vickes, Charles 189
Vickus, Charlotte 127
Vicus, John 91
Vier, Faney 48
Vincanon, Hannah 120
Vines, Sarah 117
Vinsant, Lany 113
Vires, Salley 167
Vollentine, Thomas 183
Vollintine, Marget 183
Vyers, Matilda 150
Waatts, Annis 177
Waddel, Nancy 116
Waddell, Clabon 83
  Lidia 12
  Sarah 83
Waddil, Claborn 174
Waddill, Dianna 16
Waddle, Alcy 42
  Atha 190
  C. 12
  Calborn 190
  Live 190
  Sary 12
Waddy, Kissy 196
Wade, Montelion 84
  Montillmon 187

Wadel, Claborn 15
Wades, Fanny 40
Wadkins, Andrew 79
  Clarasa 63
  Dicey 54
  Fereby 191
  Joel 122, 142, 158
  John W. 85
  Lossern(?) 198
  Rebecca 192
Wadle, Claborn 174
Waggoner, Owen 117
Wagner, James 167
Wagoner, Cathrine 13
  James 162
  Mary 153
Waid, America 117
Wainscott, Nancey 190
Waits, Jane 136
Waldon, Elisha D. 204
Wales, Rachel 120
Walk, Wilson 200
Walker, Alfred 191, 197
  Ambrose 191
  Ann 71
  Arminda 113
  Benja. 163
  Benjamin 53, 142
  Bicy 71
  Charles 73, 106, 191,
    192
  Clary 84, 157
  Cynthia C. 191
  Daly 192
  Diana 30
  Elisabeth 71
  Eliza Ann 25
  Elizabeth 3, 90, 121
  Howard 143
  Isaac 4, 4, 143, 193
  Ismeal 90
  J. B. 32
  J. D. 17
  J. F. 17
  J. P. 27
  James 15, 19, 189
  James H. 86
  Janey 73
  Jayn 151
  Jesse 43, 63, 74, 190
  Jessee 130
  John 8, 27, 50, 71, 135,
    191, 191, 193
  John J. 180
  L. R. D. 191
  Lemira 197
  Leonard 76, 191
  Liddy 100
  Lotty 76
  Lucy 19
  Mahaley 19
  Mariman 12
  Martha 164
  Mary 63, 130, 156
  Mary Eveline 47
  Mary L. 173
  Matilda 142
  Mere 19
  Milton 192
  Milton J.'9
  Mira 151
  Mitiday 104
  Nancy 1, 107
  Overton G. 25
  Patsy 147
  Perlina G. 30
  Priscilla 123
  Randler 191

240

Walker (cont.)
  Randolph 42
  Richard 126, 192
  Robert 30, 35, 43
  S. C. 167
  S. E. 86
  Sarey 197
  Sarha 73
  Simuel(?) 191
  Susanah 32
  Tilda 90
  Turner 84
  William 47, 77
  Wilson 93, 151, 200
  Wm. 3, 164, 180
  Wm. H. 29
  Wm. T. 92
Wall, John 193
  Jonathan 109
  Joseph 196
  Leweretia 52
  Marth 52
  Susannah 203
Wallace, Edwards 69
  Lidda 134
  Prissy 53
  Salley 43, 160
  Susanah B. 172
Wallas, Ellender 106
  Vary 154
Waller, Rachel 137
Wallice, Dianah 147
  Susanna 5
Wallin, Salley A. 71
Wallis, Richard (see Wallace)
Walls, Elizebeth M. 64
  Jacob 175
  James J. 193
  Jane 175
  Jinsa T. 120
  John 48, 202, 202, 203
  Joseph 48, 144
  Mary 48
  Moses 133
  N. J. 48, 48, 140, 193
  Nancy 46
  Nancy P. 69
  Nathan J. 28, 48, 193
  Susan 175
Wals, James 32
Walser, Susanna 2
Walsh, A. J. 185
  Bennet B. 167
  Calvin 193
  Elender 167
  Elizabeth 59, 71, 193
  Elizabeth Evaline 71
  Elza 85
  Fanny L. 17
  George B. 55
  Harry 194
  Harvy 194
  Martha(?) 90
  McAlpin 184
  Merry W. 80
  Miry W. 184
  Peggey 156
  Philip 185
  Phillip 140
  Rachel 184
  Samuel 35, 80, 185
  Susanna 194
  Thomas 179, 193
  William 144, 193
Walter, Aly 80
  Joel 80
  Rachel 177

Walter (cont.)
  Rebecca 80
Walters, Elizabeth 108
Ward, Dice 58
  John A. 67
  Nathan 112, 129, 180
Warran, Peter 113
Warren, Alfred 18, 54, 61, 95, 189
  Catharine 193
  Elisabeth 104
  Francis 36
  Hampton 204
  J. H. 195
  James P. 67
  Lucinda 101
  Matilda 204
  Nancy Jane 79
  Robt 194
  Sarah 95
  Sary 9
  Susanah 204
Waters, Aily 175
  Ann 186
  Elizabeth 6
  Hannah 116
  Jane Amanda 45
  Joel 185
  John W. 108, 109, 150, 198
  Leah 75
  Lewis 75, 116
  Malinda 76
  Marthy 198
  Molly 82
Watkins, E. 179
Wats, Lydia 119
Watson, Catharine 195
  David 16, 49, 54, 81
  Elihu 194
  Elihue 16
  Eliza 80
  Elizabeth 81
  Fanny 106
  Francis 76
  Gille 135
  John 16, 153
  Lewis 81
  Lucindy 81
  Malinda 75
  Mandy 74
  Marthy 39, 63
  Mary 16, 131, 153, 153
  Rebecca 81
  Selah Adaline 195
  Susan Miranda 197
  Susanna 172
  Thomas 195, 195
  Thos 194, 195
  William 32, 39
  Willis 195
Watters, Nancy 126
Watts, Benjamin 195
  Elizabeth 94, 145
  George 147, 196
  Jacob 196
  James 84, 146, 196
  John 11, 196
  Luisy 147
  Lurener 196
  Lydia Adeline 196
  Margerett E. 195
  Maria 57
  Presila 99
  Rebecca 196
  Ruben 84
  Sarah 196
  Sarah H. 196

Watts (cont.)
  William 46, 84, 115
  Winey 196
  Wm 11
Waugh, H. O. 6
  H. P. 38
  J. 13
  Wm. P. 73, 112, 116
Waver, John 196
Web, Nelley 106
Webb, Cary 134
  Ede 80
  Elizabeth 18
  Francis 186
  John 185
  Naomy 101
Webber, Amelia E. 106
Webster, Elijah 66
  Molly 134
  Sarah 181
  William 181
Weeb, Francis 195
Welborn, Catherine 188
  Claranner 51
  H. M. 188
  Isaac 51
  John 7
  John M. 30
  L. D. 200
  Lee Davis 139
  Lewis 157
  Malinda 76
  Maryann 187
  Nancey D. 188
  Nancey E. 82
  S. C. 124
  Sarah 197
  Thos S. 197
Welburn, Isaac 12
Welch, J. C. 47
  McAlpin 154
  Polley 154
  Rachel 93
  Rebecca 40
  Susannah 50
Wellborn, Abel R. 157
  Catharine 143
  Daniel 21
  Danl. M. 25
  E. M. 175
  Eloirah 150
  Hugh Montgomery 150
  J. W. 145
  James 3, 10
  John 107
  Lucinda 108
  Mary 24
  Nancy 17
  Nancy M. 177
  Rachal S. 32
  Rebecca 182
  Rebecca M. 68
  Rebecka 136
  S. 197
  S. C. 124
  S. Chaply 140
  Saml. 160
  Samuel C. 124
  Sarah 21
  Susan 21, 57
  Susan S. 119
Wellcoxson, Eliza E. 122
Wells, Elizabeth 81
  Hardy 63, 106, 107, 107
  Holley 121
  Miles 197, 197
  Samuel 165
  William 121, 138

Welsh, W. Calphin 140
West, A. B. 90
  Catherine 197
  Eliza Caroline 98
  J. W. 11
  Malinda 45
  Margaret 90
  Mary Ann 11
  Melinda 152
  Wm. 93
Westloch, Hila 150
Westlock, Catharine 159
  Jane 63
Whatley, George, Jr. 19
Wheatley, Amelia M. 169
  G. 3
  George 101
  George, Jr. 169
  James 156
  Mason 107
  Milley 122
  Polly 122
  Salley 102
  Willis 86
Wheatly, Betsey 94
  Elizabeth 10
  Matilda 90
  Nancy 88
  Sarry 1
Wheeler, Absolom 198
  Martha 188
  Matilda M. 188
  Richard 165
Wheler, Elizabeth 76
White, Danl 107
  Elisabeth 167
  Elisha 39
  John L. 205
  Tabetha 20
  W. W. 134
Whiteman, Joseph Tanner 189
Whitesides, James 132
Whitington, Caroline 62
  James H. 150
Whitley, Nancy 171
Whitly, Elizabeth 1
Whittenton, Allen A. 62
  Calvan W. 146
  Emly C. 188
  James 199
  James R. 58
  John 56, 109
  Mariah E. 188
  Marthy 32
  Salley 49
  Sarah 56
  W. R. 188
  William R. 188
Whittington, A. G. 60, 62, 102
  Alexander 167
  Alexr. G. 85
  America E. 167
  Benjamin F. 199
  Eliza 102
  Elizabeth M. 10
  John 110
  John W. 22, 115
  Leander E. 150, 150
  Mary Mailsey 115
  Nancy E. 42
  Sarah 176
  W. R. 28, 53, 122, 168
  Wm. 57
  Wm. R. 85
Whitty, Elizabeth 36
Wiatt, Victory 23

Wiet, Nancy 76
Wiett, Elizabeth 31
Wiggins, Abraham 187
  John 200
Wilborn, A. R. 200
  Abel R. 190
  Harrison 200
  Lucindy 139
  Mary 140
  Mary E. 35
  Randal 125
  Susana 7
Wilburn, Lucy 12
  Mary M. 147
  Wm. 12
Wilcockson, Daniel 197
  Salley 174
  Sary 23
  William 70, 200
Wilcox, Ailcy 205
  Fanney 159
  Nancy 81
Wilcoxen, Martha 130
Wilcoxon, Margarett L. 105
  Mary C. 59
Wilcoxson, Elizabeth 164
  Harriet 84
  Isaac 164, 200
  Jane 124
  Martha 2, 109
  Mary 192
  Sarah Jane 15
  William C. 15
  Wm. 160
Wildes, William 60
Wilds, Elizabeth 2
Wiles, J. A.(?) 200
  James 84, 192
  Levina 190
  Nancy 15
  Polly 125
  Rachel 189
  Sarah 19
  Susannah 29
  Thomas 14, 15
  Viry 16
  W. H. 200
  William 29, 189
  Winna 115
  Wm. 122
Wilkins, David 91, 38, 38, 102
Willcox, Francis A. 167
Willcoxson, Jesse 46
  Martha A. 109
  Polly 124
  Wm. C. 122
Willcoxon, Daniel 124
Willey, Elizabeth 150
William, Francis 83
Williams, Anea 201
  Anthony 197
  Aquilla 136, 204
  Charity 52
  Drucilla 89
  Elizabeth 49, 96
  Hugh R. 108
  James 201
  Jas. 186
  Jos. W. 201
  Juda 197
  Judah 10
  Marcy 94
  Martha 12
  Mary 10
  Mima 197
  Moses 91

Williams (cont.)
  Olley 144
  Quiller 44
  Robert 123
  Salley 106
  Sally 147
  Sarah 147
  Sealy 45
  Viney V. 127
  William 186
  Wm. 3
Williamson, Alexander W. 50
  Martha C. 112
Willson, Nancy 176
Wilson, Anna 95
  Catherine H. 41
  Elizabeth 19
  Hannah 41
  James 64
  John 126, 202
  Maria Louisa 109
  Martha 199
  Mary 10, 202
  Nancy 57, 64, 160
  Rebeca 143
  Rebeckah 182
  Saley 204
  Samuel 36, 164
  Tarlton 48
  Th. 109
  Th. W. 18, 68
  Thomas W. 187
  Ths. W. 202
  William 39, 65, 204
Windle, Henry 6
Winfree, Elisabeth 19
Wingler, Adaline A. 109
  Amelia 204
  Elijah 95
  Elisabeth 49
  Lucinda 151, 162
  Sary Jane 205
  Suzanna 95
Winglor, Sally 95
Winkler, Cay 187
  Salley 198
  Susanna 141
Witherspoon, Betsey 123
  Flora 122
  James 83
  Jane 41
  John 122, 202
  Mary Jane 9
  Nancy 9
  Polley 83
  Sarah 55, 162
  Thos. 40, 73, 104, 121, 128, 129
  William P. 9
  Wm. P. 89
Wittington, L. C. 42
Wolf, Pharaby 75
Wolis, Samuel 157
Wood, Betsy 90
  Elizabeth 153, 202
  Francis 173
  James 97
  James F. 192
  Jean 30
  Jos. 203
  Joseph 65, 103, 203, 203
  Lafat 77
  Lindsey 153
  M. R. 120
  Manson 20
  Mary 203

Wood (cont.)
  Nancy L. 191
  Nathaniel 202
  Patsey 79
  Peggy 29
  Rissy 103
  Ruth 120
  Salley 29
  Tabitha 123
  Thos 79
  William 202
Woodde, Bryan 203
  Jonathan 203
Wooddy, John B. 196
Woodel, Taton 109
Woodey, Luiza 92
Woodruf, Lucinday 38
Woodruff, D. C. 124
  E. M. 149
  G. M. 163
  Jane H. 23
  Martha E. 63
  Prudence E. 2
Woodward, Peggy 157
Woody, Jane 120
  Jonathan 167
  Jonathan P. 149
  Martha 149
  Martha Malissa 149
  Nancy 204
  Ruth 167
  Susan 92
Woolf, Tennessee 88
Woolfolk, Fanny 4
Wooten, Abner 141
  Elizabeth 141
  John 204
  Sarah 204
Wooton, Mary R. A. 30
  Nancy 26
  Temperance 72
Wootten, Fannay 148
Word, Sarah J. 194
Woten, Sarah 83
Wotten, Icy 84
Wray, Jesse (see Ray)
Wright, Amelia M. 21

Wright (cont.)
  Dianah 147
  Elizabeth 68
  Isabella 106
  James W. 21
  Jerusha 184
  Maryan P. 204
  Nancy 122, 126
  Thomas 204
  W. W. 191
  William 185
Write, Matilda 100
Wyat, George 205
Wyatt, Aaron 167, 205
  Ann 39
  Emeline 167
  George 2, 22
  Leaner L. 141
  Leonard 48
  Leucy 202
  Libby 41
  Lucey 98
  Mary 83, 159
  Melvina 162
  Nancy 2, 157
  Nancy E. 35
  Nathan 205, 205
  Nelson 167
  Polley 167
  Sally 35, 101
  Sarah 167, 203, 204
  Vicrey 35
Wysong, Elizabeth 21
Yarber, Elizabeth 150
Yarnell, Aron 205
Yates, Adalade 37
  Anne 187
  Barnard 199
  Barnet 205
  Elisabeth 205
  Elizabeth 150
  Jemima 149
  Jerusha 117
  Jesse 60, 145
  John 101, 123, 152, 205
  L. A. 64

Yates (cont.)
  Leuisey 101
  Louisa 151
  Mary 139
  Mary V. 117
  Nancy 200
  Polly 199
  Rebecah 10
  Robert 104, 115, 117, 205
  Robt 187
  Robt. H. 123
  Salley 123
  Sarah 61
Yeakle, Annie P. 31
Yeargain, Benjamin 4
  John 199
Yeates, Jesse 37
  Leafy 12
Yeats, Alston 79, 120
  Aly 199
  Austin 45
  Caroline 153
  Elizabeth 7
  Francis 199
  Hugh 200
  Jesse 61
  John 7, 131
  Milly 79
  Salvy 131
  Sarah 110
  Tillman 149
York, Dolly 169
  Elizabeth 182
  Henry 102
  Lewis 166
  Mary R. 182
  Matilda 116
  Salley 169
  Zilpah 54
Younce, Rebecca C. 14
Young, Adaline M. 44
  Louisa 132
  Patiance 94
  Rebeca 184
  Rebeckah 139
Younger, Nancy 75
Yrpleth, Jane A. 33

ADDENDA

Powel, Rachel 195   Powel, Rebecca 145

www.ingramcontent.com/pod-product-compliance
Lightning Source LLC
Chambersburg PA
CBHW070247230426

43664CB00014B/2435